THE NAVIES OF
ROME

THE NAVIES OF ROME

by

MICHAEL PITASSI

THE BOYDELL PRESS

First published 2009
The Boydell Press, Woodbridge
Reprinted in paperback 2010, 2012

ISBN 978 1 84383 600 1

The Boydell Press is an imprint of Boydell & Brewer Ltd
PO Box 9, Woodbridge, Suffolk, IP12 3DF, UK
and of Boydell & Brewer Inc.
668 Mt Hope Avenue, Rochester, NY 14620, USA
website: www.boydellandbrewer.com

The publisher has no responsibility for the continued existence or accuracy of URLs for external
or third-party internet websites referred to in this book, and does not guarantee
that any content on such websites is, or will remain, accurate or appropriate.

Images accompanying the highlighted sections in this book are reproduced
by courtesy of the Master and Fellows, Trinity College, Cambridge

A CIP record for this book is available from the British Library

Papers used by Boydell & Brewer Ltd are natural, recyclable products
made from wood grown in sustainable forests

Printed in Great Britain by
CPI Antony Rowe, Chippenham and Eastbourne

CONTENTS

List of Plates   VII

List of Maps & Illustrations   VII

Introduction   IX

General Chronology   XV

Chapter 1:   Beginnings: Foundation to the First Punic War, 753 to 264 BC
             Foundation and the Etruscans   1
             The Early Republic   8
             A Roman Warship   18
             The Navy Board   30

Chapter 2:   A Great Naval Power: The First Punic War, 264 to 218 BC
             Growing Tensions   43
             The First Punic War   51
             Victories and Disasters   61
             A Disastrous Year   68
             The Romans Prevail   73

Chapter 3:   Interbellum & The Struggle Resumed, 218 to 201 BC
             The Adriatic   83
             The Second Punic War   87
             Cannae - Roman Lowpoint   91
             The Tide Turns   102
             The Final Act   106

Chapter 4:   The Growth of Empire, 201 to 86 BC
             War in the East: Macedonia   119
             War in the East: Seleucia   123
             Various Operations   130
             The Third Punic War   136
             Naval Run-down and Marius   140
             The Rise of Piracy   144

Chapter 5:   The Road to Civil War, 86 to 44 BC
             The Growth of Piracy   151
             Pompeius: War Against the Pirates   156
             Caesar in Gaul and Britannia   159
             Caesar Versus Pompeius   165
             The Alexandrine War   175

Chapter 6:   End of the Republic, 44 to 13 BC
              Filling the Vacuum   183
              The War Against Sextus   186
              Octavius versus Antonius   191
              The Principate   197
              Imperial Fleets   201
              Expansion - New Fleets   213

Chapter 7:   The Early Empire, 12 BC to AD 70
              Germania   219
              Tiberius   221
              Britannia   227
              Nero   236
              Civil War: Confused Loyalties   238

Chapter 8:   Apogee and Nadir, AD 71 to 285
              The Flavians   253
              The Antonines: High Point of Empire   259
              Troubled Times   265
              Instability and Invasion   270
              Three Empires in One   277

Chapter 9:   Renewal and Decline, AD 285 to 476
              Diocletian: a New Beginning   285
              Constantine   294
              The Empire Divided   300
              The Final Acts   307

Appendix I: Kings and Emperors of Rome   315

Appendix II: Navy Personnel Ranks   318

Appendix III: Suggested Crew Levels of Ship Types   320

Appendix IV: Glossary of Place Names   323

Appendix V: Glossary of Nautical Terms used   328

Bibliography   331

Index   337

LIST OF PLATES

between pages 196 and 197

Plate I   The statue base of Valerius Valens, Praefect of the Misenum Fleet

Plate II   Warships as motifs on coins

Plate III   Wall painting showing warships at sea, Herculaneum

Plate IV   Wall painting showing warships leaving harbour, Pompeii

Plate V   Suggested reconstruction of the Corvus

Plate VI   Marble sculpture of a ram, Ostia

Plate VII   Wall painting showing warships entering harbour, Pompeii

Plate VIII   Panoramic view of Misenum

Plate IX   Typical Roman merchant vessel

Plate X   A Trireme of the early Empire after the Pozzuoli Relief

Plate XI   Petroglyph at Alta, Norway

Plate XII   Portus Adurni (Portchester Castle), Hampshire

Plate XIII   4th century AD Rhine Fleet patrol vessel

Plate XIV   The Column of Arcadius

LIST OF MAPS & ILLUSTRATIONS

Rome and her Surroundings up to 264 BC	6/7
The Diekplous Attack	14
The Periplous Attack	16
The Gastrophetes	19
Rowing Systems	33
Torsion Spring Artillery	37
The Battle of Mylae, 260 BC	58
The Battle of Ecnomus, 256 BC	62
Drepanum	67
Lilybaeum	68
The Battle of Drepanum, 249 BC	71
The First Punic War, 264 to 241 BC	78
Syracuse, 214 BC	97
Patterns of Marine Shields	99
Carthago Nova, 209 BC	103
Tarentum	104

The Boarding Gangway 109
The Carthage Campaign, 204 to 202 BC 113
The Second Punic War, 218 to 202 BC 116
The Battle of Myonnesus, 190 BC 129
Evolution of the Ram 133
The Roman Six 135
The Siege of Carthage, 146 BC 139
Naval Operations, 2nd Century BC 147
The Aegean, 203 to 190 BC 148
Brundisium 166
Oricus, 48 BC 172
Alexandria, 48 BC 177
Marine Shield types 181
The Actium Campaign, 31 BC 195
Misenum 205
Ravenna 207
Ribbons of Rank 223
Later Torsion Spring Artillery 235
The Revolt of Civilis, AD 69 241
Imperial Fleets from Augustus to Diocletian 249
Pontus Euxinus, The Black Sea 257
Distribution of the Fleets, 1st to 3rd Centuries AD 281
The Northern Frontier 295
Disposition of the Fleets, 4th to 5th Centuries AD 312

INTRODUCTION

Some nations, in their development and in the exercise of power, are destined to become essentially 'land powers', whilst others can be considered to be 'sea powers'. So it is that Great Britain as an island nation, where the furthest point in any direction from the sea is no more than 75 miles (120km), has always been regarded as a sea-faring nation. At the other extreme, Russia, amid the vast Eurasian landmass, has of necessity developed primarily as a land power. There have been times when Britain has deployed great armies and Russia great fleets, but geography has always been the main factor which has dictated the overall main focus of each nation's efforts and imposed those fundamental differences in outlook which have gone so far in defining the course of their histories, and the direction of their endeavours.

When considering Rome, and the Roman world, one of the most enduring images is of Legions of Roman soldiers tramping along straight Roman roads. The Legions helped transform the known world; building great fortresses, towns and cities that, to this day, form both the real and ideal foundations of many of our own settlements. It is perhaps this tangible link with our Roman past that brings us to consider them as having been an essentially land based power. The conquests of Rome, her Empire, her civilisation and her exercise of power by the medium of her armies are recorded in great detail and an extensive literature. However, the consideration of Romans as seafarers, and as the creators of one of the largest navies the world has ever seen, is generally regarded in a passing way and, more usually than not, dismissed as a comparatively trivial part of the whole.

This is to do less than justice to the seafarers and ships that made up the navies of Rome. From the traditional founding of Rome in 753 BC, to the 'official' end of the Western Empire, with the dismissal of its last emperor in AD 476, there was a period of some one thousand two hundred years during most of which time Rome, whether as a Republic or as an Empire, maintained and operated a navy that first made her, and then kept her as, the supreme naval power throughout Europe, North Africa and western Asia.

The city of Rome was established where it is because of water. It is built on a peninsula where one can never be more than 70 miles (112km) from the seas, into the middle of which it projects, and whose people have been affected from the earliest of times by its influence. Indeed, it may well be that some of its earliest inhabitants arrived by sea. Rome's first acquisition of territory beyond the city limits was towards the sea, and she went on to build an empire at the literal centre of which was a sea. The securing and control of that sea was, from beginning to end, the often overlooked or neglected, but nevertheless essential, factor in the health, and ultimately the survival, of that empire. To build her empire, Rome had to be in control of the sea. To keep it she had to maintain that control and, in the end, when she lost that control, the Western Roman State quickly ceased to exist. A 'land' power maybe, but it was upon the sea that she ultimately depended.

Throughout most of its existence, the Roman state poured a vast amount of manpower, money and resources into its navies, and used a great deal of ingenuity and invention in the usage of water for its military operations, both for offence and defence. The State made use not only of seas great and small, but also of rivers, and invariably suffered whenever it neglected the maintenance of a sufficient level of investment in the military security of them. Observation will lead to the conclusion that, to the Roman mind, the difference between a river and a sea was only one of degree, of size. Both were waters, whether salt or fresh, and capable of use for military as well as for civilian purposes. Water was used on the one hand for the ability to easily transport large quantities of goods and materials which would prove infinitely more difficult over land. On the other hand it was the natural barrier that secured its borders and protected its people and commerce. The water-borne operations on the Rhine were as much a matter of the exercise of naval power as those in the Mediterranean. Strategically water was one of the key elements that defined the way in which the Empire grew; and exactly how far it would expand. The Rhine and Danube are wide, deep and swift; the Caucasus was probed to find such a river to use as a boundary, without success; a large length of the eastern border ran along the course of the Euphrates and Western Europe itself forms a peninsula bounded by seas. The borders of the Empire wherever possible rested and relied on rivers and seas.

Another matter of which one must not lose sight is what is meant by 'Roman'. At first, of course, they were the inhabitants of that city state, then natives of the Italian Peninsula. As the 'Roman' world grew, so did the compass of peoples from among whom the 'Romans' were garnered. An ever greater diversity applied so that at the height of Empire a 'Roman' could be by race, inter alia, a Celt from Gaul, a Semite from Syria, a Berber from North Africa, a German from the Rhine or a Greek. They were all 'Romans' and they and the Empire looked upon itself as one state. In naval matters, the absorption of Etruscan, Italiote and then Greek seafaring traditions and influences had great effect, but the achievement was 'Roman'. The freighter following the monsoon winds on the spice route to India, built by the Red Sea of timber from Lebanon and Cyprus and with a complement of Greeks and Egyptians; the French-built double-ender trading into the Baltic for amber and crewed by Celtic Britons and Dutch and Germans from the Rhine Delta; or the Greek-built ship in the Black Sea with a crew from Northern Turkey delivering goods to Georgia and the Crimea; if one asked any of these men who they were, they would all have replied 'Romans'.

It is with the military operations of the Roman state upon water, whether salt or fresh, that this book is concerned. It is an attempt to put into perspective the extent and importance of those operations that frequently justified that state in expending as much as a quarter to a third of its total military effort upon them. Such operations are not often delineated in detail, or indeed at all, by contemporary writers, yet much can be garnered from examination of their commentaries, from the course of historical events as they unfolded and from the nature and geography of the operational areas, to reveal the usage of 'naval' forces in successive contexts. Much may be inferred from the course of campaigns, although it is earnestly hoped that the too-easy trap of inferring too much has been avoided in the interpretation of events having a marine element.

By the First Punic War the Romans had already realised that control of the seas would give them control of the lands whose shores were washed by them. They had therefore adopted the policy of seeking out and destroying enemy ships wherever they were. The pursuance of this policy into the Second Punic War meant that for all of Hannibal's tactical genius, Carthage could not win. It was control of the seas that dictated the course and outcome of the later Civil Wars, and it was a naval battle that settled them and started the Imperial Period. The fleets were instrumental in the growth of the empire and the maintenance of its trade and security. It was the freezing of the Rhine in AD 406 that neutralised the fleet there and enabled the barbarians there to migrate westward in numbers which proved too great to be ejected. This presence within the borders disrupted the former cohesion of the State and largely initiated the final collapse of the Western Empire. Conversely the strength of naval forces on the Danube enabled the line to be held there and was a factor in the survival of the Eastern Empire. Finally, the lack of an effective navy in the West by this time enabled the barbarian invaders to dismember it and consolidate their hold on power in Hispania and Africa, without which, Rome itself fell. It is worth noting that the control of the seas around the continent has remained a fundamental and often determining factor in almost every major war in the subsequent history of Western Europe.

This work was conceived as a very traditional military history, for which

I make no apologies. With dozens of available general works dealing with the history of Rome itself, or with achievements of the Roman army, I felt that a more general maritime history, that brought together much of the material relating to Rome's naval achievement, was justified. The narrative of the work is set out in chronological order. Additional notes have been included at the appropriate historical junctures, relating to ships, weapons, seafaring, navigation and trade. Although these notes do not form part of the narrative, it is hoped that they will serve to provide background information and to set elements of the story into context.

No detailed specifications of Roman warships survive and the extant contemporary, brief descriptions were penned by non-naval writers. Added to this, no remains of a sea-going Roman warship have yet been discovered and the surviving iconography on coins, statuary and even paintings is hardly photographic in detail. The matter of describing ships therefore must remain an inexact process and to rely on what one hopes to be reasonable in the circumstances and based on the little that is available. It is hoped that as the various notes herein on the development and evolution of the warship are followed, the definitions will become clearer. However, on the whole I have adopted the convention of referring to types in Roman service by their Latin names, such as quinquireme or trireme (rather than the Greek Trieres). A reme (from the Latin word remiges, rowers) is a horizontal row of oars along the side of a ship, thus mono-, bi- and tri-remes (three being the maximum that was built in ancient times) and where respectively, one, two and three such horizontal rows were superimposed. This is also to distinguish from the medieval and later practice of referring to a monoreme where each individual oar was manned by three men as a 'trireme'.

In relatively recent decades the number of Roman ships discovered by archaeologists has vastly increased our knowledge of early vessel design and ship building techniques. However, in no documented case has any of these vessels proved to be a purpose built warship. Therefore, trying to ascertain what a Roman warship actually looked like (and in the thus-far total absence of surviving accurate, contemporary drawings, descriptions or specifications) one can only try to draw the best interpretation from contemporary illustrations of ships on wall-paintings, coins, mosaics and statuary. Most of these renditions are impressionistic or stylised at best, and there thus remains the need to allow considerable leeway in interpretation, the use of informed supposition and educated guesswork.

For the author's models of examples of Roman ships included in this book, plans and drawings have been prepared from the sources, subject always of course, to a constant and overall consideration of the demands of practicality and the limits imposed by the materials and technology of the time. The starting point has been to try and decide what type of ship the original artist has sought to depict and thus the type to be drawn and modelled. This is not always easy as, more often that not, the artist was simply showing 'a ship' with no particular regard as to type. This in turn dictated the oar system in use and number of rowers that had to be accommodated and around which the hull could be formed. The models represent the author's own personal interpretation of the ancient sources and iconography and no claim is or can be made to any particular authenticity or that they in any way represent definitive renditions of their prototypes.

The Roman names of places have mostly been used, giving modern equivalents where they exist, and have preferred the Latin 'Hispania' for the whole peninsula which now includes both Spain and Portugal, likewise Britannia for the British Isles. Whereas Euxine, Danubius and Rhenus seem to fit so well into the narrative, 'Oceanus Germanicus' for the North Sea is just too much of an encumbrance; for this and such other idiosyncrasies the author makes no excuse, hoping that the flow of the history is not thereby prejudiced.

The present work I happily acknowledge, has depended so heavily upon the oft-times amazing scholarship and copious research carried out by the authors of so many of the books that I have read on the subject of the 'ancient world', and the seafaring that was such an important part of it, and to all of whom I am duly indebted. Having said that, I do not necessarily concur with all of the interpretations and conclusions drawn by them and have presumed to settle on some of my own, for which I accept full blame and proffer the pious hope that not too many conclusions have been 'jumped-to' unjustifiably

Navigare necesse est, vivere non est necesse.

To sail is necessary, to live is not.

Gn. Pompeius Magnus

General Chronology

CHAPTER I

BC	
753	Traditional date of the founding of Rome.
642–616	Bridge across Tiber and expansion to the sea.
616–510	Etruscan period at Rome; first quays built; commercial shipping at Rome which becomes a trading centre.
535	Etruscan and Carthaginian fleet defeats Greeks.
524	Etruscans defeated by Greeks at Cumae.
509	Expulsion of last king from Rome; foundation of the Republic; first treaty with Carthage.
492	Rome imports grain from Cumae.
488	Rome imports grain from Sicily.
474	Etruscan fleet defeated by Syracusans off Cumae; Etruscan seapower broken.
453	Syracusans raid Etruscan coast; Carthaginians in Corsica and Sardinia.
394	First record of a Roman warship.
348	Rome renews treaty with Carthage; foundation of Ostia.
343–341	First Samnite War.
340–338	Latin War.
338	First Roman naval action; victory off Antium.
323	Treaty with Tarentum; Roman ships restricted in south;
326	Alliance with Neapolis.
326–304	Second Samnite War.
326	Samnite naval raids on Roman coast; Roman experiments with naval forces.
312	Latin colony on island of Pontia.
311	Appointment of *Duoviri Navales*.
310	Roman naval attack on Pompeii and area.
306	New treaty with Carthage.
304	End of Samnite War, Romans acquire an Adriatic coast.
298–290	Third Samnite War; extension of Roman coastlines on east and west of the peninsula.

295   Plot by draftees for the fleet fails.

282   Roman warships in Gulf of Taranto defeated by Tarentines.

280–275 Pyrrhic War.

278   Punic fleet visits Ostia; treaty with Carthage.

276   Pyrrhus defeated by Punic fleet.

273   Diplomatic relations established between Rome and Egypt.

272   Tarentum surrenders to Romans.

CHAPTER 2

272   Punic fleet appears off Tarentum.

267   Four *Praefecti* of the Fleet appointed.

264   First Punic War; naval landings on Sicily; Punic fleet blockades Messina; fleet lands Roman army on Sicily.

262   Roman alliance with Syracuse, Agrigentum captured; Punic fleet roams and raids at will.

260   Battle of Mylae; C. Duilio defeats Punic fleet.

259   Romans on Corsica and Sardinia; Punic fleet off Olbia.

258   Roman fleet wins battle off Sulci.

257   Fleet raids Melita; Punic fleet defeated off Tyndaris.

256   Battle of Ecnomus; Roman victory; Regulus lands army in Africa; fleet withdrawn but returns to evacuate army after it is defeated; Romans win Battle of Hermaeum.

255   Fleet almost totally lost in storm.

254   New fleet aids in capture of Panormus.

253   Raid on African coast; fleet wrecked in storm on return.

250   Fleet reinforced; attempted blockade of Lilybaeum.

249   Battle of Drepanum; only major Roman naval defeat of the war; Punic fleet attacks remnants of Roman fleet and storm wrecks more, fleet effectively ceases to exist.

247   Public loans raised to rebuild navy.

242   New Roman fleet sails for Drepanum.

241   Battle of Aegades Islands; Punic navy defeated and is broken; end of war; Rome supreme naval power in central Mediterranean.

CHAPTER 3

238   Operations to annexe Corsica and Sardinia and in Liguria.

238–230 Operations in Liguria.

236–220	Control of Adriatic coast extended past Padus Delta.
229–228	First Illyrian War; Illyrians storm Corcyra; fleet in Dalmatia; captures Corcyra; landings near Apollonia; Roman protectorate in Southern Illyria.
226	Embassy to Carthaginians in Hispania; Iberus treaty.
220	Illyrian fleet attacks Pylos and Aegean; Second Illyrian War; navy ferries army across Adriatic and clears it of pirates.
219	Punic seige of Saguntum.
218	Start of Second Punic War; Hannibal marches on Italy; Gn. Scipio founds navy and army base at Tarraco.
217	Romans beat Punic fleet at mouth of Iberus; fleet raids and landings along Hispanic coast; fleet reinforced.
216	Battle of Cannae; Marines of fleet bolster army; fleet cruises Sardinia and Corsica and raids African coast; sails to Illyria to counter Macedonians; enemy ships with dispatches captured; 50 ships sent to Tarentum.
215	First Macedonian War; legion transported to Sardinia; Punic fleet damaged in storm; war against Syracuse; fleet in Sicily increased.
214	Fleet operations in Illyria, Macedonians burn boats; 100 extra ships authorised; wealth tax to pay sailors; fleet foils Hannibal's attempt to seize Tarentum; Punic fleet apppears; Seige of Syracuse, fleet attack fails.
213	Hannibal seizes Tarentum; citadel supplied by sea.
212	Counter-attack by Syracusan fleet beaten off; grain shipments from Sardinia to Italy.
211	Punic fleet appears off Sicily; fall of Syracuse; Roman fleet attacks Utica; Scipios beaten, killed in Hispania.
210	Eastern fleet takes Zakinthos and Aegina; Sicilian fleet raids African coast; Romans beaten at sea by Tarentines.
209	Navy and army jointly take Carthago Nova; Eastern fleet raiding Gulf of Corinth; naval diversion supports recapture of Tarentum; Sicilian fleet raids Africa.
208	Re-organisation of fleets; naval raids on African coast; defeat of Punic squadron there.
207	Raids on African coast, Punic fleet beaten there; Eastern fleet and allies in Aegean. Hannibal blockaded.
206	Battle of Ilipa; first Roman ships in Atlantic; battle in straight of Gibraltar; Mago escapes; Scipio's embassy
205	Mago sails to Genua; Eastern fleet reinforced; end of Macedonian War; Punic relief convoy for Hannibal captured; fleet raids Africa.
204	Fleet escorts Scipio and his army to Africa.

| 203 | Scipio's ships feint at Utica; Punic attack on fleet fails; Hannibal leaves Italy; Mago evacuated from Gaul. |
| 202 | Fleet in Africa reinforced; Battle of Zama; end of the war; Punic fleet surrendered. |

Chapter 4

201	Rhodes and Pergamum attacked by Macedonia, appeal to Rome for help; operations in Liguria.
200	Second Macedonian War; fleet sent East, captures Chalcis and joins local allies.
199	Fleet attack Chalkidiki; capture Oreus; supreme in Aegean.
198	Allied fleet captures Eretria.
197	Battle of Cynoscephelae; end of war; Macedonian fleet surrendered; insurrection in Hispania.
195	Roman and allied campaigns against Sparta; surrender of Spartan fleet.
194	Romans withdraw from Greece; squadron left in Aegean, fleet in Sicily reinforced.
192	Antiochus lands in Thessaly; attack on Romans causes war.
191	Roman army returned to Greece, defeats Antiochus; Aegean squadron reinforced; battle off Cape Corycus, Syrian fleet defeated and driven to Ephesus.
190	Syrians attack Rhodian squadron; Hannibal's fleet defeated; Romans and allies win major battle off Myonnesus; Romans extend their control in Adriatic.
189	Battle of Magnesia; Antiochus beaten and his fleet surrendered; end of war; naval intercession in Crete.
188	Anti-piracy operations and seizure of Cephallenia; Romans withdraw again from the east.
178	Fleet active in north Adriatic campaign.
177	Istria annexed with naval support.
176	Insurrections in Corsica and Sardinia; troops transported and supported there.
172	Third Macedonian War; fleet operations in Aegean.
170	Fleet captures Abdera in Thrace.
169	Fleet fails to support army in Greece; Macedonian ships operate along Anatolian Coast.
168	Operations on Illyrian coast and Aegean; Battle of Pydna ends war; Romans withdraw; Delos as duty-free port; decline of Rhodian sea-power starts; Roman coastline extended to Massilia. Unrest between Syria and Egypt.
161	Roman treaty with Israel.
156–155	Campaigns in Illyria; Romans extend control of Adriatic.

154 Naval operations in the Atlantic; campaigns against Lusitani; campaign against Ligurians.

151 Start of Third Punic War.

149 Macedonia becomes a province; fleet transports army to Africa and supports seige and blockade of Carthage.

148 Greece overrun; marine's landing at Carthage repulsed.

147 Fleet at Carthage seizes sand-bar to seal harbour; Punic fleet escapes but is caught and beaten; Roman marines secure bridgehead on Carthage harbour.

146 Final assault and fall of Carthage; sack of Corinth.

139 End of Lusitanian war; 'Atlantic fleet' operates as far as northern Pyrenees.

133 Fall of Numantia, end of war in Hispania; naval manpower and fleet strength reduced; run-down of the navy starts; mercantile traffic increases; Ostia becomes civil port.

130 Province of Asia acquired.

125 Campaign against Ligurians, Roman–controlled coast extended to Hispania.

122 Fleet action in capture of Balearic Islands.

117 Campaigns in Balkans and Africa; Jugurthine War.

107 Marius starts army reforms but navy run-down, neglected.

102 M. Antonius operates against Cilician pirates.

98 Marius retires.

96 Cyrene becomes Roman possession.

90 'Social' War in Italy; navy stays loyal; marines used against rebels.

88 End of war; Sulla given Eastern command.

CHAPTER 5

86 Mithridates of Pontus overruns Asia, attacks Greece and has a fleet in the Aegean. Lucullus sent to gather a fleet; Sulla retakes Athens, beats Mithridates who withdraws; Lucullus' fleet sails to the Hellespont.

85 Fleet supports Sulla's advance into Anatolia; peace with Mithridates who surrenders 70 ships.

84 Sulla returns to Rome; Lucullus' fleet disbanded; plans for naval garrisons in East not completed.

83 Sulla joined by Pompeius; civil war in Italy.

81 Sulla Dictator; fleet backs Pompeius' campaign in Africa

80 Seige of Mytilene; allied ships used.

79 Sulla retires; fleet in anti-piracy sweep off Cilicia.

78 Anti-piracy campaign continues.

77	Vatia defeats pirates off Lycia.
76	Vatia attacks pirate coastlines; Pompeius has naval support in Hispania.
75	Vatia reduces Isauria; Caesar taken by pirates.
74	Varro on western shore of Euxine; Cyrene annexed; Bythinia bequeathed to Rome; war against Mithridates, Vatia's operations cease; fleet and army sent East both defeated; M. Antonius sent against pirates.
73	Pontic Fleet in Aegean; part destroyed at Lemnos; remainder withdraws; Mithridates beaten and war ended.
72	Antonius loses to Cretan pirates; pirate raids on Italy.
71	Slave revolt in Italy.
69	Navy in poor state; piracy rages unchecked; Delos attacked; Metellus takes Crete.
67	Anti-piracy *Lex Gabinia* enacted; Pompeius commands; Ostia attacked by pirates; navy's decline halted, it is built up anew; Pompeius' naval campaigns destroy pirates; navy established as a permanent force.
66	Pompeius defeats Mithridates, marches to Armenia; Romans control Euxine Sea; Euxine and Aegean squadrons founded.
63	Pompeius annexes Syria, settles Judaea.
61	Caesar in Hispania; Roman control extended to northern coasts.
60	The First Triumvirate in Rome: Caesar, Crassus, Pompey.
58	Navy suports annexation of Cyprus; Caesar's first campaign in Gaul reaches the River Rhenus.
57	Caesar in Gaul; sea-routes supply his winter camps.
56	Revolt in Brittany; Roman fleet prepared in Western Gaul; Battle off Quiberon Bay, Gauls defeated; Biscay coast brought under Roman control.
55	Caesar's first expedition to Britannia.
54	Caesar's second expedition to Britannia.
53	Caesar in eastern Gaul; Crassus defeated in Parthia.
50	Caesar settles Gaul; naval force established in English Channel; Caesar and Pompeius generate factions.
49	Civil war between Caesar and Pompeius who moves to Greece; Caesar to Hispania, navy split between them; Pompeius' fleet wins victory in Adriatic; seige of Massilia and naval battle; Caesar leaves Hispania
48	Caesar crosses to Greece; besieges Pompeius but siege broken by his fleet; Battle of Pharsalus, Pompeius defeated; Caesar in Egypt.
47	Egyptian fleet defeated; Caesar in Judaea, Pontus, Rome.
46	Caesar made Dictator, defeats rebels in Africa

45   Caesar Dictator for life; intends war against Parthia.

44   Murder of Caesar.

Chapter 6

44   M. Antonius controls Rome, Sextus in Hispania; plotters flee to Greece; Octavius in Rome as Caesar's heir.

43   Sextus given command of navy; Second Triumvirate: Octavius, Antonius, Lepidus; Octavius forms own fleet.

42   Octavius and Antonius land in Greece; defeat plotters; Sextus in Sicily, seizes Sardinia, controls shipping.

40   Treaty between Octavius and Antonius

39   Triumvirs meet Sextus; Octavius readies a fleet for war.

38   Corsica and Sardinia defect to Octavius; battle off Cumae, Octavius beaten; appoints Agrippa admiral; he founds new naval base near Misenum, rebuilds fleet.

37   Triumvirate renewed; Octavius receives part of Antonius' fleet as reinforcement.

36   Attack on Sicily; Lepidus in the west, Agrippa wins sea battle off Mylae; sea battle of Naulochus, Sextus defeated; Octavius supreme in west, Antonius in east.

35   Naval sweep of Adriatic.

33   War between Octavius and Antonius; Antonius at Actium, joined by Egyptian fleet.

31   Agrippa seizes Corcyra; Octavius in Greece, blockades Antonius; Agrippa captures Patras, Corinth, Leucas; Battle of Actium, Octavius victorious.

30   Suicide of Antonius and Cleopatra in Egypt; Octavius sole ruler of Roman world.

29   Octavius' Triumph; military reforms commence.

28   Advance up to First Cataract of Nile.

27   Octavius becomes Augustus.

26   Expedition down Red Sea to Sabaea.

25   End of Red Sea expedition; Nile border advanced to Second Cataract; Galatia annexed; peace with Parthia; reform of navy; founding of *Classes Praetoriae*.

22   Founding of Italian fleet bases at Misenum and Ravenna.

17   Bosporan affair; Roman and allied fleet land marines, dominate Euxine; Pontus annexed.

16   Noricum occupied.

15   Advance to line of Danubius; establishment of *Classis Pannonica* and *Classis Moesica* on upper and lower Danubius.

| 13 | Military reforms completed. |

CHAPTER 7

| 12 | Advance into Germania; Roman fleet on Dutch lakes and North Sea; founding of *Classis Germanica*. |
| 9 | Advances in Germania; fleet on German rivers and North European coasts to Baltic entrances. |

AD

6	Judaea annexed; Herod's navy absorbed.
9	Defeat in Germania; Rhenus made into permanent border.
14	Death of Augustus; Tiberius succeeds; fleets support campaigns in Germania.
16	Further operations in Germania and northern coasts.
19	New provinces in Anatolia.
28	Frisii revolt; Balkan command reformed.
37	Tiberius dies, Gaius succeeds; builds pleasure ships; bridge from Baiae to Puteoli.
40	Gaius' at the English Channel.
41	Gaius assassinated, Claudius succeeds; administration reorganised; starts to build Portus, Rome's new harbour.
43	Invasion of Britannia; *Classis Britannica* founded; army dependent on fleet for supplies.
44	Fleet operations along coasts of Britannia
45	Naval expedition to Bosporan kingdom.
46	Thrace annexed, temporary fleet formed for the operation; *Classis Moesica* extends into Euxine.
47	*Classis Britannica* rounds southwest of Britannia.
52	Operations in South Wales.
54	Claudius dies; Nero succeeds.
61	Revolt in Britannia; Praetorians in Egypt.
62	Storm damages ships at Portus; canal proposed for Gaul.
64	Pontus annexed; *Classis Pontica* formed.
65	Nero forms two legions from Italian fleet personnel.
66	Revolt in Palestine, Vespasian given command there.
68	Nero's suicide; Galba emperor; naval legions attacked.
69	Galba murdered, Otho succeeds; supported by Misene Fleet. Vitellius declared emperor; fleet attacks Liguria; first Battle of Cremona; Otho's suicide, Vitellius succeeds; Vespasian declared emperor; Civilis' revolt; Ravenna Fleet joins

Vespasian; second Battle of Cremona, Vitellius defeated; Misene Fleet at Tarracina; Vitellius killed; Civilis' revolt suppressed.

Chapter 8

71	*Classis Britannica* in North Sea.
74	Operations in Wales; start of move into Agri Decumates.
78	Agricola in Britannia, advances northward; *Classis Pontica* secures Euxine.
79	Death of Vespasian, accession of Titus; Vesuvius erupts, Misene Fleet in rescue work.
80	Colosseum dedicated, navy crews operate awnings; operations on east and west coasts of Britannia, which is circumnavigated.
81	Death of Titus, Domitian succeeds; navy pay rises.
82	Reconaissance of Caledonian and Hibernian coasts.
83	Agricola in Caledonia; combined operations.
84	Fleet off north coast of Caledonia. Mons Graupius.
85	Dacian incursions; Agricola and troops withdrawn; further eastward advance of German lines.
89	Incursions across Rhenus defeated by *Classis Germanica*.
93	Peace restored; Domitian's reign of terror.
96	Death of Domitian, Nerva succeeds.
98	Death of Nerva, Trajan succeeds.
101	Start of Dacian campaigns.
106	Completion of Dacian Wars; Red Sea–Nile canal restored; Nabatea annexed; Roman ships in Indian Ocean.
117	Trajan dies following Parthian campaign; Hadrian.
122	Hadrian in Britannia, defines new border with his wall.
127	Ptolemy's map of the world; navy ships in Red Sea.
130	Expedition to Bosporan Kingdom, garrisons placed there.
132	Revolt in Judaea.
138	Death of Hadrian, Antoninus succeeds.
142	Border in Britannia advanced to Antonine Wall.
161	Antoninus dies, Marcus Aurelius and Lucius Verus succeed. *Classis Pontica* moves to Cyzicus; naval build up in East.
162	Parthians attack the East; Verus captures Armenia.
169	Barbarian incursions across Danubius; death of Verus; Misene Fleet operations off Mauretania.
170	Invasions across Danubius, Emperor campaigns in opposition.

174	Start of barbarian raids on north European coasts.
175	Navy enlistment term extended.
180	Death of Marcus, succeeded by Commodus, abandons settlement of new provinces in Central Europe.
185	Fleet supports punitive campaign in Caledonia.
192	Commodus killed; Pertinax emperor, killed; Severus, Niger and Albinus proclaimed; Praetorians 'auction' Empire; Severus marches on Rome, defeats Niger.
195	Albinus in Gaul, defeated by Severus, who becomes sole Emperor; border in Britannia returned to Hadrian's Wall.
197	Severus campaigns against Parthians.
208	Severus in Britannia for conquest of Caledonia.
211	Severus dies, succeeded by sons Caracalla and Geta.
212	Caracalla extends citizenship.
213	Emperor on Rhenus, campaigns in Germania.
215	Caracalla in the East.
217	Caracalla assassinated. Macrinus emperor.
218	Macrinus killed, Elegabalus emperor
219	Attempts to usurp; fleet promotes one usurper.
222	Elegabalus killed, Alexander Severus succeeds; unrest and indiscipline in army; fleets neglected.
230	Raiding and piracy in North Sea; start of northern coastal defence system; North Sea coastline changes.
231	Mutiny on Danubius; indecisive campaign in East.
233	Attempts at mass migration of Germanic tribes starts; Rhenus frontier breached.
235	Alexander tries to buy off invaders and is killed; Maximinus Emperor.
236	Emperor campaigns in Germania.
237	More campaigns across Rhenus and Danubius.
238	Maximinus killed opposing pretenders; Gordian III emperor; Goths cross Danubius; raid on west Britannia coast.
241	Persians invade; Gordian defeats Goths.
243	Persians defeated and driven out.
244	Gordian killed, Philip emperor; campaign across Danubius.
248	Rome celebrates 1000th anniversary of founding; uprising by Balkan legions.
249	Decius commands in Balkans, restores order; campaign against Goths; Decius declared emperor, defeats Philip.
250	Goths cross Lower Danubius; Decius opposes them.

251	Emperor killed in battle; Gallus emperor; Goths overrun Bosporan Kingdom, Roman control of Euxine weakens.
252	Persians invade Syria; Goths attack, defeated by Aemilius who is declared emperor.
253	Gallus killed; Aemilius killed; Valerian emperor with his son Gallienus.
254	Gallienus campaigns on Danubius; Goth sea raids in Euxine.
257	Emperors campaign against Persians and on Rhenus.
259	Juthungi invade Italy and are defeated; Goths attack Moesia and Thrace; Goth fleet in Aegean.
260	Juthungi expelled; Persians capture Valerian; Franks cross Rhenus; Alemanni threaten Italy; revolt in Africa put down by Misene Fleet; Postumus restores Rhenus, himself emperor in Gaul, Hispania and Britannia.
261	Romans defeat Persians; Palmyrenes put down revolt.
263	Gallienus recovers Rhaetia; Agri Decumates abandoned.
265	Gallienus tries and fails to recover Gaul.
266	Palmyrenes defeat Persians; piracy in the Levant, shipping declines.
267	Odaenathus of Palmyra defeats Goths but dies.
268	Palmyrenes defeat Gallienus; barbarian invasion of Moesia and Thrace, Athens attacked; Gallienus defeats them but is killed; Claudius II emperor, destroys invaders; Goth sea force beaten in Aegean.
269	Claudius campaigns against Alemanni and Goths; Postumus killed; Victorinus eventually succeeds; Hispania, part of Gaul recovered by Claudius.
270	Rival Palmyrene empire; Claudius dies, Aurelian emperor.
271	Invasions across Danubius and Rhenus defeated; 'Aurelian' walls around Rome.
272	Aurelian defeats Goths on Danubius; Dacia abandoned; Palmyrenes defeated and east restored.
274	Aurelian defeats 'Gallic Empire', Empire reunited.
275	Invasion across Danubius defeated; Aurelian assassinated; his successors campaign in Balkans against invaders.
276	Probus emperor; invasion of Gaul; three year campaign to defeat invaders and restore borders.
279	Probus defeats invasion across Danubius; revolt in Egypt.
282	Probus killed, Carus succeeds.
283	Campaign on Danubius; Carus defeats Persians but dies; Carinus and Numerian succeed; Numerian dies, succeeded by Diocletian; Carinus campaigns on Rhenus and Danubius.
284	Carinus in Britannia; defeated and killed by Diocletian.

CHAPTER 9

285	Diocletian emperor, adds Maximian as co–ruler.
286	Carausius commands *Classis Britannica*, secedes; reform of army and navy; Danubius border reorganised.
288	Campaigns on all borders.
290	Peace with Carausius, who extends shore defence system.
293	Constantius and Galerius as Caesars; Constantius recovers north Gaul; Carausius replaced by Allectus.
294	Forts built on left bank of Danubius.
296	Attacks on Africa and Armenia; Constantius invades Britannia, ends secession; punitive cruise by fleet.
297	Galerius defeats Persians; reform of administration.
305	Emperors retire; Constantius and Galerius joined by Maximinus and Severus.
306	Constantius dies, Constantine declared emperor; Severus killed, Maxentius in Rome; piracy and raiding in Gaul.
308	Emperors' conference to resolve power sharing.
311	Galerius dies; Constantine defeats Maxentius.
316	Civil war against Licinius; Constantine invades Balkans.
323	Naval battle of Hellespont; Licinius defeated.
324	Final defeat of Licinius, Constantine sole emperor; founding of Constantinople; army reforms.
328	Campaigns across Rhenus; border reinforced.
332	Campaigns across Danubius.
336	Campaign in Dacia.
337	Constantine dies, empire split between his sons.
353	Civil wars, Constantius II sole emperor; raiding across river and coastal borders; Julian campaigns over Rhenus.
360	Julian sends forces to restore Britannia; end of Bosporan Kingdom; Julian declared emperor.
363	Julian uses a fleet on Euphrates to attack Persia.
364	Emperors Valentinian in West, Valens in East.
367	Barbarian conspiracy, invasion of Britannia.
369	Theodosius restores Britannia, defences strengthened.
375	Valentinian dies, Gratian succeeds.
378	Battle of Hadrianopolis; Theodosius Emperor in East.
383	Gratian killed; western fleet supports usurper in Italy.

386	Battle on Danubius destroys Goth migration.
388	Theodosius defeats Magnus; battle between rebel and eastern fleets off Sicily, rebels defeated.
395	Death of Theodosius; Empire divided, Arcadius in East, Honorius in West; control of northern seas lost by now.
396	Stilicho restores Britannia.
397	Expedition to supress rebellion in Africa.
401	Goths invade west; Troops withdrawn from Britannia.
406	Rhenus freezes; mass influx of barbarians into Gaul; Honorius moves to Ravenna.
407	Usurper takes troops from Britannia to restore Rhenus.
408	Alaric the Goth beseiges Rome.
409	Britannia invaded; barbarians enter Hispania.
410	Goths sack Rome.
413	Count of Africa's invasion of Rome defeated.
418	Visigoth kingdom in Aquitania; Franks settle north Gaul; barbarians control parts of Hispania.
423	Honorius dies; Aetius exercises power.
429	Vandals cross to Mauretania.
432	Count of Africa's challenge for power in Italy beaten.
439	Vandals take Carthage and build a navy.
440	Vandals take Sicily, Sardinia and Corsica; Eastern Emperor sends fleet, which is defeated by them.
451	Attila the Hun invades Gaul and is defeated; Anglo-Saxon kingdom in Britannia.
456	Romans defeat Vandal fleet off Corsica.
457	Vandal fleet defeated at Ostia; Roman fleet destroyed while fitting out in Hispania.
467	Joint East and West Roman fleet recovers Sardinia, beaten by Vandals; last action by a western Roman fleet.
476	Last emperor of the West leaves office; 'official' end of the Western Empire.

BEGINNINGS

Foundation to the First Punic War
753 BC–264 BC

Tradition has it that Rome was founded in 753 BC. Certainly the peoples inhabiting at least some of the Roman hills came together to form a conurbation at about that time and they established a monarchy that would rule over them for nearly two and a half centuries to come, until 510 BC.

753 BC

The newly founded city was strategically placed on the left bank of the River Tiber that divides the central western part of the Italian peninsula. The location is based on defensible hills adjacent to the lowest crossing point of the river and also the highest point to which it was navigable by the seagoing ships of that time. The embryo city was thus placed to control not only an essential element of the land trade routes, but the river crossing with its traffic upriver along the Tiber valley and downriver to the open sea. Control of the Tiber valley gave access to sea and, as a result, to the international trade beyond.

To the north of Rome, the city-states of the Etruscans were dominant and expanding their horizons. To the south the Greeks were establishing and extending their colonies in the 'heel' and 'toe' of the peninsula, in Campania and on Sicily (the Italiote Greeks). The Phoenician colony of Carthage (founded in about 814 BC) had expanded its ambitions both as to territory and as to domination of sea-trade and occupied parts of Sicily and Sardinia.

642 BC

Tradition again has it that there were seven kings of Rome, the fourth of whom was Ancus Marcius, who reigned from 642 to 616 BC. It was in his reign that the first, probably wooden, bridge was built across the Tiber. Ancus Marcius is also considered responsible for extending Roman territory along the south or left bank of the river the fourteen miles to the river's mouth, at what would eventually become the site of Ostia. Rome thus directly met the sea for the first time. The move is thought to have been to gain control of the salt beds at the river mouth and to secure freedom of navigation on the Tiber. However, these expansions of territory antagonised the Etruscans who immediately seized control of the north bank.

By now the Etruscans were expanding their domains rapidly, they captured Rome and moved southward across Latium and Campania to Pompeii and Surrentum (Sorrento), by-passing the Greek colonies at Cumae (Cuma) and Neapolis (Naples). These moves brought them into contact, rivalry and eventually conflict with the Greeks.

At Rome, the last three of their kings were Etruscan and they represent a period of a century of almost continuous Etruscan domination. The Romans undoubtedly gained greatly from this period and many Etruscans settled in Rome. The Etruscans were an advanced and inventive people who brought to Rome their varied and considerable abilities. Some of the most notable of these were in the area of civil engineering, which the Romans would go on to develop and utilise in the centuries to come, including ways that would enable them to operate a large portion of their empire by using water for both transport and the projection of power. The Etruscans were already a seafaring people of long standing, and it is again from them that the Romans probably had their first practical introduction to the design, building and operation of ships intended for waters beyond the Tiber, rather than simply acting as hosts to the visiting seagoing ships of other peoples.

Archaeology indicates that it was during this period that the first wharves were built at Rome on the flat land between the ends of the Palatine and Aventine Hills. Fairs were held where people from the city and its surrounding area could meet with traders from overseas, whose ships had made their way or been towed up-river to the quayside at Rome. Trade, and with it the importance of Rome as a trading centre, increased (foreign trade goods have been found there dating from the period 575 to 500 BC). The Tiber ran more deeply than today and small and medium-sized ships could reach the city. The larger ships would have had to moor at the river mouth and offload their cargoes onto barges or lighters for onward carriage to Rome. It has been calculated that a small barge could carry about five tons, operated by a crew of five, one to steer and four on the riverbank pulling it by ropes.[1] The crew would also of course, load and unload the barge.

Rome not only expanded but the horizons of her people must surely have been widened as they progressed from minor backwater to mercantile centre. Doubtless Carthaginian ships visited and the links with Carthage were formed at this time that would lead to the three hundred year alliance between the two cities.[2]

It seems inconceivable that in the hundred years or so of the Etruscan period, no Roman, or Etruscan settler in Rome owned, operated or at the very least, served aboard ships, some of which must have been based there. It is from this period that the first 'Roman' ships are likely to date. There must also have grown up a body of shipwrights, sailmakers, riggers and the other trades connected with the fitting-out, repair and victualling of the shipping

MERCHANT SHIPS

Merchant ships of various sizes and types will have become familiar sights to the Romans, ranging from small, open, rowed vessels and barges to the larger open vessels with raised stem and sternposts, broad of beam and mounting a short, stout mast which carried a yard bearing a single, rectangular sail. Several oars were positioned on each side, to assist when becalmed or to manoeuvre in restricted waters or harbours. The sternposts were commonly decorated and carved into animal-head shapes. The ships were equipped with a single mast, but in the early fifth century BC the Etruscans introduced a second foremast, the earliest depiction of a two-masted ship being in an Etruscan tomb at Tarquinia, just north of Rome, and dating from this time. Later on, larger ships came into use, with decked-over hulls and also mounting a second mast, or *artemon*, forward. This mast was raked forward and carried a yard with a second sail. The Greeks in particular also employed many sleek, principally oar-powered, ships for trading, giving them the added possibility of some buccaneering or low level piracy if opportunity arose.

NAVIGATION

Most navigation at that time was by following coasts but the Egyptians had conjectured, from seeing sails disappear over the horizon, that the Earth was 'curved'. The Phoenicians had for some time, navigated by observing the constellation of the Great Bear or Plough, the Pole Star not having achieved its present, central position at that time, and they were able to draw astronomical charts. They had ranged far and wide to extend their trade routes and had dared the seas beyond the Pillars of Hercules (Straits of Gibraltar) and founded a colony at Gadir (Cadiz), whence they could trade with the local kingdom of Tartessos or Tarshish, as well as with the Atlantic seaboards of what are now Portugal and Morocco. The concept of maps had been long-established and the earliest known which show the cardinal compass points date from circa 2300 BC Mesopotamia.[3] Scales of distances on maps emanated from Babylon. Similarly, observations of the changes in the passage of the sun and stars through the seasons and that they varied according to location, gave rise to the development of the concept of latitude and that this could be used to determine one's position relative to north and south.

NILE–RED SEA CANAL

In about 610 BC, the Egyptian Pharoah Nekau or Necho II, had a navigable canal dug between the easternmost or Pelusiac branch of the Nile Delta (which has since dried up when the river changed course), from a point near to modern Zigazag to Lake Timsah, then by the Bitter Lakes (a distance of perhaps 35 miles (52km)) to join the northernmost tip of the Gulf of Suez, a distance of sixty or so miles (100km) at Rome and on the river. Local builders of the small riverine craft used on the Tiber may well have extended their repertoire to build ships for Roman-Etruscan owners.

Beyond their river mouth the Romans would have seen three powers vying for control of the sea-trade of the western Mediterranean, the Etruscans, the Greeks and the Carthaginians. For over a century, Greek seafarers had frequented the coasts of Sicily and southern Italy, establishing settlements and colonising the coastal areas. The earlier voyages were for plunder or trade and insofar as piracy could be termed 'trade by other means' the seafarers would seek such opportunities as presented themselves; trade with a powerful entity or kidnapping to obtain slaves, ransom or plunder against a weak one. Flotillas of these adventurers would sail together, enough to deal with all but the strongest of local opposition. This appears to have resulted in the native population largely abandoning the coasts and moving to defensible settlements inland. Archaeologically, these settlements tend to be characterised by the way in which buildings were erected around a perimeter, facing inward, and presenting blank, strong, continuous walls to the outside; a feature still commonly found in Italian villages. A good example is the Etruscan city of Tarquinia, built and fortified on a mount a few miles from the coast, while its port, Pyrgi, on the coast is little more than a few insubstantial quays and jetties and appears not to have been intended to be defended. The Greeks were able to settle and colonise the resulting empty coastal sites. For their part, the Phoenicians established trading relations with the Etruscans and started to colonise Sardinia and Sicily; a process that was inherited by their Carthaginian successors. Unlike the Greeks, they did not however, plant colonies on the Italian mainland, although they probably had trade representatives at various ports there.[4]

600 BC   In about 600 BC the Greeks founded a colony at Massilia (Marseilles) and were becoming increasingly interested in Corsica. The Etruscans objected to these incursions into their area of influence and concluded an

535 BC   alliance with Carthage. In 535 BC, their joint fleets defeated the Greek fleet off Alalia in Corsica and, although Massilia survived, Greek expansion was halted. The Etruscans, it seems, were content with their coastal trade and the Carthaginians were left with a virtual free hand in the rest of the western Mediterranean.

In connection with the loss of ancient warships (apart from those wrecked on shorelines, foundered in storms, were destroyed by fire, broken up or which just rotted to bits), it is convenient to refer to those lost in battle or similar circumstances as having been 'sunk'. In our age of steel-hulled ships, it is easy to imagine a holed ship plunging to the sea bed, as the water rushes in displacing the air inside the hull, and metal being heavier than water, it sinks. An ancient merchantman, when holed, was dragged down overall and linking the Mediterranean with the Red Sea and beyond. Ships could be rowed, depending upon the span of their oars, or pulled by their crews or teams of animals on towpaths. The canal may have been widened later by the Persian King Darius I after the Persian invasion of Egypt, nearly a century later. Its use depended greatly upon the attention given to constant dredging and maintenance by successive rulers as it was prone to rapid silting. It was further improved by Ptolemy II Philadelphus (reigned 285 to 246 BC), who added locks. The year after it was built, the Pharoah commissioned a fleet of Phoenician ships to sail south from the Gulf of Suez, down the African coast. About three years later they re-appeared on the Mediterranean coast of Egypt, having circumnavigated the continent.[5]

SHIP BUILDING

For many centuries the practice when building a ship's hull has mainly been to erect a skeleton of frames and ribs and to then cover it. Throughout the ancient world the reverse was done in that the 'shell' was built first, the shipwrights fashioning and fitting each plank on either side to build up the outer hull, setting up the shape with battens for guidance. Only after the shell was completed would frames and strengthening timbers be fashioned and fixed inside the hull. The planks of the hull were joined edge to edge by cutting a great number of mortices or slots at frequent, matching intervals in the edges of both planks then fitting a wooden tenon into each mortice on one plank and pushing the two together, engaging the tenons in the corresponding mortices in the other plank. With the planks pushed into a tight join, the tenons were secured by drilling a hole through each plank and tenon and driving in a retaining dowel. The method gave a strong hull, relatively free from built-in stress and needing little or no caulking, for which tow was used. On the other hand, it was extremely labour intensive, required highly skilled shipwrights, and was wasteful in materials (as much as three quarters of a piece of timber could be cut away to fashion it into a fit). The method had, however, been universally used in the Mediterranean since at least 1350 BC (the date of the oldest wreck so far found, built using this method) and would continue almost unchanged as the method of construction for both merchant and warships until the first century AD.[6]

The Mediterranean is home to ship-worm and Teredo beetle, both devastating to an unprotected wooden hull, and to protect them from marine parasites, they were therefore smeared inside and out with pitch from tree resin or a pitch and wax mix. Alternatively tar, which is found welling to the surface in natural tar pits at places such as Zakynthos in the Ionian Islands (as recorded by Herodotus in the early fifth century BC), could be used. The tar could be dried into cakes and carried, to be melted and used as needed and, of course, was a highly tradable commodity. Later, merchant ship hulls were protected by thin lead sheeting, laid over tarred fabric and fixed by nails, to sheath them. Obviously such a method would have added

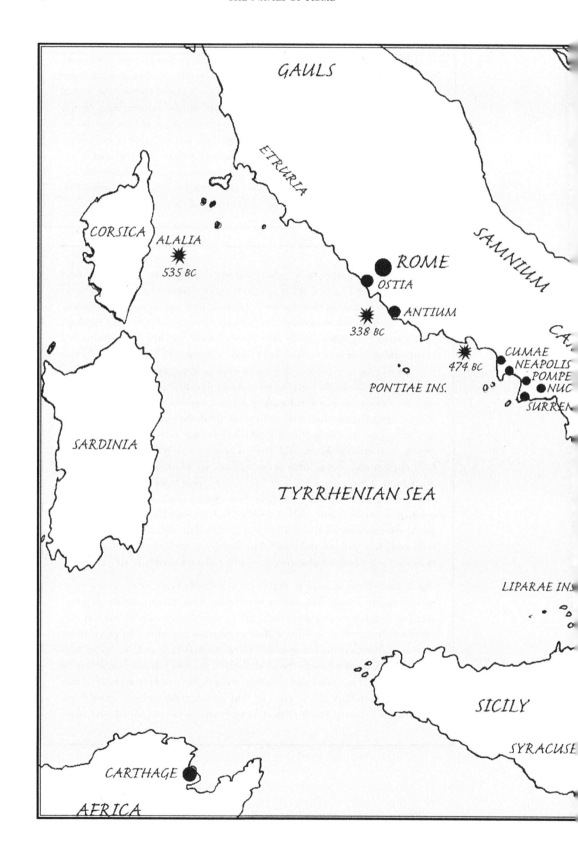

GAULS

ETRURIA

CORSICA

ALALIA
✴
535 BC

SARDINIA

ROME

OSTIA

ANTIUM

✴
338 BC

✴
474 BC

PONTIAE INS.

SAMNIUM

CA

CUMAE
NEAPOLIS
POMPE
NUC
SURREN

TYRRHENIAN SEA

LIPARAE INS

SICILY

SYRACUSE

CARTHAGE

AFRICA

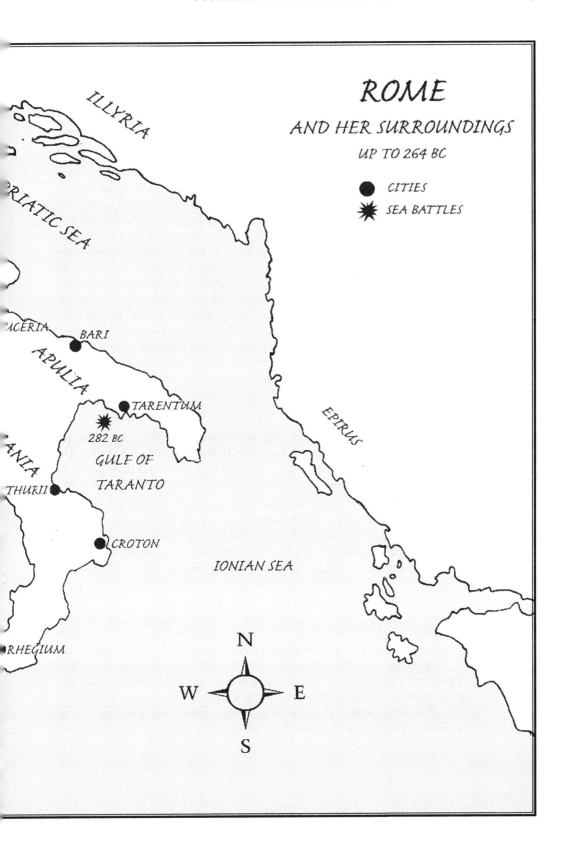

ROME
AND HER SURROUNDINGS
UP TO 264 BC

● CITIES
✱ SEA BATTLES

ILLYRIA

ADRIATIC SEA

ACERIA

BARI

APULIA

TARENTUM

282 BC

GULF OF
TARANTO

THURII

...ANIA

CROTON

EPIRUS

IONIAN SEA

RHEGIUM

N
W   E
S

by the weight of its cargo and as a result, a number of sunken merchant ships have been found underwater by archaeologists and divers. To date, no sunken remains of seagoing warships have been found. The obvious reason for this is that wood floats and has to be forced beneath the water by a weight greater than its own reserve of buoyancy. Ancient warships were all wood and carried, even with their rams, no load greater then their intrinsic buoyancy. As a result, if holed one or more times by rams, they would not 'sink' but settled to the waterline dictated by the natural buoyancy level of the wooden hull mass. In effect, they 'floated' at, or just below, the surface, well below their normal waterline, so that they became swamped, awash and unstable. Heeling towards any imbalance, waterlogged, unmanageable and helpless they were effectively lost. Such ships could be, and were sometimes, salvaged; the prerogative of a victorious fleet.[7] As the ship's main strength was in the hull shell, successive blows from rams could disrupt it sufficiently to cause it to start breaking up into a mass of still-floating lumps of carpentry. A ship which had been holed obviously took time to become swamped, during which its crew were still capable of fighting and indeed, had an extra incentive to do so. An attacker which could not withdraw quickly was itself at risk of being boarded by its victim's crew. There were occasions however when a ship settled quickly and the lowest reme of rowers could not get out of the hull in time to avoid drowning.[8]

THE EARLY REPUBLIC

524 BC

To remove it from the flank of their southward expansion, the Etruscans attacked the Greeks of Cumae, but were badly defeated in 524 BC. The Etruscans had now reached the peak of their expansion and their power in the south began to decline.

510 BC

In 510 BC, the Romans became disaffected and expelled what was to be the last of their kings, the Etruscan Tarquin the Proud, and formed a Republic. One of the new state's first acts was, in 508 BC, to conclude a formal treaty of friendship with Carthage. By this treaty, the ships of Rome and her allies were forbidden to enter African Waters west of Hermaeum (Cape Bon in Tunisia), except in an emergency, and even then, had to leave in five days.[9] Although it is hardly likely that Rome and her allies could have provided any kind of threat, either naval or mercantile, Carthage jealously guarded her trade routes. This tactic also ensured that she would not have another competitor in the western Mediterranean and at the same time, by recognising and supporting the new republic, she encouraged another opponent to her Etruscan rivals. These terms imply that Rome had ships of her own at this time and that some at least of them were capable of long-distance voyaging. There must have been some corresponding benefit to Rome, possibly and logically Carthaginian support for the young too much weight to a warship, which would hamper its speed. Wax-based paint was made, pigmented to provide white, purple, blue, yellow, red, brown and green, although having the primary colours, presumably any other colour could be mixed. For building the ships, pine, fir, oak, elm and more exotic woods such as cedar and cypress were used; rope was made from flax, papyrus or hemp and esparto grass from Spain. Sails were of canvas made from flax or hemp. Both plants are indigenous to Western Asia and Europe, hemp also providing fibre for good quality rope and cord. Cotton, indigenous to India and Central Asia, was also known and introduced and increasingly grown in Egypt for use for awnings and light weather sails.[10]

Steering for all ships up to about the twelfth century AD was effected by one or two large-bladed 'steering oars' or side rudders, mounted on the stern quarters and able to be turned by means of a tiller, fitted at right angles to the top of the vertical shaft of the oar. With surfaces both fore and aft of the steering oar shafts, these 'rudders' were, in effect, balanced, and by all accounts a well set-up ship was light to steer. However, reconstructions of ancient vessels using this rudder mechanism have encountered a number of problems, particularly in the more challenging waters of the Atlantic. There are many very ancient depictions in Egyptian paintings of boats rigged with a single rudder or steering oar slung on the sternpost, with the upper end resting in a cradle and steered by a tiller. A similar arrangement is known later on Roman river craft, but there is no indication that it was developed for use for seagoing ships. Ships had to be regularly hauled out of the water to have the hulls cleaned and re-treated against the attack of shipworm and Teredo beetle and were brought ashore for the 'closed' winter season, warships being hauled up stern-first to avoid damage to the rams. Apart from being hauled out onto suitable beaches, the construction and use of purpose-built ramps and ship-sheds was widespread.[11]

WEATHER

The Mediterranean in winter can give rise to vicious storms and mariners of old quickly learned the advisability of not sailing between November and March. Ships did sail during the winter, but prudence dictated that they did so only exceptionally. As a rule, throughout the ancient world, sea-travel was largely suspended during those months. In addition, observation of the sun and stars, so necessary for navigation, is far less frequently possible through the overcast skies of winter.

WARSHIP EVOLUTION

By this time the warship was well developed. Until about 900 BC warfare at sea had merely been an extension of land warfare; the ships being only platforms for troops to fight from. On the meeting of opposing fleets, archers and slingers would

Republic. Although they would shy at providing military help on land, the Carthaginians could, at little cost, keep open Rome's access to the sea and its trade, in which they doubtless were greatly involved. At sea, apart from Carthaginian domination of the West, the Etruscans regarded the Tyrrhenian Sea as 'theirs' and the Greeks of the south looked to their own local waters. The distinction between formal trade and brigandage remained clouded, and plundering ships of a foreign state was not necessarily regarded as any business of a ruler. In times of war between various Greek city-states, pirates and their ships were often seconded as 'navies', there being no such formal state organisations. Privateering was authorised and rights of 'reprisal' granted, amounting to state-sanctioned piracy.[12]

506 BC

The Latin peoples to the south of Rome also rose against the Etruscans and the Romans closed their Tiber crossings. In response, the Etruscans attacked, forcing the river and moved south, but were again beaten at Aricia in 506 BC. Presumably as a result of these upheavals, Rome suffered famines

492 BC

and had to import corn from Cumae in 492 BC and from Sicily in 488 BC. Although, as the Carthaginian treaty implies, the Romans had some ships of their own, it is more likely that in each of these cases the respective Greeks supplied and delivered the corn.

Elsewhere, and by 500 BC, the maritime trading nation of Rhodes promulgated the *Lex Rhodia*, the first code of law developed to govern the operation and usage of merchant shipping. It met with very wide international acceptance and many of its principles remain encoded in succeeding bodies of maritime law, right up to the present. In Greece, guilds were emerging for sailors, ship's surveyors and other maritime offices. The Persian King, Darius I, who ruled over Egypt between 521 and 486 BC, recorded that he had completed the canal linking the Nile Delta and Red Sea. As it would seem from the fact that trading towns had been established along the canal in Necho's time, it follows that the canal was completed then; as has been surmised, perhaps Darius improved or extended it, but certainly it was still in use at this time.

474 BC

In Italy Cumae, still under pressure from the Etruscans, had called upon Hieron, Tyrant of Syracuse in Sicily, for help and in a naval battle off Cumae in 474 BC the Etruscan fleet was severely beaten by the Syracusans. The southern Etruscan Empire collapsed, leaving a vacuum into which the Samnite and Sabellian peoples of central Italy poured, colonising and setting up their own confederations.

453 BC

In 453 BC the Syracusans raided the Etruscan coast and Etruscan sea-power was effectively ended. In the meantime, the Carthaginians who had acquired Sardinia, started to show interest in gaining Corsica and also expanded across western Sicily. This led them into conflict with Greek interests in eastern and central Sicily and resulted in a succession of wars engage until the ships could be grappled and hauled together, whereupon the infantry would fight it out. Whereas anything that floated and could carry armed men would suffice for such tactics, it soon became apparent that there were advantages to be had in greater speed, manoeuvrability and carrying capacity for fighting men. In reasonable conditions, a more slender hull, driven by the power of many oars was faster and better suited to offensive operations by kings and pirates alike, its rowers doubling as fighters once in contact with an enemy, or prey.

By about 850 BC the ram had been invented; a heavy, metal spike, fixed over, and projecting from, the ship's specially shaped and strengthened bow structure, at, or just below, the waterline. The ship was propelled at speed at an enemy vessel which was struck by the ram. The attacker then backed water and withdrew, leaving its holed enemy to sink or founder. With this, the ship itself had become the weapon and its design had to become specialised to make it work. The hull had to be strengthened against the shock of ramming and had to become more slender for the increased speed needed to catch its target and to make a blow effective; it also had to become longer to accommodate the extra oarsmen necessary to provide the motive power to achieve that speed. The great dividing point had finally been reached between the broad, round, capacious hull for carrying cargo and the slender, fast ship of war.

Although most warships carried one or two masts, with their yards and sails for cruising whenever the wind was favourable, the motive power in battle was provided solely by the oars. The oar was used by bracing its pivotal point against a tholepin, a hardwood pin, inserted into a hole in top of the thole or top wale and which formed the fulcrum for the oar stroke; a leather or rope thong was used to tie the oar to the pin. The only way to increase speed and ramming power was to increase the number of oars and oarsmen. This was done progressively through twenty oars, ten each side, via thirty rowers (fifteen each side), to the penteconter (fifty rowers, twenty-five per side). This proved to be the largest to which such an arrangement could be stretched, as to increase length beyond this, to accommodate more rowers in an already long, thin hull, would leave it seriously weakened. Further, the inherent weakness of the hull would have restricted its seakeeeping qualities, its extreme length-to-beam ratio making it cumbersome in manoeuvre and needing a lot of room in which to make a turn.[13]

More power demanded more rowers, however, and in about 700 BC a solution was found. This was to accept a broader, higher hull and double the number of rowers on each side by semi-superimposing the rows, or remes, of oars so that two remes were mounted on each beam. Nearly twice the motive power could thus be obtained from the same length of hull. Alternatively, the fifty rowers of a penteconter could be accommodated in a shorter, beamier hull, more manoeuvrable in action as well as more robust in a seaway. The increase in beam and hull cross-section was more than compensated by the increased power. Confusingly, ancient writers refer to ships as 'penteconters' regardless of whether they were rowed at one or two levels (i.e.

for mastery of the island; a struggle that would eventually bring Rome into conflict with both of them.

At about this time, a type of cargo ship was developed which was round-bottomed but of shallow draft, broader then usual in the beam, with the usual large square sail but having up to twenty oars per side, in a single reme, for added speed and manoeuverability. The type became very widespread and a vast number were to be built, so many in fact that regular scheduled trade routes appear to have begun at this time.

450 BC   In about 450 BC, a Phoenician, Himilco, is reputed to have sailed to south-western Britain, opening a sea-route for Celtic tin. Shortly afterwards a Carthaginian fleet under Hanno, sailed the west African coast and ventured possibly as far as Sierra Leone.

The rest of the fifth and latter part of the fourth centuries BC were marked at sea by the succession of wars between various Greek and Hellenistic states, and between Carthage and Syracuse, which resulted in what has come to be regarded as the heyday of the trireme and the perfection of ramming tactics. Thereafter, the introduction of newer and different types, as will be seen, would relegate the trireme to a still important, but essentially subsidiary, role.

Ramming required a great deal of skill in the handling of the ship, to ensure impact in the right place to cause maximum damage to the enemy ship and at the right angle, otherwise the attacker could suffer as much as the intended victim. The timing of the order for the rowers to back water was critical to prevent over-penetration by the ram, with the danger of getting stuck and/or grappled, and of having the ram twisted off by the movement of the two hulls relative to each other.[14] Grappling and seeking to board an enemy ship was always to be the prime objective (except for the Athenians) and every ship carried a number of archers and slingers, who would try to clear an enemy's deck, and a contingent of marines to effect boarding or to prevent an enemy from boarding their ship. Successful ramming could only be carried out when ships had plenty of sea-room, otherwise, if too crowded, a battle became, as previously noted, a 'floating land battle' between the respective marines and missile troops.[15]

When they met, opposing fleets would deploy in line abreast, rams towards the enemy, each ship thus presenting the smallest target. The line abreast was also a defence against ram attack. By leaving as little space between the neighbouring ship's oars as possible, given the wind and sea state, and while still allowing the ships motion for station-keeping, one ship's oars were covered by the next ship in line, leaving no room for an enemy to penetrate the line without losing their own oars. Wherever possible, a fleet would try to rest at least one flank on a suitable shore or obstacle. At first fleets simply rowed towards each other, meeting in a melee and seeking mono- or bi-reme; the author will for the sake of clarity, use the 'conter' suffix only for monoreme ships and prefer 'bireme' to differentiate the same). These 'biremes' start to appear from about 700 BC, the Phoenicians and Greeks evolving distinctive individual styles. By 600 BC Etruscan paintings show that they also had biremes, built showing Greek influence. Although the bireme became the principal heavy warship for about two hundred years, the Conter type of ship continued to serve alongside it. Some ships continued to be open whilst others had decking to various extents; from just fighting platforms in the bows, up to complete decking over the rowers as well. These were the principal types of warship engaged at the Battle of Alalia. The crews required for these ships were of course, one man for each oar mounted, together with a captain, his lieutenant, a few sailors to handle the sailing rig and anchors and a number of marines and archers; for a twenty-oar ship a total of perhaps thirty-two men, with up to seventy needed for a penteconter

As a corollary to these developments, the ram had also changed from its original pointed form. Experience had shown that it was rarely possible to make a perfect hole in an enemy hull and there was a tendency for the ram to stick, effectively disabling the attacker as well as the victim. It was better to seek to disrupt the integrity of an enemy hull, causing it to sink, and the ram was thus given a blunt end, often shaped like a boar's head. A blow from such a ram would cause a ship's side to be stove in and holed, with more serious structural damage and a higher possibility of sinking. For all of the refinement and skill invested in perfecting the ram and the ship bearing it, with a few exceptions (notably the heyday of the Athenian and Rhodian navies), it remained really the secondary weapon and one of opportunity in naval warfare. In the main, naval warfare continued to be a land battle, conducted over water. The ram could be a ship-disabling weapon and although it could be very effective in so doing, it necessitated the attacker coming into physical contact with the intended victim. This situation could be equally dangerous to an attacker, with the crew of the rammed vessel fighting their way aboard to escape their own damaged ship. Despite the later introduction of shipboard artillery and much later, cannon, the true ship-destroying weapon would only arrive with the invention of the high-explosive shell many centuries later.

EVOLUTION
OF THE
TRIREME

Between about 600 and 550 BC, the next major step in warship development was achieved with the perfection of the trireme, with three banks of oars on each beam. For a century or more, naval architects had been seeking ways to further increase the power of warships. The Greeks had found that the attachment of an outrigger along the side of a hull enabled a third, higher reme of oarsmen to be included, who sat on the very edge of the hull outboard of the lower remes. Their oars pivoted on the outrigger, i.e. outboard of the hull proper and the hull thus retained its sleek form with its speed and manoeuvrability, but had a third opportunities to ram or at least to run close in alongside an enemy and shear off his oars, thereby disabling him. The order to ship oars in the face of an enemy attempt to snap them must have been well practised and carried out with the utmost alacrity. The most vulnerable aspects of the ships to ramming were the sides and stern. To take advantage of this and, to obviate as much as possible an enemy's defensive formations, tactics were developed to place an attacker in position to attack the enemy rear; manoeuvres known as the *diekplous* and the *periplous*.

In the *diekplous* attack, co-ordination and some surprise were needed. A galley in the centre of the line would race for the gap between two enemy ships, closely followed by a second; at the last moment it would put its helm over and scrape the side of one of the enemy, shearing off its oars and causing it to slew, which left it open to being rammed by the second attacking galley. The enemy galley was sunk or at least pushed, disabled, out of the line and the attacking fleet then poured through the resulting gap to fall upon the rear of the remaining enemy ships. Such a manoeuvre was best suited to the fastest ships, which could come up upon the rear of an enemy target which was itself trying to accelerate away; the difference in speed between attacker and intended victim need not have been great to cause a breach in the hull of the latter. The counter to such a move, if one had enough ships, was to have a second line stationed behind the first.

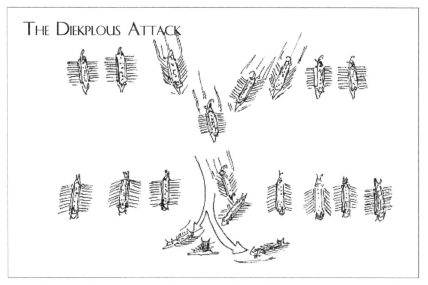

THE DIEKPLOUS ATTACK

The *periplous* attack was best suited to a fleet with greater numbers than its opponent. Whilst the enemy is pinned by the attacker's fleet at the front, the attacker extends one flank sideways, out and round the enemy, from where it can attack the enemy flank and rear. The quandary in these more motive power. In little more than the same length as a penteconter, about 120 feet (36m.), with its fifty rowers, the trireme packed 170, on three levels, with a deck above from which marines could shoot down onto an enemy. These ships were powerful, handy and fast, being able to cruise at over seven knots for extended periods and to sprint at over nine knots. They could turn through 180 degrees in only two and a half times their own length and proved to be quite fast under sail. The trireme would become and remain the fastest of the warships of antiquity. The high performance was gained at a price however, and the trireme tended to be fragile and lacked seaworthiness. In all but a calm sea, the lowest reme of oars, being no more than 18 inches (460mm) above sea level, became unworkable and the oars had to be shipped and the ports sealed with leather-covered stoppers. In seas running at three-feet (1m.) waves the ships became difficult to handle, any rougher than that and they probably did not put to sea.[16] With the perfection of the ship, came the perfection of its principal weapon, the ram, which was cast with several horizontal vanes either side of a central blade and which could thus cut into and along the grain of the hull planks of an enemy. To spread the force of impact, the bronze ram was mounted on large, long timber wales and braces, separate from the forefoot of the hull proper and led back along the sides of the hull to distribute the force of impact away from the bow and avoid the possibility of the ship damaging and effectively ramming itself. The trireme was expensive to build and an even greater drain on manpower, needing for each ship, 170 rowers, four or five officers, a crew of sixteen to twenty sailors and a contingent of anything between fourteen and forty marines, totalling some 200 men per ship. Details of the crew of early triremes in the Athenian navy survive to show that the ship had a *Trierarch* (the captain) a *Pentekontoros* (first lieutenant) a *Prorates* (bow Officer) and a *Keleusta* (rowing officer). Of the seamen crew there were two helmsmen, two stroke oarsmen, the ship's carpenter and an *auletes* (a flautist or musician). The equivalent of all of these positions later on in Roman service at least were rated as leading hands or *dupliciarii* on double-pay. There were, in addition, ten sailors, sixty thranite rowers (plus the stroke oarsmen) in the topmost level of rowers, fifty-four zygite rowers in the middle level and fifty-four thalamite rowers in the lowest level. The Athenians relying entirely on their ram, carried only four archers and ten marines on deck, but other navies had up to forty marines on board and the Romans can be safely assumed to have been in this latter group, so as to make use of their infantry. The *thranites*, or topmost oarsmen, were the senior hands and controlled the two men in the other levels below them in their 'group', the former being the only ones who could see out and direct the all-important synchronisation of their collective oar-stroke. The two rearmost *thranites* were the 'stroke' oarsmen, who would relay the rowing officer's orders and set the pace. The deployment of such an exotic type started slowly and it was not until the last third of the century that it was in service in large numbers.

This new type of warship predominated in both fleets by the time of the crucial Battle of Salamis in 480 BC, when the Greeks defeated the Persian fleet. Having proved manoeuvres was that by taking precautions against the one, a fleet laid itself open to the other. With both sides seeking to outmanoeuvre the other, most battles resolved themselves into an advance in line abreast and discharge of a shower of missiles, preceding the two lines smashing into each other bow-to-bow, the deck crews sitting just before impact to avoid being thrown about by it and the rowing masters yelling their orders to back water. Fortunate was the ship that could turn enough at the last moment to hit her opponent and to hole it below the waterline; in many cases, due to the motion of the ship and sea, the blow was struck above the enemy waterline, inconvenient but not too prejudicial. For the marines, the prospect of clambering with their weapons across the bows of two ships to get to their opponent's, who presumably were trying to do the same thing, must have seemed suicidal.

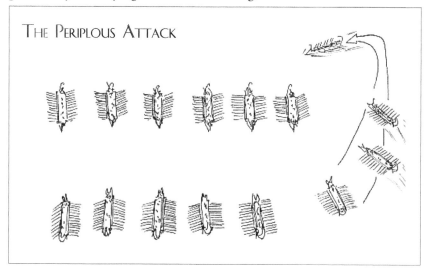

THE PERIPLOUS ATTACK

The Rhodians appear to have developed an answer to the problem of holing the enemy above the waterline. Their sailing masters perfected the trick of trimming their ships, causing the prows to dip into the water just before impact, causing its ram to strike the enemy below the waterline and the waterline wales and armour. This made the enemy heel away as the Rhodian ship rose, helping to free itself and further disrupting the enemy which would take on more water on the reverse roll. It is not known exactly how the Rhodians achieved this, but no others are recorded as mastering this technique.

As a result of battle experience in the wars of the Greeks, the trireme had been modified by building up the strength of the bows, in effect armouring them. This was achieved by building a very strong projecting structure onto the forward ends of the outriggers to prevent damage to them by a close enemy pass. Such damage would have meant that, even if the top reme itself in battle, the trireme became the standard warship type of the Greeks and other navies must have rushed to replace their remaining examples of older types, although a few undoubtedly remained for secondary or auxiliary tasks. The trireme was to dominate naval activity for the next one and a half centuries. Even when superceded by larger, newer types it continued in common usage as a naval workhorse right up almost to the mid-fourth century AD. It has been estimated that the average trireme hull had a life of twenty to twenty-five years, a testimonial to the quality of the workmanship and skill with which they were built.[17] The Athenian navy certainly classified the effectiveness of their ships by reference to their age. During its lifetime, a *trireme* could be used as a line-of-battle ship (being the fastest type afloat), as a despatch carrier, a convoy escort, for amphibious landings (being light enough to be hauled up a beach) and with reduced rowing complement, as a fast troop carrier or horse transport. Apart from its seaworthiness, a further limiting factor was that in multiplying the crew numbers without a corresponding rate of growth in the hull size, the result was that there was less space than ever to carry stores or provisions and crews had to be frequently rested and fed ashore, a factor which prevented their effective use for blockade, or for operations for extended periods off an enemy-held shoreline.

EVOLUTION
OF THE
QUADRIREME

The Carthaginians, in operations in 409 BC, introduced an enlarged version of the *bireme* with each oar manned by two rowers, namely a 'four' (*tetreres* in Greek or *quadrireme* in Latin). This increased the power yet retained much of the compactness and handiness of the type. In 404 BC, Dionysius of Syracuse followed suit, as gradually did other naval powers, until the type became popular, being adopted widely by the end of the century. Being broader and lower than a trireme for similar power, it was not as 'tender' in a seaway, although not quite as fast under oar. It was also economical and although the deck was lower than a 'five',[18] it had similar performance and was reportedly fast under sail. The type remained in use by the Romans when they attained naval hegemony and continued throughout the ancient period. However, the lower deck level of the type left it at a decided disadvantage when opposed by a 'five', the marines having difficulty in climbing aboard the latter, the marines of which could, in turn, shoot down upon them. Inferior to a 'five' and slower than a trireme, the type was nevertheless successful, being large enough to stand in the line of battle. With only two remes, it was less complicated and expensive to build and more economic in its manpower requirement; advantages that ensured that it remained in common use. The Rhodians were particularly fond of it. As a type it remained in use until about the third century AD. From Rhodian inscriptions some indications survive as to the crew of such a ship. These state that it had seven officers, ten ratings, ten sailors and about thirty marines; the number of rowers is given as eighty per *reme*, a total of 160, a total crew of 215 men.

rowers had shipped their oars in time, the blow to the outrigger would have made them incapable of use. Finally, to increase protection against ramming, belts, or wales, of extra timber were fixed along the waterlines.[19]

The proportion of *triremes* in the navies of the day had increased. For example, the Athenians deployed about two hundred at Salamis in 480, whereas they are recorded as having twice this number by the end of the century. The type remained expensive to build and, with its crew of some two hundred men, represented a considerable drain on manpower. A number of the smaller types thus continued in service in subsidiary roles.

A ROMAN WARSHIP

394 BC In 394 BC the Romans sent a votive gift for the Temple of Apollo at Delphi, in thanks for the capture of the Etruscan City of Veii. Three senators were sent with the gift in a warship which was waylaid and captured by the ships and men of the Liparae Islands of northern Sicily and taken back there. The islanders had long opposed Etruscan pirates but once aware of their captives' identity, treated them with hospitality and even escorted the Roman ship to its destination.[20]

This none-too-glorious episode is the first specific mention of the existence of a Roman warship and, although no particulars of it survive, one may venture that it was quite small to fall such easy prey to the Liparaeans, and even that it was perhaps a captured Etruscan ship, leading to their interest. Further, the ship was travelling alone even though on so important a mission and one which the Romans must have known to be long and which could be perilous; a journey which they had indeed entrusted to a warship, rather than to a merchant ship. Was this for the Romans their first naval adventure, coinciding as it does, approximately with the founding of a sea-port at Ostia and the issue of the earliest Roman coin so far discovered, which is stamped with a design showing the prow of a warship? With the one harbour and a fairly short coastline, a few *conter* type patrol ships would have been quite sufficient for the policing of Rome's territorial waters.

386 BC Shortly after this, in 386 BC, the Romans besieged Antium (Anzio) during which they deployed and used artillery, the first reference to their having these weapons in service. In Roman service they were designated as a *catapulta* for arrow or bolt shooters and *ballista* for a stone thrower. As mentioned, at about this time also (although there is evidence that it could have been earlier) the port of Ostia was established, with a fort, at the mouth of the River Tiber to act as the port of Rome.[21] With the development of a larger, deeper water port and its facilities, bigger ships could be operated which could be loaded and unloaded there. Lighters and barges, better suited to the river, could carry goods to and from Rome. Further afield it is possible **378 BC** that the Romans attempted to found a colony on Sardinia in 378 BC; the

To counter the Carthaginian threat, the Syracusans built up their navy and, in about 398 BC, they introduced longer oars and placed two men per oar in the upper two remes of an enlarged trireme, producing a five-man group or *penteres* (five longitudinal lines or files), for a total of circa 300 rowers. The ship was recorded as being at sea in 398 BC With the increase in power provided, the ships could then be built larger, approximately 150 feet (45m) long and as such, carry more troops and have still better seakeeping qualities. These larger ships were also heavier in construction and, as a moving mass, a blow from one would wreck a lighter ship, which could, in turn, do comparatively little damage to the bigger vessel. Being larger, they were also higher, with a deck about 10 feet (3m) above water-level and from which their troops could more effectively shoot down onto an enemy. The crew of such a ship would have been approximately six to eight officers, twenty ratings and sailors and between 250 and 300 rowers, together with perhaps forty marines. The exact number of marines is only attested for the Roman navy, others may well have had different numbers. On average therefore, there was a crew of over 350 men per ship.[22]

NAVAL
ARTILLERY

It was the Syracusans also who appear to have been the first to take advantage of the more substantial ships by mounting artillery aboard them. Until then, shipboard missile weapons had been the same as those for the infantry: javelin, sling and bow. The javelin could be thrown some 30 to 50 yards (27 to 45m) or, with the assistance of a throwing thong or *amentum*, up to 70 yards (64m). The sling used a lead bullet

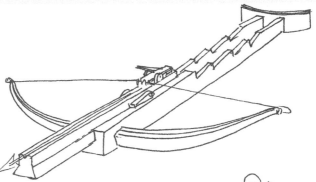

The Gastraphetes or 'belly bow' was in use from at least 399 BC. It utilised a composite bow too powerful to be drawn by hand. A slider is pushed forward to engage the bow-string in a trigger mechanism. The weapon was then cocked by the archer using his body weight to push in the slider.

attempt did not succeed and nothing more is heard of it, but the next treaty with Carthage would ensure that the experiment would not be repeated.

349 BC

Roman naval strength must have remained the same, namely fairly nominal, as they made no naval foray when in about 349 BC a force of Greek buccaneers cruised up the Latin coast, raiding and plundering.[23] As the oared ships of the time had to be beached at night so the crews could rest and get food and water, the Romans opposed the buccaneers with their army, such ships as they may have had being insufficient to face them. The army could follow the Greek ships along the coast and prevent them from landing. Had they tried to land, the Greeks would have had to face a much stronger full-scale army, or whilst on a raid, had their ships destroyed on the beach and lost their means of escape. The policy worked and forced the buccaneers to keep away from Roman coasts.

348 BC

In 348 BC, Rome renewed its treaty of alliance with Carthage. This second treaty appears even more restrictive upon the Romans than the first. They were forbidden by it to plunder, trade or found settlements west of Hermaeum in Africa, or in Hispania, and were excluded from Sardinia. The allowance for emergencies was cancelled, but Carthage was free to trade in Italy and to intervene against non-Roman cities if necessary.[24] If this is so, then something is missing from the account, for there is nothing in it for Rome. It may well be that as the supreme naval power in the western Mediterranean, Carthage undertook to keep the seas free from pirates and/ or that in return for the restrictions, Rome was given advantageous trading terms or a free hand elsewhere.

343 BC

In the First Samnite War (343 to 341), the Romans and their Latin allies came into conflict with the Samnites of central Italy in the first part of their contest for domination of the peninsula. This was followed by the Latin War (340 to 338) in which Rome gained the undisputed leadership of the Latin peoples. It is towards the end of this war that the first Roman

338 BC

naval action is reported, when in 338 a Roman fleet under the Consul Caius Maenius overcame the Latins and Volscians in a sea battle near Antium, and then went on to take the town and its port. The prows of some of the captured ships were set up in the Forum at Rome as trophies and used as *rostra* (speaker's pulpits) whilst the least damaged of the enemy ships were taken into the Roman service.

To emphasise not only that Rome had a navy at this time, but that their intentions at sea had to be considered, the major Greek maritime colony of Tarentum (Taranto) made a treaty with Rome in 338.[25] The Greeks were trying to increase their domain in Apulia, enlisting the help of King Alexander of Epirus. Although Roman territory came nowhere near to them at that time (nor were they to be interested in Apulia until the Second Samnite War, twelve years into the future) and the Roman coastline in the

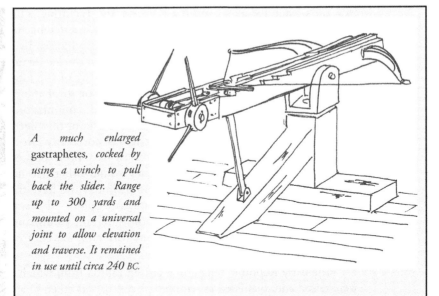

A much enlarged gastraphetes, *cocked by using a winch to pull back the slider. Range up to 300 yards and mounted on a universal joint to allow elevation and traverse. It remained in use until circa 240 BC.*

and had a range of 30 to 40 yards (36m) and the sling-staff or *fustibulus*, up to 200 yards (182m). A stave bow could cast an arrow up to 250 yards (228m) and a composite bow up to 400 yards (365m). These ranges were maxima, achieved under special conditions and it would be more fair to allow a reliable shooting range for the bows, under battle conditions, at about half of these distances. All of these weapons were best suited to short-range work and ship's rowers could be protected by light screens of leather, wicker, or wood, rigged across their access hatches and slung over the open sections of the ship's sides. The Syracusans had embarked on a drive for improved weapons, employing engineers and craftsmen from a number of sources and in about 399 BC they came up with the *gastraphetes*. This was basically an improved crossbow that utilised a composite bow that resulted in an estimated range of about 250 yards (228m), cocked by leaning against the rest on the butt end

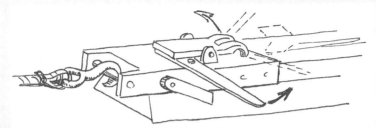

Release mechanisms contrived for use by the gastraphetes *and used in appropriate sizes for the larger machines. The trigger could be pivoted on the far side of the claw to allow release by pulling. Similar mechanisms remained in use on the later torsion-spring weapons.*

west only extended as far south as Cumae, the Tarantines must have been sufficiently concerned at the prospect of Roman interference by sea to have sought to limit the possibility of Roman expansion at sea by having them agree that Roman warships would not sail east of the Lacinian promontory (Capo Colonne), near Croton in the western part of the Gulf of Taranto and well away from Apulia. Within fifty years or so of the establishment of their first sea-port, the Romans had acquired, commissioned, and used a war-fleet. There is no record of the composition of that fleet but one can presume, with some justification, that it was not overly large; perhaps no more than twenty or so galleys. They must have been 'beaked' ships, that is warships equipped with rams, as they would otherwise not have been able to prevail over their adversary, who definitely did have them. Some of their prows were brought back to Rome as trophies. This was a common practice in the ancient world to demonstrate and commemorate a naval victory, where the extreme bow, complete with ram, was cut from a captured ship and set up as a trophy.

The early Republic relied on a citizen militia from which armed forces were raised and dismissed as required. A census was taken of all able-bodied men, each of whom had to provide their own weapons and equipment. The men were then divided into five classes of infantry, the wealthiest having full armour and equipment, down to the poorest, who had only slings. Below this again were the *capitacensi*, (literally, 'headcount'), those too poor for anything, who were employed nevertheless for ancillary duties such as bearers, cooks, trumpeters, draft animal and wagon handlers etc. Each class was further divided into centuries of one hundred men.[26] In about 400, pay had been introduced for soldiers, which enabled them to be kept in the field for longer periods. Before this the men had to return to their civilian lives after each campaign season, to work and earn their keep and support their families. The introduction of pay for the troops also enabled the men to buy weapons and equipment and the distinctions in equipment between the categories of troops, although still existing at this time, had begun to lessen. Later certainly, ship's crews were levied from the *capitacensi* (no equipment was required to man an oar) and it seems reasonable to assume this to have been so in 338.[27]

The basic and well-established system of centuries was ideal for use when organising the crew of a galley, the major part of which was employed in rowing. Thus a century of *capitacensi* could provide oarsmen for two penteconters or a bireme, or two centuries could man a trireme. To this would have to be added some of the infantry as marines and some archers and slingers and a century of each could provide contingents for several ships. Sailors and ship's captains could be levied from the Roman merchant marine, hired from among the Italiote Greeks or Etruscans, or levied from among the allies. The marines would have their own officers. Once assigned which pushed in a sliding section of the stock. An ingenious trigger was perfected for it and before long, the principle was applied to bigger and more powerful machines with huge composite bows. The push of an operator's body was replaced by a winch and the whole secured atop a mounting by a universal joint which allowed it to be trained and elevated for aiming. Two types were evolved, one to shoot large arrows or bolts and another to project stone shot, to an average effective reported range of some 300 yards (275m). These machines caused a sensation when first used in action by the Syracusans at the siege of Motya in Sicily in 397 BC.[28]

First mounted on 'fives', then on all bigger ships, these larger and harder-hitting weapons were able to damage an enemy's ship, as well as its crew, at longer ranges and with virtual impunity from beyond enemy bowshot. The introduction of such weapons made it essential to provide greater protection for the rowers. The bigger ships now carried nearly 300 oarsmen, manning about 180 oars and the sides of the ships had to be closed in with solid bulwarks and decked over to protect them. Such ships were known as *cataphract*, best translated, as it was for cavalry, to mean 'armoured' and as distinct from the open or *aphract* ships.[29] Below decks ventilation would have been a problem and the decorative frieze shown on many contemporary representations of warships may well represent louvres or opening vents designed for this purpose.[30] Vents could also be allowed in the undersides of the outriggers and be augmented by deck grilles; several large deck hatches must have been let into the upper deck to allow rapid entry and exit for the rowing crews below and for ventilation, these could be covered by lightweight, protective covers when in action. The 'big five' would become the Roman quinquireme.

EVOLUTION OF THE HEXERES

In Syracuse in about 365 BC the next, logical step in warship design was to make a small increase in the size of a 'five' and place a second rower at each oar of the remaining reme, to produce the 'six' or *hexeres*, with a crew of some 360 rowers, plus officers, sailors and marines. Although the six seems to have been subsequently adopted quite widely by various navies, it was not in great numbers or so as to displace other types and was the largest type to be taken into regular service by the Romans. These great ships, although not that much longer, were altogether more massive and carried crews of about 550 men each.[31]

TORSION ARTILLERY

By about 340 BC, a new type of artillery piece was invented by the engineers of King Philip of Macedon. Cords of animal sinew or (less preferably) hair, were stretched and wound under tension around frames in the machine, which were then twisted to form two powerful springs. Into each of these 'springs' were inserted the staves forming the bow, all of which replaced the composite bow of prior machines.

to their ship, the whole crew was treated as a century, or on a trireme or larger ship with a crew of over 200, as a maniple, which was a tactical grouping of two or more centuries.

At this time, the citizen levy was enough to provide 170 centuries of infantry, eighteen of cavalry and five or six of *capitacensi*, enough to form three legions of 5000 men. Of the twenty centuries of infantry and the six of *capitacensi* left over, if only half were used to man ships, a dozen biremes could be deployed. In the absence of direct evidence a mix of twenty or so biremes and pentaconters would appear to be a reasonable composition for this 'first fleet', although the acquisition of a trireme or two to operate as flagships, or even just for prestige, cannot be ruled out. Of particular note is the fact that the Roman navy did not use slaves aboard their warships.[32] All the navy's crews, from these earliest fleets to the end of the Empire, were recorded as being made up of free men. The galley-slave was an aberration of the sixteenth to eighteenth centuries AD and unknown to the Romans. Crews were provided by the citizen levy, by allied contingents supplied by treaty and by volunteers. Later, when the navy became a standing professional force, men joined by voluntary enlistment or conscription from the citizenry.

From the beginning, the fleet was made a consular command. Under the Republic two Consuls were elected for each year as the supreme magistrates of the state. In times of war, the Consuls commanded the armies in the field and this principle was extended to the fleet, which continued to be a command of consular rank until the late Republic. As subsidiary commanders and staff officers, the consul appointed military tribunes (at the rate of six per legion in the army) from among experienced officers having five to ten years' service. The tribunes appointed a centurion to command each century, who in turn appointed a second, junior centurion (later called an *optio*). In the naval context, tribunes rarely appear as such, but their equivalent were the officers appointed to command the larger ships and even squadrons, ranks which would become more formalised in later, imperial times as trierarchs and navarchs. These officers could deal with operating the ships and command individual squadrons and provide a backbone of experienced senior officers.

326 BC

In 326 BC Rome entered an alliance with Neapolis, the Greek commercial centre of mid-Italy. On Rome's part this was a move to counter the growing spread and power of the Samnites and to bring the largest Greek colony on the Italian mainland within its sphere. By helping Neapolis to rid itself of a Samnite garrison the Romans gained a powerful foothold in the south, together with first class harbour facilities and the best location from which to exercise control of shipping in the Tyrrhenian Sea. The Neapolitans were freed from the obligation to provide troops in return for patrolling and guarding the harbour and surrounding coasts. At a stroke the

When properly set up these machines were reportedly immensely powerful, capable of projecting their missiles to an effective range of about 400 yards (365m), more in exceptional cases. Once again, two versions were developed, one for shooting arrows or bolts, the other for throwing stone shot. For siege work these machines were built in successively larger sizes. The building, setting up and performance (which could vary) of these new pieces was more haphazard however and composite bow-powered machines continued to offer advantages, being reliable, easier to build, operate and maintain in combat readiness. The torsion-powered machines needed trained artificers to keep them in operating condition and they also deteriorated with wet or even dampness; the springs stretched after prolonged use, needing to be removed, greased and re-stretched and then re-strung onto the machine. The composite bow was not susceptible to damp and once installed, needed no serious attention other than a light oiling; not surprisingly, it remained in regular widespread service alongside the newer types and presumably especially so for sea service.[33]

THE VOYAGE OF PYTHEAS

In about 324 BC, a Greek from Massilia, named Pytheas either sailed his ship through the Straits of Gibraltar and north; or journeyed overland to the Atlantic coast of Gaul and from there, proceeded by a succession of local ships. Whichever, he reached Cornwall in Britain; he continued north and circumnavigated the British Isles and visited the Shetlands and probably also the Orcades (Orkney Islands); he then went on to either (probably) Iceland or to Norway and even further, to the edge of the Arctic ice. This was a great feat of exploration and navigation and, during the course of his travels, Pytheas made several observations of the height of the sun and sought to chart his journey and to calculate his latitude at various points. Upon his return to Massilia, he wrote an account of his travels, sadly since lost.[34]

Although the compass was not known, if Pytheas could see recognisable stars, such as the Great Bear, he did not need one. Millennia before, the Sumerians had observed that the Earth and the Sun revolved about each other, although they knew not which; they also thought this orbit took 360 days. Therefore they divided the disc representing that orbit into the 360 segments, or degrees, still used today. Pytheas would have known this, also that the Earth is round and that if he measured the angle of the Pole Star above the horizon, this angle would equal, with a minor adjustment which he could make, his own latitude. Longitude could only be estimated from reckoning the ship's speed and course. Pytheas did note that the tides encountered in those northern waters followed the phases of, and were caused by, the Moon. For centuries after this epic voyage, Pytheas' account and observations formed the basis of the ancient world's knowledge of those northern climes.

Romans, in return for the military burden which they could accommodate, had extended into Campania, opening the way to the south, and had obtained the best base on the coast from which the sea route to Rome could be secured. The number of ships available to them, both warships and merchantmen, were augmented by the Neapolitan ships. Most important also, was the accretion of all the Neapolitan sailors and shipbuilders, with their knowledge, skill and long seafaring traditions. With the adherence of the Italiote Greeks, with their centuries-old naval traditions, it was probably at this time that the Greek names for ship's officers and crewmen of various types were adopted by the Romans, a practice that was to last throughout the imperial period to come. Up to that time, the Etruscans, with their own well-established seafaring traditions, had been the principal maritime influence on the Romans, probably with a little Carthaginian input. Thus predominantly Etruscan nautical terms were most likely to have been in use, details of which have been lost, along with the Etruscan language.[35] Latin terms do mostly survive, to which were added some Greek terms, and together composed the Roman nautical vocabulary. The heirarchy of ship's officers had been well established by the Greeks and as has been seen, a trireme had an establishment of five officers; captain (*trierarchos*), second officer (*kybernetes*), chief rowing officer (*keleustes*), paymaster or executive officer (*pentekontarchos*) and a junior or 'bow' officer (*proreus*); the senior military officer would have overall command. The Roman equivalent for these ranks were *Magister Navis*, literally ship master, for the captain, although the term *trierarch* was also used; *Gubernator* for the lieutenant and navigating officer, while the rowing officer was called the *Pausarius* and the bow officer the *Proreus*; the executive officer was the *Secutor* who was also the master-at-arms.[36]

326/5 BC   The Roman move into Campania brought them once more into collision with the Samnites and prompted the start of the Second Samnite War (326 to 304 BC). The early part of this Samnite War saw serious reverses for the Romans and much of Campania and Latium were overrun or threatened by the Samnites.

323 BC   The eastern Mediterranean had meantime seen the rise of Macedonia and the creation of the vast empire of Alexander the Great. Upon his death in 323 BC, this empire quickly broke up into wars between his former generals for mastery of its various parts, the 'successor' wars which were to last until the 280s BC. The result was that much of Asia Minor, the Levant and east became the Seleucid Empire, whilst Antigonous became dominant in Greece and western Asia Minor and Ptolemy annexed Egypt. Much of the fighting in these wars took place at sea. Seleucus was embroiled in the east trying to hold onto Persia; Ptolemy had secured most of Alexander's fleet; Antigonous built up a fleet to challenge Ptolemy's ambitions, placing his son Demetrias in command. The fleets clashed, starting the struggle for supremacy of the

SHIPS'
SIGNALS

On board ship, communication of orders was primarily by voice, but bugle calls were also employed (a method in use to this day), a practice started by the Etruscans. For military use, the Romans used four different bronze wind instruments, each with a different and distinctive sound, the *bucina, cornu, tuba* and *lituus*. Only the first two are so far attested in naval use, their players being known respectively as a *bucinator* and a *cornicen*.[37] In the army, combinations of instruments and calls were used to signal orders for a great variety of activities and manoeuvres and could even be tailored to individual units. Such systems were easily adapted for use at sea and, in addition, ships carried ranking officer's flags and pennants (as they still do). Later, we learn of Scipio using lanterns for station-keeping and identification whilst sailing at night. The use of burnished shields as a heliograph, to flash messages is recorded in 307 BC and signalling by flag was well established in the army. All of these methods can be and doubtless were, used to signal between ships at sea and between ship and shore; all of them however, presuppose the establishment of fixed codes and the training of signallers, an ability extant in the army.

HEMIOLIA

The 'fours' and 'fives' introduced by the Syracusans and Carthaginians had already grown to 'sixes' and these types were becoming more common in the fleets of the rivals, but bigger was yet to come. To complement the bigger ships, a smaller type had also been evolved, a development of the single reme 'conter' type, known as *hemiolia* or 'one and a half'. Probably starting with the pirates of south-west Anatolia, it could have had each of the centre sections of oars manned by two men, allowing a beamier ship, with improved sea-keeping and a greater number of fighting men, yet retaining the same performance. Although the trireme remained the fastest of the warships, it was still expensive and the small ships were efficient for use as scouts, despatch boats, for penetrating shallow waters and even, in sufficient numbers, for attacking stragglers and damaged ships on the periphery of a battle.

EVOLUTION
OF THE
POLYREME

In the East, the naval rivalry between Antigonous and Ptolemy had become furious. In 315 BC Antigonous built the first 'seven' and by 301 BC had developed 'eights', then 'nines', 'tens', 'elevens' and was building a 'thirteen'. In 288 BC, he built a 'fifteen' and then a 'sixteen', whose speed and performance were said to be remarkable. Ptolemy was not far behind with 'twelves' and 'thirteens' of his own. It is convenient to refer to these great ships as polyremes. Nothing larger than a 'ten', of which quite large numbers were built, are known to have been in action. With no examples or identifiable iconography of any of these big ships having so far been found, nor any eastern Mediterranean and Aegean and prompting a naval arms race as each side strove to out-build the other with ever-bigger galleys.

In Italy, much of Campania and Latium were overrun or threatened by the Samnites and there was some naval activity by them. In 326 BC the Samnite garrison at Paleopolis (Pizzofalcone, part of modern Naples) raided the Roman coast. For their part the Romans also experimented with their sea-power against the enemy's ports and shipping. The Samnites controlled much of the Campanian coast south of Neapolis and presumably relied upon 'their' Italiote Greeks for ships and crews. No other Samnite naval activity has come to light so it would seem either that the raid was an isolated occurrence which proved not to be worth the effort, or that they were unable to employ enough ships to mount a challenge to the Roman fleet. For their part the Romans, with the assistance of their new Italiote allies, could raid Samnite-held ports and shipping and even conduct a blockade. After a pause, between 321 and 316 BC, the war was resumed with the Romans gradually regaining their former territories and re-establishing the land link to Neapolis.

312 BC

In 312 BC a Latin colony was established on the island of Pontia (Ponza), off the Latin coast. The island has a good anchorage and ships based here could screen the coast. Despite the burden of having to support and supply the colony and garrison there, it made an ideal offshore base, being situated halfway between Ostia and Neapolis, and from where it was possible to dominate the coastline with relative ease. It also secured communications between Rome and Neapolis in the event of the Samnites once more reaching the sea in the Gulf of Gaeta and severing the recently re-established land routes.

The Romans had now been operating a naval force for at least eighty years. It is unlikely to have been a standing navy as we know it, but, like the army, would have been mobilised as and when needed and stood down, with its ships hauled out of the water and laid up, during the winter or at the end of campaigning.

Up to now the acquisition and commissioning of warships had, in the absence of any permanent establishment, in all probability been an ad hoc business. Various ships were acquired and used as opportunities arose and circumstances dictated, being afterwards simply laid up, but with no apparent coherent strategy for the development and use of naval forces. Unlike troops that can be mobilised and equipped quite quickly, the Romans had doubtless found that a ship cannot be simply put aside until needed. For example, if a ship is hauled out of the water for any great length of time, the wooden hull will dry out and the wood shrink, causing seams to open, joints to loosen, and the whole thing to leak excessively when put back into the water. Conversely, if left in the water too long, it will become fouled by contemporary detailed description or diagrams of them; knowing that the terms by which the ancient writers described them referred to the numbers of oarsmen per vertical group of oars, there has been much discussion as to how the increasing numbers of rowers were arranged in these increasingly mighty ships. Two basic limiting facts are that firstly, no contemporary depiction of a warship shows more than three remes of oars, and there is no Greek word for any class of rower other than the three levels of a trireme, thranite, zygite and thalamite;[38] secondly it was found in the next great age of the galley, the sixteenth to eighteenth centuries AD, that it was not practical for more than eight men to man one oar.[39] Within these parameters, one can have any sort of combination up to three levels of eight-man oars, that is a 'twenty-four'. Much ink has been expended on the subject but the fact is that no hard evidence survives or has been discovered to date as to how these ships were organised or the method by which, for example, a quinquireme was rowed; thus it could have been a monoreme with five men to one oar, a bireme with perhaps three men to the topmost and two to the lower oars of a 'group' or a trireme with two men to each of the upper two oars and one man to the lowest. There is no record of the Romans ever using a ship larger than a 'six' or *hexeres* as a part of their regular fleet. These ships with their ever-increasing rowing crews nevertheless, did not rise correspondingly higher out of the water as their height was always limited by the constant factor of having to have their two or three remes of oars operated as near-to-horizontal or parallel-to-the-water as possible for efficiency, while maintaining as much freeboard as possible for seaworthiness. This height of the 'engine-room' dictated in turn the height above water of the main deck, which remained at a maximum of about 10 feet (3m). Similarly, overall length grew to little more than 150 feet (46m.); where these ships did gain was in beam and 'massiveness' and the increased numbers of troops and artillery that could be embarked. Ramming as a tactic, rather than an opportunity, was not their purpose, they were floating fortresses.

Once again, a corresponding light, fast warship was developed, the *trihemiolia*, which, following logically from the *hemiolia*, was a bireme with either an extra half-reme of rowers 'doubling-up' at the upper oars, or, it is suggested that the half-reme was added at the lowest, *thalamite* position to make the ships a three-reme type, although there would seem to be little point in producing what would have been an underpowered trireme. Finally, if *hemiolia* referred to one and a half *remes* per side, logically, *trihemiolia* meant three and a half remes, which would suggest a trireme with a doubling-up of rowers on half of the *thranite* oars. However configured, the new type was designed to have the ram as its principal weapon and, with the original trireme-type being by now too light and flimsy for use in battle against the huge, armoured multi-remes, it was heavier and better protected to be effective against them. The type was popular and widely used by the Hellenistic navies, particularly the Rhodians, but does not appear to have commended itself to the Roman service.

weed, barnacles and other marine growth, perhaps even become afflicted by ship-worm and eventually rot. Any ship, and particularly a wooden one, requires constant maintenance to keep it seaworthy, which in turn requires the skilled tradesmen to carry out the work, the stores of materials for them to use and the shore facilities to support the whole enterprise; in short, an entire framework of logistical support. The extension of Roman hegemony had encompassed towns with their own naval and shipbuilding traditions, enabling warships to be built and maintained in what were now 'Roman' yards. Here the Romans themselves would also have quickly learned, if they did not already know, that the building and equipping of a warship was a complex and expensive matter that took time and forethought. Finally, with an extended coastline to be patrolled with any sort of continuity, a properly constituted and equipped naval force would be required.

THE NAVY BOARD

311 BC
It was obvious that the former arrangement, such as it was, could not achieve this desired result and thus, in 311 BC, a small naval board was set up. Two officers, named *Duoviri Navales*, were appointed whose duty it was to provide and equip a fleet and to keep it in repair. With the realisation that an armed service distinct from the army had emerged and become a reality, had come the recognition of the need for a permanent and strictly naval organisation to run it, freeing it from the constraints of being merely a floating part of the army. The navy had available the remaining ships from the action at Antium in 338 BC and Neapolitan ships. Twenty war galleys were commissioned to protect Roman shipping against Samnite raids and pirates and there were presumably others to patrol the coasts and support the offshore garrison.[40] In any event the Romans had secured their coasts, communications and ability to continue trade, and could now support their land route to the south.

Over the years, certain of the centuries of the citizen levy who had manned the ships several times would probably have become identified with the navy and been posted to it whenever called up, becoming in effect, purely naval centuries. Furthermore, the men of those units would have become experienced and some of them at least would have acquired the skill of the sailor and have been promoted to become sailors in their own right or even ship's officers. Likewise, certain centuries of soldiery of the more lightly armed classes (the heavily equipped men would always be required as the backbone of the legions) may have been habitually assigned to shipboard service, becoming de facto marines. All of this is conjecture in the absence of any firm evidence, but in the light of later known developments, seems not unreasonable, given the constant desire to maximise the use of manpower and the basic system of organisation and mobilisation.[41]

As the galleys got bigger they became less handy, slower to react to changes and less manoeuvrable, and their ability to ram suffered accordingly. The importance of ramming was reduced but the ships could carry larger numbers of marines and missile troops (archers, javelin men, slingers) as well as being fully decked in and mounting bulwarks to protect the rowers who now plied their oars in a virtual armoured box. Alexander the Great had mounted catapults on some ships to help in his seige of Tyre in 332 BC and the Syracusans had mounted light catapults. The power and shock of discharge of these machines would have shaken and damaged the earlier, more lightly built ships but the bigger ships now being built could mount heavier artillery and it was probably Demetrias of Macedon who at about this time added stone and arrow shooting heavier catapult artillery as standard fittings to his ships of the line, a practice that inevitably spread, even some merchant ships having catapults for defence against pirates.

A barrage of darts and stones could clear an opponent's decks and if it could be shot into the rowers, would cause losses which would (more importantly) disrupt their stroke. It has been calculated that a 'five' could mount up to ten catapults, each capable of shooting a 27-inch (69cm) long arrow and two stone throwers, each hurling a five pound (2kg) shot up to 400 yards (365m). The bigger ships could of course, mount more and bigger machines and the biggest could throw a half hundredweight (25kg) shot some 400 to 500 yards (457m). As a postscript to these developments, the Athenians in 306 BC, perfected a torsion-powered catapult that could be adapted by the substitution of interchangeable sliders, to shoot either six feet (2m.) long arrows or stone shot. Although its advantages seem obvious, lack of further references to this type would indicate that its performance was lacking and that it did not find general acceptance.[42]

The West did not share the Eastern predilection for ever-bigger ships and apart from the odd bigger ship, seem to have settled on the 'five', or quinquireme for the Romans, as their standard heavy warship, with the *trireme* continuing in use in significant numbers and the four being popular in the Punic navy. As the Roman ships grew old and were scrapped, their replacements, now being built in their own yards, would have been of these more modern types.

Why did the Romans and Carthaginians not seek to emulate the Hellenistic seapowers and deploy the larger types of warship, settling instead on the five or quinquireme (with a very few sixes) as their standard line-of-battle ship? Obviously the only logical reason to build the larger types was if they gave a clear advantage in combat. The ships themselves must have been incredibly expensive to build and required huge numbers of crewmen. For Rome the expense was possibly a limiting factor and for Carthage, whose manpower was always stretched to the limit, crewing was likely to have been a problem. Neither of these limitations however would have precluded either side from deploying just a few eights or tens perhaps, if to do so would have given them a clear advantage in fleet actions.

310 BC   In 310 BC the Romans sent a small squadron to attack Pompeii and to
          raid the area around Nuceria (near Salerno); this expedition was commanded
          by one of the *Duoviri*, Publius Cornelius, the only time such an operational
          command is mentioned for a *Duovir*. It seems the expedition met with little
          success. Nuceria being located inland, the landing force ventured too far,
          and after meeting increasing opposition, was forced to abandon its booty
          and flee to the ships.

          Apart from the original Roman manpower, much of the increase in navy
          manpower at this time probably came predominantly from the Italiotes as
          they are omitted from army rosters of the period. These rosters set out the
          details of military contingents to be supplied by Rome's allies and federated
          states. Maritime Italiote cities therefore omitted would have probably, like
          Neapolis, been required to maintain a number of ships at sea in lieu of
          providing troops. Overall, seaborne operations during the war were minor,
          but significant for the Romans who recognised the importance of the
          sea even in a predominantly land war such as this. Always an eminently
          practical people, the Romans had seen the advantages of a secure coastline
          and water-borne communications along it; that this control could ensure
          a continuation of their trade and the ability to import necessities; that
          well-placed naval bases could support a fleet and that a proper naval staff
          could ensure that it all worked. They had seen that sea-borne raiding and
          joint naval and military operations were possible and had built up a pool of
          experienced 'navy' men.

306 BC   In 306 BC the Romans once again entered a treaty with Carthage.[43]
          This was clearly of mutual benefit in that by now with coastlines on both
          sides of the peninsula and their navy, the Romans had almost unwittingly
          become a Mediterranean power; as indicated by the far more equable terms
          of the agreement. The Carthaginian's struggle against the Greeks in Sicily
          continued and the interests of both sides, apart from a by now traditional
          alliance, were suited by not having to rival each other. This resulted in an
          agreement that the Romans stay out of Sicily, and the Carthaginians out of
          Italy. They further agreed to divide the formerly Etruscan island of Corsica
          between them, although Rome does not appear to have taken advantage of
          this.

304 BC   The Samnite War ended in 304 with Rome victorious and spreading its
          alliances and colonies across the peninsula. Of significance shortly would be
          their planting of a colony at Luceria (Lucera, in Abruzzo) and alliance with
          the Apulians of south-east Italy.

          The Samnites, although reduced, were not yet finished but the Third
          Samnite War (298 to 290 BC) saw the eclipse of their independence. Their
          attempted alliance with the Etruscans and Gauls in the north saw the defeat
          of them also and the extension of Roman coastal dominion northwards to

ROWING SYSTEMS

Mono-reme or 'conter' type. A single line of rowers sat one behind the other along each side of the ship, up to a maximum of 25 per side (a penteconter)

Doubling the rowers at each oar increased power but as the length of the oar stroke is dictated by the inboard man, the outboard man can only add 3/4 'man-power' as opposed to the bireme arrangement.

Bireme. By semi-superimposing another reme slightly outboard of the first, the ship's oar-power was doubled for little increase in length.

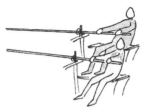

'Four' or quadrireme. Logical development of the bireme. By doubling the rowers at each oar in an enlarged hull.

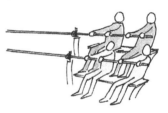

Trireme, added a third reme above and outboard of the others, their oars worked across an outrigger projecting beyond the ship's side.

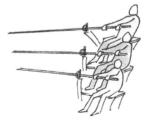

The quinquireme or 'five'. By doubling the rowers per oar in the upper two remes. The standard line-of-battle ship of the Punic Wars.

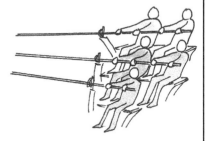

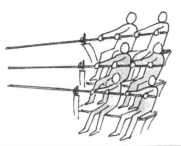

The 'six', the largest type known to have been in service with the Roman Navy.

a line roughly from La Spezia on the west coast to Rimini on the Adriatic, from where their coastline ran south to Bari.

Although there was no naval activity reported during this war, the navy was mobilised; in 295 BC a large number of Sabellian levies from coastal Campania and the south had plotted trouble when they were brought to Rome, on their way to service with the fleet. The plot failed, but of interest is that there were 4000 of them.[44] They were rated *socii navales*, that is, naval allies, and at an average of 200 men to man a trireme, represent enough to provide crews for twenty ships. The Sabellians were related to the Samnites and it was an obvious move to get them aboard ships lest they be tempted to join the Samnites. At the same time, we must assume that the Romans would not have allowed their naval force to be manned by a preponderance of unreliable men. Even being generous and estimating that the levy was half of the service's manpower, enough crews for a fleet of forty or so ships emerges.[45]

The Roman alliance with the Apulians provoked tension with the Greek maritime colony of Tarentum, while in the south-west, a struggle between the Syracusans and the Bruttians (of Calabria) caused some of the Italiote Greek towns of the south to look to Rome for protection and alliance. This in turn caused Rome to look further to the south and in 285 BC, Thurii (on the western side of the Gulf of Taranto) appealed for help.

Thurii again appealed for help in 282 BC and this time the Romans responded. For their part, a port in this position would be a useful base for the navy in transferring ships, now that it had both west and east coasts to patrol and the Adriatic was prone to piracy. With the Romans now in 'their' Gulf, the Tarentines became extremely nervous. Whether it had become obsolete, or the Romans were adventuring, it seems they chose to ignore their treaty with Tarentum of 338 BC

During 282 BC, a Roman squadron of ten ships was cruising in the Gulf and was close to Tarentum. In the city there was an internal political struggle between pro- and anti-Roman factions. The presence of the Roman ships may have been provocative or they may have simply been going past enroute to the Adriatic; in any event, their presence triggered a violent response by the Tarentines, who manned their ships and attacked the Roman squadron, sinking four ships, capturing one and scattering the rest. The Romans had suffered their first naval defeat. Although there is no account of the size of the Tarentine fleet, corollary evidence would suggest between fifteen and twenty ships, presumably most of which would have been available to attack the Romans. Regardless, the Romans had been unable to escape before being roundly beaten, losing a sizeable portion of their fleet strength. Flushed with success, the Tarentines took and sacked Thurii. Roman peace envoys were then refused audience, leading to war.

The only conclusion is that the huge polyremes of the Hellenistic powers were built more for prestige and to overawe each other, rather in the manner of the battleship races of the twentieth century. In other words, the biggest ship was intended only to oppose the enemy's biggest ship; the limitations inherent in galley warfare dictated that it could not actually control the seas and anything smaller would simply avoid it. To confirm this, the surviving accounts of their operations are limited to set-piece battles, where their presence does not provide the deciding factor and they certainly do not prove to be the fleet-smashing weapon, sweeping all before their awesome size and power (note the account of the Battle of Chios in Chapter 4). Further, their deployment against the Roman and allied fleet in the Eastern Mediterranean (see Chapter 4) failed to prevent the fleet of which they were an integral part from being beaten. Even in their last foray at Actium in 31 BC, when Marcus Antonius found some tens for his fleet, they lost. Time and again, a few smaller ships would combine to destroy one of the giants; at Chios, two fives attack and destroy a ten; at Actium, three or four of Octavian's smaller ships overwhelm one of Antonius' big ships.

Although impressive, perhaps these ships' sheer size ironically in fact, worked against them. The essence of the ram-equipped ship was that it was swift and manoeuvrable enough to be able to catch its opponent and strike a (preferably) fatal blow. As the ships became bigger, heavier and more ponderous the degree of 'swift and manoeuvrable' declined in inverse proportion. For such a ship to be able to ram, its target either had to be stationary or to blunder close in front of it. The big ships could of course carry many more marines, but to be effective, they had to board an enemy and the smaller ships could keep clear. They could also mount increased quantities of heavier artillery pieces. Although these could cause prodigious damage (witness the missile damage to the stone walls of Pompeii reputedly caused by Sulla's artillery in 89 BC)[46] it was not until the invention in the nineteenth century of the high-explosive shell that artillery became a true ship-destroying weapon.

One can only conclude that the quinquireme was the optimum size for a heavy-weight warship which, while being able to be built and manned in quantity, nevertheless was effective and able to defeat larger ships, yet retained enough of the 'swift and manoeuvrable' to be able to catch most smaller ones.

MERCHANT
SHIPS

Merchant ships had continued to grow and by this time averaged some 250 tons and some very large ones could carry as much as 1000 tons. With their broad, round hulls and one or two large sails they could make about three or four knots, but also made much leeway and were difficult to handle in rough weather, when the masts could strain the hull and cause leaking.[47]

281 BC   In 281 BC the Romans started to march on Tarentum, which appealed
to King Pyrrhus of Epirus for help. This led to the Pyrrhic War (280 to 275
BC) when the King crossed unhindered with an army to Italy and in the
ensuing campaigns, the Romans suffered severe casualties. It is tempting
to think that by laying up the fleet, enough manpower would have been
released to form the equivalent of an extra legion; alternatively however it
may have profited the Romans more to maintain ships on the Adriatic coast
to disrupt Pyrrhus' communications and lines of supply to his homeland.
There are no reports of naval activity during this war, so this remains pure
conjecture. After his inconclusive campaign in Italy, Pyrrhus made a quick
peace with Rome and crossed to Sicily to help the Greeks there against the
Carthaginians, who had overrun most of the island. Elsewhere in 280 BC,
the Pharos of Alexandria in Egypt was built, the first recorded lighthouse
and one of the wonders of the Ancient World.

278 BC   In 278 BC the Carthaginians sent their admiral, Mago, with 120 ships
to Ostia to help Rome, but Pyrrhus was already in Sicily and it was not
needed. Since Pyrrhus posed no naval threat to Rome, this action by the
Carthaginians seems curious and perhaps represented a show of force to
deter the Romans from being tempted to use pursuit of the Epirote king as
an excuse to intervene in Sicily. The numbers were clearly excessive for a mere
diplomatic mission. The allies did agree to help each other wherever Pyrrhus
attacked; Carthage was to provide ships and maritime support and they did
in fact transport five hundred Roman troops to reinforce the garrison at
Rhegium (Reggio Calabria). Even if available in the area, the Roman fleet
would have been no match for the combined Syracusan and Tarentine fleets
fighting with Pyrrhus, but the presence of the huge Carthaginian fleet could
guarantee their non-interference in this operation.

275 BC   Whilst Pyrrhus was in Sicily the Romans forced the rest of the Samnites,
the Lucanians and the Bruttians to submit to them; thereby extending their
rule over most of the south and acquiring most of the peninsula coastline
in the process. Pyrrhus tried to cross back from Sicily into Italy in 276 BC,
using a fleet of 110 ships, but he was defeated by the Carthaginian fleet,
losing all but forty of his ships. He managed to withdraw to Tarentum but
after some minor campaigning, finally withdrew to Epirus in 275 BC.

With the withdrawal of Pyrrhus and with Syracuse facing the
Carthaginians, the Romans could renew their pressure on Tarentum
uninterrupted. It is logical to assume that the ships of the fleet were
concentrated to provide a blockade in the Gulf of Taranto. Such blockades
were rarely totally effective in ancient times. The inability of ancient oared
warships to keep station at sea for long periods of time, and the large numbers
needed to maintain any kind of constant patrol (which were rarely available),
together with the problems caused by night and the weather, enabled

Between 270 and 265 BC the Syracusans built two exceptional ships. The first was a giant merchant ship, possibly over 200 feet (62m.) in length and having luxurious passenger accommodation, with cabins with mosaic floors, promenades, gymnasium, baths, library and chapel. It could carry 2000 tons of cargo and had three masts and carried towers and catapults for self-defence.[48]

They followed this by having a 'twenty' reme warship built for them at Corinth. This ship carried four masts and eight catapults. Both ships were presented as gifts to Ptolemy of Egypt, whose love of vast ships was well known and one must assume that such expensive presents supported Syracusan diplomacy in seeking help against the Carthaginians, or perhaps as payment for help given.

Inspired, Ptolemy went on to build two 'thirties' and one 'forty', the biggest ever; these two freak types were evidently two 'fifteens' and two 'twenties' respectively, joined by a bridging deck, catamaran-style. They were not used in action and although totally unrepresentative, do indicate the range of imagination and sophistication as well as the abilities of the ancient shipwrights who actually built them.

At about this time also, Ptolemy's military engineers achieved an important step in the further development of artillery. As has been mentioned, the potential power of torsion-spring artillery had not been fully realised; the juggling of the relationship between the size, length and positioning of the springs, the length of the bow-staves and of the stock and the size of the missile to be projected being a matter of guesswork and performance a matter of chance. Ptolemy's engineers perfected formulae whereby, upon specifying a missile size, the relative sizes of all of the parts of the piece would be dictated and the machine, made accordingly, would give a reliable, known performance. Although still needing regular, expert attention, the dependability of these new 'formula' machines led to their widespread adoption and the phasing out of the composite bow-powered artillery pieces.[49]

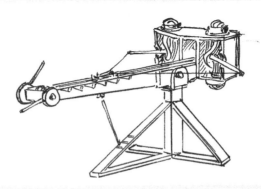

blockade running to go a long way towards keeping a town supplied, given a reasonable amount of luck. In 272 BC Tarentum surrendered and Roman hegemony was established over the whole peninsula and consolidated in the next few years.

In the east, the long drawn-out successor wars had petered out and the Macedonians and the Egyptians remained as the two major sea-powers. The vast expense of building, maintaining and operating great fleets of huge galleys must have exhausted and all but bankrupted the antagonists and could not be kept up. The huge galleys had to be laid up and their brief era had passed.

273 BC   In 273 BC Ptolemy II of Egypt established diplomatic relations and friendship with Rome. The island state of Rhodes had emerged as a naval power which held the balance of power at sea in the east. The Rhodians had a very large merchant fleet and a quite small, but extremely efficient, navy to protect it, suppressing piracy and developing the fastest of ships and tactics to deal with them.

Ptolemy II of Egypt extended his maritime trade in the Red Sea, bringing him into conflict with the Nabateans of north-west Arabia, whose prosperity depended upon caravan trade. They took to piracy and Ptolemy, circa 275 BC, had the Nile–Red Sea canal renovated and sent a fleet, including quadriremes, into the Red Sea to suppress them, giving an indication of the size and capacity of the canal at that time.

The navy had now become a part of the normal armed forces of the Roman state. From the experience gained by Roman crewmen aboard Etruscan ships and warships; from the familiarity with the shipping using Rome and her river; from the long association with Carthage and the Italiote Greeks; all had led to the first tentative experiments with the use of naval forces and to their first naval victory in 338 BC, as well as to their first naval defeat in 282 BC.

Obviously the ad hoc collection and commissioning of ships was inefficient and most likely incapable of providing the ships needed, which led to the establishment of the Navy Board in 311 BC. From then on the Romans had the basis of a permanent naval organisation. Although their naval actions were not, to say the least, overly distinguished in the years that followed, doubtless a valuable body of experience was acquired, upon which foundation could be built the great navy that would follow.

The naval forces available to the Romans were by now, like the army, in two parts. Firstly there were the Roman's own ships, the squadrons raised and organised by the *Duoviri* on behalf of the state and manned by Romans, equivalent to the Legions of the army. It was the duty of the *Duoviri* to ensure that a force of ships was maintained and would be available for use when needed; ships do not last for ever and logically, they would have had new ships built as required to replace those lost by action, accident or misadventure or which were simply worn out. This force probably remained at about twenty to thirty ships.

In addition, there were now further forces available. Just as Rome's allies and federated states were liable to provide certain military contingents, called *auxilia*, to serve alongside the legions (but never within them) so too the maritime allies provided ships and crews. These vessels, provided by such allies as Neapolis, Paestum, Tarentum and Thurii, would have doubled the available naval strength. It seems possible that allied manpower was used to augment the numbers of rowers and seamen on 'Roman' ships but otherwise the extent to which Roman and allied contingents were mixed probably followed the army's practice, i.e. that they served alongside each other in separate formations and were not merged. In other words, Romans mostly manned Roman ships and allies manned allied ships. As for the army, Roman and auxiliary units operated together under the unified command of a Roman officer, a Consul or a deputy appointed by the Consuls. During the 'closed' season for navigation (November to March) the ships would have been laid up and refurbished, ready for the next season's duties. Such men as were not required for this work would have been disbanded and sent home. With a coastline now including most of peninsular Italy, the ships of the fleet were now only just sufficient to patrol and police Rome's territorial waters. Rome and her erstwhile ally, Carthage (Punica to the Romans, a Latin corruption of the name Phoenicia) were now the two dominant powers in the western Mediterranean. Strains in their long relationship had grown with the growth of Roman power and it was perhaps inevitable that one would have to prevail at the expense of the other. The stage was thus set for the epic struggles between them, struggles in which sea power would prove to be decisive.

NOTES

1. See Selkirk, *The Piercebridge Formula*.
2. For the story of Rome's beginnings, Livy (59 BC to AD 17) , Books I–III, remains a most important source, especially when evaluated and interpreted, both as to ancient sources and as to archaeology by e.g. Grandazzi, *The Foundation of Rome*; also Scullard.
3. Maps and diagrams have been found from as early as the Stone Age and a map on pottery from northern Iraq dated to 2300 BC has the cardinal points clearly marked; James & Thorpe, *Ancient Inventions*.
4. From Pyrgi come inscriptions on gold sheets in Etruscan and Phoenician dedicated to the Goddess Uni of the former, the latter's Astarte; and see Barker and Rasmussen, *The Etruscans*.
5. The sources do vary and several aver that the canal was built by Darius of Persia but the earliest reference found to it is to Necho's Canal. See Casson, *Travel in the Ancient World*, quoting from Herodotus.
6. For more detailed explanations, see Casson *SSAW* and Bass, *A History of Seafaring*, for examples of wrecks recovered, confirming this method of construction.
7. E.g. following the Battle of Arinusa in 406 'Athenian ships … were detailed to recover the wrecks' Rodgers, referring to Diodorus.
8. That most men got out of a stricken ship is perhaps confirmed by the specific mention of occasions when they failed to do so, eg. at the Battle of Chios in 201 (chapter 4) and the second Battle of Massilia in 49 (Chapter 5).
9. Polybius III.22.
10. Casson, *SSAW*.
11. Such installations have been found, e.g. at Piraeus and an excavated example can be seen at Admiralty Island, Carthage.
12. See Ormerod, *Piracy in the Ancient World*.
13. For an examination of the iconography of the evolution of warships, see Morrison & Coates *GROW* also Casson *SSAW*.
14. There are several references in the literature (eg. Polybius) to ships losing their rams (that is the castings) and the cast bronze ram discovered underwater off Athlit in Israel is an example (Casson).
15. See description of the Battle of Chios in Chapter 4.
16. The 'Trireme Debate' on the precise form of these ships was long and often heated and the suggested interpretations many. See eg. Torr, *Ancient Ships* and the (included therein) views of Tarn. The question was surely settled by Morrison and Coates in *The Athenian Trireme* and other volumes and by their actually building and sailing one, the Greek Navy's *Olympias*. Still there are dissenting views, see Tilley, *Seafaring on the Ancient Mediterranean*.
17. Casson, *SSAW*.
18. Polybius III.22.
19. The strategy and tactics of trireme warfare are related by Thucydides in *The Peloponnesian Wars* and expounded in Rodgers. It is illuminating to undertake wargaming with models representing them (Hague, *Sea Battles in Miniature*).
20. Livy V.28.
21. See Calza and Becatti, *Ostia*.
22. There are contrary views (eg. Rodgers) but this seems to now be the generally accepted pattern of development. See Morrison & Coates *GROW*.
23. Livy VII.
24. Polybius III.24.
25. See Scullard, a standard history for this period.
26. The framework of the system had been introduced by Servius Tullius (ruled 578 to 535) the penultimate King of Rome.
27. Livy I.43 and Polybius VI.19.
28. Marsden, *Greek and Roman Artillery*.
29. The term actually means 'un-fenced' and cataphract is 'fenced-in' (Casson) or 'open, un-decked' and 'decked' (Morrison), although the latter is stretching the meaning to suit.
30. Later wall paintings also confirm this.
31. Again, see Morrison & Coates *GROW*, Casson *SSAW*.

32. All of the authorities agree on this. As if in confirmation, the one occasion when slaves were used deserved especial mention (in 38 BC, Chapter 6).

33. Marsden, *Greek and Roman Artillery*.

34. Cunliffe, *The Extraordinary Voyage of Pytheas the Greek*.

35. Livy V.34.

36. And see Casson, *The Ancient Marines*.

37. Such methods are recorded (inter alia) by Polybius; also see Connelly, *Greece and Rome at War*; as to the navy, see Starr.

38. Casson *SSAW* and Morrison & Coates *GROW*.

39. But see Portuguese fishing boats in Tilley.

40. Scullard.

41. By the Second Punic War this seems to have become so, Livy XXII.57 refers to a 'marine legion, the Third'.

42. The two volumes of Marsden give a comprehensive account of ancient artillery, illustrated in Connelly, *Greece and Rome at War*.

43. Polybius III.25.

44. Salmon, *Samnium and the Samnites*, commenting on Livy and Orosius.

45. There may have been more as the fleet would have had ships smaller than and needing a lesser crew than a trireme; conversely a few quadriremes or quinquiremes would need more. The figure is thus posited as a reasonable average.

46. Russo, *89 A.C. Assiedo a Pompeii*.

47. Casson SSAW.

48. Athenaeus, quoted in full in Casson *SSAW*, for which also see descriptions of the other 'monster' ships.

49. Marsden, *Greek and Roman Artillery*.

A GREAT NAVAL POWER

The First Punic War
264 BC–241 BC

Carthage had grown into an empire that by this time included most of modern Tunisia (its heartland) and parts of the north African coast of what is now Libya, Algeria and Morocco; it encompassed a large part of southern Spain, the Balearic Isles, Corsica, Sardinia and western Sicily. Its ships had ventured into the Atlantic Ocean, as far as Madeira, the Canaries and perhaps even to the Azores. It was essentially a sea-borne trading empire with a population of some five million people. With the eclipse of Etruscan sea-power and the reduction and limiting of that of the western Greek colonies, together with the treaties with Rome which had effectively restricted her freedom at sea, the Carthaginian fleets dominated the western Mediterranean, making it a virtual Carthaginian lake, policed by her huge navy, the seamanship and skill of whose sailors and crews was legendary.[1]

At Carthage, the Punic navy had its own military harbour, built about a circular lagoon and adjacent to the civilian harbour with which it connected and which was protected by walls. There were ship building and repair yards, stores, workshops and all the other installations of a complete naval dockyard, needed for the maintenance and operation of the Navy. Surrounding the lagoon and also in an artificial island built in the middle, were ship sheds and slipways, capable of holding 200 warships.[2] The fleet totalled up to 250 warships, some of which were posted to squadrons stationed at places about the empire, such as Lilybaeum (Marsala) in Sicily. The fleet had a 'seven' as flagship and numerous triremes and 'fours', but their main warship type was the 'five' or to the Romans quinquireme.

272 BC   In 272 BC, during the Roman siege of Tarentum, a Punic (Carthaginian) fleet suddenly appeared offshore for no apparent reason, then just as quickly sailed off. This may have been an exercise in opportunism, to see if they could turn the situation to advantage, or they may have turned up to support the Romans in accordance with the Treaty of 278 BC. However they made no attempt to land troops and Carthage later apologised for what the Romans regarded as an incursion. Tension was mounting between the two powers.[3]

Rome had mastered Italy and controlled a population totalling some three million people. She had maintained and operated a naval force for some 130 years and had inherited the skill and expertise of the Italiote Greeks, to add to those of her own people, the Italians and Etruscans. The navy had been placed on a permanent footing by the appointment of the *Duoviri Navales* in 311 BC and in 267 BC, just before the war, four *Praefecti* or Prefects of the fleet were appointed. It is not clear whether these officers were appointed in substitution for the *Duoviri*, or in addition to them; logically it was the latter as otherwise firstly, the number of existing officers would simply have been increased to four (and called *Quattroviri?*); secondly the 'new' officers were entitled *Quaestores Classici*,[4] literally 'Fleet Treasurers', a quaestor being principally a financial officer; thirdly, they were posted to various areas, one at Ostia, one in Campania and the other two presumably at other locations, perhaps Tarentum and the Adriatic, certainly after the coming war, one was posted at Lilybaeum in Sicily. One of the four was made *Quaestor Ostiensis* and placed in command of the naval installations and personnel there. Ostia was the original 'home base' of the navy and its position ensured its prime importance and that it be a centre of command. The other three Prefects' duties included attending to the navy and allied contributions to it together with naval installations and ship building and repair, in their respective areas. Each command probably had a number of warships assigned and in permanent commission for patrol and communications duties, with the main body of heavier ships kept ready and in repair to be mobilised and concentrated when needed.

The navy had outgrown its earlier organisation and the administrative structure was expanded to now comprise the two *Duoviri* in Rome, overseeing the four *Quaestores*, each with his own naval district and so, despite, or perhaps because of, its somewhat inauspicious earlier operations, the Romans thought the navy to be of sufficient importance to thus reinforce its institutions. Operational command of the fleet remained a consular appointment in the same way that a Consul commanded the army. Although a Consul, as the supreme magistrate of the Republic, had total authority in the execution of his command, the disadvantage was that his term of office was only for one year, so no-one had the opportunity to become an experienced naval commander or admiral. This problem was later partly alleviated by extending the consular command authority or *imperium* into a second year, when the officer would be entitled a Pro-Consul and subject only to the Consuls for that year. The organisation of ship's officers was typically, the *Magister Navis* or Captain (in this regard the term 'Trierarch' may already have been preferred, after all *Magister Navis* could be the captain of any ship whereas a Trierarch could only be Captain of a warship). Next was the *Gubernator* or navigating officer, in charge of the helm and the after part of the ship and second in command; the next senior officer was the

The quinquireme was a galley of about 130 to 150 feet (39 to 45 m), that is not much longer than a trireme, but with a higher deck over the rowers from which the marines could fight, up to ten feet (3m) above water and with a broader beam, perhaps of 25 feet (8m) across the outrigger. The ship needed 270 to 280 rowers, pulling on either three remes with two men manning each upper and middle oar and one man the lowest oar, or in two remes, with two men on each oar in one reme and three on each in the other, although the former arrangement seems the more likely. These ships, it has been estimated, could sprint for short distances at up to eight knots and cruise for prolonged periods at nearly seven knots.[5]

The ship would have about twenty sailors and half a dozen or so officers, together with a contingent of marines, Roman ships of the type having forty. In Roman service, officers were the Captain or *Magister Navis*, the helmsman or navigating officer, known as the *Gubernator*, a *Proreus* or bow officer, in charge of the forward section rig, anchors and depth-taking; a sailing master in charge of the seamen and rig and a rowing master, who was called the *Hortator* or *Pausarius*. Under the former was the ship's carpenter, sail maker and other tradesmen; under the latter, apart from the rowers, were the ship's musicians, the rhythm of whose playing would help keep the rowers in time and probably whose specific calls would relay orders along the ship, in the manner of the army's bugle calls; the musicians were called by the Greeks *Auletes* or flute-players and, despite the popular modern image, drums are not attested. It must have been difficult for a rowing master to control so many rowers by shouted orders alone which could not have been audible from end to end of the ship; even with the men silent, the noise of the oars being worked, the natural creaking and movement in the hull and of its passage through the water would be enough to overcome the loudest shout, let alone the noise of battle. As well as the calls of the musicians, therefore, it seems more than likely that there were sub-officers or senior ratings at intervals among the rowers, to control their particular section of men and to relay orders. A crew of a *quinqireme* thus totalled about 350 men.[6]

Whereas there is no evidence of the actual organisation of Roman crews at this time, applying the system of centuries would logically suggest that rowers be split into two centuries, port and starboard, marines forming a third, with the deck crew attached. Although 'century' of course means one hundred, the effective strength of an army century was eighty men. If strictly applied therefore to a quinquireme crew, the rowers with their supernumeraries would divide into two port and two starboard, each with seventy-odd men, the marines a half-century and the sailors and artificers another half-century. No account of the exact manner of in which crews were organised aboard these ships has survived and we can only guess at it by trying to apply the known system of centuries.[7] Once in action, the sailors and other non-rowing crew, other than the helmsmen, could have been a vulnerable encumbrance and must therefore have been armed and employed in protecting the helmsmen with their shields and in supporting the marines, perhaps as archers,

Proreus or *Proretus*, the bow officer in charge of the lookouts, depth taking and the forward part of the ship. The rowing officer was the *Pausarius* or *Celeusta* (from the Greek), while the marines were commanded by their own *Centurio* and his *Optio*, smaller units perhaps by an *Optio* alone.

Clearly the Romans were already thinking in terms of the future expansion of the navy and perhaps had already started to do so at this time. The first task of the expanded naval administration was to establish shipyards, manpower and the supply of materials to increase the building capacity for warships. Additionally, yards for the victualling, repair and maintenance of these ships, together with facilities to house, feed and train their crews had to be expanded and organised.

278 BC It would seem likely that the visit by the Punic Admiral Mago with a fleet of 120 ships in 278 BC and the pressure that he was able to exert and indeed, did exert on the subsequent negotiations (with the fleet at his back and the Romans unable to challenge it), offended their pride and caused them to resolve not to be in such a position again. The appointment of fleet officers was evidence of a further change in Roman attitude towards their navy. The navy had started as and grown to be essentially a force for coastal defence and communication, looking principally ashore to deal with hostile coasts, rather than out to sea to deal with enemy fleets. Carthage was a naval superpower and the Romans could envisage the day when they would be at odds with her. To be able to effectively oppose Carthage, Rome would have to become the same. Hitherto, Rome had developed as a basically land-based power with its main military effort directed to the army. It would now have to effect a radical change to become a maritime power and to direct a massive effort towards the build-up of a world-class navy. This change had to be fundamental if success was to be gained in that for a sea-power the objective is to dominate the seas by beating the enemy fleet or denying it movement, defending against invasion, blockading the enemy yet protecting one's own shipping and finally, operating in conjunction with the army in the projection of power to any chosen point having access to the sea.

This the Romans set out to do with their customary efficiency, setting out to build 100 quinqueremes and twenty triremes. Polybius, writing just over one hundred years later, famously relates that the Romans copied a Punic warship that had been washed ashore, but this is highly unlikely and if not apocryphal, would only have yielded some possibly useful intelligence as to the specification of an enemy ship. In any case this is probably a duplication of the reference to the capture of the Rhodian blockade runner in 249 (see below).[8] The Romans had already started building their new ships with the aid of the peoples of the peninsula; their contact with Egypt kept them aware of developments in the east and finally, of course, their 300-year relationship with Carthage herself would have left them well-informed as to the Punic operating catapults and grapnels and generally adding to the ship's fighting strength. As to the vulnerability of helmsmen, several contemporary renditions of warships, particularly of the smaller types, show a cuddy in the stern, shaped like half a beehive, which are likely to have been shelters to protect the helmsmen and officers from the rear.

Armament would be principally the ram and by now the mounting of catapults was standard. The type powered by a large, composite bow was being superseded by torsion-spring powered types, built according to the recently perfected formulae for producing reliable machines and in convenient sizes for shipboard use. Types such as a three-span catapult, for shooting a large arrow, some 27 inches (69cm) long, together with stone throwers capable of hurling a five pound (2.5kg) shot were mounted. These weapons, although unable to destroy or seriously damage a ship to the point where it was a wreck incapable of action, were intended to clear enemy decks and to shoot in amongst the rowers, the hitting of a very few of whom would interrupt the essential rhythm of the oars and throw the others into confusion.

navy. It is further not unlikely that the Romans and if not, their Italiote allies already had some quinquiremes of their own. When the Romans' new ships started to appear, they were in any event unlike the Punic ships, being heavier-built and not having such fine hull lines and, as a result, they were more unwieldy than their Punic counterparts. However, their larger and heavier construction was deliberately designed for a specific purpose, as will be seen later. As for the triremes, these were still widely used by Mediterranean navies and being lighter and faster, as well as needing smaller crews, were valuable as scouts for a main force – or as despatch vessels. Additionally, smaller ships such as *penteconters* although no longer having any part to play in a battle-line, were still employed in small numbers for the various minor roles and duties for which a large warship was unsuitable or an expensive luxury.

The composition and disposition of a fleet operation was in many ways analogous to the deployment of an army, with the conters as the equivalent of the *velites* or light infantry skirmishers, well ahead of the main body, dropping back to report sightings or contact with an enemy; the triremes, the fastest ships, being equivalent to the cavalry, operating on the flanks and in pursuit; finally the quinquiremes, equivalent to the heavy infantry and artillery, to get to grips with the enemy at close quarters. With all of this, the relative speed of the different types of ship had to be considered. It has been more or less established that the trireme was the fastest type by a noticeable margin; among the others, there was little difference in speed between say a conter and a 'six', although the bigger ships could of course maintain a better speed in heavier seas. Assuming that an advancing fleet sent a screen of conters out a day before its own departure, with orders to stay ahead but to report back to the fleet any sightings of the enemy, every one of them that did thereafter fall back to report, would weaken and leave a shorter screening line. Having done so it would not have the speed advantage to enable it to return to its station ahead of the fleet, even if the latter were making way at a leisurely pace to conserve their rowers. Conversely, the enemy would have its own screen of scouts ahead of it, also anxious to sight an enemy and report and in turn to prevent the other side's scouts from doing so. The scouts might well clash and if some got through the screen and closer to the enemy main fleet, the latter could detach some triremes which could overhaul and catch them. The scout might assume the presence of the enemy fleet from the presence of their scouts and feign retreat, seeking to entice the enemy scouts onto their own fleet. The permutations are many and the whole was to be repeated in the tactics evolved for the great battle-fleets of the First World War, where conters were replaced by cruisers, then battle-cruisers, and the same cat and mouse game played out.

It is not easy from the, of necessity, limited available accounts, to keep track of the relative strengths of the opposing navies as the war progressed and much has been written on the subject. Among the writers of ancient times are tendencies to be partisan, to duplicate figures, or to exaggerate. Many of their modern counterparts tend to assume that all of a navy's ships are always concentrated in one place, so that annihilation is always total. They also fail to keep in mind that a ship cannot be used, put aside and be ready for instant use again later almost at a whim, in the same way and with the same simplicity say as an infantryman's sword and shield. Finally, there is a tendency to overlook the fact that, having built a system of shipyards and a skilled work-force dedicated to the production of warships, these could not simply be activated and dismissed at will or switched off like a machine, and that to keep these yards in existence, a continuous programme of naval construction was required.

267 BC   From 267 BC therefore, the navy was increasing its shipbuilding capacity and equally, having established such an operation, it follows that the building of warships was a continuous process throughout the coming war. From the figures that have been provided by the ancient sources, it is possible to ascertain an approximation of the production capacity for warships. By taking this larger overall view, such statements as that by Polybius that the Romans built 120 ships in two months, which on the face of it appears unlikely, can become reasonable and feasible. If one accepts the not unreasonable view that if the larger Navy Board started to increase warship building capacity in 267, when the *Praefecti* were appointed, and

that by 265, had six yards in operation; then Polybius actually meant that it took two months to build one ship (so they were all 'built in two months', but *each*) i.e. if a ship took sixty days to be built, the shipyard would at that rate, build six ships a year, half a dozen yards would build thirty-six and so on. Even if he exaggerated and it took three months to build a ship, those six yards would build twenty-four ships in a year and therefore, starting in 265 BC, the 120 new ships would all be ready, as they were, for use together in 261 BC. Taking the war as a whole and the ancient sources' figures for new construction (and allowing for, in addition to the 'natural' annual wastage of old ships at the end of their lives, those lost by accident or misadventure that had to be replaced) then the Romans' annual average production of new ships was about twenty-five ships.

There was a possible increase in the period 260 to 258 BC, but home production could well have been augmented by orders for additional ships placed with shipbuilders of the Hellenistic east, an option denied later in the war due to the continued drain on the economy which it caused. Even this possibility becomes unnecessary however if one accepts that there was a regular annual production of new ships. The provision of measured lengths of timber by various cities and from the state forests in the quantities required for the continuous building effort quickly exhausted the supply of seasoned wood and necessitated the use of improperly seasoned or 'green' timber (which was preferably cut in winter when the sap was out). The ships built from this poorer quality timber needed constant maintenance and drying-out and were also heavy; natural movement of the timber as it matured could also cause structural weakness or even damage and such matters can well explain the dreadful losses of ships in storms, which well-founded ships may have weathered.[9] However, more recent experience had demonstrated that green timber was preferred, being easier to work and fashion as it was more supple[10] although requiring a greater degree of skill on the shipwright's part in anticipating the future conduct of the timber being used, an ability that may have been insufficiently widespread in the very rapid build-up of ship numbers.

New ships were not sent into the war zone piecemeal, but were husbanded by both sides, until a major force had been built up which was then deployed en masse. Polybius' assertion that the Romans built 120 ships in 261 BC should be varied to say that they were probably built *by* 261 BC, which would once again fit the available evidence and add credence to the existence of an established and viable shipbuilding industry. An average production rate of twenty-five or so ships a year for the duration of the war, plus the repair and re-commissioning of, say, two thirds of captured enemy ships is enough to provide all the numbers of ships reported to have been deployed by the Romans during the war. It would appear to be the loss of men rather than ships that caused the major reductions in Roman naval activity from time to time during the war. As to the financial crises that were to be caused by enormous ship losses, it follows that such losses meant a prolongation of the war and of its costs and that further capital had to be raised to replace those losses.

For the Carthaginians there is even less information available but they undoubtedly started the war with a much larger number of warships than the Romans, possibly as many as 250 ships. On the face of it, the Roman effort to build up their fleet by 120 ships to oppose such apparently overwhelming numbers, would seem to have been pointless unless they knew that it would be enough to at least equal the Punic fleet available for use in Sicilian waters. The main problem for the Carthaginians was manpower. Unlike the Romans with their citizen levy and their allies, which made every able-bodied man liable for military service, Carthaginian citizens were exempt, except in cases of extreme emergency, from military or naval service. They provided officers but otherwise relied on mercenaries and drafts of men from subject and allied peoples. This system set a financial and numerical limit on manpower which had to be balanced between the needs of the army and those of the navy. With their long-established and sophisticated naval establishment, the Carthaginians had building yards for warships producing them on a regular basis, if only to replace worn-out ships. Like the Romans, their building capacity must have been increased during the war but certainly did not match that of the Romans, who were to consistently out-build them. Consideration of the figures for the Punic navy as a whole would suggest that they normally kept a battle fleet in commission of one hundred or so ships and augmented this as needed by fitting out and commissioning more from a large reserve of ships, for the maintenance and keeping of which they had excellent facilities at Carthage. At the outbreak of the war, the active Punic fleet was increased to about 150 ships, with a hundred or so in reserve which could be used to provide replacements for losses; if they stepped up their building rate to an average of fifteen ships per year and on the assumption that they maintained this up to 249 BC, this would provide all the ships that they are actually recorded as having deployed. It is also possible that they could have had recourse to the shipbuilders of their Levantine ancestral ports to augment their own production although there is no record surviving of their having done so.

It must be borne in mind that when mentioning 'the fleet' in connection with various specific operations, one is referring to the main combat formation of the navy, but not the whole navy, of either antagonist. As with for example, the Royal Navy's Grand Fleet in the First World War, although it was the principal striking formation of the service, stationed to cover the North Sea as the expected major scene of action with their enemy's main fleet, there were other fleets and ships performing other duties around the world. So it was with both the Roman and Punic fleets, who had their main fleets concentrated to oppose each other in the Sicilian theatre, the most important area of operations of the war, but also, throughout the war both sides had other warships and squadrons of warships of varying strengths operating in other areas (there would also always be a number of ships in port, undergoing repairs or refitting). For the Punic navy, the Carthaginian trade routes along the African coast and to the eastern Mediterranean had to be protected and their merchant ships escorted, perhaps in convoys; in the west, contact had to be maintained with the other Punic colonies on the north African coast and most importantly, with their large possessions in southern Hispania, the source of much of their supplies, manpower and wealth, also the place from which their trade with northern Europe operated. Initially their presence in Sardinia and Corsica had to be protected, a burden that would pass to the Romans later. For the Romans, their Adriatic seaboard and its shipping had to be protected against the all-too-prevalent Illyrian pirates; shipping along the western coastline of Italy had to be protected against possible Punic raids or even a Punic attempt at invasion and the lines of supply and communication to their garrisons had to be maintained. The transports maintaining the army in Sicily had to be escorted and the normal trading routes of Roman merchant ships patrolled.

THE FIRST PUNIC WAR

264 BC   The long struggle for Sicily between Carthage and the Greeks, led by Syracuse, had continued and by 264 BC, most of the island was once more in Punic hands. When they put a garrison into Messina, the controlling faction there, of Italians, not Greeks and known as Mamertines, appealed to Rome. It was clear that Punic mastery of Sicily would threaten Roman interests in southern Italy and impinge upon her and her allies' ability to trade freely. Rome had to do something and this was to be her opportunity.

Until their new ships were built, the Roman fleet was no match for the Punic navy; nevertheless, their first operation had to be to cross the strait to get to Messina. The strait is deep with strong currents running southward on the surface with a tidal surge of up to a foot (300mm) in height, twice a day; the current runs at between one and four knots. It is also subject to whirlpools and turbulence as the current changes, which were much worse then than they are today, the formation of the sea-bed having been changed by an earthquake in AD1783. Even so it was reported in AD1824 that the famous whirlpool of Charybdis was strong enough to spin a British three-deck '74' sailing ship of the line. The strait is 24 miles (39km) long but only two and a half miles (4km) wide at its narrowest. The crossing from Rhegium to Messina is about four miles (6.5km).[11] Punic ships had been operating from Messina, the only good harbour on the north-east Sicilian coast. Foolishly the Punic ships left the harbour and on hearing this, the

Romans took the opportunity and sent a Tribune, Caius Claudius, with a small force which made a night crossing and landed then ejected the Punic garrison from the city. This bold action stung the Carthaginians into action and they despatched a further army to Sicily and moved the fleet to blockade Messina, the harbour of which was garrisoned by the Romans and denied to them; they also managed to engineer an alliance with their old enemy, Syracuse.

With no harbour nearer than Mylae (Milazzo) on the north coast, the Carthaginians had to rely on beaching their ships north of Messina, near to Cape Pelorum, where the beaches are steep and covered in shingle and rocks, a most unsatisfactory and exposed position. Whereas a trireme could, in calm conditions, just about be pulled up a beach sufficiently to keep it secure overnight and to allow the crew to get ashore to rest and prepare their food, a quinquireme, although about the same length was nearly twice the beam and very much heavier and more massive altogether. It follows that beaching could only be considered in calm conditions and involve only grounding the very stern of the ship (not the bow, to avoid inevitably causing damage to the ram) and even so would risk damage to the hull on the stone-covered beaches. More likely the ships would have to be moored close offshore.

The difficulties inherent in keeping ships on an exposed coast were to recur and afflict the Romans as well. On the east coast of Sicily the winds generally come from the west or south-west but can suddenly drop off the high land onto the sea, producing very strong squalls, as fearsome as they are sudden. From August to October, the winds are most likely to come from the south, the scirocco, which later in the autumn can become dangerous, building up seas all the way from the north African coast hundreds of miles away and producing sudden gales, thunderstorms and even waterspouts.[12] The speed and unpredictably with which these seas can arise make this area treacherous and dangerous for even quite large vessels, circumstances that would levy a heavy toll of ships of the Roman navy in the years that followed.

The Punic fleet had made its fatal mistake in leaving the harbour of Messina unguarded and although when the Consul, Appius Claudius tried to cross with his main force to Messina, he was unlucky enough to be caught by them, he lost only a few transports before safely returning to Rhegium, which is close by. The Consul had only to wait a short while however and when the Punic fleet had to retire to its beaches he successfully ferried two whole legions by night across to Sicily. The Romans proceeded to make systematic progress on land, expanding the territory held by them and pushing the Punic forces south and westwards. The Punic fleet was unable to blockade the Strait of Messina and withdrew to Mylae, being content to make the occasional sweep of the Strait.

SHIP
BUILDING

The ships continued to be built on the shell-first principle and recent evidence indicates that parts were pre-fabricated.[13] Designs were fairly standard and the use of jigs on which the hulls could be set up and formed seems logical. As with the mass-production of small craft in World War II, given a standardised design with standard parts, their manufacture en masse could be placed with non-specialist carpentry, metal and other works. Such preformed parts would be sent to the shipyards who, freed from having to prepare their materials, could concentrate on assembling the parts into complete ships. A whole additional portion of the national effort was thus focused on ship production. Livy gives a 'shopping list' for the preparation of a fleet for service indicating that each town was detailed to provide certain stores, equipment, cloth, grain, timber and so on, for the equipping of the fleet.[14] Included in this list is the requirement for Volterra (in Etruria) to provide grain and 'timber for keels and garboards' (presumably to a stated specification) and which is evidence that standardised components for ships were sent to the yards for assembly. Volterra is over twenty miles (32km) from the sea and yet rather than simply requiring baulks of timber, actual ship's components were specified. The contracting and co-ordination of all of this was the responsibility of the Navy Board. For crews, the Romans already had a nucleus of experienced men, but with a trireme needing about 185 oarsmen and sailors and a quinquireme requiring about 300, the new ships would need another 34000 men, quite apart from marines. As to the provision of these extra crews, to the nucleus of experienced navy officer and men could be added sailors and skilled ranks from the maritime and allied maritime contingents; the mass of levies, who could be from anywhere, would be trained on land to row,[15] where dummy ship's sides were set up for this purpose, then allocated en bloc to a ship. Some further sea training then took place along the Italian coast before ships and crews were considered to be ready for service.

263 BC

During 263 BC, the Punic fleet, still based at Mylae, continued to make sweeps of the Strait of Messina but were unable to intercept either of that year's Consuls when they crossed with their armies to Sicily. The Carthaginians did raid the Italian coast and when the Consul Marcus Valerius marched on Syracuse, they sent a squadron to prevent the Roman navy from blockading the city. This rather begs the question, what had become of the Syracusan navy? The fact that the Carthaginians only sent a squadron suggests that the Roman fleet was superior to that of the Syracusans, but that the extra squadron was enough to tip the balance against the Romans. As to that, it follows and bears out the earlier contention that the Romans had ships of their prewar fleet operating in the war zone from the beginning, scouting and helping in ferrying troops and supplies to Sicily. In the face of Punic superiority they were held in a protected harbour or could always fall back into the Gulf of Taranto, to re-emerge literally when the coast was clear.

262 BC   In 262 BC the Punic fleet, operating from its bases in northern Sicily, again raided the Italian coast but to little effect and was again unable to cut the Roman lines of communication to Sicily. Also in 262 BC, the Syracusans ended their unnatural alliance with Carthage and became allies of Rome, giving her another valuable naval base as well as the aid of the Syracusan navy and their technology. It will be recalled that this had spawned the growth of the war galley beyond the trireme. Later in 262 BC, Agrigentum (Agrigento) on the south coast of Sicily and one of the main Punic bases, was captured and the Romans secured the whole eastern half of the island. The Carthaginians were left with the western end and the northern coastal strip which is separated from the rest of the island and protected by a mountain chain to the south of it.

It was obvious, from the history of the long struggle between the Greeks and Carthaginians, that the war could only be finally resolved by taking the whole of Sicily. It was equally obvious that this could not be achieved and secured whilst the Punic navy was intact and roaming and raiding the coasts of Sicily and Italy at will, as they had been doing, and retaining overall and unchallenged command of the sea.

By now the Romans' efforts had resulted in their planned expansion of their war fleet by some 120 ships, mostly quinquiremes. The ships were mostly new, but so were most of the crews and the Romans had foreseen that their lack of experience would leave them unable to compete and indeed at the mercy of the swiftness and ramming ability of the Punic ships; something would have to be done to enable them to stand any chance of victory. They would have to counter with their own advantage, their superior infantry, and to invent ways for it to be used which would turn the sea-battle back into a land-battle. To do this, they firstly built their ships more strongly and heavier than their Punic counterparts. This enabled them to increase the number of marines per ship.

The Greeks at Salamis, two hundred years before, had carried only about fourteen archers and soldiers on a trireme, this had increased with the larger galleys but in a navy such as the Punic, whose skill with the ram was its prime weapon, the number of marines was not likely to be much more than that needed to man the catapults, perhaps no more than thirty or forty. The Romans placed a contingent of 120 marines on each quinquireme. The normal complement of marines of a quinquireme was forty men, but for major action or campaign, a complete century of marines or legionaries from the army, eighty men, was posted aboard. This number would be varied to an equivalent weight according to the number of catapults and their ammunition carried.

It is not easy to imagine what it must have been like for troops aboard these warships, especially on extended sea voyages. A ship of say 140 feet by 25 feet beam (41 x 8m) of which say 130 feet by 20 feet (39 x 6m) is the extent of the upper deck, this is of course tapered fore and aft and from that area must be deducted space at the stern for the officers and helmsmen and from the bow for the seamen to work the anchors, cables and rig which would likely be wet in a seaway. Also to be deducted was space amidships to step the mast and standing rigging supporting it and for the seamen to work the rig and sails, more if an *artemon* or foremast was rigged, which was likely; the sailing rig would be used wherever possible to rest or augment the rowers. In addition there were catapults on deck, towers on the larger ships and many large deck hatches left open to allow maximum ventilation for the 300 or so men below and also to allow a rapid exit for them in an emergency (these could be covered by protective screens of leather or timber in action). All of this must have reduced the deck space available for the troops and their kit by at least a third, leaving perhaps 1300 square feet (123 m²) to accommodate them.

Further, imagine what it must it have been like to be one of 120 or so men, each with their armour, helmet, shield, weapons and personal pack of cloak, food, water bottle, mess tin, etc., on this remaining available moving deck space for hours on end. It was medieval practice that 2000 square feet (189m²) of deck space was reckoned to be enough sleeping room for 250 men, which translates as 18 inches by 5 feet 6 inches (45cm x 1.8m) per man in which to lie, hardly enough. The Roman soldier on board thus had a little more, 2 feet (61cm) in width, still little enough for him and his gear. Obviously they could not all seek to lie down to sleep at once, but all of this was on a constantly moving platform completely open to the elements; in light weather, awnings could be rigged to give some shade and it is conceivable that lightweight collapsible benching could be carried to seat the troops but none such is mentioned in any of the sources, nor shown in any extant illustrations. None of the sources give any inkling as to the nature of the sanitary arrangements (if any). In many illustrations of both war- and merchant ships an extended and sometimes stylised stern platform is shown projecting at upper deck level, beyond the stern of the ship and overhanging the wake. In the absence of any other obvious function for this feature, it is not unreasonable to surmise that it served as the 'heads' for the ship. Certainly much later medieval and Arab ships had projections built outboard of the stern quarters for this purpose. The troops and men on deck had, as much as possible, to sit to obviate the effect of the 'pulse' of the oars at the catch, the shock of a couple of hundred oars 'digging' into the water at the same time (Greek marines on triremes had been trained to throw their javelins from a sitting position and to sit just before ramming). Spears could be stowed in bins but shields must have been stowed in a more protected way and certainly not hung on the outside of bulwarks, although this is shown in some illustrations, perhaps for a short inshore or ceremonial trip; a long sea voyage would not take long to destroy a glued wood and leather shield.

There is an account of an exceptionally rapid voyage by a Roman squadron transporting marines from Brundisium to Corcyra, a distance of 110 miles (176km) in eleven hours, running under sail and with the decks crammed with troops. This voyage was incredibly fast, enough to warrant mention as outstanding. Cruising under oars alone was much slower; an Athenian fleet hurrying to a siege made 31 miles (50km) in twelve hours, only two and a half knots; on another occasion a fleet took 18 hours to cover fifty miles (80km), a similar speed; again, a sailing from Chios to the Hellespont, 142 miles (227km) in 32 hours sailing time was comparatively rapid at an average four and a half knots.[16]

260 BC   By 260 BC the Romans felt ready to test their new battle fleet by provoking a confrontation with the main Punic fleet which had been causing them acute embarrassment by cruising off northern Sicily and the Italian coast. Having given their crews basic training on land, the Roman fleet spent a few weeks gaining experience at sea, 'working up' before sailing for Sicily in the late spring of 260 BC. Of the Consuls for 260 BC, Caius Duilius commanded the army and Cnaius Cornelius Scipio commanded the fleet. Lipara and its island group had been much-used by the Carthaginians as a well-placed location from which their fleet could oversee the whole north Sicilian coast, easily link up with Sardinia and have ready access to the Italian coast. The receipt of a report that the Punic fleet had vacated the islands, which might come over to Rome, was too good an opportunity for Scipio to pass up and he took a squadron of seventeen ships to investigate. As the main part of the Roman fleet was still massing off the Italian coast, it seems likely that Scipio's force was a light reconnaissance squadron of triremes that went ahead; the squadron anchored at Lipara and put parties ashore. That night the Punic commander, Boodes arrived with a force of twenty or so quinquiremes and triremes and trapped the Roman ships, most of the crews of which had gone ashore for the night. The watch crews aboard the ships were surprised and quickly overcome, followed by the capture of the rest of the crews and of the Consul.[17]

The command of the fleet now devolved upon the other Consul, Caius Duilius. As the main Roman fleet sailed south along the Italian coast the Punic commander, Hannibal, took a squadron of fifty ships to reconnoitre but, overconfident, blundered into the Roman fleet itself and suffered a few losses before managing to extricate his ships and return to his own main fleet. The Romans continued to Messina, their base for the campaign. As soon as it was rested and ready, the fleet sailed and encountered the Punic

The final problem for the Romans was how to get their men onto the enemy ship. This they solved by inventing the *corvus* or raven. The *corvus* was a gangplank, mounted on a pivot on the foredeck and able to swivel about 200 degrees from abaft the port beam to abaft the starboard beam and slung from a vertical post set into the deck. The gangway was about four feet (1.22m) wide, enough for two men to cross abreast, and included a knee-high protective screen along the side, above which the troops were protected by their shields as they crossed. Up to about 36 feet (11m) long, it was hinged at the pivot end and the outboard end was raised by a rope and pulley; at the outboard end was a large metal spike (the actual *corvus*, or raven's beak) and probably a weight to add impetus.[18] The tactic was to draw up alongside an enemy, preferably with the attacker's port side to the enemy, drop the *corvus*, the spike of which pierced the enemy deck, locking the ships together, when the Roman soldiers would swarm across it and board the enemy ship, presenting their shielded side as they crossed. The complete installation was large and heavy and could only be mounted on the big quinquiremes.

To reinforce this, the Romans mounted towers on their ships' decks on which they stationed archers to shoot down onto the enemy decks. These towers were made from wood and covered with canvas which was painted to resemble stonework.[19] Siege towers had on previous occasions been mounted on ship hulls and on barges to approach sea walls and defensive towers had been built on the huge Syracusan merchant ship;[20] this however seems to be the first time that using the deck-mounted tower as an offensive feature on a warship was introduced. Each tower could accommodate up to half a dozen archers and/or javelin-men. Artillery could not be mounted on them as there was insufficient room for its use; the absorption of the shock of discharge would have necessitated an overly heavy structure and, fatally, the design of the catapults meant that they could not be depressed to shoot down on an enemy at closer ranges. The artillery was accordingly mounted on the deck or perhaps on a slightly raised platform and with a protective bulwark or parapet. The obvious advantage conferred by towers led to them becoming almost standard fittings for warships of quinquireme size or greater and even on some 'fours'. Some of the larger ships had two or more and some had them mounted on either beam, partially jettied out over each side.

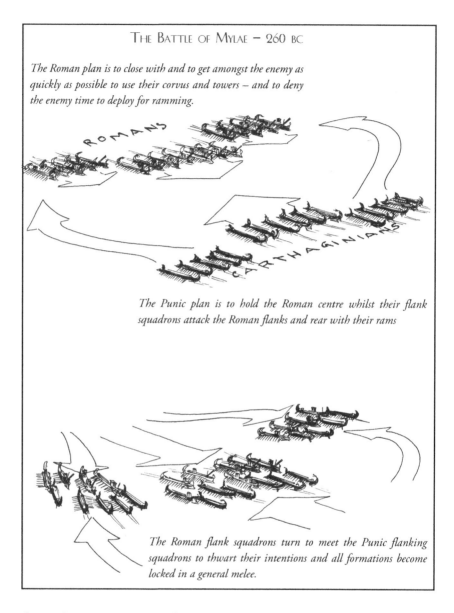

THE BATTLE OF MYLAE – 260 BC

The Roman plan is to close with and to get amongst the enemy as
quickly as possible to use their corvus and towers – and to deny
the enemy time to deploy for ramming.

The Punic plan is to hold the Roman centre whilst their flank
squadrons attack the Roman flanks and rear with their rams

The Roman flank squadrons turn to meet the Punic flanking
squadrons to thwart their intentions and all formations become
locked in a general melee.

fleet off Mylae. The Punic fleet numbered about a 130 ships, the Romans
slightly more at 143, indicating that they had a 'pre-war' fleet of forty ships
on station, which were joined by the 'new' fleet of 120, less the seventeen lost
at Lipara. Both fleets comprised mostly quinquiremes with some triremes,
Polybius relates that the Punic flagship was propelled by a single reme with
seven men to each oar, although it possible to have been based on a 'six' with

an additional man per oar at the topmost of the the three remes; the ship was in fact a prize captured from their victory over Pyrrhus in 276.[21] Confident, no doubt, of their superiority, thirty of the Punic ships were detached from their main fleet to attack the Roman van. The Roman ships were rowed straight for them and they met head-on. The Romans dropped their *corvus*, their marines swarmed aboard the Punic ships, overwhelming the smaller contingents of Punic marines and capturing nearly all of them. Meanwhile, the main body of the Punic fleet came round to try a mass ramming attack on the sides of the Roman ships but they were also met as the Roman ships turned to meet them, swinging their *corvi* to grab them and using the same grappling and boarding tactics. The Romans sank fourteen Punic ships, captured another thirty-one, including their flagship, killed over 7000 of their men and captured a further 3000. They lost one ship and suffered only a few hundred casualties.

It was a great victory and with it, the centuries-old Punic domination of the western Mediterranean was at an end. For the Romans, they had stepped into the first rank of world powers, having successfully challenged a world power in its own medium. The first ever naval triumph was awarded in Rome to Caius Duilius together with a *Corona Navalis*, a coronet decorated to represent laurel leaves and ship's prows; a column was erected in the Roman Forum (the tablet from which is now in the Capitoline Museum), decorated with projections fashioned to represent the prows of captured ships and the public speaker's platform in the Roman Forum was decorated with the rams cut from captured ships.[22] Duilius' name is commemorated in the naming of ships of the Italian navy to this day.

For the Carthaginians, the shock of having been so convincingly beaten in their favoured area, the sea, and by an upstart naval power, and of losing the assumption of naval supremacy was shattering. Although they still had a powerful navy which could still outnumber the Romans and could thus replace the seventy or so ships that they had lost, they lost belief in its supremacy. To emphasise the depth of shock caused by the defeat and the inertia that resulted, the Carthaginians took no action when in the following year, 259 BC, the main body of the Roman fleet, commanded by the Consul Lucius Cornelius Scipio, transported an expeditionary force which took Corsica and most of Sardinia. The Punic stronghold of Olbia on northern Sardinia managed to hold out until a Punic fleet eventually appeared and the Roman advance was temporarily halted. On this occasion, Scipio refused battle although the fleets were approximately evenly matched at about one hundred ships each. Scipio had landed marines at Alalia on Sardinia and his fleet was thus under strength, also, he had as yet no base on the island upon which to fall back and if driven off, his troops would have been marooned.

259 BC

The next year, 258 BC, saw the Roman fleet, commanded by Caius Sulpicius Paterculus, again operating in Sardinian waters, where it found and attacked the Punic fleet off Sulci, defeating it again and signalling the end of Punic power in Sardinia, only Olbia and its immediate area remaining. In this battle, involving again about a hundred ships on each side, there was a sea mist which enabled the Roman fleet to sail by apparently unaware of the Punic fleet's presence and thus lure it out for what it thought would be a surprise attack on the Romans. As their enemy came out however, the Romans turned and attacked. After suffering some losses, most of the Punic fleet managed to retire to port. The Romans sailed off into the mist where they waited until the enemy crews went ashore, then they attacked the moored ships. The Carthaginians lost about forty ships in these encounters.

          The war in Sicily had become bogged down and thus for these two years, 259 and 258 BC, the Romans directed their attentions elsewhere and although seemingly away from the main theatre of war in Sicily, for good reasons. Firstly, the western Italian coastline could never be secure so long as the Carthaginians held Corsica and Sardinia or either of them; secondly, the Romans could conquer the islands at little cost, the main Punic Army effort being concentrated in Sicily; thirdly, in doing so, they could reduce the enemy empire's area, population and resources, especially the timber for shipbuilding which those islands could yield from their pine forests. Finally, whilst denied to their enemy, those same resources would now be available to Rome.

In 257 BC the fleet was withdrawn from Corsica and Sardinia, which had been effectively neutralised and, now under the Consul Caius Atilius Regulus, returned to operations in Sicilian waters. A Phoenician outpost, Melita (Malta) had been taken over by Carthage in the sixth century as Phoenician power waned and it had ever since served as an important Punic naval base. Obviously it could not be permitted to remain intact, only sixty or so miles (100km) off the Sicilian coast. From it the enemy could threaten the south and west of the island and dominate the trade routes and so the fleet attacked and sacked it. Leaving Melita, Regulus returned to Mylae but near there was confronted by the Punic fleet, off Tyndaris. Regulus had apparently intended to make a further attempt at taking Lipara but the Cathaginian fleet under Hamilcar had sailed from Panormus (Palermo) to defend it.

          The Roman fleet was anchored off the Punic-held town of Tyndaris when the enemy fleet sailed by and, without waiting for the whole of his fleet to be ready, Regulus took only ten ships into the attack. Not surprisingly, the enemy fleet surrounded this small force and crushed it, nine of the ten ships being sunk, the flagship barely escaping. This impulsive act had not been entirely in vain as the Punic fleet had stopped and broken formation for the fight and the rest of the Roman fleet were thus able to catch up and fall upon them. In the ensuing battle, the Romans sank eight and captured ten more Punic ships and secured their third naval victory.

In Sicily, the land war had once more stagnated into a hard, slow slogging match and the Romans, now confident of their naval ability, looked for a way to circumvent the campaign and execute a decisive action to bring the war to a close. They decided on a bold stroke, no less than the landing in Africa of an army to march on Carthage itself. The fleet had continued to grow with the addition of more new construction and the commissioning of captured ships and by now numbered just over 250 warships; the crew and marine requirement had now grown to some 100,000 men, who had been thoroughly trained in preparation for the coming major undertaking, the greatest yet to be embarked upon by the navy. Still smarting from their recent defeats and doubtless aware of the Roman naval build-up, the Carthaginians had also increased their fleet in Sicily to over 200 warships, under the joint command of Hamilcar Barca and Hanno.

VICTORIES AND DISASTERS

256 BC

In the summer of 256 BC, the Roman fleet was ready and, commanded by the Consuls, Marcus Atilius Regulus and Lucius Manlius Vulso, massed at its east Sicilian bases of Messina and Syracuse. The fleet comprised two 'sixes' as flagships and about 250 warships, mostly quinquiremes but including some triremes, about twenty of which had been stripped and rigged as horse transports. There were also eighty transports for some of the invasion troops and their stores. A merchant ship of the time could sail, in reasonable conditions, at four to six knots and the warships, capable under oars of up to seven knots, could keep station around them using only some of their rows of oars at any one time, as well as sails, to keep their crews rested. With reasonable weather, the crossing to Africa might take a day to a day and a half.

The Carthaginians now knew of the Roman plans and that their fleet would sail along the mostly friendly southern Sicilian coast, embark its army there and sail west to Africa; a slightly longer sea-route but safer than having to run the gauntlet of the Punic strongholds and islands to the far west of Sicily, just to take advantage of the shorter crossing to Africa (90 miles, 150km). Operating from their forward base at Eraclea on the south coast, they were well placed to watch out for the Romans and when they came, were able to form up their fleet for battle and confront them off Cape Ecnomus (Licata).

The Romans, doubtless with intelligence that the Punic fleet was in the area and in any case knowing that they must pass by the enemy coast, formed into four squadrons, the leading two in a 'V' or wedge formation

THE BATTLE OF ECNOMUS – 256 BC

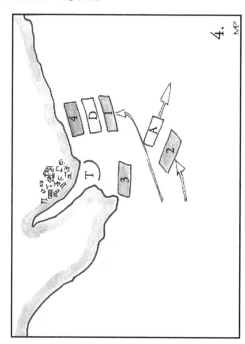

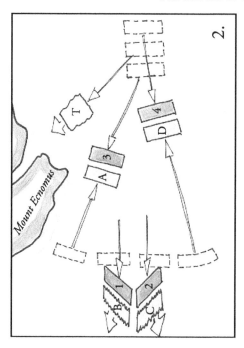

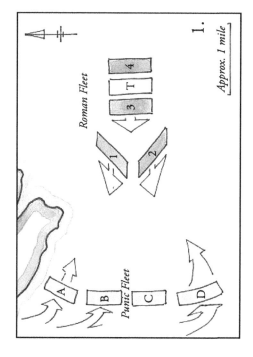

and the transports sandwiched between the third and fourth squadrons for protection and in this defensive formation, advanced westward. The Punic ships, informed by lookouts probably on Mount Ecnomus, formed up behind it to the west into four columns and came out quickly to surprise the Romans. Swiftly they changed into line abreast for their attack, seeking to tie down the Roman centre while they sent a flanking squadron around each side to attack the transports in the Roman rear. The Roman's own formation however, with its two rearmost squadrons, meant that they could deploy against these flank attacks and thus provide an opponent for each of the Punic formations, leaving the transports clear to make their escape. The leading Roman squadrons crashed into the Punic centre which they drove back, inflicting losses, the *corvus* again having been used to effect. In the meantime however, the other Punic divisions had managed to attack the Roman squadrons covering the transports and push them back towards the shore. The transports, not being engaged by the enemy, managed to slip into the shelter of the estuary and harbour of nearby Licata. Seeing all of this, the leading Roman squadrons broke off their fight and rowed at full speed to catch the Punic ships attacking the Roman third and fourth squadrons in the rear; one of these Punic squadrons managed to evade and mostly escaped but the other was enveloped and annihilated.[23]

At the end of the day the Romans had lost twenty-four ships, all to the ramming tactics of the Carthaginians. They had however, inflicted another crushing defeat on the Punic navy, sinking thirty of their ships also by ramming, thus more than matching the Punic ability at ramming, and capturing another sixty-four by the use of the *corvus* and boarding. When the Romans could close and board the result was a foregone conclusion and the Carthaginians had no answer to the *corvus*.

The route to Africa was now open and after briefly refitting the ships and repairing battle damage, including refitting forty-four of the captured Punic ships, more than replacing losses, the Romans embarked an army of over 15000 men and 500 cavalry and landed them safely near Hermaeum, just east of Carthage. They captured Clupea and secured the area. Leaving Regulus with a squadron of forty ships, Vulso and the bulk of the fleet withdrew, not wishing to be left on an exposed enemy shore and having to maintain much larger supply lines to supply itself as well as the army; it would be better in its own bases in Sicily, from which it could cover the expeditionary force easily during the coming winter season and return, fully refitted, to commence a blockade of Carthage in the following spring. At home, Vulso was able to celebrate a naval triumph but in Africa after some initial successes, Regulus was badly beaten by the Carthaginians, the remains of his forces managing to fall back to Clupea, where they held out.

255 BC The fleet was recalled to Africa in the spring of 255 BC to extricate them.

Under the two Consuls for the year, Servius Fulvius Nobilior and Marcus
Aemilius Paullus, a fleet of about 200 ships and presumably some transports[24]
sailed on its rescue mission. It was waylaid off southern Sicily by a storm,
blown off-course and driven to the Punic island of Cossyra (Pantellaria),
which they took the opportunity to plunder. It is likely that whilst there,
the Romans learned that the Punic fleet had been massively reinforced since
its defeat at Ecnomus and was once more some 200 ships in strength and
cruising off Hermaeum, presumably in the hope of blockading Regulus
and of intercepting any rescue mission. Without this knowledge, had the
Romans gone directly to Clupea, they could have easily been surprised and
caught whilst in harbour evacuating Regulus' army. The Consuls therefore
ordered the fleet to make for Hermaeum to seek out the enemy fleet, at the
same time sending a fast despatch ship to Clupea, to order the forty ships
there to rendezvous with the main fleet, which they did.

When the two fleets met off Hermaeum, the Punic fleet's comparative
lack of training and poor morale soon told and the Romans managed to
outmanoeuvre the Punic ships and jam them against the shore, denying
them the sea-room to use their rams. The Carthaginians were again heavily
defeated, the Romans using the *corvus* to great effect and destroying or
capturing no fewer than 114 of their ships. The Roman losses are not known
but are unlikely to have been heavy. After the battle, the fleet, with Regulus'
squadron and such of the captured ships as were seaworthy, a total of well
over 300 ships, plus the transports,[25] went to Clupea and evacuated the
remnants of the invasion army, with its sick and wounded. Even with the
Punic prisoners rowing (of whom there were a great number), the sheer
number of ships meant that the Roman sailors were stretched thinly and
many of the ships must have been undermanned by seamen for the return
journey.

On the return journey, between Melita and the southern-most tip of
Sicily, the fleet encountered an enemy that ignored their fighting ability
and military skill and exploited their heavily laden ships, packed as they
were with troops, horses and equipment and already top-heavy with their
towers and heavy *corvi*, namely a great storm. The ancient writer Petronius
described the loss of a large merchant ship with details presumably garnered
from survivors, which occurred in the first century AD just to the north of
this event thus: 'the sea roughened, clouds hurried up from every quarter
of the sky and the day was obscured. The sailors scattered to their posts in
a panic and shortened sail before the gale. The wind veered and drove the
waves this way and that and the helmsman was unable to hold his course.
One moment we went fast towards Sicily but generally the wind came from
the north off the shores of Italy, took possession of the ship and twirled her in
all directions ... the storm was roaring to its height, it shattered and stripped
the ship. No mast, no rudder, no rope or oar remained. The hulk tossed

and tumbled at the will of the waves like a piece of untrimmed timber.'[26] It was a disaster. Of a fleet which must have numbered nearly 400 ships, only eighty of the warships and some transports survived to limp into port to tell the tale. With no such thing as lifeboats or any other form of life-saving equipment, as many as 100,000 men perished, their ships foundering on or being dashed onto the rocks of south-east Sicily.[27] It was, and remains to this day, the greatest known loss of human life in a single incident of shipwreck in the history of seafaring.

By a supreme irony, having by its victories reduced the once-mighty Carthaginian navy to only about seventy ships, the Romans main battle fleet had itself been reduced to a nominal strength and, even more importantly, the majority of its experienced crews had been lost. Some small and unforeseen compensation however, and one which would become of increasing importance, was in hearing that Regulus' expedition had not been a complete failure. Indeed, his intervention in Africa had seriously disrupted Carthage's control over its surrounding territories, whose peoples had been encouraged to disaffection if not, as yet, open rebellion.

Undaunted but unable to capitalise on the advantages gained by their naval victories, the Romans had to restrict their activities until the building of new ships to replace those so tragically lost could produce enough to reconstitute the battle fleet. In the meantime, the survivors of the fleet had remained in Sicily on active service following the storm disaster, maintaining morale but also having to persuade the Carthaginians that nothing was amiss. The surviving ships, together with as many as could be trawled from other commands, with allied and hastily repaired captured enemy ships, would have been conspicuously paraded in safer areas to give that impression. Agents of both antagonists possibly toured the shipbuilding centres of the east to buy or commission the building of warships to feed a naval war that was consuming them at an incredible rate.

254 BC
By the spring of the following year, 254 BC, the Romans had at least 170 ships ready for sea although probably no more than a third of these would have been first-class ships and allowing for those undergoing refit, training and needed for use in other areas, barely half of that total would have been available for use in Sicily. Although able to replace the lost ships, replacement of their combat veteran crews was not possible and the new fleet had to be gradually eased into a combat role. It first saw action in supporting the army in its capture of Panormus in Sicily, rather than seeking the enemy's fleet or operating far from home and while it gained experience, the Carthaginians meanwhile, were facing revolts in Africa and with their attention thus diverted closer to home and available resources focused there, could only build a few ships and certainly not enough to enable them to challenge even the reduced Roman fleet and take advantage of the disaster that had befallen it.

253 BC   In 253 BC, the Consul, Cnaius Sempronius Blaesus, commanding
the fleet, raided the Punic coast, attacking Tripolis, near Carthage. Such a
mission would of course serve to encourage and foment anti-Carthaginian
activities in Africa, preventing them from releasing troops to reinforce Sicily
and draining the resources which could otherwise be utilised in building
ships. The raiders inflicted a great deal of damage, as well as seizing plunder
and gaining intelligence. The mission proved to be ill-fated however and
the fleet got into difficulties in shallow waters in the Gulf of Sirte.[28] They
managed to extricate themselves but on the voyage home to Italy, ran
into a severe storm off Cape Palinuros (Palinuro on the Cilento coast of
Campania).[29] It would seem that after their long African cruise, the ships
were returning to home bases in Italy to off-load their booty and for refit
and resting of the crews. Caught off the rocky and inhospitable coast, the
fleet could either run for the lee of the Cape itself, which extends out to sea
and curves northwards, providing a sheltered anchorage behind it; or could
run the twelve miles (20km) or so northward to the safety of the harbour
of the then major port of Velia. In any event it again suffered severe losses,
twenty-seven ships floundering and being lost.[30]

Both sides were now nearing exhaustion and the Roman navy, although
victorious, could not quickly replace a second successive heavy loss of crews;
the lost ships carried the best part of 10,000 men. For the next three years,
there was a relative lull in naval operations. The fleet was used in several
small squadrons in attempts to blockade the Punic possessions in Sicily
which had been reduced to a few enclaves in the west. They proved unable
to stop the Carthagians from later bringing in substantial reinforcements.
251 BC   As the fleet recovered, it was used progressively more actively and in 251
BC, commanded by the Consul, Caius Aurelius Cotta, captured the Liparae
islands and the now isolated outpost of Thermae (Termini Imerese). In 250
BC it had regained strength and confidence sufficiently to meet the Punic
navy and again beat it in an action off Panormus, although this action was
more likely to have been between squadrons rather than the main fleets and
in the nature of a skirmish only.

250 BC   By 250 BC, the Romans had managed to commission another fifty ships
and had levied an extra 10,000 men from their naval allies. It had been learned
that for all its undoubted value, the *corvus* made their ships dangerously top-
heavy in heavy weather and the Romans started to dispense with it, their
newer ships also being lighter and faster and better suited to ramming. The
Carthaginian possessions on Sicily had by now been limited to the western
end and depended upon the two strongholds of Lilybaeum (Marsala) and
Drepanum (Trapani), covered by the offshore Aegades (Egadi) Islands. The
Roman plan for 250 was to be for an assault by the army from Panormus
to Lilybaeum, supported by the navy. Hasdrubal, the Punic commander,
moved first however and attacked towards the east. He was heavily defeated

and the Romans isolated and invested Lilybaeum by land. The navy was now called upon to operate in the very west of Sicily for the first time but with no adequate Roman-controlled harbour and few anchorages nearby. Drepanum was a major enemy naval base, only fifteen miles (25km) north of Lilybaeum by sea and twenty miles (31km) by road. For the remainder of 250 BC, units of the navy doubtless made probing sweeps of the area seeking blockade runners, but could not consider attempting a close blockade until they had established that they could operate there and had concentrated a sufficient force. Indeed, the Carthaginians were able to ferry reinforcements and supplies in to increase the garrison of 7000 troops; before the end of 250 BC a squadron of some fifty ships had brought 4000 men and supplies from Carthage, the ships then withdrawing by night to Drepanum. To do this the Punic ships sailed to the west of the offshore Aegades Islands where they awaited a favourable wind from the west. The prevailing winds in this region especially during the summer are from the north-west or westerly, making it easy to make a dash into the harbours and correspondingly difficult for an opposing force; additionally if the wind should shift southward then fog is not uncommon and which would also be of obvious advantage to blockade runners.[31] With this, they crammed on all sail and made a dash for the harbour, sweeping past the Roman guard ships who were unable to intercept, being held back by the same wind and unable to engage for fear of being swept into the hostile harbour with them. Another squadron followed with another 10,000 reinforcements for the garrison and evacuated the now-useless 700 cavalry, with its horses, again going to Drepanum.

The problem for the fleet was that Lilybaeum stands on a promontory, the entrance to the harbour is difficult and dangerous to anyone not wholly

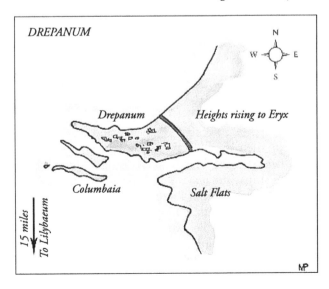

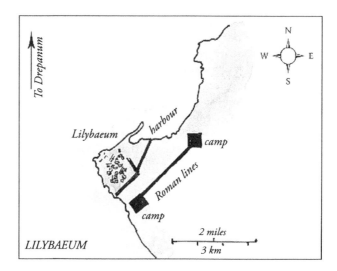

familiar with the approach, to the south the coast is open, rocky and exposed, whilst to the north there are shoals, shallow lagoons and islets, ideal for ambush by the Punic fleet from Drepanum, who were familiar with these waters. The Romans were unable to storm Lilybaeum and the siege dragged on into the winter. Most if not all of the navy's ships withdrew to secure harbours for the closed season and for refit, ready for a major blockading effort in 249 BC They had no sheltered anchorage nearby and unlike the lighter ships of an earlier age, the heavy Roman quinquireme could not be hauled wholly up a beach beyond the reach of the waves without a prepared slipway. A few of the lighter ships may well have been kept on station but the effort in feeding and housing thousands of naval personnel in addition to the besieging troops during the winter was simply not justified.

A DISASTROUS YEAR

249 BC   For 249 BC, the navy had built up and earmarked a total of some 240 warships solely for the war in Sicily. The major effort of the year was clearly to be the taking of Lilybaeum, the fall of which would make the remaining Punic presence in Sicily untenable and, it was anticipated, end the war by forcing their complete withdrawal. One of the Consuls, Publius Claudius Pulcher, was sent directly to take command at Lilybaeum, backed by a fleet of 123 ships. The remaining 120 ships were to be commanded by the other Consul, Lucius Iunius Pullus, who was to gather a large convoy of transports with reinforcements and supplies for the siege and escort them to Lilybaeum. Pulcher's fleet was believed to be more than enough to start the blockade of Lilybaeum and outnumber any Punic naval forces at Drepanum, but the enemy proved to be too elusive for him, and without needing to force a

major fleet action, were able to keep Lilybaeum well supplied. By again using their local knowledge and the onshore winds blowing from the north-west, the Carthaginian captains came from behind the offshore island of Aegusa (Favignana) and under combined sail and oar power, dashed the barely eight miles (13km) straight into the harbour entrance at Lilybaeum, which faced north, a journey of only fifty minutes to an hour. Further, by using fast, light and handy ships, they could evade the heavy, unwieldy Roman ones, for whom it was difficult to row up into the wind in attempting to intercept the fast-moving blockade runners, without themselves being trapped by it and forced onto the enemy shore. They did, however, try. Roman attempts at blocking the harbour mouth by trying to tip rock and rubble to form a mole largely failed.[32] They were not entirely unsuccessful in that a Punic 'four' ran aground on it when trying to get out by night and was captured and added to the Roman fleet. A greater prize however followed shortly when they managed to intercept and capture the most famous and audacious blockade runner, the quinquireme of Hannibal the Rhodian. This ship was the fastest of all and the Romans learned much from her design which would influence their own later designs; this important ship which had been effortlessly evading and out-running their guard ships many times was sent immediately to the Roman shipyards in Italy for study.[33]

Pulcher knew that the Carthaginians had also been building up their navy and that they now had about 100 ships, commanded by Adherbal, one of their best admirals, at Drepanum. Although he still outnumbered his enemy's fleet, Pulcher realised that while it was intact and so close, he had to keep his own ships concentrated against a surprise attack and as he was still without an adequate harbour he could not therefore effectively blockade Lilybaeum. The other effect was, however, that by tying down the Punic fleet at Drepanum, Pulcher's fleet was preventing it, in turn, from trying to intercept Iunius and his convoy. As before, Iunius would take the south Sicilian coast route, where he would be screened by Pulcher's ships. Once they had united at Lilybaeum, the two Consuls' combined warfleet of 244 ships would give them overwhelming superiority.

Before these fine schemes could come to fruition however, Pulcher learned that the Carthaginians had amassed a second fleet of some seventy ships which, commanded by the able Carthalo, were en route to join Adherbal at Drepanum, who, with 170 ships, could overwhelm the Roman fleet. For Pulcher the solution was simple; order his fleet to withdraw along the south coast and join up with Iunius. Their combined fleet would still greatly outnumber the combined Carthaginian fleet and be able to achieve its immediate objective of seeing the convoy to its destination. Pulcher was an impulsive commander, hot-headed and ruthless, and there was no personal glory to be had in such a move. He resolved to attack the Punic fleet at Drepanum, before reinforcements could reach it and thus whilst his own fleet still outnumbered it and despite the fact that many of his rowers and seamen were newly-arrived replacements of little or no experience. The priests warned Pulcher that the omens were bad for his venture as the sacred chickens would not feed, whereupon he threw them over the side of the ship, saying that if they could not eat, they could drink. He could not ensure his ability to intercept the reinforcements far out to sea and destroy them first and indeed his tactics may well have been influenced by a concern that they would approach through the Aegades and attack his own ships in the rear. The deployment of four or five of his swiftest ships as a scouting screen, which could well be afforded, would have covered such an eventuality and adequate reconnaissance of the enemy location, which any experienced admiral should have conducted, would show that an attack upon Drepanum from any angle except that chosen by Pulcher would have trapped the Punic fleet and ensured a Roman victory. Pulcher managed to approach from the only direction that left his fleet vulnerable.

The Romans mustered 123 ships which sailed by night, hoping to catch the Punic fleet at dawn at its moorings in Drepanum harbour. They sailed in a long line, one astern of the other towards Drepanum, the Consul in his flagship at the rear of the line to prevent stragglers; unfortunately this meant that he was the last to see the unfolding situation and could neither lead nor order his fleet. As the Romans made to attack the enemy ships in the roads, they were seen by the Carthaginian crews who managed to scramble aboard and man their ships and narrowly avoid being trapped in harbour and against the shore by manoeuvring around a small islet just offshore which screened them from the Roman advance. This brought the Punic ships to the seaward side of the Roman line whereupon they fell upon the exposed sides of the Roman ships which were strung out in line ahead parallel to the shore. Pulcher had clearly not thought out his tactics and on seeing this, made matters worse by trying to order a withdrawal. This threw his line into further confusion as the ships were being forced into the shore and could hardly turn. There is no mention of the use of the *corvus* in this battle and one must assume that they were no longer fitted. The Carthaginians pressed home their attack and forced the Roman ships onto the shore. The Romans lost ninety-three ships but fortunately a large number of their men were able to get ashore and returned to their own lines overland. The shoreline here is flat and lined with large saltpans and the adjoining plain could be covered by Roman cavalry to help rescue the crewmen. Pulcher escaped with thirty ships, having suffered the only Roman naval defeat of the war. Had he attacked from any other angle, the Carthaginians could not have emerged from behind the islet without being picked off one by one and their fleet would have been either trapped in the harbour or, if it tried to escape southward, driven ashore in the same way as were the Roman ships. The readily repaired captured Roman ships, some of which could

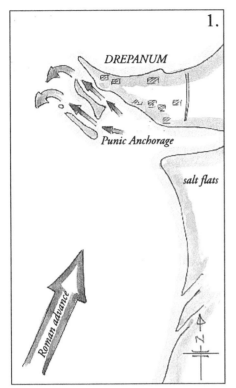
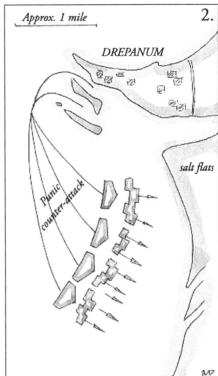

THE BATTLE OF DREPANUM — 249 BC

have originally been captured Punic ships, were sent to Carthage, although shortage of manpower meant that they did not reappear in Sicilian waters as reinforcements.

Pulcher's troubles were not yet over as, upon his return to Lilybaeum the Punic reinforcements of seventy ships, appeared and attacked his surviving ships. The attack was made at dawn and although the Romans managed to fight them off, they suffered a further four ships destroyed and five captured and towed away by the Carthaginians. In the meantime another Punic squadron had sailed along the north coast where it intercepted and captured a convoy of Roman transports off Panormus. The Punic fleet now redeployed, keeping fifty ships at Drepanum to ensure their command of the seas of western Sicily and that they could supply Lilybaeum unhindered. Obviously they had heard about the Roman plans and so the remaining 120 ships, commanded by Carthalo, were then sent to search for the other Consul, Iunius' fleet off the south coast. The Carthaginians still held the small south coast town of Eraclea which, although a poor anchorage, could at least give some support to their fleet and enable the crews to be rested ashore.

Iunius had mustered his fleet at Syracuse. He had gathered a massive fleet, carrying reinforcements and supplies for the troops at Lilybaeum, of as many as 800 transports and, even allowing for the ancient writer's propensity for exaggeration, it must have nevertheless been very large. The escort consisted of 120 warships in two divisions, which suggests that the remainder of the navy had been stripped to provide them and that therefore some at least of them would have been smaller, second-line ships. The problem for Iunius was that he had to safely get this huge fleet around the rocky and exposed south-east corner of Sicily and the length of its southern coast, which has no good natural harbours and only a few smallish anchorages for shelter. He had to achieve this now knowing that a victorious Punic fleet at least equal in strength to his own, was looking for him and that he could now expect no help from his fellow Consul. Incredibly, Iunius decided to divide his fleet, sending half of the transports, escorted by part of his fleet, on ahead to Phintias (Licata), where they could seek the shelter of the river estuary. Before long the Punic fleet appeared and attacked the anchorage and despite a spirited and hard-fought defence, managed to sink fifty of the transports and seventeen of the Roman warships, damaging another thirteen, some beyond repair. Carthalo retired to Eraclea, only 44 or so miles (70km) away by sea, to rest and await his next opportunity.

Iunius next arrived at Phintias with the rest of his fleet and transports. Although the bulk of the transport fleet was intact, Iunius had dissipated his warships and had only 90-odd to face the enemy; he knew he could not hope to get the convoy safely past them and elected to try and return to Syracuse, a decision hastened by the approach of the Punic fleet. The Romans burned the damaged ships that could not be readied to sail in time and doubtless off-loaded the ship's cargoes, then fled eastwards. The pursuing Carthaginians were faster and overhauled the Romans, burdened as they were by the slower transports, by the time they had crossed the Gulf of Gela. In the open sea and with the wind from the west and plenty of sea-room, the Punic navy was at last able to exercise its famous skill and by using only manoeuvre and without actually fighting, managed to force the Romans onto the rocky shore south of Camarina.

The Romans took up defensive formations off the rocks of Camarina but the Punic ships then suddenly broke off the action and set sail and ran before the following wind to the east towards Cape Pachynus (Correnti). The Roman fleet did not enjoy the Punic commander's ability to anticipate the approach of a storm and to take action to avoid it and they were left in the open Gulf to face its fury. The storm (and as has been seen, they can blow up very quickly in these waters) came from the west, i.e. from the open sea towards the shore, and Iunius' fleet, which was already close inshore, was driven onto the rocks. With the exception of two warships (including the Consul's) and a few transports, the entire fleet was wrecked on the shore. Most of the men managed to scramble ashore but once again the weather had accomplished what the Carthaginians, for all their recent success, could only dream of. Of the 240 or so ships with which the Roman navy had started the year's campaign in Sicily, twenty were left and as the secondary squadrons had been stripped, she was effectively without a navy.

Iunius did partially redeem himself and provided the Romans with their only success of this disastrous year by taking the mountain-top town of Eryx (Erice), which overlooks Drepanum and effectively isolates it. For his part in the year's activities, Pulcher was prosecuted and fined heavily. He was lucky; the Carthaginians had the habit of crucifying unsuccessful admirals. Iunius committed suicide in the following year. For all their great naval victories the Romans had suffered yet another appalling loss from a storm, plus a naval defeat; the Punic fleet had emerged as still the strongest and Roman enthusiasm for naval matters was, not surprisingly, at its lowest.

THE ROMANS PREVAIL

The war once more lapsed into stalemate with both sides glad of some breathing space. The Romans were drained by the serious losses of manpower suffered as well as by the experience of the war, which by now must have appeared never-ending. They were unable to consider accelerating the rebuilding of their navy even had their enthusiasm been greater. Fortune was to smile on Rome however as the Carthaginians were prevented from making use of their now overwhelming naval superiority by the outbreak of major wars in Africa. Political factions in Carthage wanted to secure a solid base in Africa before making further efforts abroad. The continual unrest in Africa was a result of the weakness of the Carthaginian system; unlike the Romans, they did not bind their subject peoples with the complex system of rights and duties which made them a part of something which was to their advantage and to which they could be loyal. The Carthaginians could not rely on their subject peoples to provide dependable troops as could the Romans and had to rely heavily upon mercenaries; to pay for this they had to tax the people heavily, which in turn fomented unrest. Being unable to depend upon the loyalty and patriotism of a citizen levy like the Romans, imposed a limit on manpower, according to what could be paid for. They simply could not afford both a large army and a large navy. There was a further factor in that the Carthaginians would react to crisis but once it had passed, relaxed; against their traditional Greek foes this had sufficed since the Greeks would advance, invariably quarrel among themselves and could then be pushed back; the Romans were, however, unremitting.

Against this background, Sicily took second place and Lilybaeum and Drepanum were left to hold out with only enough of the Punic fleet retained in commission to supply them and maintain superiority over the remnant of the Roman fleet and to carry out the occasional raid on the Italian coast; perhaps fifty ships would have been more than enough. The remainder of the Punic fleet was laid up and the crews drafted for use as troops in the African wars. The shipyard effort which had gone into building new ships had now to be concentrated on maintaining the large number of laid-up ships and the rate of new building dropped to only a couple of new ships a year for the duration.

In 248 BC, Carthalo attempted to raid the Italian coast but was thwarted by Roman troops following him along the coast and preventing landings. Also in 248 BC, Rome renewed its treaty of friendship with Syracuse. In 247 BC, the Punic commander, Hamilcar Barca, again tried raiding the Italian coast, but as with his predecessor, met with scant success. In order to relieve the pressure on Drepanum, Hamilcar next made a landing west of Panormus and occupied and fortified Mount Hierkte, which had an anchorage beneath it for his ships. The identity of this mount has not been fully established but, in view of the recent discoveries of pottery fragments and the remains of a fortified camp, the most likely location would seem to be[34] Mount Pecoraro.[35] From this position, and supplied by his fleet, Hamilcar was able to raid and harass the Romans both by land and sea and could intercept the shipping using Panormus. He was not strong enough to attempt an attack upon the city itself and although he managed to hang onto his position at Hierkte for three years, the nuisance that he created did not justify any major Roman offensive against it. Indeed whilst the Romans were unable to challenge the Punic squadron, any major attack on Mount Hierkte would simply have been foiled by the squadron quickly evacuating the enemy troops before the Romans could destroy them. At least while they remained there, the Carthaginian forces did not have the strength to attempt any major break-out at either Drepanum or Lilybaeum, which continued to be contained.

Although not strong enough to risk a challenge to the Punic fleet in Sicily, the Romans must have learned that the larger part of the enemy navy had been laid up and so, it is said, sanctioned 'privateers' to raid the African coast.[36] This is a curious and illogical choice of expression and the only time in the Punic Wars that it appears; one may conjecture that perhaps buccaneer captains with their crews and ships were hired from the east to cause some mayhem whilst the Romans rebuilt their strength. For its part, the navy certainly had residual strength and as had happened previously after a disaster, it undertook progressively more aggressive operations to rebuild experience and confidence. So once more, with the Punic navy's active strength in Sicily, the way was open for the Romans to range further afield. Several raids were mounted and at least one, against Hippo Zarhytus (Bizerta) was a major operation, the raiders attacking and setting fire to store buildings on shore and to ships in the harbour. This Roman force must have been reasonably confident of its ability as, on its return, off Panormus it surprised and captured two Punic warships, who were doubtless keeping a watch on the port and waiting in the hope of waylaying some merchantmen.

In 244 BC, Hamilcar evacuated his forces from Mount Hierkte by sea, landing them near to Eryx, part of which he managed to take, although he was unable to break the Roman hold on Drepanum. The Romans knew that the war could ultimately only be won at sea. After the disasters of 249 BC, the Carthaginians had probably their greatest opportunity of the war, but had preferred to concentrate their efforts in Africa and had totally failed to exploit their advantage. Of Sicily, they held only Drepanum, Lilybaeum and the Aegades Islands. The Roman navy had recovered somewhat, its morale rebuilt along with at least some new ships to enhance its strength, which

244 BC

FLEET REBUILDING

Once more, the Romans set out to rebuild their navy into a major fleet but the massive cost of the losses to date had left the treasury sadly depleted. To overcome this and enable the building programme to continue, loans were raised from the people, repayable in the event of victory. It is a considerable testimonial to the loyalty and confidence of the people that sufficient funds were raised to build and equip 200 warships and many transports. The fleet building programme went ahead at maximum productivity but it was to be several years before these plans came to fruition. The ships that were built were quinquiremes of fast, lighter build, incorporating the design features of the captured Rhodian ship and were well and carefully built. Although the *corvus* had given the Romans their early victories, it had made their ships into deathtraps in bad weather; without it their heavily-built earlier ships had been unwieldy and vulnerable to the handier Punic ships. The new ships did without the *corvus*, instead, they would have had light boarding planks so the marines could still grapple and attack enemy ships. These, however, could be stowed flat on deck when not needed, instead of adding to topweight. The form that these took is not known but many later depictions of warships show a deliberate gap in the bulwark on either beam, just aft of the bow section and at the forward end of the oarbox, suitable for a gangway to be run out when the ship was alongside a quay or an enemy. Adding that feature to the mention of a 'boarding gangway',[37] which must, by definition therefore, be placed to span between the decks of two ships in action, it is easy to imagine a lightweight boarding plank perhaps twenty feet in length (6m) to be practical and able to be manhandled into position by three or four men when going into action. It could for example, have lugs on one end and be held in a simple deck-edge bracket at the other, held upright by guy ropes and dropped onto the enemy deck, perhaps even with small spikes in that end to grasp it, a much simplified and lighter *corvus* in effect.

would grow inexorably. Heartened no doubt by its recent raids on Africa and its enemy's reduction of their own naval forces, the time was becoming right for the war to be pursued at sea once more.

By the summer of 242 BC, the new fleet was ready for operations and under the command of the Consul, Caius Lutatius Catulus, with the Praetor Quintus Valerius Falto as second-in-command, sailed to seek out the Punic fleet. The fleet escorted a large supply convoy to Sicily, then sailed to Drepanum but found no Punic ships there. The Punic fleet that had been operating in Sicily was evidently elsewhere; it must not only have learned of the Roman fleet's approach, but also of its strength and had fled back to Carthage to raise the alarm and to seek reinforcements. Learning that the Romans were once more at sea in force and had once more blockaded their Sicilian strongholds, the Carthaginians managed, with difficulty, to man between 170 and 200 ships; they took some eight months to gather this fleet and have it ready to sail for Sicily, commanded by Hanno. The ships they were able to refit and re-commission from all those laid up six years previously, most of which had been safely kept in the military harbour at Carthage, with the addition of a few newly-built ships. The fact that these ships were capable of being returned to seagoing duty would indicate that most of the laid-up ships had in fact, been reasonably kept and maintained in the interim. Even so, of the 230 or so ships (including captured Roman ships) that they had at the end of 249 BC, fifty or so had been active in Sicily and of the remaining 180, between 120 and 150 were now commissioned.

The biggest problem for Carthage was, as always, manpower. The crews, oarsmen and marines of the laid-up ships had been drafted into the army for action in Africa and had, in all likelihood, long since lost any identity or cohesion as naval personnel. On this occasion, as well as taking men from the army and merchant marine, many citizens had to be impressed into service to man the ships; even so, they were under-manned when they sailed and with hastily convened and poorly trained crews.

Hamilcar and his men on Sicily were by now hard pressed and greatly in need of supplies, the supply ships being unable to sail freely to him with a Roman navy which had the strength to enforce an effective blockade of Lilybaeum and Drepanum. The Romans had increased the pressure of their sieges but an attempt to storm Drepanum failed. The fleet took advantage of the enemy's delay by training and exercises and was kept in first-class condition and readiness for action. The Carthaginians loaded their fleet with supplies for Sicily and intended to take them to Hamilcar, from whom they would take some of his troops to augment their marines, the fleet's complement of which was under strength, before they went to face the Romans.

The Carthaginians sailed in March of 241 BC and made for Hiera

241 BC (Marettimo) the westernmost of the Aegades Islands, hoping for a westerly wind to blow them past the blockade and the 25 or so miles (40km) into Drepanum.

Unfortunately for the Punic fleet, the Romans found them before they could land and on the tenth of March, attacked them off the Aegades Islands. The westerly wind was blowing and the Romans had to advance into rough head-seas to intercept their enemy; their adoption of the lighter, more seaworthy type of ship was to be well justified. Whether or not the Romans knew their enemy's ships to be under-manned, they could see them to be laden and could not pass up the opportunity to attack and stop the supplies from reaching Drepanum.[38] With the wind astern, Hanno's ships were committed and could not turn back; the Romans formed a line abreast into the wind and advanced towards the enemy. Hampered by their heavy freight and lack of marines, the Punic fleet was quickly defeated by the Romans who were able to use ramming tactics and sank fifty of their ships and captured seventy more. The rest managed to escape back to Africa after the wind shifted to the east. Back in Carthage, the unfortunate Hanno was crucified. The Romans had lost about a dozen ships.

Without the supplies, Hamilcar could not hope to hold out and for Carthage it was the final blow. Her naval power had been broken and she could not match the Roman ability to replace losses and had not the manpower for another fleet even if they could build one, which was doubtful. In any case, no fleet could have been prepared in time to prevent the fall of their remaining footholds in Sicily. It must also have occurred to Carthage that, despite the allegedly superior skill of her admirals and seamen, she had been beaten in all but one naval battle of the war and even though the Romans had suffered the most catastrophic losses at the hands of the weather, they kept on and on producing replacement fleets, one after the other. Polybius estimated that throughout the war, Rome had lost some 700 warships (nearly 400 of them to storms) and Carthage some 500[39] and yet Rome still managed to end the war with the stronger navy. These figures appear to be a little exaggerated but nevertheless validly make the point: the Romans lost just under 600 ships and the Carthaginians lost about 450 ships; of those losses however, the Romans lost about 200 to combat, whereas all 450 of the Punic losses were in combat, over twice as many. It must have been most dispiriting for Carthage to have to consider that seemingly no matter what losses the Romans might suffer, they kept on coming back with more and beating the Punic fleets, which could not be replaced.

Peace was negotiated and Carthage finally evacuated her last possessions in Sicily although she retained Melita, having agreed to pay an indemnity to Rome. A further restriction was that warships of Carthage and her allies were banned from Roman waters, which now included all of Sicily.[40] Carthage

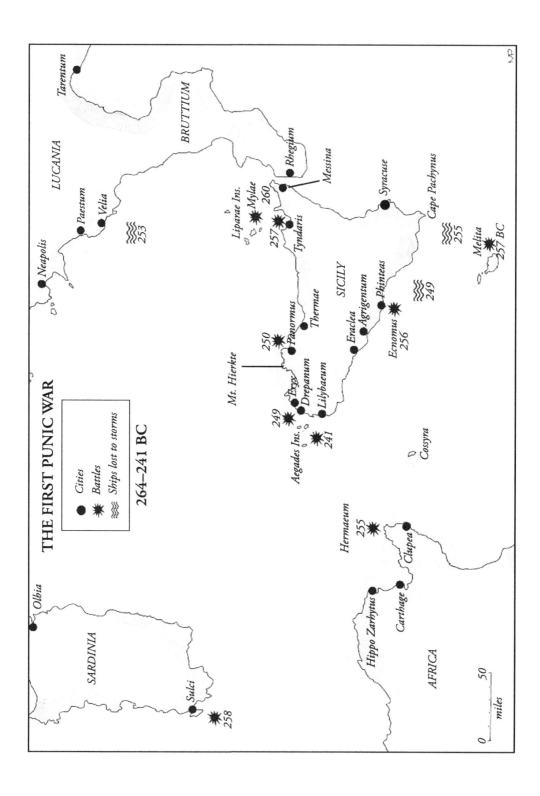

THE FIRST PUNIC WAR

Cities
Battles
Ships lost to storms

264–241 BC

was permitted to keep what was left of her fleet, which now comprised the five quinquiremes and four quadriremes or fours that she had left after the loss of most of them at Aegades and the five triremes and lighter ships left over. No restriction was however placed on her future naval plans or ability to build ships, a mistake the Romans would make but once.

The Roman navy had ended the war as the supreme naval force of the central and western Mediterranean and one of the greatest in the world. For the next twenty years, its very existence would ensure Roman security, and its operations, although comparatively minor, would enable Roman power and prestige to be projected at will.

Notes

1. Harden, *The Phoenicians*; Moscati, *The World of the Phoenicians*.
2. Described by Appian and confirmed by archaeology, One of the excavated slipways can still be seen although only the barest outline of the harbours remain.
3. Polybius (c.200 to 120 BC) is the prime ancient source for the Punic Wars, being actually present for the Third one. For the First and Second Wars he had sources available which are now lost to us, but nevertheless there are inconsistencies in some of his accounts, also sections of his works are missing. However, when he describes the ships he must be talking about what he saw and any confusion equally must arise from subsequent translation or transliteration.
4. See Scullard.
5. Once again, the interpretations follow Casson *SSAW* and Morrison & Coates, *GROW*.
6. No exact figures other than the marine contingent are known and this estimate is drawn from the known crew of a 'four' or quadrireme.
7. Starr, referring to the later Imperial navy states that a complete crew was classified as a 'Navy Century', regardless of numbers but presumably this was a convenient administrative term while the men served together; once paid off they would revert to their original (shore-based) centuries.
8. Salmon, *Samnium and the Samnites* agrees: 'assuredly too it was not the fortuitous stranding of a Punic warship on an Italian coast that led to Roman victory in the war at sea, but the creation of a fledgling navy almost half a century earlier to raid the territories controlled by the Samnites ...'; confirming the author's view.
9. Some writers (e.g. Rodgers) have argued that the numbers were exaggerated and tried to suggest lesser numbers or smaller sizes of ship but these devices are not needed if a regular production programme is accepted as reasonable.
10. Welsh, *Building the Trireme*; Morrison & Coates, *The Athenian Trireme*, for accounts of a recently built reproduction, using the ancient system. Also Theophrastus (quoted in Casson SSAW) states 'in shipbuilding, because bending is necessary, wood which is rather green must be used.'
11. See Bradford, *Ulysses Found*, for a personal account of sailing a small boat in Sicilian waters.
12. See Bradford, as above.
13. The remains of two Carthaginian ships found at Marsala in Sicily bear marks on the various timbers which were to aid assembly (and see Note 29).
14. Livy, Book XXVIII and see below.
15. Livy I.21.
16. The Corcyra voyage is related in Livy XLV.41; the Athenian voyage, Thucidides VI; 18 hours/50 miles is in Xenophon, *Hellenica* I.I.13; Chios to Hellespont, see Chapter 4. A good further selection can be found in Casson *SSAW*.
17. Polybius I.21 et seq. Also see Scullard, Part IV and Rodgers and Thiel (selectively) are based upon his account.
18. Polybius I.22.
19. The painting to resemble stonework, reported by Pliny (1st century AD) may well have come later.
20. See Chapter I, Note 40. Towers on ships for siege work, i.e. static, had been used e.g. by Athens at Syracuse in 415 and by Alexander at Tyre in 332. Silius Italicus (writing in the 1st century BC) reports towers on Roman ships at Mylae and that the Punic 'seven' captured there had towers added by the Romans and was in use in that form in the Second Punic War in 212 BC. It has to be admitted nevertheless that the assumption of the use of fighting towers this early is otherwise based on flimsy evidence.
21. Polybius I.23.
22. The Latin word for a ram, *rostrum*, having been applied to a speaker's platform ever since.
23. There are several interpretations of the account of this massive battle, which overlook or are unaware of the local geography, which enabled the Punic fleet to engage so quickly. Seeing the location has influenced the author's interpretation herein.
24. They are not specifically mentioned, but the army is likely to have evacuated as much of its stores, horses and plunder as possible.
25. Polybius says 364 (I.37).
26. Petronius, *Satyricon* (quoted in Bradford).
27. Polybius relates that the fleet sailed along the south Sicilian coast to return to its bases from which it had set out 'against the advice of the pilots'. They had in fact no alternative as (a) that is where the bases were, with the required

facilities; (b) to go west about the island would make them run the gauntlet of enemy territory and strongholds and (c) as Panormus was still in enemy hands, they would have a much longer voyage to Tyndaris for a safe haven.

28. This occurrence is generally translated (e.g. see Thiel op. cit.) as the Romans having become grounded on a falling tide. However, observation of the area will quickly reveal a rise and fall of tide of only a few inches. It will also show the area to be shallow with shifting sand bars and these are likely to have been the cause of the Roman's discomfiture. Also confirmed by the description of this coast in Sallust, *The Jugurthine War* VII.79, for a more contemporary view.

29. The author has stood on this coast in mid-September and watched a balmy, sunny, still day turn into a raging storm within twenty minutes.

30. Polybius claims (I.39) that they lost 150 ships but this must be exaggerated as (a) they did not have that many; (b) the Cape is only dangerous if caught by an onshore wind off the south-west side; (c) there is a harbour to the south-east and if the Cape could be rounded (d) a lee behind it.

31. See Bradford, *Ulysses Found*, relating personal experience of sailing in these waters.

32. The remains of two ships, identified as Punic and of this period, have been excavated from near here. They had cargoes of stone identified as from Italy and it seems most likely that they were ships captured by the Romans and used in this attempt.

33. It is this ship that the Romans famously copied according to Polybius.

34. Scullard, quoting Giustoli, Palermo 1975, etc.

35. Of the other favoured candidates, Monte Pellegrino is too close to Panormus and too big to be easily defended; Monte Castellaccio is too far from the sea and the essential anchorage could not have been protected from there; Monte Gallo remains a good possibility.

36. Scullard

37. Athenaeus V.206–209 '…had three levels of gangways .. The next, the highest was for the men-at-arms aboard…'. Gangways are shown on iconography and see Appian, *Civil War* V.106.

38. It is claimed that they did know and thus wanted to attack before the best Punic troops could be put aboard; if so, their intelligence gathering must have been first class.

39. Polybius I.63.

40. Polybius III.27.

INTERBELLUM

The Struggle Resumed
241 BC–201 BC

238 BC

For Rome, peace was to be but short-lived, for in 238 BC the Sardinian mercenaries in the little that was left of Punic Sardinia, who had been left unpaid, revolted and appealed to Rome. Rome seized the opportunity and annexed the whole island. Carthage, with little or no fleet and prostrate after major revolts in her African territories, was powerless to protest and had to yield any final interest in both Sardinia and Corsica. The consolidation of the islands in fact took until 231 BC, during which period the navy continued to provide the escort for supply ships, to support coastal forces and to ensure the integrity of the coasts against rebels and pirates. Rome now controlled all the lands around the Tyrrhenian Sea.

Rome's attention was next directed to the north-west, where the Ligurians, of the lands bordering the Gulf of Genoa, had been pushing into Etruscan territory, engaging in piracy and threatening the interests of one of Rome's oldest friends, the Greek colony of Massilia, which maintained its own fleet of as many as forty warships. Operations were conducted against the Ligurians between 238 and 230 BC. The nature of the terrain, for much of which the mountains almost literally meet the sea, restricted this campaign to the coastal strip and was well suited to the employment of units of the navy. Although there is no direct evidence that they did so, it seems highly probable that Massilia also contributed ships to the campaign. Apart from the well established duties of supply and transportation of the army, and of securing its seaward flank and communications, the large contingents of marines on warships were ideal for raiding and effecting landings in the enemy's rear, seizing villages and establishing bridgeheads. Indeed until the 19th century, some of these villages remained inaccessible save by sea or precipitous mountain path. In the absence of any naval opposition, the landing parties could be easily increased by replacing one of the remes of rowers by extra troops. Such landings would disrupt the enemy and allow the land forces to leapfrog them and link the bridgeheads, without having to wait for supplies, which could come in by sea ahead of them. The campaign

230 BC   extended Roman power and the coast controlled by it northwards, which, by
230 had been secured as far as Luna (La Spezia) which offers an anchorage
well sheltered, save from the south-east.

On the Adriatic coast, the Romans were expanding their territory
towards the valley of the River Padus (Po) and after war with the Gauls of
the area, occupied it. Their coast now extended north past the delta of the
river which itself formed a convenient border.

With her navy supreme and unchallenged on the west coast, the
Romans could now turn their attention to a long-standing problem, namely
the Illyrian pirates who, operating from among the myriad islands of the
Dalmatian coast, infested the Adriatic. These peoples had lived principally
by piracy for centuries, darting out in their light, fast galleys to attack
hapless traders. The original Illyrian name for these boats is not known and
it is convenient to use the Greek term *lemboi*, (although this term was used
generally for anything from a ship's tender to a seagoing boat) or the Roman
term *lembus*, the similarities in which might well indicate the original.
With the decline of Greek sea power in the area, the Illyrians had built up
a kingdom extending south to Epirus. When this 'pirate kingdom' took to
raiding southern Italy, Rome sent envoys to protest but they were rebuffed
by the Illyrian Queen Teuta and were attacked on their way home, one being
killed. The Illyrians went on to attack Epirus and then stormed Corcyra
(Corfu), defeating a Greek naval force which had been sent against them.
This action is interesting for the use made of their small ships by the Illyrians
against the Greek ships. The Greek squadron was of ten warships, fours and
fives. After an initial, indecisive action against the seven regular warships of
the Illyrians' allies, the Greek ships turned on the lemboi, which had been
lashed together in fours, presenting a beam to the Greek rams. This was
just too tempting for the Greeks who obliged, but their rams became stuck
and enmeshed in the comparatively flimsy structure of the several lemboi
deliberately sacrificed to each ram, giving their crews enough time to swarm
aboard and take the Greek ships. Four lemboi could carry about 200 men
and they overwhelmed the few dozen Greek marines on each ship, taking
five of the Greek ships.[1]

229 BC   The slight to Roman prestige caused by the treatment of her envoys,
together with mounting pressure from her merchants finally stirred Rome
into action and in the summer of 229 BC the navy sent the major part of
the fleet, 200 ships under the Consul Cnaius Fulvius Centumulus, against
Corcyra, which surrendered. Meanwhile the other Consul, Lucius Postumius
Albinus, sailed from Brundisium (Brindisi) with 22,000 troops and 2000
horse, landing on the coast adjacent to Apollonia (near Fier in modern
Albania), which also promptly surrendered. The fleet then shadowed the
army as it moved north up the Dalmatian coast to Epidamnus, then on to

ADVANCES
IN
NAVIGATION

The art of navigation at sea had continued to develop and in about 230 BC, one Eratosthenes, who was librarian of the great Ptolemaic Library at Alexandria, calculated the circumference of the world. He arrived at a figure of 24,700 miles, only 202 miles less than the true figure of 24,907 miles, an error caused by the two points between which he measured his basic distance for the calculation not being, as he thought they were, exactly north and south of each other. By observing the angles of the Sun above the horizon at noon on the annual solstices and equinoxes, tables of angles were produced for the days between so that latitude, ie. relative distances north and south, could be simply worked out at any time of year.[2] With these tools it was possible to prepare more accurate maps and, for the sailor, charts. As the accurate measurement of longitude, ie. relative distances east and west, had to await the perfection of the chronometer in AD 1762; ancient maps tend to be accurate as to latitude but distorted as to longitude, depending for this, as they did, upon estimated speeds and distances.

Issa, meeting little opposition, the light lemboi being no match for the huge numbers of warships manned as they were by veteran battle-hardened crews. The fleet proceeded to take several coastal towns whilst the army moved inland and took the surrender of local tribes.[3]

The employment of the major striking force of the navy, namely 200 ships, against the Illyrians who although having a similar total only had small, light ships, would at first sight seem excessive but several factors probably gave rise to this massive deployment of naval might. Firstly, the Illyrians were supported by Macedonia and the possibility of their intervention had to be countered. Secondly the Romans were operating in unfamiliar waters and were obviously going to allow the enemy no chance to gain any kind of lucky victory. Thirdly it may have been felt necessary to overawe the other peoples of the area to keep them out of the fight by demonstrating the size of force that could be deployed. Finally, this massive force may have been employed to impress the nearby Greeks, to whom the Illyrians were also enemies. Except for a squadron of forty ships, the fleet was withdrawn for the winter, this force being considered sufficient to deal with any enemy activity; the Illyrians in fact capitulated in the following spring (228 BC).

228 BC

The Illyrian Queen Teuta came to terms to pay a tribute and to cede territory for a new Roman protectorate, which they established in Dalmatia, in an area roughly contiguous with modern Albania. The Illyrians were further forbidden to sail south of their new southern border at Lissus with more than two unarmed lemboi. Now having bases on both sides of the Adriatic, the Romans could control it and ensure that the suppression of the piracy that had been achieved could be maintained. The Adriatic had effectively been made into a Roman lake and the Roman sphere of influence could extend across it into the Balkan peninsula; finally, Macedonia had been thwarted in any attempt to extend westwards, a fact that was not to be lost on its kings. A further by-product of the new protectorate in the Balkan peninsula was that Rome was now in direct contact for the first time with the Greek homeland and embassies were sent to the Greek states, where they were well received, their navy having dealt with the common enemy.

Carthage had, during the latter part of the Punic War, suffered the disaffection and desertion of much of her Hispanic territories. Hamilcar (with his young son Hannibal) was sent to recover the position, which he did, leading to the conquest by them of most of southern and eastern Hispania. The Romans watched carefully as the Carthaginians rebuilt and extended their power, in the knowledge surely that, after the experience of the recent war, the existence of two expanding empires in the western Mediterranean could not last. Sooner or later they would once more clash. The Romans sought to limit total Punic hegemony in the west by forming an alliance with the native city of Saguntum (Sagunto) and also to bolster their treaty with Massilia; all were nervous of Punic expansion northwards up the eastern Hispanic coast and thus towards Italy, where they might encourage the Gauls and Ligurians to attack them.

226 BC An embassy was sent and in 226 BC a treaty secured whereby the Carthaginians agreed not to advance north of the River Iberus (Ebro) and the Romans, not to interfere south of it.

Further trouble broke out in the Adriatic when Demetrius of Pharos, encouraged by Macedon, sought to extend his kingdom by invading Roman territory and taking the town of Dimale. He then went on to gather a fleet 220 BC of some 90 lemboi and in 220 this fleet sailed south, attacking Pylos in the Peloponnese, before proceeding into and cruising the Aegean. This could not be permitted, especially as relations with Carthage were again becoming strained. The two Consuls for 219 BC, Lucius Aemilius Paulus and Marcus Livius Salinator, sailed with the fleet and an army, attacking and storming Dimale and then Pharos itself. The Roman forces arrived at night and the fleet secretly landed troops who hid in woods. At daybreak, twenty ships sailed deliberately past Pharos and then ostentatiously landed troops near to the town; the garrison, assuming this to be the assault force, came out to offer battle whereupon the hidden troops emerged between the garrison and the town. Opposition collapsed and terms were dictated and imposed on the Illyrians, Demetrius fled to Macedonia and his lands were added to the Roman Protectorate.[4]

It had been a lightning combined operations campaign and was completed with the defeat of the pirate leaders and the clearing once more

THE LEMBUS

> As a useful type of warship, the lembus must have impressed the Romans, who had captured many of them. It had originally been a lightly built, open galley, carrying about fifty men and rowed in a single reme and without a ram. It had evolved into a ship with a ram and some decking and protection for the rowers, with the centre section of oars on each side manned by two men per oar (hemiolia or 'one and one half', to the Greeks); the type had fine lines, particularly forward for speed and although not as fast as a trireme, still faster than other classes of light warship. The Romans took some into their service and adopted the type for reconnaissance, scouting and communication duties, also adopting the name for the type in its Latin form of *liburna*. The Illyrians may well have had bireme versions of the ship but nevertheless the Romans did develop a bireme warship of light to medium dimensions and scale, which they also called a *liburna*. The type evolved into several variants at different times and in different theatres of operation, all retaining the same generic name and remaining in service as such for centuries but in forms which probably had nothing in common with the Illyrian original, save the name.[5]

of the Adriatic of this scourge. It had also confirmed Rome's territory in Illyria as permanent but it had brought her thereby into contact and in fact, into confrontation with the interests and ambitions of the powerful King Philip of Macedon. For the present however, the Adriatic was under Roman domination and the lines of supply and trade to the east were secure and unchallenged.

THE SECOND PUNIC WAR

219 BC

In Hispania the Carthaginians had continued to make territorial gains and had a new general in the field, Hamilcar's son, Hannibal. In 219 BC, he laid siege to Saguntum, which fell after eight months. Saguntum lay south of the line of the River Iberus and Hannibal therefore regarded it as a legitimate target, but he must have been aware that the city was an ally of Rome and an exception from the treaty terms. Whether deliberately provocative or not, the move had the same effect and proved to be the final straw. The tension between Rome and Carthage now boiled over and it was time to seek conclusions. War was declared in 218 BC.

218 BC

In anticipation of the resumption of hostilities with Carthage, the Romans had been planning major operations for the navy; a fleet of sixty warships would support the landing and operations of an army in Hispania against Punic possessions there; another fleet of up to 160 warships would support and safeguard operations via Sicily to Africa itself to attack the enemy homeland.[6] As a preliminary step in this plan and to obviate a future problem, the Consul Tiberius Sempronius, in command of the fleet, attacked and occupied Melita,[7] where the small, isolated garrison surrendered and the archipelago passed into the Roman domain. The Carthaginian navy was past its peak, but still had to be regarded as formidable, with about 100 ships and 25,000 personnel of which about fifty were in Hispania and the remainder in home ports. What the Romans did not know was that its confidence, shattered in the first war, had not recovered. For their part, the Roman and allied navy had over 220 ships with 50–60,000 personnel and its morale could not have been higher. Victorious in the last Punic War and having been in almost continuous successful operations since, all of which had served to keep it in a high state of efficiency, it knew the enemy's fleet was smaller and was confident of its ability to beat it once more. Of its other enemy, the weather, which had caused such dreadful losses, it had to be more philosophical and rely on its improved ships, experience and seamanship.

Whereas up to now, command of a fleet had been exercised by a Consul or by one of the Praefects of the Navy (a Praefect being of the rank of deputy Consul), a squadron or even a fleet could now be placed under the command of a *Praetor*, an officer equivalent in rank to the governor of a province (who thus had to be of senatorial rank, rather than the *equites* or 'knight' rank required of a Tribune). The commission lasted for the duration of a campaign or even just for the operation for which the fleet had been formed. When operating away from the central Italian area, as in Hispania or Greece, the command was subject to the overall military commander of the theatre of operations.[8] Rowers and sailors continued to be provided by the Italian allies and maritime colonies and marines by the allies and Latins, in addition to the Roman *capitacensi*, as previously. The service was, it seems, not popular with the Roman elite, lacking the glamour of the legions, together with the opportunities for plunder and booty, and this despite its prominent role in the recent wars. The fleet continued to employ the qinquireme as the standard line-of-battle ship. There were also triremes used, as before and a few 'fours', or quadriremes, in addition to the light *liburnae*, adapted from the Illyrian craft, these latter lending themselves to scouting and the carrying of despatches.

In the First Punic War, Rome had gained mastery of the seas and this was not to be seriously challenged in the second war, where she retained the ability to deploy her forces between theatres of operations at will and to deny the enemy the same ability. This naval supremacy would prove to be decisive. After the first war, Carthage had retained her navy, despite her defeat. The Romans learned from having to face it again, not to allow such a mistake to recur and in all of their following wars, where their adversary had any kind of fleet, it will be seen that a specific term would be imposed upon a defeated enemy for the surrender of that navy. The consistency of these terms formed a continuing policy to ensure that the Roman navy would ultimately be the only one.

The Roman navy's dominance of the central Mediterranean had an immediate effect on the new war. The Punic commander in Hispania, Hannibal, knew that he must strike first and, being denied the freedom of the sea, that he could only do so effectively by land. Thus he was forced to undertake the perilous overland route for his famous march to Italy. Starting out in spring of 218 BC, he took his army across the Pyrenees and southern Gaul and crossed the River Rhodanus (Rhone). The two Scipio brothers were sent with an army to intercept Hannibal at the Rhodanus. This was in fact the Roman navy's first operation of the war, a squadron of thirty-five quinquiremes escorting the Scipios' army from Pisae (Pisa) to Gaul. There the troops were safely landed near to Massilia, imagining that they were in Hannibal's path. Hannibal had however, already reached and crossed the Rhodanus well inland and was heading for the Alps, the Scipios not reaching the crossing point until three days too late. The Scipios re-embarked their troops and Publius returned by sea to Pisae, having despatched his brother, Gnaeus, with the army and the warships to Hispania to commence operations there. The Punic navy was not wholly inactive and despatched from Carthage two powerful raiding squadrons, one of thirty-five ships to Sicily and the other, of twenty ships, to the Italian coast. Both were intended to disrupt shipping and the flow of supplies and to interrupt the preparations for the proposed Roman invasion of Africa. The second squadron ran into a storm to the north of Sicily and three of its ships were blown towards Messana where they were captured by locally based Roman ships. From them the Romans learned of the larger fleet's proposed attack on Sicily and hurried to meet it. They caught up with the Punic fleet off Lilybaeum and in the ensuing battle, captured seven Punic ships. The remainder eventually effected a rendezvous with the smaller squadron at the Lipari Islands and together raided the Italian coast, before heading for home. Ten ships had been lost for very little return.[9]

Meanwhile, in Hispania, Gnaeus Scipio landed and established his base at Tarraco (Tarragona) where he beat off various enemy attacks to secure it and build a base for the fleet. He also cut any lines of communication between Hispania and Hannibal. Even without a secure land route established between Italy and Hispania, the navy had enabled the Romans to take the war to their enemy, rather than let Hannibal's initiative dictate the sole course of events.

The Punic commander in Hispania had fitted out and manned a fleet of between thirty-five and forty warships, having also a dozen or so more, for which he did not have sufficient crews. The fleet was composed of thirty-two quinquiremes and three triremes commanded by Himilco. He set out in 217 BC to march from his capital at Carthago Nova (Cartagena), north up the coast to meet the Romans, his flank secured by Himilco's ships close offshore. Learning of the Punic move, Gnaeus embarked a picked force of marines augmented by troops and sailed to intercept. Rome's ally, Massilia, had contributed two of their ships to the Roman fleet of thirty-five and they were scouting for the fleet when they spotted the Punic fleet anchored and pulled into the shore, about ten miles from the mouth of the river Iberus and without themselves being seen.

Scipio immediately ordered an attack and managed to get close before being spotted. The Carthaginians, many of whom were ashore, had been surprised and had to scramble to man their ships, which were in considerable confusion and well strung out when the Romans made contact. In the first rush, the Romans boarded and took two ships and rammed and swamped another four. The rest were pushed towards the shore and some at least of their crews panicked and abandoned their ships to scramble ashore. Unable to seek the shelter of the estuary, the remaining Punic ships were run ashore so their crews could also escape to the safety of their army which was there. The Romans pressed their attack and managed to tow many of the enemy ships off, away from the shore. Of the forty ships, the Romans took twenty-five and were masters of the Hispanic coast, the balance of naval power having now swung overwhelmingly in their favour.

To follow up this success, Scipio reinforced his squadron with some of the captured ships and his fleet landed marines and troops and stormed the enemy town of Onusa; they then raided the surroundings of Carthago Nova itself and the town of Longutica, destroying stores useful to the enemy and taking much plunder. The fleet next sailed to the Carthaginian isle of Ebusus (Ibiza) and although they could not take the main town, wrecked crops and looted the countryside until the inhabitants sent peace envoys and the island was thus neutralised.

Finally the fleet returned to northern Hispania, where several of the local tribes north of the Iberus gave their submission to Scipio, giving him a solid foothold in what is now Catalonia. The Hispanic theatre would be critical in the war and be fought over ferociously by both sides; its reserves of wealth, materials and manpower were essential to Carthage and without it, despite Hannibal's amazing exploits in Italy, Carthage could not win.

By his naval campaign, Gnaeus Scipio had ensured the Roman presence in Hispania and that its lines of communication and supply, which could only be by sea, were secure. In contrast, the Carthaginians there had to operate more or less in isolation from their homeland, cut off by sea and separated as they were by a very long and tenuous land route. They did receive some troop reinforcements, but no extra ships. Later in 217 BC, Publius Scipio sailed from Ostia to join his brother at Tarraco, bringing another twenty warships and many transports laden with reinforcements and supplies. With this, the Romans could go onto the offensive on land.

Meanwhile, after beating the Romans at Trebbia in 218 BC, Hannibal had entered the Italian peninsula where his army was augmented by large numbers of the Gauls of northern Italy. Roman garrisons were trapped at Placentia (Piacenza) and Cremona, isolated by the enemy cavalry forces which were roaming the surrounding plains. The garrisons were only able to hold out until the Punic army moved away to the south because they were kept supplied by ships operating up the river Padus (Po), doubtless organised and escorted by the Adriatic Squadron of the navy. Hannibal again badly defeated the Roman army at Lake Trasimenus in 217 BC, but despite this and his march through Italy, most of Rome's allies in the peninsula remained loyal to her. The planned invasion of Africa had to be abandoned and the troops earmarked for it moved north to counter Hannibal. A naval squadron was left to protect Sicily and the remainder of the fleet withdrawn to Ostia.

217 BC   In the summer of 217 BC, a Punic fleet of seventy quinquiremes sailed via Sardinia and Corsica to the coast off Pisae, intending to contact Hannibal. It managed to capture a Roman supply convoy en route to Hispania but fled upon the approach of the Roman fleet of about 120 ships from Ostia, under the Consul Gnaeus Servilius Geminus. The Punic fleet returned home by the same route, followed by the Roman fleet, around Corsica and Sardinia, to Lilybaeum, ensuring that the enemy had indeed gone home. Servilius' subsequent foray to the African coast was, however, badly handled and his fleet suffered some losses in men while trying to secure booty. The fleet then returned to Ostia where it was readied for more offensive operations, planned for the following year.

216 BC   In 216 BC, the navy duly took to the offensive and, again under Servilius Geminus, a fleet of 120 ships sailed around Sardinia and Corsica, taking hostages to ensure those islands' continued loyalty. They then sailed to Africa and raided the enemy coastline at will until one raiding party was ambushed and lost some men. The fleet returned to Sicily, having met no enemy naval opposition.

CANNAE – ROMAN LOW POINT

In the same year however, the Romans suffered their greatest ever military disaster. Their army was destroyed at Cannae by Hannibal and much of the south of the peninsula defected to him. The majority of Rome's allies did however, remain loyal and the Punic leader, despite his success, could not muster the strength to march on Rome herself. He was in any event isolated from home by Roman sea power and the inability or unwillingness of his own side to challenge it.

After their horrendous losses at Trasimenus and Cannae the Romans had to raise whatever manpower they could to block Hannibal. The Praetor of the fleet at Ostia, Marcus Claudius Marcellus, sent 1500 of his marines to bolster the garrison at Rome and from the remainder, formed a legion of his marines, some 5000 men, which he led to northern Campania to join the hastily raised army there. The fleet was left under the command of Publius Furius Philus who, with the loss of the marines, had to decommission fifty or so of his ships. Despite the shortage of men, the citizens of Ostia and Antium were the only ones who remained exempted from military service, they being needed to supply the requirements of the fleet.

Even with this reduction in strength, the navy could still dominate the seas; of the 220 ships with which they had started the war, fifty-five were in Hispania with the Scipios (who also had as many as they could repair and make seaworthy of the twenty-five captured Punic ships). Of the 120 ships of the main fleet, fifty were laid up and seventy operational; the remaining forty-five ships forming the guard squadrons at Sicily and in the Adriatic. It seems that at about this time, just after the Battle of Cannae, Punic squadrons did venture forth, perhaps on hearing of the defeat, in the hope that the Romans had been forced by their losses of manpower to have their fleet stand down completely. A squadron attacked Syracusan territory, while another appeared off the Aegades Islands to the west of Sicily; both were driven off by the presence of the Roman fleet and the Syracusans, neither of whom were able to bring them to battle.

To add to Rome's troubles, a new theatre of war now arose in the east when Philip of Macedon, who had for the past two years been moving to extend his power westward to the Ionian Sea, tried to seize a base in Illyria. He was forced to withdraw upon the approach of a Roman squadron of ten heavy ships alerted by intelligence from, and sent to give support to, their local allies. Hannibal sought to build on Philip's antipathy towards Rome and gain an ally and thus made an alliance with him whereby Philip would operate against Rome and her interests in Illyria and Corcyra, whilst Hannibal campaigned in Italy. The diplomatic contacts between Hannibal and Philip had to be conducted by Macedonian ships seeking to run, undiscovered, into secret prearranged landing-places in the Gulf of Taranto. Unfortunately for them both, Philip's envoy, an Athenian named Xenophanes and some Carthaginian officers, complete with all of their diplomatic papers, correspondence and a copy of the proposed treaty, were en route by sea to Hannibal in a squadron of five ships when they were intercepted off southern Italy by twenty-five ships of the Roman navy and, excepting one ship which escaped back to Philip, were captured. The Romans thus had as full details of the plans as Philip and Hannibal themselves. This intelligence was sent straight to the Senate, which was thus able to act promptly to prevent any linking between the new allies. Marcus Valerius Laevinus was sent, in command of another twenty-five ships, to Brundisium, there to reinforce and assume command also of the twenty-five other ships already stationed there. To cover this deployment, Hieron of Syracuse sent his fleet to Ostia. At Brundisium, Laevinus organised the setting up of a subsidiary base on the Adriatic coast, placed to allow him to operate against the coasts of Epirus and Illyria. From these positions astride the Adriatic narrows, he could blockade Hannibal and prevent any attempt at incursion by Philip, while ensuring that the routes for Roman trade to the east remained open.

215 BC   Thus in 215 BC, started the First Macedonian War which would continue for the next decade. The Carthaginian diplomatic offensive continued and they saw a further opportunity amongst their own former subjects, the restless Sardinians. In 215 they sent a fleet of sixty warships, carrying a force there to raise the island against Rome. Once again, however, the Romans must have had good intelligence as a legion was immediately transported to the island, arriving just ahead of the Punic force, who were met and defeated as soon as they landed. The Punic fleet was then damaged in a storm and had to divert to the Balearic Islands for repairs. The misfortunes of this Punic fleet were not over however. The commander in Sicily, Otacilius, on his way home from a raid on the African coast, ran into them and in a brief battle, took seven ships as prizes, the rest scattering and escaping. After this the Carthaginians made no further attempt at Sardinia or Corsica.

Later that same year (215 BC), in Hispania, Punic forces again tried to move north but were severely beaten by the Scipios. This victory forced the Carthaginians to divert forces there which could have helped Hannibal, assuming of course that they could have been landed in Italy. A summer's hard campaigning had left the Scipio brothers short of money, clothing and equipment for their troops and ships' crews. Their dispatches reporting their successes also therefore demanded money, clothing and food and replacements for lost and damaged equipment for the fleet. Private contractors were engaged to provide the supplies but public subscription had to be resorted to to help pay for them. Shipping was carried out at the risk of the state against storms and enemy action, so it can be assumed that naval escorts were provided for the merchantmen. Later on, a Punic squadron under Bomilcar did manage to evade the Romans and land reinforcements in Italy for Hannibal and escape again, the only reinforcements that Hannibal was to receive from home.

In the east, the Romans had turned to diplomacy and had put together the Aetolian League, an alliance of Greek states nervous of Philip's ambitions. These included Rhodes and Attalus, King of Pergamum in Asia Minor. Both Rhodes and Pergamum were naval powers, having substantial, modern and efficient fleets of their own which could dominate the Aegean for the allies.

Finally in 215 BC, yet another theatre of war opened up when Rome's long-term friend and ally, Hieron of Syracuse in Sicily, died. At the same time, the navy's strong squadron based at Lilybaeum sailed along the south coast of Sicily as far as Cape Pachynus, before turning and returning to their base. Although this seems no more than a regular patrol or exercise, it may have been made on hearing of the death of Hieron and to influence a favourable transmission of power. It was claimed that the squadron reversed course on hearing that Hieron was yet alive, although how they could have learned this while at sea is a mystery. Hieron was succeeded by his young son, who took the Roman action to be hostile, especially as he had pro-Punic sympathies. After some palace intrigues and the assassination of the young king, the pro-Carthaginian faction gained ascendancy, made an alliance with Carthage and brought Syracuse into the war against Rome. Reinforcements had to be sent to the garrison in Sicily and arrangements were put in hand to increase security in the Tyrrhenian Sea and to increase the fleet at Sicily to 100 ships under the overall command of Marcus Claudius Marcellus.

215 BC   As 215 BC ended, the Romans must have looked with anxiety at their situation; not only did they have a victorious enemy army rampaging about Italy and a major war to prosecute in Hispania, but their enemies were now strung across the south of them in a line from Hispania in the west, to Africa and Sicily in the south, to Hannibal in the centre and on to Philip in the east. The increase in their navy shows that the Romans well understood that it was to this service that they must look to resolve these problems. It would be essential for them to retain naval supremacy against the Syracusans and Macedonians in addition to the Punic fleet. If they could do so then they could seal each segment of the wars and deal with it in turn and in isolation when they were ready and thus always retain the initiative.

214 BC   In 214 BC, Philip moved against Roman territory and bases in Illyria; he had amassed a fleet of about 120 light galleys, many of which were in fact built by Illyrian shipwrights, who presumably produced their traditional lemboi, possibly in both mono- and bireme versions. From his domains in the Peloponnese, Philip and his forces sailed north to attack Apollonia and Oricus (Dukat). Laevinus immediately sailed from Brundisium, the seventy-five or so sea miles (110km) to Oricus. Sailing with his heavier and well-armed ships and with extra troops in transports, he met with ten ships of his Aetolian allies. In the face of this attack, Philip's ships were forced to retreat up a nearby river until the big ships could no longer follow. There they were contained, helpless, while the Romans recaptured Oricus and relieved Apollonia. Philip was forced to burn his boats and retire overland. Laevinus wintered at Oricus with his ships, thwarting any plans that Philip may have had for a counter-attack.

Philip had attacked in anticipation of the arrival of a Cathaginian fleet which must have been promised to him in the same way that a Roman fleet had been promised to Rome's Greek allies. The difference was that Philip waited in vain for his Punic fleet, without which he could not gain the initiative, nor operate effectively in western Greece, as had just been proven. Neither could he contemplate any crossing to Italy to join Hannibal, who for his part could expect no relief from across the Adriatic or Ionian seas.

It seems a reasonable conjecture that the despatches which would have arranged for a Punic fleet to sail to Philip were among those captured by the Romans the previous year. With Rome's allies all around him, Philip now had to campaign strenuously on several fronts. Roman participation had been agreed to be limited to the provision of naval support with a minimum commitment of twenty-five quinqiremes to be stationed in the area and a single legion as a garrison for their base. Once again, by a prompt and decisive naval campaign, Rome had seized the initiative and isolated the Macedonian War within its own local area. They had neutralised the impact of the Punic-Macedonian Pact and prevented it from having any impact upon Italy, or any other theatre of war. In addition to this, the Roman diplomacy had the result that the war was being fought on land by the Greeks against the Macedonians and that apart from the promised naval commitment and garrison, Roman troops were not required. Even so, a legion plus the crews of 25 quinqiremes represents approximately 12,000 men, a not inconsiderable commitment.

The Egyptians, under their Pharoah, Ptolemy IV Philopater, felt that their interests were ill-served by the war between Macedonia and the Aetolian League and sought to mediate. It was essential for Rome, which was in no position to contemplate a land war in Greece, to keep Philip occupied and separated from his Carthaginian friends and an embassy was sent to Alexandria. The Egyptians were persuaded to remain neutral; in return the Romans purchased several shiploads of Egyptian corn, which were sent to Rome. Although not essential to the Romans at this time, the extra source of supply became useful when the Carthaginians had an army in Sicily, restricting supplies from there. The grain was also useful to help Rome's allies in Greece, whose own harvests were adversely affected by the recent campaigns. Later of course, the trade in Egyptian corn would become more and more important until it would supply fully a third of Rome's annual consumption and the great fleets of huge grain ships would become a regular annual feature for centuries.

The Romans continued to build warships and Livy mentions that an extra 100 were authorised for 214 BC,[10] but they were also short of crewmen. Extra taxes were raised for the sole purpose of paying sailors' wages and were levied on a sliding scale according to wealth; they ranged from the equivalent of six months' wages for one sailor, to a year's pay for eight sailors (this last was from senators). This was the first time that a fleet had been provided by public subscription rather than loans and its importance in Roman thinking is demonstrated by the senators having imposed the heaviest subscriptions upon themselves. The fleet had long been important enough to be a consular command and without a strong fleet the Romans knew that Sicily and the islands would be lost and Philip could land in Italy, whereupon the war would doubtless be lost.

Hannibal had moved into southern Italy. He made no move to try to relieve Syracuse, although of course, once on Sicily, he could be trapped there. It is a moot point because, by now, knowing that he could not invest Rome itself, he could have joined the Punic forces being landed there and pursued the recovery of Sicily for Carthage and would have been no more trapped there than he already effectively was in Italy itself. In any event, he tried to take Tarentum to gain a secure base and harbour but the Roman fleet stationed at Brundisium was too quick and reinforced the garrison whereupon Hannibal withdrew, unable to contemplate a siege.

In Sicily, with the Roman forces on the island concentrated for the siege of Syracuse, the Punic fleet, under Bomilco, had landed troops on the south coast. He then sent fifty-five of his ships which managed to run the Roman blockade and get into the harbour of Syracuse. Once there, they were of little use and as their crews were consuming more supplies than they brought, they had to leave at the earliest opportunity, managing again to slip by the blockade. The Carthaginian army which had been landed captured Heraclea, Agrigentum and some of the surrounding area, intending to advance to the relief of Syracuse, which had been invested by the Romans by land and sea; the Syracusan fleet was bottled up in the city's Little Harbour. Although the Punic fleet made a demonstration in the area, it did not attempt to attack the Roman fleet, which continued unhindered to bring troops and supplies for the siege, including another legion and thirty more quinquiremes for the fleet. Bomilco, for his part, succeeded in running the Roman blockade on three more occasions. Marcellus took part of the besieging army and marched to face the Punic invasion force. He defeated it and it fell back on Heraclea which quickly became untenable and Bomilco therefore concentrated his fleet there to evacuate the Carthagininan army's survivors. The Roman fleet sailed for Heraclea to intercept, but Bomilco avoided contact and refused battle on their approach, (probably from the west) sending his transports to run southward for home (presumably with such of the troops as had managed to embark). His warships evaded the enemy fleet and headed eastward toward Tarentum and Hannibal.

Syracuse had been besieged by the Roman army under Appius Claudius Pulcher, while Marcellus, commanding a fleet totalling 130 ships of all types at Syracuse, planned to assault the city from the sea. He based his ships at Thapsus, a peninsula enclosing a sheltered anchorage in the bay immediately north of Syracuse and visible from its northern suburbs. His attack was

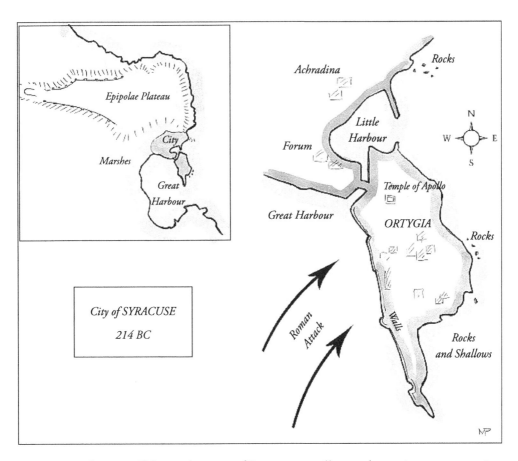

beaten off due to the mass of Syracusan artillery and contrivances emanating from the fertile brain of the great Archimedes. A simultaneous assault by Pulcher's men from landward was also repulsed, mainly by concentrated artillery fire.

For the naval attack, the Romans moved up some sixty quinquiremes, manned by archers, slingers and javelin men and armed with catapults, whose job was to stand off the city walls and give covering fire to keep the defenders off the walls. Eight other ships, lashed together in pairs and propelled by their respective outer banks of oars, moved in for the assault, having been equipped with especially built protected scaling ladders called *sambucae* or lyres. These were four feet wide (1.3m), long enough to reach the top of the walls and encased in a wooden protective 'sheath'. The ladders were laid on deck between the masts of the paired ships for their approach. As the ships came up against the walls, they were raised by pulleys slung from the masts and placed against the walls whereupon the troops, who had been sheltered by screens over the decks, would swarm up onto the walls. Scaling towers several stories high, together with battering rams, levers and hooks for attacking the masonry were also carried, along with elevated, screened platforms each with four archers, probably attached to the masts for them to be able to shoot down onto the defenders on the walls. The area of attack was dictated by the geography of the city, whose coastline to seaward is fringed by offshore rocks and shallows and heights rising from the sea to the Epipolae Plateau, all of which naturally focuses it onto the west side of the Ortygia island; even today, the strongest of the surviving old fortifications are on the west, not on the seaward side.[11]

Archimedes had prepared the defences by having many loopholes made in the walls at all levels to allow shooting by artillery of various sizes, which had been moved up, heavy for the ships offshore and light for closer-range shooting against the assault boats. The defending artillery could keep their enemy under a constant hail of missiles from about 400 yards offshore, until they could finally get below the limit of depression at about sixty yards; however, the light engines, sited in low embrasures could then engage the landing craft from there, right up to the walls themselves. Finally, on the walls he had installed contraptions consisting of a large swing-beam with grapnels or 'claws' at one end and counterweights at the other. These were used against the ships which were at the walls, grappling them and lifting one end or the other out of the water, then dropping them, causing great damage if not swamping or wrecking them completely. Another type of device was a swing-beam which carried a very heavy weight, swung by ropes and pulleys, horizontally out over an enemy deck; the weight was released, to smash down onto the deck, then raised and the action repeated; 600 pound (300kg) lead and stone weights were so used as 'wrecking balls'. At least one of the *sambuca*-carrying ships was wrecked by this method. This was an adaptation of a similar device, known as a 'dolphin', used by some merchant ships, which had stout, strong yards; a suitably equipped yard was rigged and swung over the deck of a pirate ship that tried to come alongside and the weight released (it must have been a prerequisite to only use it before being grappled as otherwise, if successful it would have necessitated the pirates having to take the ship or drown). The Roman attack was frustrated but the siege continued. Marcellus tightened the blockade with part of his fleet, while securing with the rest any other areas of the island which supported Syracuse or Carthage.

213 BC

In 213 BC, Hannibal had again made his way south and this time, with the aid and connivance of the anti-Roman faction in the city who killed the guards and opened the gates to him, successfully occupied Tarentum. This gave him a reasonable base at last from which he could re-establish links with the outside world. His success was marred however in that the Roman garrison secured itself in the citadel. To prevent any foray by the garrison

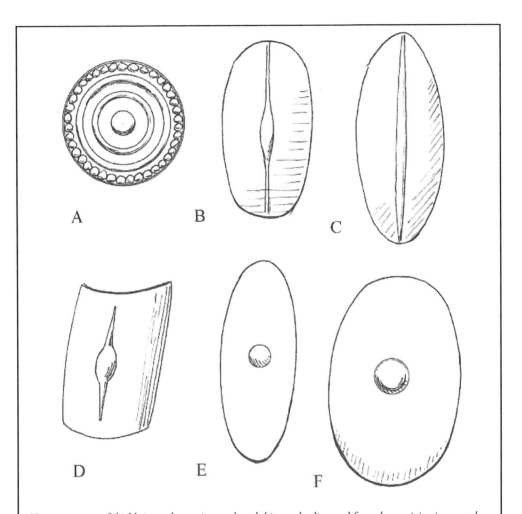

Various patterns of shields in use by marines on board ship can be discerned from the surviving iconography.

A.   *Circular with a central boss. Covered in embossed bronze sheet. 3rd century BC from funeral urns.*

B.   *Ovoid reduced-size version of the legionary body shield, with the central boss faired into the rib. 2nd century BC from a sarcophagus in the Naples Museum.*

C.   *Elliptical dished shield, shoulder to above knee, single, vertical hand grip faired into the central rib. 2nd to 1st century BC Praeneste Relief.*

D.   *Reduced-in-size version of the army's rectangular shield. From a relief, probably 1st century BC.*

E.   *Ovoid, flat with a central boss. 1st to 3rd centuries AD. From mosaics in Tunis and wall paintings in Pompeii.*

F.   *Ovoid, almost circular body shield but still with the central boss. 4th and 5th centuries AD. From the Arch of Constantine and the Column of Arcadius.*

against the city and to secure it better, Hannibal had the Romans sealed in the citadel by the building of a moat and palisade, which was completed in the face of a furious Roman attack. The Romans still held the city of Metapontum, a little way along the coast to the west and with control of the sea, were able to reinforce and keep supplied the garrison in the citadel. A further attack by them destroyed much of the siege equipment being readied by Hannibal with which to attack the citadel and he was henceforth content to contain and leave the Romans there. A second and third line of palisades and a garrison were added to deter any further attempt at a break out. The problem for Hannibal was that the citadel was placed to overlook and command the entrance to the harbour, which is deep and very narrow. Given a good artillery establishment and with some of their ships moored alongside, the Romans could attack and take anything that tried to go in or out of the harbour. There were ships trapped in the harbour, perhaps some merchant ships and some Punic ships; in any event, to gain the open sea, the Tarentines had to drag some of their lightest ships on rollers from the harbour, across the isthmus to the seaward side, roughly where the canal between the sea and harbour now is. That they failed, despite the fall of Metapontum to Hannibal, to break the Roman blockade by this is demonstrated by the fact that the Roman garrison held out in the citadel until the city was recaptured, four years later, in 209 BC Throughout this time it was kept supplied by the navy alone and Hannibal was nevertheless, by their presence, denied a secure harbour.[12]

212 BC   In the spring of 212 BC, the Romans stormed part of Syracuse's defences and gained a foothold, beating off counter-attacks, including an attempt by the Syracusan fleet to break out of the harbour.[13]

Meanwhile, also in 212 BC, grain was being shipped from a now-pacified Sardinia, assuring not only that Rome could not be starved out, but that she could feed her Italian allies whose lands had suffered greatly at the hands of the Carthaginian army of Hannibal. The main fleet by now numbered some 200 ships and 50,000 men.

211 BC   In the next year (211 BC) the Carthaginian fleet of over 100 warships, with a supply convoy, presumably intended for Syracuse, made another appearance, again commanded by Bomilcar. It appeared off Sicily, but sailed away again in the face of the approaching Roman fleet. In Sicily itself, after a two and a half year siege and with no hope of relief, Syracuse finally fell in 211 BC and the whole island was pacified by the following year. With the Syracusan threat removed, it was time for the navy to resume the offensive and a fleet of eighty quinqiremes under Titus Otacilius Crassus sailed from Lilybaeum to Utica, attacking the harbour and shipping there and capturing and towing away as many as 130 laden transports as prizes. These cargoes would have been too late for Syracuse which had fallen a few days before,

but ironically they were used to feed its inhabitants following the siege and until regular supplies could be arranged.

The failure of the Punic navy to take any form of initiative, or even to seriously support its erstwhile allies in Sicily and Illyria, had lost them those allies and the war in both theatres. The naval initiative had belonged solely to the Romans, who had never wavered in their commitment to naval supremacy, even in the dark days following their defeats by Hannibal. As a result, Rome retained unquestionable control of that vital 'bridge' between Italy and Africa, namely Sicily.

In Hispania in 211 BC, the Scipios had advanced southward, capturing Saguntum, but their forces had become depleted and upon the defection of their unreliable local allies they were each beaten and the two brothers killed. The remnants of their armies were forced back northward, but managed to hold the line of the Iberus, their starting point. The Roman naval superiority in the area, apart from providing a ready reserve of troops, must have inhibited the Carthaginians and ensured the Romans' flank, communications and supply routes. Reinforcements of two legions were sent later in the year by sea from Puteoli to Tarraco to secure the line, presumably with a strong naval escort.

210 BC   In 210 BC in the east, Laevinus' fleet captured the island of Zakynthos and the towns of Oeniadae and Nassus on the mainland, which he handed over to the Aetolians and then himself withdrew to Corcyra. Laevinus was then appointed to command a squadron of the fleet at Sicily, being replaced in Corcyra by Publius Sulpicius Galba. The new commander sailed his fleet into the Aegean and captured the island of Aegina, off the coast near Athens, which became an important base for the Romans and their allied ships. He failed however to relieve the town of Echinus (Lamia, opposite northern Euboea) which was being besieged by Philip's force. Aegina was left in allied hands and Galba returned to the Gulf of Corinth.

From Sicily, Valerius Messalla, commanding fifty ships, carried out further raids on the African coast, taking Carthaginian prisoners from whom the Romans learned much of the enemy situation at home and of their plans for relieving Hannibal. These plans were to fit out a fleet of fifty ships, each with a detachment of over a hundred marines, providing a force equivalent to a legion and which could be doubled by arming and landing a third of the rowers.[14] At Tarentum the Romans still holding the citadel had become short of supplies. A provisioning fleet was gathered at Rhegium with an escort commanded by Decimus Quinctus. Originally allotted two triremes and three smaller ships for the escort, he was reinforced by three quinqiremes and twelve small allied ships from Rhegium, Velia and Paestum, for a total of twenty ships of various sizes. When about fifteen miles off Tarentum, the Tarentines, under Democrates, also with about twenty ships, all of which must have been dragged overland to the sea, sallied forth to challenge them. The Roman ships stowed their sails and prepared for action upon sighting the enemy. Both squadrons were arrayed in line abreast and met head-on; a furious fight ensued during which the Roman flagship was boarded and Quinctus killed; a second Tarentine ship then boxed the flagship in and it was captured.

The remaining Roman and allied ships tried to extricate themselves but some of them were rammed and sunk in open water and some of the others were forced ashore and lost. Most of the transports had made sail and escaped out to sea under the cover of the fight. This was to be the sole Roman naval defeat of the war and says much of the desperation of the Tarentines and of the poor standard of Quinctus' own ships' crews who despite having three quinquiremes and two triremes, was beaten by a force which could only have contained ships limited in size by having to be small enough to have been dragged across land to be launched in the sea.[15]

THE TIDE TURNS

210 BC Publius Cornelius Scipio the younger was appointed to command in Hispania and sailed from Ostia early in 210 BC for Empuriae (Empurias), with a fleet of thirty quinquiremes and transports laden with reinforcements and supplies. These ships would augment the ships already in Hispania and Scipio appointed his friend Gaius Laelius to command the fleet, which was by now some eighty ships in strength. Scipio decided to start with a bold stroke, no less than the capture of the capital of Punic Hispania, Carthago Nova itself, which, it had been learned, only had a small garrison. The town lay on a peninsula, jutting into a round bay, with the best natural harbour on the east Hispanic coast, part of the north side of which was shallow and could be waded. Scipio's troops marched south in 209 BC, their arrival timed to coincide with that of Laelius' ships.

209 BC The troops sealed off the isthmus to the east and the ships to the south and west. A sally by the garrison was beaten back, as was the first Roman attack on the walls. A renewed assault was more co-ordinated and while the army carried out an assault from landward and troops forded the lagoon to attack from the north, the ships came up to the city walls on the south, which were then scaled by their marines. One of the highest of military decorations of the time was the *Corona Muralis*, awarded to the first man over enemy walls in a siege. Scipio awarded two after the fall of Carthago Nova, one to a legionary centurion and the other to a marine of the fleet. With the capture of Carthago Nova, the Romans had won the key position in Hispania; the Carthaginians withdrew to the west and south, but had lost control of the wealth-creating potential of the country as well as the allegiance of many of the tribes who went over to Scipio.

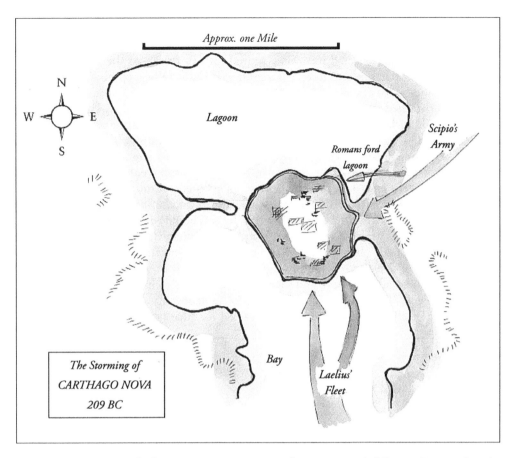

Approx. one Mile

N
W · E
S

Lagoon

Romans ford
lagoon

Scipio's
Army

Bay

Laelius'
Fleet

The Storming of
CARTHAGO NOVA
209 BC

With the city, vast quantities of war material fell into Roman hands, over 450 artillery pieces, together with over sixty merchant vessels and eighteen warships in the harbour. The marines of the fleet stood guard whilst Scipio rested his troops after the capture of the city.

Laelius was sent to report to Rome on this success, taking a quinquireme and six other ships, laden with booty and captives. At first the Hispania fleet was kept efficient and battle-ready by holding exercises, mock battles and manoeuvring practice, but with no enemy left to fight, most of the ships were hauled ashore and their crews used to bolster the army. If needed, Scipio could mobilise nearly one hundred warships but for now, in the absence of any enemy naval challenge, he needed only sufficient to escort the transports to and from Italy.

Elsewhere in 209 BC, the fleet in Illyria, still commanded by Sulpicius Galba, carried out raiding operations in the Gulf of Corinth against Macedonian-held shores and on one occasion, a thousand marines were sent

209 BC   to reinforce the Aetolians who were trying to block a southward advance by
          Philip's forces.

          Hannibal had meantime moved into Bruttium so the Romans seized
          the opportunity to recover Tarentum. This was to be a combined operation
          and whilst the army set up the siege of the city, thirty quinquiremes were
          detached from the main fleet at Sicily and, commanded by Fabius, moved
          to blockade Tarentum and to guard against any attempt at relief from the
          sea, or against any further sally by the Tarentine ships that had so surprised
          Quinctus. Some of the ships were equipped with siege artillery and some
          of the transports that accompanied the squadron were also equipped with
          artillery and oars for manoeuvre, all in preparation for an assault. They
          approached the city mainly as a diversion for the intended assault by the
          army and from the citadel, but the city was betrayed and surrendered before
          this took place. With Tarentum back in their hands, the Romans once more
          had a major base linking their fleets in Sicily and the Ionian Sea and could
          patrol the Gulf of Taranto more effectively, all of which helped to isolate
          Hannibal even more and increased the dangers to his blockade runners. In
          Sicily, Laevinus commanded a fleet of some seventy ships; with his deputies
          Messalla and Cincius they again raided the African coast in 209 BC.

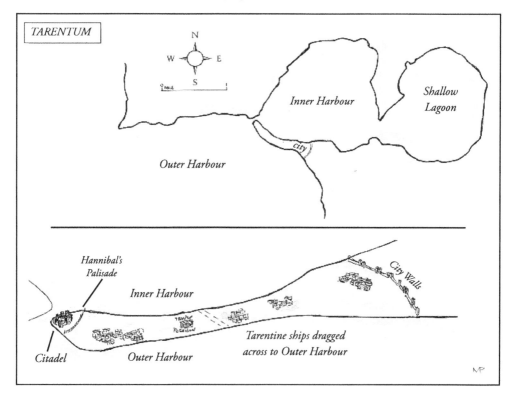

In 208 BC the Romans believed once again that the Carthaginians were preparing a naval offensive and as a precaution, fifty ships of Scipio's command in Hispania were recalled and stationed at Sardinia, from where they could quickly deploy, as needed, west to Hispania, east to Rome or south to Sicily. The thirty ships from Tarentum rejoined the main fleet at Sicily, which continued to patrol the gulf between Sicily and Tarentum. A further thirty ships were sent to Ostia for refit and repair and to join the twenty newly constructed ships being fitted out there, to form a reserve home fleet of fifty more ships.[16]

Laevinus took his Sicilian fleet (totalling a hundred ships) and again raided the African coast. On his return voyage, he came upon the Punic fleet of eighty-three ships, attacked and defeated it, capturing eighteen ships. Unfortunately, no details survive of this, the first large naval battle of the war.

In the east, Sulpicius Galba continued to support the Aetolians and with fifteen of his ships, crossed from Navpactos to Cyllene, in the Gulf of Corinth at night. There he landed 4000 troops, who proved to be a decisive surprise to Philip in the following day's battle, and caused Philip to lose it.

For 207 BC, Laevinus continued his naval raids on the African coast and once more, during a return voyage, the fleet came upon the Punic fleet at sea. This time the enemy had some seventy ships and Laevinus about the same. In the ensuing battle the Carthaginians were again beaten, the Romans sinking four of their ships and capturing another seventeen, the remainder escaping. Unlike their operations off Sicily earlier, on both of these occasions the Carthaginians, being closer to home, were prepared to engage in battle with the Romans who were, in turn, far from their own bases. Even with matched numbers, the Roman navy, obviously now at the very peak of its power and efficiency, could beat a Punic navy whose morale and abilities were evidently poor by comparison and could never again match it.

In Hispania, Scipio defeated the Punic commander Hasdrubal, who managed to escape with the remainder of his army and marched to join Hannibal. He got as far as Metaurus in northern Italy where he was caught and utterly destroyed (207 BC). For his part, Hannibal was now effectively blockaded in Bruttium by land and sea and increasingly powerless to influence events. Despite his brilliant successes, he was to all intents and purposes neutralised, unable to prevent the Romans from carrying on the war as they saw fit and wherever they liked.

In Greece, the naval war had moved into the Aegean and half of the Roman squadron sailed to their base on the island of Aegina then went on to the island of Lemnos. There its twenty-five ships were joined by thirty-five ships of King Attalus of Pergamum. Although Philip had a fleet, it would be no match for the joint fleet and he wisely kept it well out of the way.

The allied fleet could now attack the Macedonian's long Aegean coastline at will. The fleet sailed to Euboea, where it attacked the town of Oreus by making an amphibious landing on the seaward side, with ship-borne artillery support, whilst the Greek allies attacked by land. Although Philip was advised of the attack, he was unable to cross to the island with his troops in the face of allied naval power. The attack was successful and the Macedonian garrison was rounded up and shipped home. The fleet next sailed into the Gulf of Euboea, to the stronghold of Chalcis (Khalkis) but the defences were too strong and the anchorage too exposed, so the fleet withdrew to Locris, on the mainland. Chalcis is a location that will recur in the struggles for Greece, due to the peculiarity of its position. The large island of Euboea is separated from the Greek mainland by a strait (actually two flooded valleys, one opening from each end) which averages some ten miles (16km) in width; roughly in the centre of the overall length however, the strait suddenly narrows to become a channel called the Euripus, only some forty yards wide, with some rocks in the middle and which has been bridged from the earliest of times. This constriction gives rise to a fierce tidal bore, which runs at six or seven knots, seven times per day. The narrows are dominated by the fortress of Chalcis and prevent the passage of the gulf from end to end by ships, which can thus only approach from one end or the other.[17]

Unable to achieve any more, the allied fleet then left the dangerous, narrow Gulf of Euboea and returned to Lemnos and then to their base on Aegina. Philip now moved with his navy, entering the gulf from the north, where he held the shores. Philip's fleet was a mix of types, with three quadriremes ('fours') and three biremes provided by his Achaean allies and seven quinquiremes and over twenty of the light boats, brought back earlier from the Gulf of Corinth, where they had waited in vain for the expected Carthaginian fleet. After cruising in the gulf and encouraging his garrisons, Philip sailed north to Demetrias (Volos). Significantly and in acknowledgement that every move that he had tried in the recent campaigns had been thwarted by Roman and allied naval superiority, he also ordered the building of 100 more ships at his yards in Chalkidiki.

Attalus, meanwhile had withdrawn with his ships to his kingdom, to deal with troubles there, and it seems that, with no other objectives in the Aegean, the Roman squadron returned to its bases in Illyria.[18]

THE FINAL ACT

206 BC

In 206 BC, Scipio inflicted a crushing defeat on the Carthaginians at the Battle of Ilipa and then proceeded to complete his conquest of the Punic empire in Hispania. Towards the end of the campaign, the Punic forces under Hannibal's younger brother, Mago, had been pushed back to Gades

(Cadiz) with their remaining ships. The Romans planned to advance on the port, while Laelius attacked by sea, for which operation he mustered a quinquireme and seven triremes. This force, out of the fifty or so warships available to Scipio, seems almost nominal but must have been thought sufficient to deal with the Punic ships known to be sheltering at Gades. In view of the size of the force that it later met (a quinquireme and eight triremes) and which was only part of the Punic naval strength at Gades, it could be suspected that Roman intelligence reports were at fault; alternatively that further Roman naval forces were following Laelius.

After some delays, the operation got under way and Laelius led the first Roman warships to have operated beyond the Mediterranean, out into the Atlantic. The Carthaginians had meantime uncovered a plot to betray Gades to the Romans and put the plotters aboard a quinquireme which was ordered to take them to Carthage. The ship sailed, followed shortly by a squadron of eight triremes, commanded by Adherbal. The Romans had not gone far beyond the Pillars of Hercules before the Punic ships ran into them. Laelius attacked at once, but all the ships were under the influence of the current which runs strongly into the Mediterranean, rendering tactics all but impossible and sweeping the ships along, virtually unable to manoeuvre. The Mediterranean Sea loses by evaporation far more than it gains from the rivers that flow into it and the difference is made up by a huge, constant flow of water from the Atlantic Ocean, inward through the Straits of Gibraltar. The Punic quinquireme which had been leading went by and could not turn back against the tide to assist and whilst the two groups of triremes tried to battle it out, the Roman quinquireme, which was in formation with its triremes, was better able to manoeuvre, having greater oarpower than the triremes, and managed to ram and sink two of the Punic triremes and shear the oars off from the side of a third. Adherbal managed to get away with the remaining five triremes to the African coast and escape.[19]

For Mago, Hispania was lost and he managed, in addition to having thirty warships, to obtain enough ships to extricate the remainder of his army and to evacuate Gades, the last outpost of Punic Hispania. After an abortive attack on Carthago Nova, he reached the Balearic Islands, where they wintered. It seems likely that the sacrifice of the triremes in the recent action off Gades was a deliberate cover for the escape of the quinquireme. Surely the transport of a few traitors, who could have been simply dealt with by Mago, disguised the true nature of the mission, namely to take Mago's report on the loss of Hispania and details of his plans to join Hannibal, back to Carthage. The absence of naval activity by the superior Roman fleet is curious, especially with such a capable admiral as Laelius in command. No attempt seems to have been made to blockade Mago in Gades, nor to intercept his evacuation. Perhaps the Roman effort was needed to secure the more important new acquisitions, enabling Mago to escape in the confusion; his 'army' of course need not to have been any more than a token surviving force by this time.[20]

Scipio next sailed with Laelius to Africa to seek an alliance with Syphax, a powerful ruler of Numidia in what is now northern Algeria. They sailed in two quinquiremes, arriving on the African coast to find seven Punic triremes, commanded by another Hasdrubal, about to enter harbour. Before the Punic ships could turn to engage the Romans in the open sea, Laelius ordered full speed and the two ships entered the harbour. The Carthaginians dared not attack the Romans in the neutral harbour, especially as they were also on a mission to curry favour with Syphax. Scipio managed to conclude a treaty with Syphax and his successor, Massinissa and sailed for Hispania under cover of stormy weather, four days later. We do not know if or how the Punic ships tried to stop him, but by all events, they did not do so.

205 BC   In 205 BC, Mago left the Balearics and sailed to Liguria, where he attempted to incite the Ligurians and Gauls against Rome, intending then to try to join Hannibal in Italy. Scipio meanwhile, now that Hispania was secure, was able to send troops back to Italy. In the east the Romans renewed their alliance with Pergamum in 205.

The Macedonian War had been winding down for some time and finally ended in 205 BC, helped by the arrival of Publius Sempronius with substantial numbers of fresh troops and thirty-five warships at Dyrrachium (Durazzo, Durres). Fifteen of the ships were detached and sent to Aetolia, the remainder reinforcing the squadron previously stationed in the east. The Romans wanted to concentrate all of their energies on the coming campaign which they were planning for Africa and this extra show of force was to indicate that either the war was to be resolved now or they would pull out of the Macedonian War completely and regardless. The Greeks were also tired of the war and peace terms were finally agreed. So far as Rome was concerned, for a minimum investment in warships, a potential major ally of Carthage had been neutralised and Rome's essential trade routes to the east had been kept open.

Carthage did try to send reinforcements and supplies to Hannibal in 205 BC, but the ships of their convoy were driven before a storm to Sardinia and captured.[21] They were successful however in sending twenty-five warships with reinforcements to join Mago and his thirty warships in Liguria, further confirming that they had his despatches with his plans, sent before his escape from Hispania, to know that he was there.

Scipio was elected as a Consul for 205 BC and he resolved to finish Carthage off. Having concluded the war in Hispania and Greece and isolated Hannibal in Bruttium, it was time for an offensive against Carthage itself. Whilst Scipio concentrated and trained his army in Sicily, Laelius,

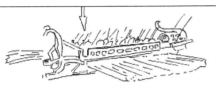

Above: from a wall painting at Pompeii showing the position for mounting of a gangway or bridge.

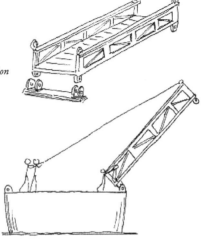

Gangway is raised and manhandled across the deck.

The lower lugs are secured to the deck brackets and it is ready to be dropped onto an enemy deck.

 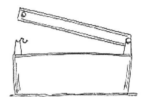

Above: this method would allow it to be deployed on either beam without having to be manhandled across the deck.

Below: an even simpler solution which would allow for a greater length of gangway.

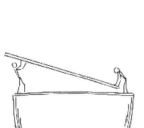  

THE BOARDING GANGWAY

The corvus, *though highly successful in battle, proved to be disastrous to a galley's seagoing abilities, particularly in rough weather. As a result the navy developed the 'boarding gangway'; a device that could operate much like a* corvus *but had the advantage of being stowed away during normal sailing. No direct evidence of the construction or design of these gangways survive and the three suggestions offered above are based upon only limited pictorial and textual references.*

commanding the fleet, carried out raids on the enemy coast and in particular, the area of Hippo Zarhytus (Bizerta). These raids caused some panic in Carthage, where they must have had wind of Scipio's preparations in Sicily. Although the raids caused little real damage to the Carthaginians, other than some dismay and considerable unease, the main purpose would have been to gather intelligence of their strength and dispositions, in anticipation of the coming invasion.

In Sicily, the navy had to oversee the gathering of sufficient transport ships to convey the army to Africa, with all its stores, equipment and food and to maintain it for the duration of its stay there. These ships all had to be victualled, fitted out and made seaworthy and their crews instructed in the tasks which would be required of them; finally, they had to be loaded for the voyage. The navy had to ensure that its own ships were battle-ready and to maintain constant patrols and be in readiness to face any attempt by the Punic navy to interfere in the preparations, or the invasion itself. Many of the allied towns of Italy donated various stores, such as sail-cloth, pikes, grain and timber for the fleet.[22]

204 BC   All was ready by the spring of 204 BC and the fleet sailed for Africa. There were nearly 400 transports and the naval escort comprised Scipio, with his brother Lucius with twenty ships on the right of the fleet and Laelius, as admiral with his Quaestor, Marcus Portius Cato as second in command with another twenty ships on the left. This was the close escort for the transports and the main battle-fleet would have been nearby, having detached smaller, fast ships to watch the enemy coast against a sortie by the Punic navy, a task ideally suited to the newly introduced *liburnae*. For the crossing during the hours of darkness, warships were to show one light, transports two lights and the flagships, three. The crossing was uneventful and the fleet safely made the African coast; they had set out after dark and after the following day and night at sea, landed just after sunrise on the second day, 110 sea miles in forty-eight hours. The fleet landed Scipio with an army of some 30,000 men near to Utica.

Scipio established a base on a defensible promontory jutting into the sea which he named Castra Cornelia. Although it had not been much in evidence, the Punic navy still existed and in considerable numbers, with its home bases very near. The campaign got under way slowly at first, the Romans being intent on securing their bridgehead and the navy closely watching out for their seaward side and guarding their essential line of supply. As there was no question of being able, even in part, to live off the land, the maritime supply route was the only one and if it was cut, Scipio and his army would be lost.

203 BC   In 203 BC, to cover the invasion of Africa, the Roman navy deployed 160 warships, requiring more than 30,000 men for crews and rowers, plus

marines. Apart from the forty ships under Laelius with Scipio in Africa, a further forty, under the command of Pomponius, were allotted for the defence of Sicily; these two squadrons could reinforce each other as needed and co-operate in covering the supply convoys to and from Africa. A further thirteen ships were later transferred to Pomponius' command so that the squadrons could be kept up to strength whilst ships were systematically withdrawn for overhaul.

For the Sardinian area and to cover any move by Mago's ships, Gnaeus Octavius was given command of another forty ships with 2000 marines. Finally, Marcus Marcius commanded a further forty ships with 3000 marines, guarding the Italian coast. These numbers would suggest that the complement of marines on each ship had been halved to provide troops to replace or augment those in Scipio's command.

At this time, Rome had an army of twenty legions, which with allied contingents, totalled about 120,000 men. The extent to which the navy formed a major part of the military establishment is demonstrated by its employment of a third of the state's military manpower in addition to supporting shore bases and the vast costs of its ships and their gear. Throughout the war the Roman fleets seem to have averaged about 240 ships of all types, requiring, with marines, some 60,000 personnel.

In Africa, Scipio began to increase pressure on the Carthaginians and loaded his ships with catapults and siege equipment and made a feint as if to assault Utica from the sea. The enemy army came out to fight and was defeated. From Utica, Scipio advanced to Tunis, very near to Carthage itself, from where the Punic fleet at last made a sortie and tried to attack the Roman fleet. The Romans were still digging in to their new positions when the enemy fleet was sighted. The Roman warships were moored bow-on to the shore to be able to use their siege equipment with which they were still heavily loaded as well as with booty from Utica; they could not be cleared and turned around and got to the open sea for action in time. Scipio ordered the ships to be pulled as close into the shore as possible and for the transports to be lashed together with their masts and spars stepped and lashed horizontally across the decks between them ship to ship; the transports were so lashed, forming a four-deep cordon around the warships and making a floating fortification onto which troops were put.[23]

The Carthaginian fleet meanwhile had inexplicably and most obligingly made anchor some way off, delaying their attack and thereby giving the Romans the very time they needed to complete their own preparations. The next morning the Punic fleet formed up for a formal naval engagement and waited, but no Roman ships emerged. Finally the Carthaginians attacked but as the decks of the unladen transports were higher than those of the warships, it was as if they were attacking city walls. Small Roman assault craft darted out from between the transports to counter-attack the Punic ships, but only got in the way and were withdrawn. The Punic attack failed and they backed water and withdrew.

Later they attacked again and this time concentrated on trying to grapple the transports and pull them out of formation and in this way they managed to cause some disruption. The Romans, unable to stop them, with difficulty cut the grappled ships free and some sixty transports were lost and towed off by the Carthaginians. The Punic triumph was illusory however as the remaining three lines of transports were intact and the warships secure and undamaged.

Hannibal was finally recalled from Italy and he managed to improvise a fleet to transport his army home. This he managed to do, evading any Roman patrols. However, to do this, instead of heading directly toward Carthage, he had to swing well to the south-east to land safely at Leptis Minor.

His brother Mago had failed in his attempt to stir up the Ligurians and Gauls against Rome and although he advanced to the valley of the Padus, 203 BC he was defeated and had had to retreat to the west coast. In 203 BC in the only successful large-scale Punic naval operation of the war, he and his forces were evacuated. Mago died of wounds on the return trip and some of his ships were intercepted and captured off Sardinia by Octavius' squadron; the remainder managed to land and join Hannibal.

Talks were opened between the antagonists about an armistice, one of the peace terms proposed by the Romans was for the surrender of the Punic fleet. When part of a Roman supply convoy was driven ashore by a storm, near to Carthage, some Punic warships were sent out to round up some of the beached and wrecked Roman transports and to seize their cargoes, a belligerent act in breach of the armistice. At the same time, a Roman quinquireme carrying envoys to the talks was sent from Tunis to Carthage and was welcomed there; when it sailed upon its return, Carthage provided an escort of two triremes, who turned for home when they sighted the Roman camp.

The main Carthaginian fleet however, had been laying somewhere to the west off Utica and three of its quadriremes[24] came in from seaward and attacked the Roman ship as she approached the camp.[25] The Roman successfully evaded their rams and as her decks were higher, she could not be boarded; despite putting up a fight, the Roman ship was forced onto the shore, now lined by their troops. The ship was lost on grounding but the crew was saved. It is not known what induced this attack, whether a Punic captain, knowing nothing of the armistice talks, saw an opportune target present itself or a pro-war faction deliberately out to sabotage the talks (Polybius was certain that it was the latter). In any event it proved to be the last foray of the Carthaginian navy. The armistice was off.

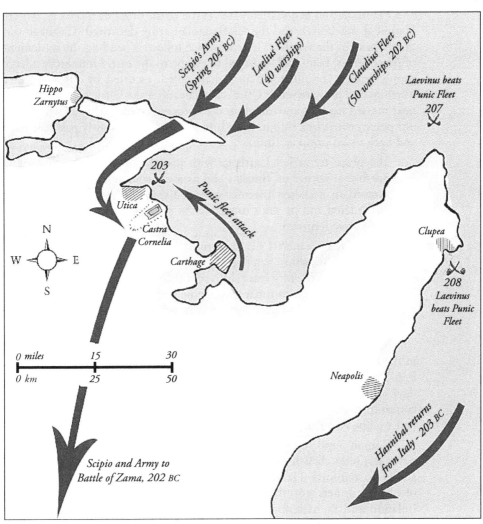

THE CARTHAGE CAMPAIGN, 204–202 BC

202 BC   For 202 BC, Claudius was given command of fifty quinquiremes to be sent to join Laelius in Africa, which together would give the Romans overwhelming naval superiority. The ships came mainly from the squadron at Ostia and so twenty of the ships of the Sicily squadron were withdrawn to Ostia to replace them. Faced by even more Roman ships and with Scipio's army over-running the other Punic seaports along the African coast, their navy had become effectively confined to Carthage and made no further attempt to intervene in the war.

Hannibal and Scipio finally met at the Battle of Zama in 202 BC, where Hannibal was beaten and the Carthaginian army destroyed; Carthage was finally beaten, the war lost. An armistice followed pending the settlement of peace terms. Hannibal managed to escape to the east. From Sicily a large supply convoy, bound for Scipio, had sailed, escorted by the fifty extra warships and they arrived at Utica a few days after the Battle of Zama. Scipio next massed his fleet and sailed on it in procession to Carthage, which sent out peace envoys in a ship to meet him; he then sailed slowly past Carthage and back to his camp at Tunis.

The peace terms left Carthage with just the territory surrounding it (the north-east corner of Tunisia) and as a dependant 'ally' of Rome. She was allowed to keep ten triremes as guard-ships but otherwise her navy was surrendered and its ships towed out to sea and burned. The captured transports were returned.

201 BC   For the next year, 201 BC, the armed forces were reduced to fourteen legions and 100 warships. Scipio remained in Africa with the original thirty-nine warships and the fifty extra ships sent there were recalled, forty of them being returned to their commands at Rome and Sicily and the other ten sent under Marcus Fabius to join the Sardinia squadron. The other ships were paid off and decommissioned.

The great war was ended with Rome not only the supreme naval power in the western Mediterranean (which she had effectively been after the First Punic War) but the only one. From start to finish and even in their darkest days after the losses of Cannae, the Romans had never wavered in their commitment to maintaining the strongest navy, a commitment that alone had swallowed an eighth of their annual national expenditure.

Roman naval superiority had proved to be absolutely crucial and was never seriously challenged. They were able to deny the Carthaginians the ability to reinforce Hannibal, their allies to help him and even though blockade runners got through, the inevitable result was his increasing isolation and the deterioration of his position. Ultimately it was also his increasing irrelevance as the Romans dictated the course of the war. They were able to secure Corsica, Sardinia and eventually, Sicily and use the produce of the islands to underwrite their food and supplies, at the same time denying similar succour to Carthage. They could field support and supply their armies in Hispania, dictating that the main theatre of war should be there and forcing their enemy to maintain its maximum effort there, away from Italy.

Finally, the continuous raids and operations on the African coast ensured that they always had intelligence of events in the enemy homeland, which although suffering only superficial damage, was left feeling insecure. The trade routes upon which Carthaginian prosperity depended were severely damaged, while Roman trade could continue uninterrupted. The once-great Punic navy had never recovered from the destruction of its morale in the First Punic War, not even building up its numbers, and at no time mounted a serious challenge. The Romans retained the initiative at sea throughout and the naval supremacy that they maintained largely ensured their eventual and complete victory.

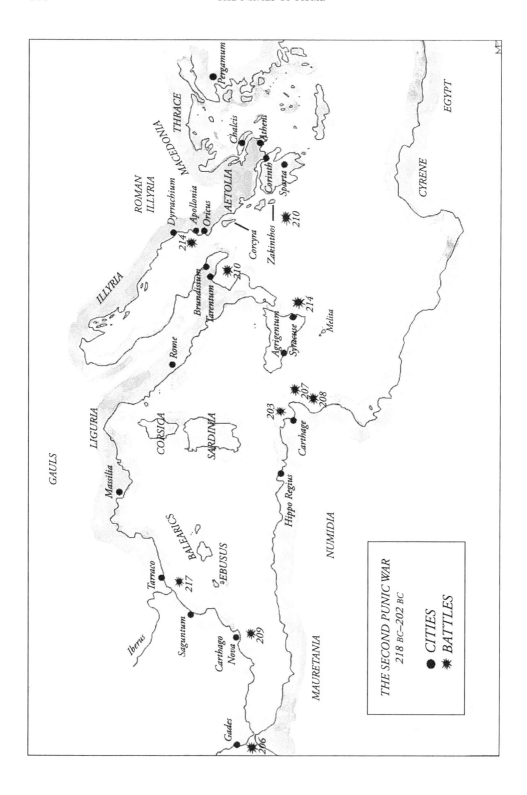

THE SECOND PUNIC WAR
218 BC–202 BC

● CITIES
✸ BATTLES

NOTES

1. Polybius II.10.
2. James & Thorpe, *Ancient Inventions*; Sprague de Camp, *The Ancient Engineers*.
3. Polybius II.11.
4. Polybius III.19; see also Scullard and Rodgers.
5. This interpretation arises from a general consideration of the sources and authorities.
6. Polybius III.41; Livy XXI.17.
7. Gaul, *Malta, Gozo & Camino*.
8. Casson *SSAW*; Starr; Peddie, *The Roman War Machine*.
9. For the general course of the varied operations, both Livy (XXI to XXX) and Polybius (III) are the prime sources and have been followed, together with the commentary in Rodgers.
10. Livy XXIV.11. Presumably referring to the reasoning as to the annual production of warships in Chapter 2, this was a programme for future building over the course of the next few years, eg. twenty-five per annum for four years or such like.
11. Livy says (XXIV.34) that the naval assault was on the district of Achradina but it is bounded to seaward by cliffs and offshore by shallows and rocks and is unsuitable for approach. There are also no remnants of walls to be seen, which would indicate that it had not been thought needed there. An assault on the (protected) mole of the Little Harbour is a possibility but limited in frontage and open to flanking fire from both sides. The only prominent surviving fortifications (medieval atop ancient foundations) are along the western side of Ortygia and this is averred to be the target of the assault, being the only sizeable approach offering clear, reasonably deep water. Polybius (VIII.4) also states that Achradina was the point of attack but his geography is faulty more than once and again, why would Marcellus, having made such careful preparations, send his ships over rocks to attack a cliff? A walk around the seaward perimeter of the city reveals much.
12. A road bridge now closes the original harbour entrance, which is no more than 150 yards across and thus well within bow shot.
13. There is no information on the size or composition of the Syracusan fleet at this time, but it was contained in harbour throughout the siege by the overwhelming strength of the besieging Roman fleet.
14. This shows that each ship to be used had approximately 300 rowers and were thus quinquiremes.
15. Quinctus' formation must have been very second-rate. Interestingly, Livy (XXVI.20) mentions the Punic fleet being ordered to blockade the city of Tarentum in 211. They failed in this but if they or some of their units were there, might they not have been the cause of Quinctus' defeat? This is offered by way of explanation, not excuse as if it were so, Quinctus' lack of reconnaissance was at fault.
16. Rodgers has calculated the Roman navy to have had 280 ships in commission, with 60,000 personnel in 280 but the numbers of men needed for such a fleet must have been greater than this.
17. See Norwich, *A History of Venice*.
18. Livy XXVIII.8. Polybius' account of this period is lost.
19. Livy XXVIII.30 as to the battle and Bradford, *Ulysses Found* as to sea conditions.
20. Although Livy reports (XXVIII.46) that he had 14,000 troops and captured Genua.
21. If they were bound for Hannibal it is a mystery how they could end up in Sardinia. Either they were meant for Mago, or as another attempt to foment trouble in Sardinia.
22. Livy XXVIII.45, sets out the full list, including the laying down of ten quadriremes and twenty quinquiremes, presumably to counter anticipated losses.
23. Livy XXX.9.
24. Polybius (XV.2) says that they were triremes.
25. Although Livy (XXX.25) says that they came from the west, these attacking ships must have been to the east, to be able to see, let alone intercept, Tunis being to the south-south-east of Carthage.

THE GROWTH OF EMPIRE

201 BC–86 BC

I f the Romans thought that they had earned a respite to repair the ravages of the long wars and to enjoy the fruits of their hard-won victory, they were soon to be disappointed.

In the eastern Mediterranean a precarious balance of power had been maintained between Macedonia, the Seleucid kingdom in Anatolia, the Levant and Ptolemaic Egypt and lesser leagues and independent states. In 203 BC, Ptolemy IV of Egypt died, to be succeeded by his five-year-old son Ptolemy V. That winter, Philip V of Macedon formed an alliance with Antiochus of Syria (the Seleucid king) to exploit this and seize Ptolemaic possessions in the Aegean and Levant respectively. In 202 BC Antiochus invaded northern Palestine whilst Philip, using the new fleet that he had ordered to be built in 207 BC, attacked some cities along the Propontis (Sea of Marmara). Philip's fleet now had over fifty major ships and apart from his quadriremes and quinquiremes, had a 'ten' as flagship, together with some 'sevens' and 'eights'. He further supplemented this fleet by hiring some pirate captains to harry the Rhodians.[1]

In 201 BC Philip, having moved into the Hellespont, annexed the Cyclades and occupied the island of Samos, capturing some ships and destroying an Egyptian fleet there, thereby ending the Ptolemaic naval presence in the Aegean. He next attacked the territory of Pergamum; at sea he was beaten in a battle off Chios by the joint Pergamene and Rhodian fleets under Attalus, King of Pergamum. Philip in turn later defeated them near Miletus and advanced into Caria. This victory was however Pyrrhic as it cost Philip about a half of his combat fleet in losses and he was unable to thereafter seriously challenge the allies at sea. Rhodes and Pergamum, both allies of Rome, appealed to her for help.

There survives a near-contemporary account of the battle off Chios, written by Polybius about fifty years after it, which illustrates only too vividly the chaos of a battle between giant galleys dominated by traditional ramming tactics.[2] The allied fleets had sixty-five heavy ships and a dozen or

203 BC

201 BC

so triremes and smaller types, while Philip had fifty-three heavy and about 150 light, open boats. The fleets formed up in line abreast and then came together in a general melee:

> 'Attalus' ship attacked an eight and getting its blow in first, struck it mortally below the waterline; although the marines on its deck kept fighting for a long while, eventually he sank it. The flagship of Philip's fleet, a ten, fell into the enemy's hands in an unexpected fashion. A trireme class galley came into its path and it rammed the vessel with a mighty blow amidships, below the thranite oars, the ram however, stuck fast since the commander was not able to keep a check on his ship's impetus. So, with the vessel hanging from it, it was in a hopeless situation, utterly unable to move.
>
> 'At that moment, two fives fell upon it and wounding it fatally, one on each side, they destroyed the ship and all aboard, including Democrates, Philip's admiral. At the same time that this happened, Dionysodorus and Dinocrates, brothers and admirals on Attalus' side, launched attacks, one on an enemy seven, the other on an eight and suffered strange experiences in their combats. In his attack on an eight, Dinocrates' ship received a blow above the waterline, since the opposing vessel had his bows elevated, but struck the enemy below the waterline. At first he was unable to break free, despite repeated attempts at backing water and since the Macedonian marines were fighting courageously, he was in the greatest danger. Attalus came to his aid; by delivering a blow on the enemy ship, he broke the embrace of the two vessels and Dinocrates was in this unexpected fashion, set free. The enemy marines all fought courageously but they were destroyed and Attalus' men took over the undefended ship. Dionysodorus, charging with great force to deliver a blow not only missed doing any harm but, being carried on past the enemy, lost his starboard oars and the timbers supporting his rowers were shattered. As soon as this happened, enemy vessels surrounded him. Amid shouts and confusion the ship was destroyed with all aboard except for Dionysodorus and two others who managed to swim to a small ship that came to their aid.'

The description serves to illustrate the various effects of a well-delivered ram attack; in the first instance, the attack on an eight caused the big ship to settle slowly because the marines on board were able to keep on fighting. The later instance where a ship 'was destroyed with all aboard' indicates that the victim was broken and settled quickly. The thought of the hundreds of rowers below decks scrambling to escape (in the absence of any evidence that life-saving devices were carried) once in the water, trying to find and hang onto some flotsam in the hope of eventual rescue, defies description. On the other hand, the possible disastrous effect of a mis-timed ramming attack on the attacker is also illustrated by the fate of Dionysodorus' ship. A few more interesting points emerge: firstly the great variation of height in the impact of the rams, from below the waterline to just below the thranite or uppermost tier of oars, when Philip's 'ten' hit a trireme; the pitching and roll of the ships and the rise and fall of the seas could make all the difference between a blow proving fatal or not. Secondly, although most if not all of the bigger ships must have been so fitted, no mention is made of the effect of artillery shooting. Presumably it is included in the general description of 'fighting' but was not decisive enough to warrant specific mention. Finally, when a ship was stopped and immobile or disabled, none of the now-redundant rowers are mentioned as coming on deck to join the fighting to augment the marines. On both sides the only 'tactic' employed was to charge at the enemy and join in a general and unstructured melee and to use the ram whenever an opportunity could be seized; it was only when ships became stuck together that an infantry fight took place. In contrast, the Romans always sought to grapple and seek an infantry fight by boarding.

201 BC   In north-west Italy, the Ligurian tribes were again proving troublesome, threatening the Padus valley and Etruria. In 201 BC the Romans marched against them with naval backing and secured control of Luna and Genua (Genoa), two important ports which would and did enable rapid deployment by sea in the event of recurring trouble in the area.[3]

For their 'peacetime' naval dispositions, the Romans at this time maintained an active fleet in Sicily of as many as fifty combat ships, mostly quinquiremes. Other active units of varying strength were kept in the lower Adriatic and Tyrrhenian seas but the Sicily fleet was the navy's lynch-pin. From that strategic, central position ships could be deployed in any direction and it was there that naval forces were to be concentrated in preparation for operations further afield. From the way in which substantial numbers of ships would be re-commissioned from time to time, it is clear that a large fleet of reserve ships was maintained in very good, indeed seagoing, order. This presupposes the organisation of naval dockyards with personnel and facilities for ship-upkeep at various ports in Italy.

200 BC   In the east, the alliance of two of the three powers there against the third had upset the balance of power and troubles continued to mount in Greece and in Athens in particular. A Macedonian squadron seized four Athenian warships. Rome's allies, Rhodes and Pergamum, supported Athens, who thereupon declared war against Philip and also appealed to Rome for help.[4] Philip sent one of his generals into Athenian territory, following which he crossed to Asia Minor and took the Pergamene seaport of Abydos on the Hellespont.

The Romans appointed their veteran commander of the First Macedonian War, Publius Sulpicius Galba, who crossed with two legions to Apollonia, supported by a fleet of thirty-eight ships from the Sicily squadron, under Laevinus. The Romans had already previously operated with the Pergamene and Rhodian navies; now they also had Athens with her fleet as an ally and the base facilities that she could provide on the western side of the Aegean. Despite Philip's fleet, Rome and her allies together would have naval superiority from the start. The allied fleet, with Laevinus in overall command, comprised Roman ships making up half of its number and the other half allied ships. Immediately after landing their troops, a squadron was dispatched to Athens carrying a thousand of the troops (presumably in addition to its regular complement of marines). Twenty triremes were sent and were joined at Athens by three Rhodian quadriremes. Having thus secured the seas adjacent to Athens and bolstered its garrison, the Roman squadron proceeded to mount a surprise attack on, capture and sack the Macedonian stronghold of Chalcis on the island of Euboea. With insufficient troops to garrison their prize, the Romans then withdrew. Philip meanwhile, advanced toward Athens, to find that he had been pre-empted by the strengthened garrison there and with Galba advancing from the west on his flank, he had to withdraw to Macedonia for the winter.

199 BC   In the coming year (199 BC) the allies planned for the fleet to attack the enemy in its home ports of Chalkidiki, whilst Galba advanced overland from the west. The naval campaign met with only modest success, but did capture Oreus and generally held control of the Aegean, Philip's fleet failing to make any challenge. The Romans sent more warships to strengthen their 'Eastern Fleet', increasing it to fifty ships. The allied fleet was composed of the fifty Roman warships, to which was added twenty-four Pergamene and twenty Rhodian ships. Most of the Roman and Pergamene ships were quinquiremes, whereas the Rhodians favoured quadriremes; the rest were most likely triremes although there were, in addition, liburnians and several dozen small mostly open 'conter' type large boats rather than ships, for ancillary duties. Philip's navy never exceeded twenty heavy fighting ships, plus many smaller and thus could never hope to seriously challenge the allies.

198 BC   In 198 BC, Galba was replaced by the Consul Titus Quinctius Flaminius who drove Philip from central Greece. The allied fleet, commanded by the Consul's brother, Lucius, concentrated at Andros, then sailed to attack enemy coasts and captured Eretria on Euboea, following which it sailed back to Corinth to meet Flaminius and support his attack upon it. Corinth was massively reinforced however and the siege abandoned. The fleet withdrew to Piraeus, where the allies wintered, the Romans carrying on to Corcyra for the Winter.

197 BC   The Flaminius brothers continued in command for the following year (197 BC). Lucius with the fleet attacked and captured the island of Leucas in the Ionian Sea, thereby dominating the adjacent Greek coast and the entrance to the Gulf of Patras and Corinth, forcing Philip's forces back into the hinterland. The Rhodians attacked Philip's forces in Asia Minor and finally, Titus decisively defeated him at the Battle of Cynoscephalae. The war

was at an end and Philip, as part of the peace settlement, had to surrender all but six ships of his navy, described by Polybius[5] as 'five light vessels and his huge flagship in which the men rowed eight to an oar', in fact a 'sixteen'. In 195 BC Nabis, the Tyrant of Sparta who had sided with Philip, was forced to surrender Argos and his fleet after an allied campaign. The Romans, having settled affairs, evacuated Greece by 194 BC, with the exception of the naval squadron which remained in the Aegean, but reduced in strength to twenty-five ships.

195 BC

At sea the Roman navy with its allies had held unchallenged naval supremacy in the Aegean throughout the war, but only had limited opportunity to play a part in what had been an essentially land war. Nevertheless, the surrender of enemy naval forces were again a prominent item of the peace terms and at its end, the war left one less naval power.

From 197 BC there had been insurrection in Hispania and the army there was increased to four legions, the supply convoys and their escorts increasing accordingly.

WAR IN THE EAST– SELEUCIA

Antiochus, the Seleucid king, with the defeat of Macedonia, thought that there was a power vacuum and thus an opportunity. He marched his army along the coast of Asia Minor in 197 BC, carefully going around Rhodian and Pergamene lands, although he took and secured the important neutral port city of Ephesus, which lay between their respective territories, as an Aegean base. He then besieged the cities of Smyrna and Lampsacus, who appealed to Rome. The Romans issued a warning, which Antiochus ignored, and crossed the Hellespont and in 196 BC, seized part of the Thracian coast. Rome had, with her settlement of Greek affairs, become de facto protector of the Greek states and although Antiochus had assiduously not encroached upon Rome's friends, it was one step too far. There followed some complex diplomacy, not helped by Hannibal, who had appeared at Antiochus' court and who was not unreasonably suspected of fomenting war. The Aetolians, disappointed that despite their war efforts their demands had not been met by the peace, sought to combine Philip of Macedon, Nabis of Sparta and Antiochus in an alliance against Rome.

Philip, after his recent defeat, was not interested; Nabis was willing but broke his treaty and moved too soon and the Achaeans defeated him on land, supported by the Roman squadron which, with allied ships, attacked his naval base of Gythion, landing troops. By 194 BC, the last Roman garrisons had been withdrawn from Greece, only the twenty-five strong Aegean Squadron remaining on station. Antiochus did however, encourage the Aetolians in their designs. In Rome it seemed that despite all their efforts to have peace in the east, they were again being drawn into a

194 BC

war there. The Romans set about preparing an army and increased the fleet at Sicily to seventy quinquiremes, to form a strong reserve of ships which could be sent to the east. Ships laid up after the Punic War were refitted and recommissioned as part of this build-up and a programme was instituted to build thirty new quinqiremes.[6]

192 BC   Despite suffering some reverses, the Aetolians seized Demetrias in Thessaly, thus providing a base for Antiochus' ships and late in the year (192 BC) he finally landed troops there, supported by a fleet of forty heavy and sixty light warships, covering 200 transports with nearly 11,000 men. The Roman squadron was on the Boeotian coast, south of the landing site and on the mainland opposite to Euboea. Antiochus set about attacking Chalcis but one of his generals on the mainland made the mistake of attacking a Roman detachment, marching to join the ships. It was open war; the main Roman fleet, under the Praetor Atilius, was in the lower Adriatic between Brundisium and Corcyra and two legions with a close escort of another thirty ships made ready to cross to Apollonia.

191 BC   Antiochus had gained Euboea and Boeotia and most of central Greece, but the Romans secured the co-operation of Philip of Macedon who, having so recently been beaten by them, was in no hurry to repeat the experience and also no doubt, mindful that his 'ally' had not exactly hurried to help him and who was in fact more of a rival than a friend. In early 191 BC, the Roman army was once more transported across to Apollonia and started to force Antiochus back across central Greece. They and their Greek allies finally caught Antiochus at Thermopylae and soundly beat him, after which he fled, with the remains of his army, back to Asia Minor, nevertheless losing a supply convoy to interception by the Roman squadron.[7]

The war would now have to be concluded in Asia Minor, but before this, mastery of the seas would have to be secured against a new enemy who had a powerful navy. Claudius Livius Salinator was put in command of a fleet of fifty quinquiremes and triremes and, according to the chronicles, six Carthaginian ships. This seems to be a curious report as the peace treaty only allowed Carthage a total of only ten triremes and it seems unlikely that she would risk the majority of her scant naval resources on such a foray. It may well be that the surviving account is incomplete and, perhaps, the reference is in fact to Roman ships manned by drafts of Carthaginians, or to Roman ships withdrawn from a guard squadron at Carthage. Alternatively of course, it may just be correct although curiously perhaps, they are not mentioned again in the sources. This fleet sailed to Aegina in the Aegean to join the fleet of Pergamum (now ruled by Eumenes, the son of Rome's friend Attalus). Livius was there reinforced by the Roman squadron already in the Aegean, bringing his total strength up to seventy-five Roman ships and further by the decision of Rhodes to join Rome, with her own considerable navy. Antiochus was then at the Hellespont with his fleet of seventy large ships, under the command of his admiral, Polyxenidas. This fleet he sent to his base at Ephesus, which, although secure, was far removed from the Hellespont. In doing so, however, Antiochus had relinquished possession of the Hellespont, which was of course, the key strategic objective as whoever held it dictated who could cross it or pass through it. From Ephesus however, Polyxenidas intended a sortie against Livius to attack him before the Rhodian ships could join him.

The fleets met off Cape Corycus in September 191 BC, the allies having superior numbers, with their seventy-five Roman and twenty-five Pergamene ships. Sailing south with Livius in the van, followed by Eumenes' ships, the allied fleet came upon Polyxenidas' fleet drawn up ready for battle with his right flank towards and protected by the shore. Livius' ships downed sails and cleared for action, deploying into line abreast of about thirty ships and stood to to give Eumenes time to bring his ships into line to seaward of the Romans. Two 'Carthaginian' ships got ahead of the formation and were promptly set upon by three of the enemy, who raked the sides of one of them, breaking its oars and rendering it immobile; the ship was then boarded and taken, the other escaping. The rest of the Roman line then came into a general engagement as the two fleet met and by grappling and boarding the Romans soon got the upper hand. As Eumenes' ships came into the attack to seaward and started to outflank him, Polyxenidas broke off the battle and fled back to Ephesus. The allies' victory had cost them the loss of one ship, but the enemy lost ten destroyed and thirteen captured.

The following day the Rhodians arrived, adding their twenty-seven ships to the allied fleet and giving it overwhelming superiority. Antiochus had lost command of the sea and with it, the ability to prevent the Romans from crossing to Asia and to maintain their presence there. The allies conducted a naval parade just off the coast by Ephesus which, not surprisingly, failed to tempt Polyxenidas to come out and offer battle. Being unable to achieve anything more, the allies withdrew, the Rhodians homeward and the Romans and Pergamene ships north to a harbour on the strait between the island of Lesbos and Pergamene territory on the adjacent mainland, from which they could control the approaches to the Hellespont and which they proceeded to fortify as winter quarters for the ships and crews.[8]

190 BC   For 190 BC, Lucius Cornelius Scipio, brother of the victor of Zama, was elected Consul and put in command of Greek affairs; command of the fleet was given to the Praetor, Lucius Aemilius Regillus and an additional twenty warships with a thousand marines and an additional 2200 troops were to be sent with him as reinforcements. The eastern fleet would have ninety-five warships, plus its allied contingents and any former enemy ships that had been re-commissioned. The Roman ships were mostly quinquiremes, with

some triremes. The Pergamene fleet included a few of the larger Hellenistic ships, sixes or sevens; the Rhodians, with a grand total of some fifty ships, preferred their lighter threes and fours. After effecting an armistice with the Aetolians and re-affirming the co-operation of Philip, the Consul's army started its march to the Hellespont from where it would cross to Asia Minor.

First however, the naval campaign would have to be completed, for although badly defeated, Antiochus' navy had spent the winter building up its strength. Polyxenidas now had nearly ninety ships, including two sevens and three sixes, under his command at Ephesus and Hannibal was raising another fleet in Antiochus' Phoenician and Syrian domains. Obviously if at all possible, the two had to be prevented from uniting. The Roman and Pergamene ships had spent the winter keeping Polyxenidas cooped up and in doing so, were themselves just as trapped; if they moved off station to intercept Hannibal, Polyxenidas could slip by them to join him or to seize the Hellespont; this left Rhodes alone to deal with Hannibal. Despite these constraints, in March of 190, thirty Roman and seven Pergamene ships were despatched to deal with some hostile shipping in the Hellespont which could have been used to disrupt any crossing. The squadron swept the area, to demonstrate its power and, securing the acquiescence of local ports, returned to their own base before their enemy could learn of, let alone try to take advantage of, their absence.

In the meantime, in their winter base the Roman and allied ships had been refitted and readied for use in the coming season. They experimented with the mounting of long booms or poles, extended forward beyond the bows of the ships, from which were suspended iron braziers or baskets filled with burning material and capable of being dropped on an enemy. Such a device is shown in a graffito at Alexandria of the first century BC, but otherwise is only mentioned twice by the sources in use as a weapon. Perhaps for obvious reasons it did not become popular, the risks outweighing its possible advantage; the graffito could in fact just as well be showing the device in use as a navigation light.[9]

190 BC   In April of 190 BC, despite the watch on his movements, Polyxenidas managed to slip out of harbour and fell upon a Rhodian squadron of twenty-seven ships which had come too close. The Rhodians were in a harbour just south of Ephesus, probably Panormus (approximately modern Kusadasi) and thus out of contact with their allies to the north. By first landing a strong force of troops to outflank them, the Rhodians were forced to man their ships and to try and break out of the harbour, where Polyxenidas' fleet was waiting for them and pounced as they emerged piecemeal from the narrow entrance. At least seven of the Rhodian ships broke through the gauntlet by suspending the braziers of burning material on long booms either side of

their bows; the other twenty ships were lost or captured by the trap.[10]

On hearing of this defeat, Livius had to move south and return to the blockade of Ephesus with his ships. Anticipating that Livius would do this, Polyxenidas sailed northward, intending to find and hide behind a suitable promontory and to ambush the rear of the Roman fleet line as it passed. Although the fleets came within sight of each other, the plan was frustrated by rough weather which forced them back to their respective bases. The new commander, Regillus joined the fleet but with only two extra ships, the rest having had to be stationed at various points en route from Italy to secure and keep the sea lanes open in the face of an upsurge in piracy. A last foray by Livius against the Lycian coast was unsuccessful, as was a cruise southward to Rhodes by the fleet under Regillus a little later. Antiochus' forces meanwhile had attacked Pergamum itself and Eumenes had to withdraw his fleet to defend his homeland. Although the immediate threat to Pergamum was relieved by the arrival of allied Achaean troops, it was decided by the allies that while the Roman and Rhodian fleets watched Polyxenidas, Eumenes' fleet should proceed to the Hellespont to cover the Roman army which was now nearing there.[11]

In June it was learned that Hannibal had sailed with a fleet of forty-seven ships, including three sevens and four sixes, ten triremes and thirty quinquiremes and fours from Phoenicia and was heading westwards along the Cilician coast. The Rhodians concentrated their fleet of thirty-two fours and four triremes, to intercept and despite their inferior numbers, were avenged by defeating him off Side. Hannibal's ships advanced in line of battle, with their right to shoreward and Hannibal on the left wing, to seaward. The Rhodians approached in sailing columns and their leading ships, under Eudamus, deployed to seaward to form up for battle. These ships, the Rhodian right, came into action against their opposite numbers quickly and before the rest of the Rhodian ships could deploy into line abreast. Accordingly any movement away from the shore was prevented and the rest of the Rhodian ships did not have room to form line abreast; instead they seem to have formed into short columns of a few ships in line ahead and forced their way between and behind the Syrian ships, effecting thereby a series of *diekplous* attacks.[12]

Although mostly smaller, the Rhodian ships were the fastest and their captains and crews the very best; their lightning attacks on the enemy's right wing completely overwhelmed it, just as Eudamus' ships offshore were themselves hard pressed and signalled for help. The Rhodian ships inshore now switched their attack to support Eudamus and, realising that he was hopelessly out-matched, Hannibal had to order retreat. Although the Rhodians only managed to capture one of his ships, a 'seven', and damaged and disabled about a dozen more. Hannibal had had enough and made no further attempt westward. The linking of the two fleets never took place. The Rhodians kept a squadron of twenty ships on the Cilician coast to watch for any repeat attack from the Levant, but none came.

By October 190 BC, allied naval strength watching Antiochus' fleet was reduced, some Roman and the Pergamene ships having been withdrawn to the Hellespont, as well as through the natural attrition caused by the long blockade. The fleet watching Ephesus now numbered fifty-eight Roman ships,[13] commanded by Regillus, supported by Eudamus of Rhodes with a squadron of twenty-two lighter ships and totalling some 20,000 men. The Syrians had not been idle and had built up their fleet with new construction, to a total of eighty-nine ships including three sixes, with 24,000 men and Polyxenidas was therefore ordered to break out and to attack the allies.

After attempting to stalk the Roman fleet, Polyxenidas just failed to catch them in harbour, the allies managing to man their ships and get to sea in time, and the fleets met off Myonnesus. Polyxenidas extended his line of ships so that his superior numbers would envelop the Roman right which was offshore. To counter this Eudamus led most of his Rhodian ships to protect the flank and Rhodian ships then harried and held the Syrians' offshore wing, whilst the Roman ships broke their centre in a classic *diekplous* attack, using their 'grapple and board' methods. The tactics were in fact, a virtual repeat of those used to defeat Polyxenidas at Corycus the year before. The battle developed into two distinct areas. On the one hand the Roman seaborne infantry battled methodically, overcoming one enemy, then moving onto the next and repeating the process; on the other hand the Rhodians used their swift, handy ships to attack with the ram and missiles and possibly even the threat of their fire baskets, while avoiding becoming entangled with the enemy. At the same they frustrated every attempt by the Rhodians to envelop the Romans who could thus concentrate on doing what they did best. Before long, Polyxenidas' left (offshore) wing was in retreat and the survivors of his fleet soon followed, back to the haven of Ephesus. Polyxenidas was defeated, losing thirteen ships sunk or burned and another twenty-nine captured, nearly half of his fleet. The Romans lost two ships with several more damaged and the Rhodians one.[14] With these two naval victories, Rome and her allies now controlled the Aegean and the coasts of Asia Minor. Antiochus managed to evacuate Thrace but could not stop the Romans from crossing, escorted by thirty Roman and the Rhodian ships, safely into Asia. Once across, they proceeded southward along the coast, where the navy could support and supply them. In a final operation for the year, the fleet laid siege to and took the enemy city and harbour of Phocaea (Foca) on the coast north of Smyrna, to use as a winter base and in anticipation of the arrival of the army.

Elsewhere, the Romans were re-establishing themselves in what is now

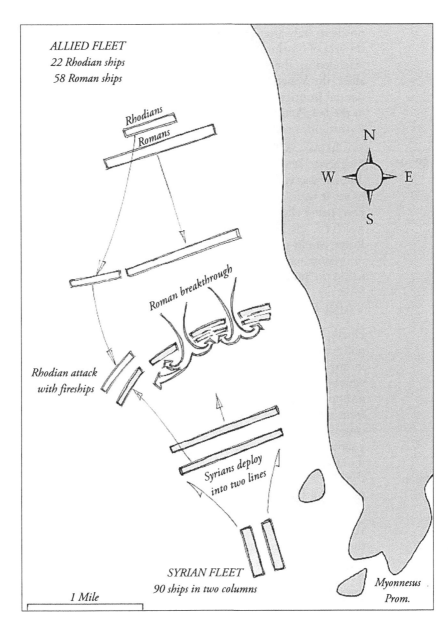

ALLIED FLEET
22 Rhodian ships
58 Roman ships

Rhodians

Romans

N

W   E

S

Roman breakthrough

Rhodian attack
with fireships

Syrians deploy
into two lines

SYRIAN FLEET
90 ships in two columns

Myonnesus
Prom.

1 Mile

THE BATTLE OF MYONNESUS – 190 BC

northern Italy after the Punic War and by 190 BC had pacified and settled the area of Cisalpine Gaul north-west to the Alps; in the north-east they had extended up the Adriatic coast past the Padus delta to meet up with their allies, the Veneti, at the northern end of that sea. Beyond the Veneti, the natural frontier of the Istrian peninsula, which had been subdued, but lost in the last Punic War, was falling prey to raiding tribesmen, who had to be warned off.

189 BC   In Asia Minor, the Romans finally met Antiochus at the Battle of Magnesia (Manisa) in January of 189 BC, where they destroyed his army. The war was ended and Antiochus had to vacate most of Asia Minor. Once more, it was a key element of the peace terms that he had to surrender his fleet, being allowed to retain only ten ships which were not allowed to sail west of Cape Sarpedonium on the Cilician coast. The rest were burned. Rome would not permit even her faithful allies to acquire these ships and to become naval powers with fleets big enough to be tempted to challenge her in the future.

VARIOUS OPERATIONS

Finally in 189 BC, the navy was called upon, and was the agent of Rome's policy, when it intervened to settle internal dissension in Crete. After this its attention was focused on the Ionian island of Cephallenia (Kephalonia) which had been a lair of pirates. The navy desired the island as a base, its position at the entrance of the Gulf of Corinth making it an ideal point from which the whole of central Greece and the Peloponnese could be covered. To achieve this, and to dispose of the pirates at the same time, a naval force reinforced by troops besieged it, taking the island after four months in the January of 188 BC. The Greeks meanwhile had been left to 188 BC   their own quarrelsome devices but perhaps the Romans anticipated that it would not be long before they would again have to intervene.[15]

Once more the Romans evacuated Asia Minor, having in less than ten years defeated two of the great Hellenic monarchies, successors of Alexander the Great, and yet another naval power had ceased to be. With the third, Egypt, she had been on friendly terms since 267 BC.

178 BC   The Romans established a colony at Aquileia at the northern end of the Adriatic Sea but this stirred the tribe of the Istri to raiding, and Manlius Vulso was therefore sent in 178 BC to deal with them. He commanded a fleet and two legions and in addition, had 2000 Gallic allies. He camped close to the shore when the Istrians mounted a surprise attack; the troops panicked and fled to the sanctuary of the ships. Steadied by the marines, the troops reformed and Manlius led a counter-attack and then proceeded to advance into Istria. The fleet had plenty of good anchorages in the peninsula and could closely support the advance. The campaign was concluded in the

TRADE
DEVELOPMENT

With the evolution from smallish city-states to the large Hellenistic empire-states of the eastern Mediterranean, there had developed increasing markets for luxury and manufactured goods in addition to those for basic comestibles such as grain, oil and wine. Additionally, the increasing power and territories of Rome extended those markets to the western Mediterranean. A great increase in maritime trade had accompanied this growth to serve the markets, which had also led to a corresponding growth in the average size of merchant ships which now commonly carried 2–300 tons of cargo each, with many far larger. These bigger ships could not be beached and unloaded and many ports had to be enlarged with quays, cranes, breakwaters and warehouses to accommodate and handle them.

following year (177 BC) with the conquest and annexation of the whole of Istria. In 177 and 176 BC, the navy was called upon to arrange the urgent

176 BC transport of troops to deal with insurrections in Corsica and Sardinia.

Philip of Macedon had again built up his military strength, but had died in 179 BC, to be succeeded by his son, Perseus. Tension had been building up for some time and the Third Macedonian War (172 to 167 BC) finally broke out in 172 BC. For the war, the Sicilian squadron was

172 BC reinforced by the re-commissioning of twelve laid-up ships and brought up to combat readiness, to act as a reserve and as always to cover the lines of communication and supply between Italy and Greece. For the Aegean fleet, thirty-eight ships were prepared in Italy and sent east under Gaius Lucretius, collecting various allied ships on the way. Upon reaching the Gulf of Patras, the fleet was put under Gaius' brother, Marcus and sailed around the Peloponnese to Chalkis on Euboea, whence it ferried troops to attack enemy cities on the mainland. Perseus had only a small navy, incapable of opposing the Roman and allied fleet and thus, in the absence of opposition, the allied ships were not needed and sent home. The Roman fleet continued to operate from the base at Chalkis and had to content itself with plundering the enemy-held Boeotian coast. In 170 BC, the fleet captured Abdera in Thrace, who promptly complained to the Senate in Rome that they were friendly to Rome, which they certainly were now.

In 169 BC, the army broke through from the west and reached the

169 BC Macedonian coast capturing Heracleum on the Aegean coast. The fleet, now commanded by Gaius Marcus Figulus, was moved to this forward base to attack Perseus' harbours in the northern Aegean. Thessalonica was attacked but was too strong to be taken. Reinforced by twenty Pergamene and five Bithynian warships, the allies next attacked Perseus' naval base

at Cassandeia nearby, but the base was relieved by small boats operating as blockade runners. Being late in the season, the fleet retired southward, raiding the enemy coast as it went, and returning to its base on Euboea for the winter. Having left a detachment on the island of Skiathos to act as a forward observation post and keep a watch on the northern Aegean, the allies returned home. Following complaints as to their conduct among the local populace and the attack on Abdera, a Senatorial mission was sent to Greece to inspect the Roman forces there and had to report back that the army was under-strength and the fleet in poor condition after three years of constant operations.

It will be recalled that after the First Macedonian War, the Macedonian navy had been reduced to six ships. Some additions to this total had been made, perhaps by purchase or by some clandestine building, probably some of both, adding several dozen 'conter'-type ships. This fleet was still not very large and sought no confrontation with the Roman navy, but started to operate off the coast of Asia Minor with a fleet of over forty such craft. On one occasion they freed a convoy of Macedonian grain ships from its Pergamene captors and on another, near to Chios, intercepted and captured a convoy carrying cavalry horses for the allied army in Greece. This appearance was timed to coincide with Perseus' attempts to cause disaffection among Rome's allies, at a time when the Romans were sadly lacking any significant success in the war. Perseus was also pursuing an alliance with Antiochus IV, the Seleucid king and the cruise by the Macedonian ships was timed as a useful demonstration in support of Perseus' diplomacy.

168 BC More efficient commanders were appointed by the Romans for the next year, 168 BC and one, the Praetor Anicius, had to deal with a new threat; the Illyrian king, Genthius, having been persuaded to join Perseus, had mustered an army and a fleet of *lemboi* at Lissus (Lezhe, in Albania). Anicius' forces went straight onto the offensive and stormed Scodra (Scutari, Shkoder), capturing the king and then marched south into Epirus; the campaign was concluded in thirty days. The other commander, Aemilius Paullus, sought to turn Perseus' position. The navy made a feint to suggest that the Romans were embarking a force at Heracleum, which had the desired result of persuading Perseus to divert some of his forces to protect the coast. Aemilius marched his army to Perseus' rear, to a place called Pydna. The next day, 22 June 168, battle was joined, the Macedonian army was cut to pieces and Perseus fled.[16]

167 BC The war was ended in 167 BC and Macedonia was divided into four republics; Illyria was also divided, into three republics. Greece was otherwise left independent and Roman forces once again withdrew. In a Macedonian shipyard, the Romans found the 'sixteen' that had been built for Demetrios in about 289 BC in the age of the great naval arms race. The old ship had not

EVOLUTION OF THE RAM

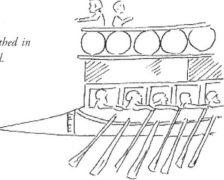

Phoenician. 8th century BC. Sharply pointed, sheathed in metal and intended to pierce and hole an enemy hull.

Greek. 6th century BC. Bronze casting of a stylised animal form but with a blunt end intended to stove-in an enemy hull.

Hellenistic. 4th century BC. Highly developed as a massive bronze casting with a vertical spine to break into an enemy hull and horizontal vanes to cut the shell planking along the grain and joints.

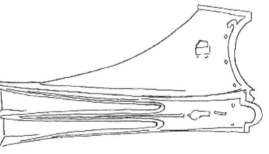

Roman. 2nd century AD. Unopposed by armoured hulls, this was intended to cut into light or open enemy hulls.

Late Roman. 4th century AD. Not intended to puncture but to ride up and over the bulwark of an enemy and to submerge it.

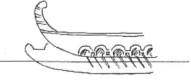

been to sea for nearly seventy years but must, amazingly, still have been in reasonable condition (even at the grand old age of 120 years) as the Romans took it to sea and in fact sailed it to Italy, where they took it up to Rome as a trophy and curio.

As part of the settlement of Greece, the Romans handed the island of Delos to Athens, but decreed that it should be a free port. In a short time it grew into a major trading centre and Rhodes, through the consequent loss of trade, went into decline. As Rhodes declined so did its navy, one of whose main functions had been to keep piracy down. Without this constraint, piracy began to increase, firstly in the areas previously controlled by the Rhodians and then spreading their depredations ever wider.

In the north-west of Italy, the Romans could now secure more of the coast and extended their road from Pisae and Genua to Massilia. The navy still accounted for about ten per cent of the annual military expenditure, which itself amounted to about three quarters of the whole of the Roman Treasury.

161 BC Rome was approached by Jerusalem and concluded a treaty with Israel, promising help if they were attacked (161 BC). This was useful as a counter to continuing dynastic problems in Seleucia, which was becoming weaker (the long struggle between it and Egypt finally ended in 145 BC).

After the Third Illyrian War in 168 BC, the Romans held the eastern Adriatic coast as far north as the River Narenta (Naretva, north of Dubrovnik) and from 177 BC, the coast south to Fiume (Rijeka). The Dalmatae, the tribe that lived in between, began to harry their neighbours and in 156 and 155 BC, campaigns brought their territory and part of Pannonia, inland from it, under Roman control. The whole of the Adriatic was now a Roman lake with all but a tiny part of its coastline (included in 129 BC) brought under their control.

155 BC In 155 BC, Crete fought against the declining power of Rhodes. Crete was one of the chief centres for piracy which Rhodes was no longer able to control. Rome did not intervene, even though Rhodes was an ally, an omission that would prove costly later.

Rome's attention had been diverted to Hispania, where they were to become embroiled in a succession of campaigns that drew them ever further across the peninsula. Most of the warfare was in the interior, where the Lusitani had raided Roman territory. They occupied the area of modern Portugal, north of the River Tagus and the Lusitanian War which broke out in 154 BC thus took place adjacent to the coast so the navy was brought in to carry out its by now well-developed role of supporting and supplying the army. The campaign required the navy to operate in the Atlantic Ocean and it started by operating out of Gades. There was a town at Osilipo (Lisbon) in the Tagus estuary and although there were no proper installations there

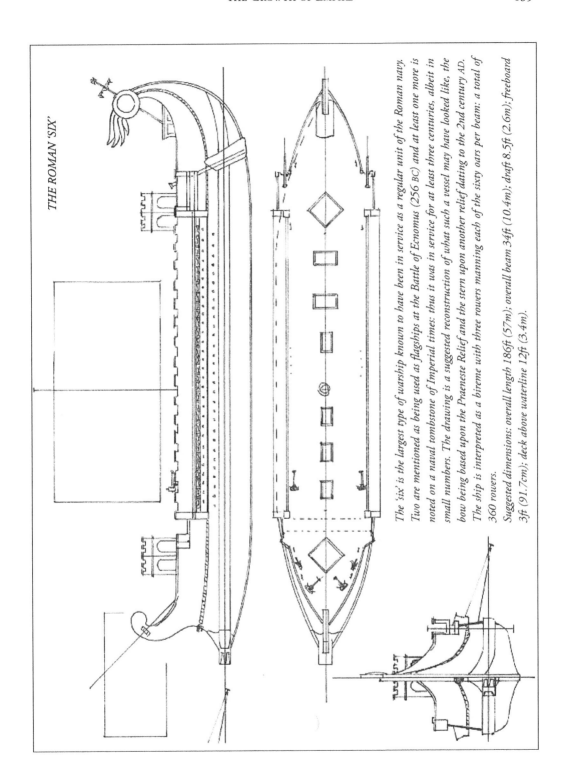

THE ROMAN 'SIX'

The 'six' is the largest type of warship known to have been in service as a regular unit of the Roman navy. Two are mentioned as being used as flagships at the Battle of Ecnomus (256 BC) and at least one more is noted on a naval tombstone of Imperial times: thus it was in service for at least three centuries, albeit in small numbers. The drawing is a suggested reconstruction of what such a vessel may have looked like, the bow being based upon the Praeneste Relief and the stern upon another relief dating to the 2nd century AD. The ship is interpreted as a bireme with three rowers manning each of the sixty oars per beam: a total of 360 rowers.

Suggested dimensions: overall length 186ft (57m); overall beam 34ft (10.4m); draft 8.5ft (2.6m); freeboard 3ft (91.7cm); deck above waterline 12ft (3.4m).

as yet, it was useful as a forward base and close to the area of operations.[17] There is no record of any special ship-types being developed for use in the Atlantic at this time and it can only be assumed that Mediterranean ships of existing types were used.

154 BC
Also in 154 BC, the Ligurians again became restive and raided Massilian ports at Antipolis (Antibes) and Nicea (Nice). The Romans marched against the Ligurians and defeated them, securing the land route to Massilia.

149 BC
Greece erupted again in 149 BC when a pretender, Andriscus fought to succeed Perseus and to become King of Macedon. A small Roman force sent against him was defeated, but the two legions that followed quickly ended his career. Macedonia was then declared a Roman province and Illyricum and Epirus were added to it.

THE THIRD PUNIC WAR

In Africa, Massinissa, the ambitious King of Numidia and loyal ally of Rome in the Punic War, had been grabbing pieces of the remaining rump of Carthaginian territory. Carthage was forbidden to go to war by the peace treaty, but in 151 BC she could tolerate affairs no longer and marched against Massinissa. Despite the provocation, Carthage had broken its treaty and attacked a friend of Rome, which now prepared for the third and final Punic War. In 149 BC the fleet, composed of fifty old quinquiremes and about a hundred triremes and smaller craft and commanded by Lucius Marcus Censorinus, escorted and transported a huge army of 80,000 men to Africa. They landed at Utica, which had already surrendered, and by the summer had laid siege to Carthage. The city was protected by massive defensive triple walls and ditches right across the isthmus, behind which was the residential area of Megara. Beyond this was the older part of the city, Salammbo and the acropolis of Byrsa Hill, between which was the forum and administrative centre and government buildings. Much of the promontory was further protected by curtain walls along the seashores. To the north the city was bounded by a shallow marshy lagoon, at that time still open to the sea, which was not fordable or accessible to any but the smallest of craft; the north-east point was dominated by a hill with steep cliffs to seaward which secured that corner of the city. The city was well supplied with water cisterns and a freshwater spring and had stockpiled foodstuffs; in any event, as seen so many times, sea blockades were never total, and some runners could be expected to get through. The fleet was stationed by the southern shore of the peninsula upon which Carthage stood, by the Lagoon of Tunis, to blockade the city from seaward. The Lagoon was however, stagnant and unhealthy in summer and Censorinus was forced to move his ships out to sea. The defences across the isthmus comprised a ditch and strong palisade; then a cleared zone before a second line of a fairly low wall with regularly spaced bastions

PUMPS AND
DRY DOCKS

> Two new nautical developments of this period were an efficient, double-acting pump, which by an ingenious arrangement of chambers and valves, enabled water to be pumped by both the up and the down strokes of a lever; the other was the invention of the dry-dock for ships, which could be simply floated in, the lock gates closed and the water pumped out quickly, to leave the ship dry for work to proceed on the hull.[18]

for the troops supporting the palisade; finally a wall some fifty feet (17m) high and ten feet (3m) thick, reinforced with projecting towers four floors in height, every 200 feet (60m), i.e. within bow shot of each other, behind which were the barracks, stables and stores for the garrison. Additionally, the old town probably had another defensive wall and the harbour area was defended by more walls on the seaward side, ending with a rectangular fort on the seaward side of the harbour mouth.[19]

148 BC   The following year (148 BC), widespread trouble broke out in Greece once more. The Romans therefore overran the rest of Greece and sacked Corinth. Initially under the Governor of Macedonia, it later became a province in the following century.[20] Greece, with its great maritime tradition, was now Rome's; the naval formations of the former Greek states were doubtless reduced, but retained a nucleus of ships and trained men who could be levied as auxiliaries for duty as required, which would happen in the civil wars of the next century. The insufficient level at which such levies were to be provided would also become apparent; possibly not a few of them in fact joined the increasing incidence of piracy; after all, inactive ships and crews could be 'borrowed' for a little profitable extra-curricular activity.

In Africa, in 148 BC the blockade of Carthage by land and sea continued. The new Fleet Commander was Lucius Hostilius Mancinus who decided to attack Carthage from seaward where the defences were lightest and out-flank its massive defensive walls. His marines effected a landing on the north-east of the peninsula, scaling a poorly watched section of wall and taking a water-gate, and penetrated the suburb of Megara, where they were heavily assailed and got into difficulties and had to be extricated the following day by ship.[21]

147 BC   Scipio had been appointed Consul and Commander-in-Chief and in the spring of 147 BC, ordered the strengthening of the Roman siege lines across the isthmus and the construction of earthworks to seal Carthage off completely by land. Scipio dispatched the historian Polybius, accompanied by a philosopher, Panaetius, with some ships to reconnoitre the African coast. This was seemingly a private scientific venture, but any cruise would have yielded useful intelligence to the Commander, for instance, to confirm that no enemy ships were lying in other ports. The occasional blockade runner had been getting through and, to seal the city off completely by

sea, Scipio established the fleet, reinforced by extra troops, on a sand bar south of the city and adjacent to the harbour entrance. They then started to build a mole by tipping boatloads of rocks, north-east across the harbour-mouth of Carthage. Both the civil and military harbours were served by one entrance only, seventy feet (21m) wide, which could be closed by chains. Blocking this would completely seal and isolate the city. When they realised the Romans' plan, the Carthaginians, in a frenzy, cannibalised the ships and whatever materials they had in the harbour and city and managed to produce fifty useable warships; also, to obviate the Roman mole, they cut a new channel to the sea from their inner harbour, the remnant of which, much silted, can be seen today. It seems likely that this channel already existed as a narrow sluice to help flush the otherwise landlocked harbours which had only the one entrance and would otherwise have silted. If this was the case the defenders enlarged the sluice enough to permit the passage of their ships. The high city walls screened this activity until the last minute demolition of the outermost screen and the Romans were completely surprised to see this last Punic fleet put to sea.

Instead of taking advantage of this surprise and attacking immediately, the Punic admirals made the cardinal mistake of cruising about to work their ships up. The Romans were, of course, also prepared and, three days later, brought the Punic fleet to battle off Carthage. The Punic ships with their 'scratch' crews proved no match for the well-trained and experienced Roman fleet and were soon beaten. The Punic ships either tried to get back through the narrow channel into Carthage, or were driven onto the shore near it and destroyed. Some Carthaginian ships backed onto their shoreline with their rams towards the Romans, who, having made a ram attack in the confined space, had difficulty in rowing astern to withdraw for a further attack and had no room in which to turn. To overcome this problem and maintain their momentum, they therefore first dropped an anchor, paying out a line astern as they made their ram attack, then withdrawing by pulling against the anchor and kedging out clear to set up for another attack. The Roman marines, in driving the enemy ships onto the shore, followed them in and after some tough fighting, managed to get onto the shore and fortify a position there, taking the large rectangular fort and section of walls commanding both the original harbour entrance and the new channel and thereby dominating the harbour. The outer works protecting the harbours from seaward had been effectively made into an island by the cutting of the escape channel and once they had secured it, the Romans could be supplied from the sea and overlook the harbours and the centre of the city itself. Carthage was completely sealed.

146 BC   The following spring (146 BC) saw the final assault on, and fall of, Carthage. The city that had once commanded the western Mediterranean and North Africa was then systematically destroyed by the victorious

ADVANCES
IN
NAVIGATION

In about 145 BC a Greek, one Hipparchus of Bithynia, working in either Rhodes or Alexandria as an astronomer, codified and settled upon a method of describing the position of places upon the Earth's surface by reference to imaginary lines drawn upon it, from north to south and from east to west, i.e. longitude and latitude. Whereas the principle of latitude had long been understood and was able to be fixed with certainty, the accurate measurement of longitude would be an achievement of the far future. This inability was less of a problem over the comparatively limited east–west distances involved in closed seas such as the Mediterranean or Euxine as sailing directions could be expressed, for example, by knowing that sailing due west for so many days at a certain latitude from say Cyprus, would bring landfall on Crete, provided of course that the weather stayed reasonable. He also compiled a star catalogue, invaluable for night-time navigation.

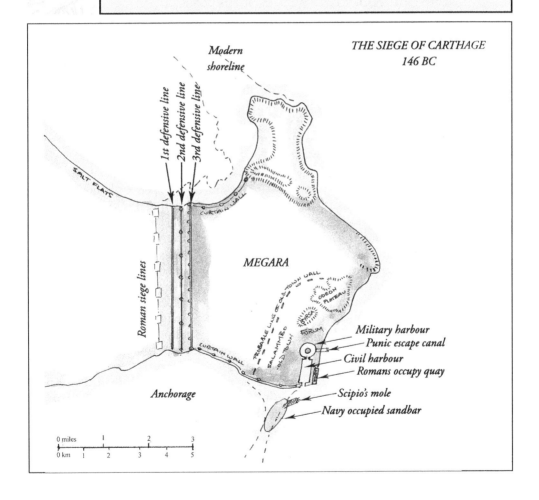

Modern shoreline

*THE SIEGE OF CARTHAGE
146 BC*

1st defensive line

2nd defensive line

3rd defensive line

SALT FLATS

Roman siege lines

CURTAIN WALL

MEGARA

PROBABLE LINE OF OLD-TOWN WALL

SALAMMBO OLD TOWN

ODEON PLATEAU

BYRSA

FORUM

CURTAIN WALL

Military harbour
Punic escape canal
Civil harbour
Romans occupy quay

Anchorage

Scipio's mole
Navy occupied sandbar

0 miles   1   2   3
0 km   1   2   3   4   5

Romans until nothing but ruins remained and its territory was made into the province of Africa. The two halves of the Mediterranean were now linked by the power in the centre, in Italy.[22]

139 BC   In Hispania, the long and treacherous Lusitanian War ended when they were finally overrun. In 139 BC, D. Iunius Brutus advanced through what is now Portugal with his army whilst the fleet advanced up the coast alongside it, to the River Douro. In the following year they continued up the coast, defeating the Callaici and taking modern Galicia, with the harbours of the north-west corner of the peninsula. They fortified Osilipo and established a settlement at Valentia on the River Oblivio (Minho). The fleet once more practised its well-tried tactics of continuously out-flanking the enemy as well as supplying the rapidly advancing army.

NAVAL RUN-DOWN AND MARIUS

133 BC   With the fall of Numantia in 133 BC, the long drawn-out campaigns in Hispania ended and after over a century of almost non-stop major warfare, the resulting Roman hegemony in the Mediterranean area brought relative peace. Much of the vast military establishment could be stood down and disbanded. For the navy, with the final defeat of Macedonia, the Seleucids and Carthage and with Egypt and the remaining Hellenistic states as allies, there was no foreign navy left to challenge it. The military transports to Hispania no longer needed escort and provincial officers and couriers on state business could as well travel by merchant ship.

Along with the army, the navy's manpower was reduced, the men discharged and sent home; older ships were scrapped and surplus ships decommissioned and hauled ashore and the building of replacement ships curtailed. A reducing core of active ships remained as the service adjusted to a peacetime role. It was also a matter for the navy to actually find a peacetime role for, having been permanently on war service for so long, it was hard to return to the old system whereby land and sea forces were only mobilised in time of actual war and that, in its absence, neither existed as a normal part of society. Rome had now grown into an empire in fact – if not in name – and it was no longer possible to return to being a state that did not have armed forces as a permanent institution. At the end of the Second Punic War, the navy had been reduced to 100 ships of all types. This fleet had seen almost continuous action since then and had proved only barely sufficient to carry out the tasks allotted to it, divided as it had been between operations in both the west and the east. The western part of the fleet now had no other naval forces to contend with and apart from the various operations mentioned, could provide a flexible presence to deter the depredations of pirates in the Tyrrhenian Sea. In the east, the fleet had to be kept concentrated to oppose its enemies' fleets and although it was only

THE
GROWTH
OF OSTIA

With the ravages of the Second Punic War and the draining of Italy's manpower for long campaigns, the old agricultural structure of Italy had been disrupted and the importation of grain from Sicily and Sardinia had become more commonplace, indeed essential with a consequent increase in sea traffic, augmented further by the elevation of Rome to be the capital of an empire. With the reduction of the navy and the increase of civilian traffic with Rome, Ostia grew and became a mainly commercial centre and port, instead of the primarily naval base of former times. At Rome, the wharves and merchant emporia developed along the river banks and extended downriver alongside the Aventine Hill.

TRADE
WITH INDIA

For many years, trade had been conducted with India, goods having been brought to ports in the Near East by Indian, Persian and Arab ships, utilising the monsoon winds; from May to September it blows from the south-west, enabling passage from the Red Sea to India; from November to March, it reverses to blow from the north-east, allowing passage back. In about 120 BC, the Greeks learned the secret of using the monsoon winds to enable a direct cross-oceanic voyage to and from southern India, instead of a longer, coasting voyage to the northern part of the country. The resulting trip was shorter, faster and far enough from land to be free from the threat of piracy. Greek and Roman merchants, with control of the Red Sea ports, could now trade direct and set up trading stations in India itself.[23]

proper for the Romans, if they were to fight for them, to require their allies to contribute ships to an allied fleet, nevertheless their own contribution had only just proved sufficient. They had been lucky. The concentration of ships in the east had diverted attention away from the pirates, who could operate unmolested in areas such as the Adriatic, where there was little or no naval presence. The navy was already overstretched and these further reductions exacerbated this situation.

130 BC   In 130 BC Pergamum became the new province of Asia, giving Rome a foothold in the east. In 125 BC, Massilia appealed for help against local tribes of Gauls and Ligurians. There followed a series of campaigns that resulted in the acquisition by 125 BC of the Mediterranean coast of Gaul, which would become the province of Gallia Narbonensis, finally securing the land route to Hispania.

122 BC   The Balearic Islands had become home to pirates and the navy's next major action was in 122 BC when, commanded by Quintus Metellus, it dealt with them and planted Roman colonies there.

The following years saw an extension of Roman holdings in south-west Gaul and campaigns in the Balkans and in Africa. This latter, the war against the native King Jugurtha, had progressed but the lack of sufficient troops and the difficulty of raising additional recruits had prevented its

107 BC successful conclusion. In 107 BC, Gaius Marius was elected a Consul and given command of the war. To quickly raise the extra troops needed to finish the war, he opened recruitment to the legions to any citizen, regardless of property qualifications, and placed upon the state the liability for the provision of all arms, armour and equipment, which had previously rested upon recruits, according to their class. The old distinctions of differently equipped classes of infantry were also abolished and all legionaries would henceforth be uniformly equipped.

The poor, the landless, the unemployed, the dispossessed, with the possibility of making a career of the service, flocked to join up. Previously, men in the higher propertied classes had been anxious to be discharged at the earliest possibility, to return to their homes, farms and businesses; for the new, poor recruits the army offered a career and security and a discharge was the last thing that they wanted. Marius had abolished the property classes and in doing so had laid the foundation of the professional, standing army. That was not to be all, for a further change in attitude resulted in that the soldiers of this army now looked to their commanders, rather than a return to civilian life, for their welfare and it was to these commanders, rather than to Rome that they gave their loyalty.[24]

The navy by contrast, had always relied on the lowest classes of the citizen levy, the *capitacensi*, for its recruits and it had also long recruited non-citizen allies, even for its marines, and since about 200 BC, increasing numbers of Greeks had enlisted. Unlike the army, where non-citizens were disqualified from the legions and had to be in separate units, in the navy such division was not possible on a ship. The service had never been concerned with property qualifications; rowers needed no equipment, other than the oar which, like the sailor's gear, was part of the ship's inventory. Marines had to be equipped by the service if they had originated among the *capitacensi* and their arms, like the extra shields and weapons kept for use by the rowers if opportunity arose, were probably also part of the ship's stores. Although naval strength had been reduced, the navy had, like the army, become in reality a permanent service and many of its men had already made a career of it. The navy was not therefore, affected by Marius' reform having always had the burden of providing everything needed by its men. For his part, Marius appears not to have included any provisions in his scheme that applied to it.

104 BC Having successfully concluded the war in Africa, Marius was again made Consul in 104 BC and given command of the army which was to be

SUNDIALS

> Since the introduction of the sundial in the 290s BC, the Romans had considerably developed this device. Normally fixed in a sunny position, with its gnomon or pointer aligned north and south (the shadow from which falls onto a scale, indicating the time) they perfected a small portable version, more complex and with a specialised gnomon and an additional, moveable calibrated ring. Lacking the true compass, they produced a dual-function sundial; used conventionally, with the gnomon lined up north–south, the dial indicated the time in the normal way; used in reverse however and with one of the rings calibrated as to latitude and the other as to declination of the sun and given the current time, it would indicate true north, enabling one to navigate.[25]

sent to oppose the bands of Germanic tribesmen who had entered southern Gaul and inflicted defeats on the Roman forces there.

Before setting out and to finish his work of reform of the army, Marius embarked upon a complete reform of its training, equipment, formations and tactics. Training continued through Marius' third Consulship in 103 BC 102 BC and in his fourth, in 102 BC, he marched his 'new look' army to Gaul, where it utterly defeated the Germans. Marius next employed his troops in digging a channel to by-pass the mouth of the River Rhodanus, which was prone to silting. This enabled shipping to navigate into and up the river, and facilitate the support of future armies as well as improve trade. The use of the military to effect works of civil engineering was already well established, particularly in road-making. In this instance, several factors came together to make these works of particular significance for the future shape of the empire.

Before the war with Hannibal, the River Iberus in Hispania had been established as the border between Rome and Carthage. In the early part of that war the River Padus in Italy had been used as a lateral line of supply to maintain garrisons along it. Many times before, armies operating adjacent to coastlines had been supported by fleets, enabling rapid penetration of new territory. With the opening up of the Rhodanus to sea-going navigation, a convenient border-line could be drawn around the western Alps, which nevertheless allowed penetration up into central Gaul and to the north of the Alps, with the ability to supply garrisons and for a major trading route.

As mentioned previously, the reforms of Marius appear not to have affected the navy. Recruitment was effectively without qualification, either of property or (except for officers) citizenship and drawn from all Roman territories. Marius' abolition of the various classes of infantry was likewise irrelevant to the marines of a ship's complement. His extension of the number of years' service for which a man might join the legions, making possible officially a long-term career in the army, merely formalised for that service what had already become a common practice in the navy.

Marius was above all a soldier and the navy, which had played so pivotal a role in the extension of Roman power around the Mediterranean, attracted little or none of his attention and continued to be reduced and even neglected.

THE RISE OF PIRACY

Throughout the Mediterranean, but particularly in the east, the run-down of naval power had left the service incapable of adequately policing the seas. With the destruction and reduction of other naval powers a vacuum was left. With nothing to check it, the scourge of piracy had spread apace and was an ever-increasing threat to shipping and to coastal settlements. There were two problems in attacking a merchantman; firstly, the largest could take more open-sea routes, far from land, out of sight and beyond the reach of the less seaworthy but faster rowing pirate boats and ships; secondly the prey could be in ballast or carrying a cargo of little or no value to a pirate. An attack on a coastal town however could yield captives to be ransomed or sold as slaves, almost guaranteed supplies and all manner of other valuables; conversely, it could yield a payment not to attack. The numbers of pirates and pirate ships proliferated, there was no shortage of unemployed members of various now defunct Hellenistic navies and doubtless some of those navies' redundant warships were 'acquired'. The pirates had been driven from the Tyrrhenian and Balearics and after destruction of their ships and control of the coast by the Romans, had been severely limited in the Adriatic, although the myriad islands and islets of the Dalmatian coast could still provide plenty of hiding places. The pirates congregated and set up whole communities particularly along the southern coasts of Asia Minor, nominally part of the failing Seleucid kingdom, but in fact almost a no-man's-land. This is rugged and rocky with many inlets and protected from incursion from inland by mountains to its rear. These forested mountains also yielded timber for construction and repair of their ships. From here, whole fleets of pirate ships, the equal of naval squadrons, ranged far and wide, even into the western Mediterranean as well as into the Adriatic. Other pirate formations operated from Crete, long a favourite haunt. Normal maritime commerce was reduced to chaos, coastal towns lived in constant fear of attack and the pirates virtually ruled the seas.[26]

102 BC   In a belated and seemingly half-hearted attempt to curb this growing menace, the Praetor Marcus Antonius (father of his namesake, of Anthony and Cleopatra fame) was sent in 102 BC, with proconsular *imperium* and a small force to establish shore bases on the coasts of Pamphylia and western Cilicia (the present south coast of Turkey). His grant of *imperium*

MEDICINE

> A shipwreck of a merchant ship, found off the Tuscan coast and dating from this period held the remains of a chest of herbs, ointments and implements that had belonged to a doctor or pharmacist. Although the inclusion of physicians and medical orderlies is known later, it could be that this find indicates that the practice took place at or by this time; it could also be that this discovery was simply of goods in transit, with or without their owner and no other actual conclusion should be drawn from their presence.[27]

gave Antonius the authority of a provincial governor, who could call upon provinces and allied states in which he operated to provide such military forces and support that he might require. He could for example, call upon Rhodes to place its warships under his command and requisition men and supplies to support them. To support Antonius, at the end of 101 BC a law was enacted closing the harbours of the empire and those of its allies and client states to pirate shipping. How effective such a measure could have been is problematical, given that a pirate fleet would ignore it and attack, or have to be bought off, and a captured merchant ship, manned by pirates and sneaking into a port to sell loot or acquire supplies would hardly advertise itself as other than a legitimate trading vessel.

101 BC

The following year (100 BC) saw the return of Antonius to Rome, where he was granted a triumph for his operations against the pirates. Of his forces and operations, no detail is known but one may reasonably assume that he took a naval force, augmented it by drawing on such local forces as were available and established and garrisoned bases, with a sea-lane for supplies, probably to Rhodes and thence to the west. Operations would include raids to destroy known pirate lairs, escorting of merchant ships and patrols to seek out and attack pirate ships. His triumph signifies that Antonius had enjoyed some success in rendering the seas safer but once again, having left no permanent naval force behind when he left, his achievement was to be but temporary in effect. No major confrontation appears to have taken place, so many pirate ships, instead of concentrating to face him, were already cruising elsewhere or simply chose to evade Antonius' forces. This comparatively modest Roman campaign must have reduced the pirates' activities at least for a while, but it did not take long for them to recover and in the absence of any permanent restriction upon them, their activities were soon as bad and widespread as ever.

100 BC

After destroying the remaining Germans in Gaul in 101 and 100 BC, Marius entered his (unprecedented) sixth consulship. He had become the most powerful man in the empire but he nevertheless resigned his office and retired in 98 BC.

98 BC

In 96 BC, Ptolemy Apion, Pharaoh of Egypt, died and left the territory of Cyrene (eastern Lybia and western Egypt) to Rome, by his will. Although the bequest was accepted by the Senate, they left the territory under its local, Greek administration. The pirates soon found it to be a convenient additional location from which to operate.

Central Italy erupted into the Social War in 90 BC, an uprising of the Italians against their lack of social status, despite having been instrumental in winning Rome her empire. Despite the considerable number of Italians who must have been serving in the navy, it was not disaffected and Roman control of the seas around the peninsula was never challenged by the rebels.

There were of course, blockade runners to the rebels, one of whom, a Cilician pirate named Agamemnon, is known. In the early part of the war the Romans were hard-pressed and the Samnites burst into Campania, where there was fighting at Pompeii. The naval commander there, Aulus Postumius Albinus, was killed whilst commanding naval operations, from which we may infer that marines had been landed to defend the town against the rebels. Three Greek sea captains were honoured for services to Rome in the war. As with earlier wars, Rome's command of the seas prevented the rebels from obtaining large-scale help from abroad and Rome was herself able to rely on provincial sources of manpower and supply.[28]

The war was mostly over by 88 BC, but it had seen the rise to prominence of another military commander, Lucius Cornelius Sulla. Sulla was elected a Consul for 88 BC and given command in the east. Marius had played only a minor, if successful part in the recent war and, feeling slighted, wanted the eastern command. Political disturbances resulted in Sulla with his army taking over the city, forcing Marius to flee. Sulla then left for Asia but as soon as he had gone, trouble again erupted. The other consul, Cinna, and Marius after much serious unrest and some fighting, prevailed and by the year's end, Rome was in their hands. Marius and Cinna made themselves   Consuls for 86 BC and declared Sulla to be an outlaw. Marius died in 86 BC, leaving Cinna as the effective ruler for the next three years.

The growth of Rome's domains and of her power was stretching the structure and capacity of her government and administration far, far beyond that for which they had been designed. The arrival of career soldiers and permanent, standing armed forces provided the means to enable ambitious men to seek to control the tottering republic which would ultimately lead to its demise.

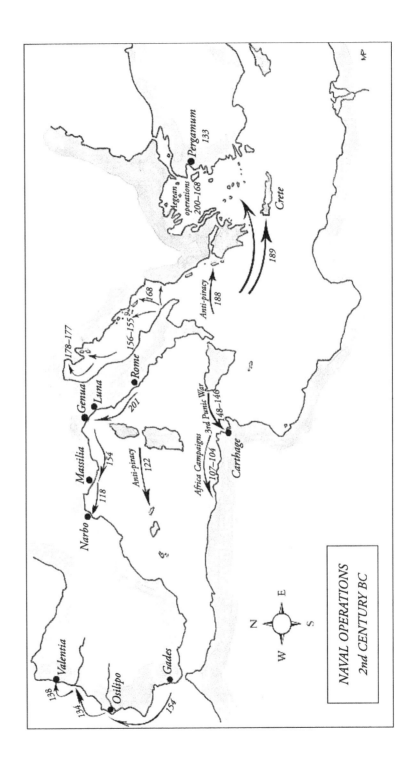

NAVAL OPERATIONS
2nd CENTURY BC

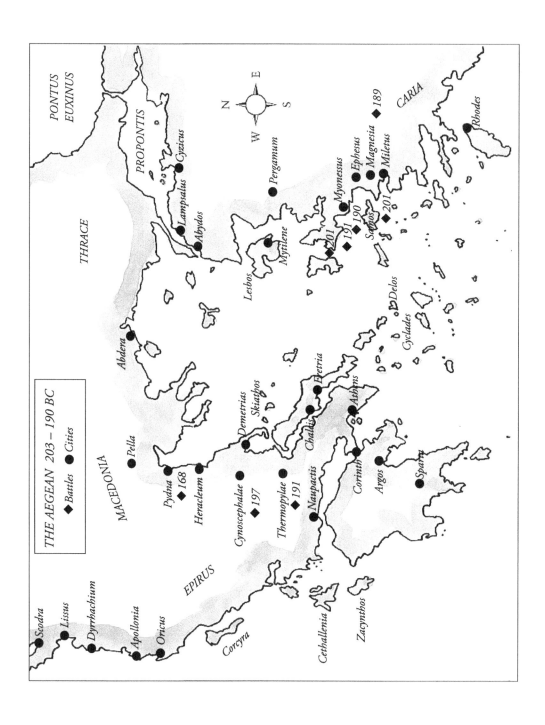

THE AEGEAN 203 – 190 BC
◆ Battles ● Cities

Notes

1. Obviously Philip's orders for 100 new ships had been optimistic but he seems to have settled for fewer, bigger ships.
2. Polybius XVI.3. There is an analysis of the course of this battle in Rodgers.
3. In fact these tribes continued to cause trouble into the 150s, but while the ports were securely in Roman hands they could be contained; and see Scullard Chapter XIV.
4. The narrative in Scullard is relied on for the framework of the course of the war.
5. Polybius XVIII.44.
6. It can be assumed that annual warship production had been scaled down at the end of the Punic Wars and a surplus of worn-out ships disposed of.
7. Rodgers and Scullard, with Meijer and Livy.
8. Morrison & Coates *GROW* quotes (no doubt amusingly) Arrian (Syr.22) as saying '…the Romans were still inexperienced at sea…' They had fought and won two major naval wars and had been in action continuously in between for seventy-five years. What was Arrian thinking? This was the world's most battle hardened, experienced and strongest navy, as the results show.
9. Graffiti at Anfushi Necropolis, Alexandria, from Casson *SSAW*.
10. Livy XXVII; Rodgers; Morrison & Coates *GROW*.
11. Much of this manoeuvring was occasioned while the Romans gathered and prepared their army in Greece and paved the way for Macedon's help in enabling it to march through their territory to the Hellespont.
12. Livy XXXVII.23/24.
13. Although the Romans had nearly 100 ships committed to the war, the rest were away on other duties or in for refit, leaving fifty-eight available for this action.
14. Livy XXXVII.30.
15. For an account of the politics, see Scullard.
16. Livy XLII, covers this conflict. Interestingly he specifies that 'Carthaginian Fives' joined Rome's allies. The peace treaty restricted Carthage to ten triremes only (see above) so either they had breached it or these (assuming Livy not to have been mistaken) were some Roman ships manned by drafts of Punic men.
17. See Scullard for a commentary on the Spanish campaign.
18. Attributed to Ctesibus of Alexandria, later examples have been found in Britain. Vitruvius X, I, 1-3 (*The Ancient Engineers*).
19. The description is from Arrian and has been partly at least confirmed by excavation. The coastline has changed drastically since then but observation of the area can still reveal the basic situation at the time of the siege, as well as the remains of the harbours. Unfortunately the part of Polybius' history dealing with the Third Punic War is largely lost, a great pity because he was there and wrote from personal experience (and see Scullard). Appian wrote a history of the wars some 200 years later.
20. Scullard.
21. Appian's account is extensively transcribed in Morrison & Coates *GROW*, which demonstrates the inconsistencies in his account.
22. For more detail of Carthage and the Carthaginian state, reference is to Harden, *The Phoenicians* and Moscati, *The World of the Phoenicians*.
23. Casson, *The Ancient Mariners*.
24. Scullard 2.
25. Selkirk, *The Piercebridge Formula*.
26. See Ormerod, *Piracy in the Ancient World* and Meijer.
27. Casson, *The Ancient Mariners* and Bass, *A History of Seafaring*.
28. See Scullard 2 for a commentary on the Social War.

THE ROAD TO CIVIL WAR

86 BC–44 BC

T rouble had been brewing in Anatolia for some time. This was due mainly to the expansionist aims of Mithridates VI, King of Pontus, whose realm extended along most of the north coast and whose navy, some 300 ships in strength, dominated the Euxine Sea. In 89 BC Mithridates had moved into neighbouring Bithynia and Cappadocia, both allies of Rome; he withdrew, only to be attacked in turn by Bithynia. Mithridates counter-attacked and in doing so, his forces overran much of the Roman province of Asia. His fleet sailed into the Aegean, sacking Delos, which never really recovered, being checked only at Rhodes. In 88 BC, Mithridates had sent forces into Greece where their initial advance was reversed by the Roman garrison. Sulla meanwhile, had landed at Epirus with five legions and advanced to Athens in 87 BC.[1]

86 BC   At sea, the Pontic navy had command of the northern Aegean and Sulla at once realised that without his own fleet to oppose it, he would be limited in his operations and thus sent his deputy, Lucius Licinius Lucullus to organise and gather naval forces. In 86 BC Sulla captured Athens and forced the Pontic forces there to withdraw but, having no ships, he was unable to prevent them from being safely evacuated by sea.

Sulla marched on Thessaly, where he beat the Pontic forces at Chaeronea. Mithridates was able to land another army in Sulla's rear on Euboea which Sulla also defeated. These defeats had effectively ended Mithridates' invasion of Greece but Sulla, still without a fleet, was unable to pursue his enemy directly and had to content himself with the long march around the northern Aegean, through Thessaly, Macedonia and Thrace, allowing Mithridates time in which to organise his further opposition.

It will be recalled that in Rome Sulla had been declared an outlaw and Cinna thus sent Flaccus with two legions directly to Asia, from which it is safe to assume that he also had an escort and support from the navy. Flaccus was murdered by his lieutenant, Fimbria, who took command and advanced northwards, beating Mithridates in a battle near the shore of the Propontis.

Lucullus had meanwhile, managed to organise a fleet. He had sailed with an escort of three Rhodian ships, from Athens to Alexandria, but despite receiving lavish hospitality, could obtain no help from Rome's ally, the Pharaoh Ptolemy IX (Soter II) who, not surprisingly, felt it more politic to stand aloof. Since Sulla had been proscribed at Rome, he could not call upon the Roman navy, which was in any case operating in support of Flaccus/Fimbria. Lucullus could and must have used Sulla's authority as Commander in the east and with Rhodes' help and ships, to requisition such warships as were in the provinces of Asia, Cyrene and Macedonia; to require allied states and the Greek islands to provide crews and to hire mercenary captains and ships. This fleet sailed into the Propontis, but Lucullus did not pause to help Fimbria, being instead intent to secure a safe crossing of the Hellespont for his chief, Sulla.[2] On the way, Lucullus' polyglot fleet raided enemy-held coasts and skirmished with enemy ships. No full battle was sought, or indeed offered, by either side.

85 BC   Now with his own naval support, Sulla was able to advance into Anatolia against Mithridates, but in view of his status there he was most anxious to return to Rome and restore his position. In 85 BC, Sulla met Mithridates near Troy and peace terms were hastily agreed, which included the surrender of seventy ships to Sulla. In his hurry to return to Rome however, Sulla neglected to organise naval forces for the protection of the eastern seas, where piracy continued to increase; they even raided the island of Samothrace whilst Sulla was actually there.

84 BC   Sulla made his way back through Greece in 84 BC and his command had grown to some 40,000 with the addition of Fimbria's troops. The naval units used to escort Flaccus were taken into Lucullus' command, together with the most suitable of the surrendered Pontic ships and Lucullus was thus able to dismiss his ad hoc fleet. Orders were given that a number of the warships be laid up in reserve in various coastal cities around the Aegean, to provide a naval force which could be quickly mobilised if and when needed. This is of course, a similar provision to that made some sixty-five years earlier, in 148 and seems to have had a similar, negligible effect on subsequent events. Nevertheless it probably represented a part of a larger overall plan of Sulla's for the long-term defence of Anatolia, which he never returned to complete.

83 BC   In 83 BC, therefore, Sulla was able to embark his army and transport it safely to Brundisium, where he was joined by Cnaeus Pompeius (known as Pompey). Civil war in Italy followed, which ended in 82 BC. In 81 BC, Sulla was made Dictator and as such, effectively sole ruler of the Roman world. With the backing of the Roman fleet, Pompeius crossed to Africa and beat the remaining rebels there. Sulla reformed the government and in 79 BC he resigned his dictatorship and retired; he died in the following year, aged sixty.

During the recent war, the city and sea-port of Mytilene on the Aegean island of Lesbos had gone over to Mithridates. The new governor of the province of Asia, Marcus Minucius Thermus intended to invest the city, which had barricaded itself against him. He needed a naval squadron to blockade the port but only had a few ships available, most likely ex-Pontic ships, which he had to man with local levies of seamen and his own troops (the Roman naval forces had returned with Lucullus). Thermus needed more ships and resolved to call upon the allied King Nicomedes of Bythinia to supply them. For this diplomatic mission, he sent one of his staff officers, the twenty-year-old Gaius Iulius Caesar, in his first military posting. Caesar secured the extra ships and crews and Mytilene was duly blockaded. The siege was successfully concluded, in the course of which, Caesar distinguished himself.[3]

79 BC

The activities of pirates had again grown to be a serious problem to the extent that in 79 BC, one of the Consuls for that year, Publius Servilius Vatia, was sent to the east in command of naval forces to attack Cilicia and reduce the pirate bases there, which had sprung up again along the very coast previously attacked by Antonius. One of the Consuls for 79 BC, Lepidus, raised an army and marched on Rome; the Senate appointed Pompeius to lead the loyal forces, who defeated Lepidus' rising. This appointment and success had the effect however of making Pompeius the de facto defender of the State and thus, extremely powerful.

78 BC

In 78 BC, Vatia commenced what was to be a three-year campaign against the pirate epidemic in Lycia, Pamphylia and Isauria. In the following year, 77 BC, he led his fleet against a pirate fleet in a pitched battle off the Lycian coast. The pirates were defeated and Vatia proceeded to reduce both Lycia and Pamphylia throughout 77 and 76 BC. In 75 BC he overran Isauria, opening the way for an attack on the final stronghold of the pirates, Cilicia, but his operations were halted by the outbreak of the Second Mithridatic War and once again, despite Vatia's successes, the opportunity for a final solution to the problem escaped.

75 BC

In illustration of the continuing activities of the pirates, it was at this time (75 BC) that Caesar sailed to Rhodes to study oratory. South of Miletus his ship was attacked by pirates, who drove it ashore and Caesar was captured. He was kept by them for six weeks and released when his ransom was paid. Before his release, Caesar promised to return and to crucify them all and a few weeks later, he returned with a force and kept his word. The force used was composed of troops from the nearest garrison in Miletus and conveyed by local merchant ships, pressed into service for the expedition, escorted perhaps by some of those same ships used at Mytilene five years before.[4]

Pompeius meanwhile had gone to Hispania in 76 BC to campaign against the rebel Quintus Sertorius. Pompeius had early on recognised the value of naval power and for the first two years he operated along the coasts, where he could rely on naval support.

Elsewhere, in 74 BC, Marcus Terentius Varro, campaigning against the incursions of Thracian tribes, advanced up the west coast of the Euxine Sea to the delta of the Danubius and defeated them there. The Greeks had for centuries navigated the Euxine Sea and had founded cities around its shores. Operating in hostile territory, Varro undoubtedly relied on Greek mariners and ships for his supplies. There was, in the absence of any form of Thracian sea-power, no need for large scale naval support.

Cyrene, in North Africa, bequeathed to Rome in 96 BC, had become a haunt of pirates who, operating between there and Crete (another of their favourite haunts) could easily attack the sea-routes between Egypt, the Levant and the West. As part of its policy against the pirates, the Senate formally annexed Cyrene as a province in 74 BC.

Finally, in that same year, the King of Bythinia died and bequeathed his country to Rome. Mithridates of Pontus had been building up his armed forces since the last war and now had about 400 ships. He was not prepared to lose control of the Bosporus and the passage it permitted between the Euxine and Aegean Seas and his army thereupon marched in and occupied Bythinia, precipitating a second Mithridatic War.

The Consuls for the year were sent east with forces to oppose Mithridates and to claim the new province; Gaius Aurelius Cotta to Bythinia and Lucullus to Cilicia and Asia. Since Vatia had been withdrawn and with Mithridates' encouragement, the pirates had renewed their activities with vigour and as a result, corn prices were already rising. Marcus Antonius (the son of the Consul of 102 BC who had campaigned against them) was given special authority to operate against the pirates (*imperium infinitum*). Cotta's forces included a fleet of sixty-four ships of unspecified type which could have included some transports. He started to conduct naval operations but rushed ahead of his colleague and was beaten on land and at sea and besieged at Chalcedon on the Asiatic shore of the Bosporus, where his ships were bottled up in the harbour by Mithridates' superior numbers. In an attack, the Pontic forces burned four of the Roman ships and managed to capture and to tow away most of the rest, many of which, ironically, could well have been ships surrendered after the first war. Lucullus meanwhile, advanced overland and drove Mithridates' forces back and then defeated him and cut his supply line, forcing his withdrawal by sea and abandonment of his siege of Cotta.

In the spring of 73 BC, Mithridates sent his naval forces into the Aegean. Lucullus was with the Roman and allied fleet when he caught and captured an enemy squadron of thirteen ships and then went on to catch another squadron of Pontic ships at the island of Lemnos, destroying it on the beach. He then drove the rest of the king's fleet back into the Euxine Sea, where the Pontic fleet suffered further losses from a storm and had to retire to their home ports in Pontus. Lucullus continued the campaign on land and sea, the fleet supporting his advance along the north coast of Anatolia. Mithridates was finally forced to flee and to seek refuge in Armenia. Of the types of ships of Mithridates' navy, nothing is known, but, on the basis that they numbered, as alleged, several hundred and that the Roman Fleet (at a maximum of sixty-four ships plus perhaps a few Rhodian allied ships) swept all before them, it must be assumed that they were mostly small boats. This would explain also why, being hopelessly outmatched, they did not put up more of a fight and also why they suffered apparently severe losses in storms.[5]

72 BC   Marcus Antonius, operating against the pirates, had concentrated his efforts on Crete but was defeated in 72 BC by the Cretan pirates. Most Roman forces in the area had of course been concentrated against Mithridates, who for his part, sought the pirates as allies and with his encouragement their strength grew and with it, their boldness. Their raids extended to the coasts of Italy itself. They attracted to swell their numbers, criminals and malcontents from all over the eastern Mediterranean and numbered many thousands. They were said at this time to have a thousand ships and had augmented their traditional lighter ships with biremes and even triremes. There was a great variety in the types employed by the pirates, from the seagoing ships of military or merchant type, to small coastal craft, according to local circumstances. In more constricted waters, such as the Dalmatian and Cilician coasts, smallish, open rowing craft of shallow draft and with or without an auxiliary rig (which could be lowered) would be employed. Manned by enough men to overpower the crew of a merchantman, the boats could be carried ashore and hidden in the face of any serious threat. It seems that the purpose-built pirate boats harkened back to the 'conter' type of warship, varying in size and carrying ten to twenty-five oars per side, being long and narrow although without a ram as their purpose was to catch and board their prey intact, rather than to ram and swamp it. 'Twos' and 'threes' were later added by the Cilicians although it is not clear whether these were in remes, in the manner of biremes and triremes, or by having two or three men per oar in a single reme. Several types which started life as pirate craft were taken over and developed into regular warships, such as the lembus of the Illyrian Coast which grew to become the liburnian of the Romans and the hemiolia, or 'one and a half', favoured by the Rhodians.[6]

71 BC   The main attention of the Romans was still focused at home by the revolt of Spartacus. Publius Licinius Crassus was appointed to lead an army against him and destroyed the revolt in 71 BC. Pompeius, having completed his campaign in Hispania, returned to Italy. When both Crassus and Pompeius had their armies in Italy the situation was tense. The Senate had to appoint

them both to be the Consuls for the year and they then disbanded their armies. With the standing down of the armies, presumably the naval force assigned to Pompeius was also stood down, weakening the service further. With Mithridates still at large in Armenia, some part at least of Lucullus' forces were maintained in the Euxine with a few ships, but most of the remaining Pontic ships which he could have used were probably scrapped or burned.

69 BC   The navy was at its lowest and piracy raged unchecked across the Mediterranean. In 69 BC, they attacked and sacked the free port of Delos and even interfered in the Sicilian Narrows with the grain ships from Africa. They attacked coastal towns and villages and the seas were virtually closed to legitimate merchant shipping to the extent that trade was all but stopped. Still smarting from Antonius' defeat, the Consul Quintus Metellus was sent in 69 BC with three legions to deal with Crete, long one of the pirates' main lairs. Metellus struck with ferocity and the Cretans surrendered, the island becoming a province linked to Cyrene.

POMPEIUS – WAR AGAINST THE PIRATES

67 BC   Two years later, the final solution to the problem was at last enacted when, in 67 BC the Senator Aulus Gabinius proposed that drastic action be taken against the pirates to deal with them once and for all. His proposed legislation provided for the appointment for three years of an overall commander with unlimited powers over the entire Mediterranean and for fifty miles inland from it, to be provided with large quantities of men, ships and money. Pompeius was the only obvious choice for the task and, despite a rough passage, the Lex Gabinia was passed by the Senate. Pompeius was confirmed in the command with increased supplies, 6000 talents, 120,000 troops, 500 ships and the right to appoint up to twenty-four legates or deputy commanders. A legate was a senior military officer, normally a senator, placed in command of a legion (one to whom authority was de-legated) by a supreme commander and was thus a senior post reserved for experienced men, in this instance acting as admirals. Additionally Pompeius appointed a *Praefectus Classis et Orae Maritimae* or Admiral of the Fleet and of Maritime Affairs. No further mention is made of the *Duoviri* and *Praefecti* and perhaps their offices and functions were merged with that of the new *Praefectus*.[7]

     Preparations were started for the coming campaign and as if to underline its necessity, the pirates actually raided Ostia, the port of Rome itself and attacked a squadron of ships which were being fitted out for service against them. The exact numbers of Pompeius' fleet is not known but it has been estimated that he deployed some 200 beaked ships and about seventy lighter ships. To the navy's own ships and every one laid up in reserve that could be made seaworthy, would have been added as many as could be trawled from the small number remaining in Greek ports; seamen and rowers could be levied from the merchant marine and allied states, but the marines would have been Roman, augmented by Roman legionaries. It is clear that the majority of the Empire's armed forces were mobilised and directed to this one purpose.

Pompeius prepared his dispositions for the campaign by dividing the Mediterranean and Euxine into thirteen sectors, each under the command of a legate, to each of whom were allocated ships and men. Each command was to isolate and attack the pirates in their sector simultaneously, leaving them nowhere to flee. Pompeius retained a mobile squadron of sixty ships himself as a reserve to support any of his legates in turn. Dividing and blockading the Sicilian Narrows, he started from the Pillars of Hercules, moving eastwards via Sardinia, coastal Gaul, Etruria, North Africa and Sicily. He swept the western Mediterranean, driving his enemies before him, into the forces of his waiting legates and crushing them in between. The west was completely cleared in forty days.

Turning east, Pompeius repeated the process, from Brundisium via Athens, Rhodes, then to Cilicia itself, sweeping the eastern Mediterranean and finally meeting and destroying the pirate fleet in a naval battle off Coracaesium in Cilicia. Coracaesium was the pirates' final and greatest stronghold, situated atop a huge rock outcrop rising 500 feet (200m) from the sea and connected only by an isthmus to the mainland. Following the battle, he captured this final mountain stronghold. He claimed to have captured seventy-one ships with over 300 more surrendering to him. Furthermore, he claimed to have killed 10,000 pirates and taken another 20,000 as prisoners. Many of these he settled in Cilicia in towns away from the sea, giving them the chance to reform and start new lives, but making sure that they were aware of the assuredly unpleasant alternative. In his later Triumph in Rome, Pompeius was credited with the taking of 600 pirate ships throughout the whole Mediterranean. Pompeius' campaign had taken only three months and was a masterpiece of well-planned co-ordinated action, the result of which was that the Mediterranean would be free from piracy for the first time, a freedom that would last for several centuries and indeed until the decline of the imperial navy.

Pompeius had organised huge naval forces which, even if they may have fallen short of the total of 500 ships authorised, represented probably the biggest Roman naval deployment yet, even allowing for the contingents supplied by allied states. Unlike previous occasions, when anti-piracy campaigns had been completed and the fleets were stood down, allowing a resurgence in pirate activity, this time a naval presence was maintained and the long period of run-down and neglect of the navy was ended. The lesson had at last been learned that the sea could not be left to take care of itself, it had to be properly and continuously policed and as the greatest Mediterranean power, Rome had to accept the responsibility to do so. The Navy had been allowed to shrink to a level at which it was unable to undertake the role but, under Pompeius, was now resurgent and would henceforth be maintained at sufficient strength. In the west, small squadrons were kept in permanent commission, including squadrons to patrol the Adriatic and Tyrrhenian Seas. Surplus ships were laid up in harbours in Sicily, Gaul, Hispania and Africa, but instead of just being dumped, were maintained in a way that would enable them to be quickly refitted and re-commissioned if needed. In the east, the more unstable political situation and threat of impending hostilities required the squadrons to be kept at full strength in active service.

Mithridates meanwhile had managed to regain his kingdom of Pontus and Pompeius, still in Cilicia with his troops, marched north and defeated him. Mithridates fled to the Crimea, leaving Pompeius in control of Pontus and giving the Romans control of the whole south shore of the Euxine Sea. Pompeius marched into Armenia, which surrendered to him, he then turned north into the Caucasus and modern Georgia. Operating so far from established bases and with the newly acquired Pontus not consolidated, the support of his fleet must have been crucial to Pompeius. It has been suggested that his advance so far into new realms was to seek a new water frontier for the east of the empire.

In any event, with control of the southern and western shores of the Euxine Sea and with the Bosporan Kingdom as a 'client' state which held most of the north shore and Crimea, Pompeius' sweep of the eastern shore confirmed the sea to be a Roman lake, which it too would remain for several centuries. Pompeius nevertheless left a strong naval presence in the Euxine Sea, stationing a squadron of warships and a garrison at Sinope on the Pontic coast, to deter any attempt by Mithridates to leave the Bosporan Kingdom and again cause mischief (he committed suicide in 63 BC). Turning once more southward, Pompeius organised a standing Aegean naval squadron, based at Ephesus. The squadron was to have two flotillas, one to cover the northern half of the sea and the other, the southern half. Pompeius thus pursued a strategy of leaving secure seas at his rear.

Both Syria and Judaea had meantime descended into states of chaos. Pompeius next marched into Syria, where he heard that Mithridates had committed suicide. Pompeius proceeded to Jerusalem to settle the power struggle there and then progressed through the East, annexing Syria as a province and settling the provinces and client kingdoms of the East. He was given the title 'Pompeius Magnus', Pompeius the Great.

In March of 61 BC, Caesar was appointed Governor of Hispania Tarraconensis, where he embarked upon the conquest of that part of the

66 BC

63 BC

61 BC

COMPUTER
NAVIGATION

It is from this period that the Antikythera 'computer' comes. Discovered in the wreck of a merchant ship off the island of that name, north-west of Crete, the device had been found to be a machine with an amazingly complex system of gears which, upon setting the date, indicates the relative positions of the Sun, Moon and stars, a kind of mechanical calendar. It is of Greek manufacture and its use as an aid to navigation is not so obvious, although given its place of manufacture and initial setting and the date, a comparison of the readings from it and observation of the heavens should enable one's distance from that place to be measured. The intricacy, accuracy and quality of its manufacture however, most ably demonstrate that the instrument makers of the time were manifestly able to produce for the mariner, navigation instruments of a quality not surpassed until recent times.[8]

peninsula not yet under Roman control, namely the north coast and its adjacent territory (the areas of Galicia, Leon and Asturias). Possession of the whole peninsular coastline allowed the merchants of the Roman world to succeed to the ancient sea-routes of the Phoenicians and Carthaginians to northern Europe and to be under the protection of Roman warships well into the Bay of Biscay and connect with the trade route from Narbo, overland to Burdigala (Bordeaux).

60 BC
At Rome, political manoeuvring and intrigue grew until, in 60 BC, the three most powerful men, Pompeius, Crassus and Caesar joined forces to form the first Triumvirate, becoming effective rulers of Rome and the empire.

Cyprus was nominally a domain of King Ptolemy of Egypt but, on the pretext (probably not unfounded) that the pirates had received help and perhaps operated from there, Marcus Porcius Cato was sent with a naval
58 BC
and military force to annexe the island in 58 BC, which he achieved without resistance and it was made part of the province of Cilicia.

CAESAR IN GAUL AND BRITANNIA

In that same year (58 BC), Caesar embarked upon the first of his campaigns that would lead to his eventual conquest of Gaul. In that first year, after defeating the Helvetii and driving German tribes back across the River Rhenus (Rhine), he extended Roman influence to that great river for the first time.[9]

57 BC
The campaign of 57 BC took Caesar north into what is now north-east France and Belgium, whilst his deputy, Publius Licinius Crassus (son of the Triumvir) went westward, into what is now Normandy and Brittany. At the end of the year's activity the legions built forts to serve as winter

quarters along the north bank of the River Liger (Loire), an obvious line of communication between them and of supply by Roman ships coming up from ports in northern Hispania. Crassus with the Seventh Legion was nearest to the sea.

56 BC

In early 56 BC the tribes of Brittany and Normandy revolted. Caesar moved quickly to prevent the trouble from spreading, sending forces into eastern and south-western Gaul; for the first time in his Gallic wars however, he also had to deal with a seaborne threat. The tribes of Brittany were experienced sailors and shipbuilders. Apart from leather-covered light skiffs and coracles and rowing boats of wood, they had developed sea going vessels. With these they traded extensively, south into the Bay of Biscay and north to Britain and the northern coasts of Gaul. These ships were flat-bottomed so that they could negotiate shallow waters and could sit upright on a shore when the tide went out. They had high sides and very high bows and sterns so they could withstand the heavy seas of the Atlantic. They were built of oak and had stout internal cross-bracing, fastened with iron bolts, and the hulls were thus very stiff and strong and later proved almost impervious to ram attack. Power was provided by leather sails, they having no canvas, and a few oars were mounted only to aid manoeuvre.[10]

Caesar had already appreciated the quality of these ships as a potential enemy and that he would ultimately need his own fleet to deal with them. When he heard of the troubles, whilst still in Illyria, he gave orders to Crassus to have warships built on the River Liger. Caesar also made arrangements for rowers to be recruited from the Roman provinces in southern Gaul and sent north to join Crassus. Crews of seamen and pilots were also procured; Caesar distinguishes these from the rowers and thus one can assume them to have come from the navy as the logical source of men experienced in the operation of warships.

The army had the manpower to fell, collect and dress the required timber and although its engineers were well able to construct barges and pontoons, Caesar once again must have procured and sent naval architects, shipwrights and naval personnel skilled in the details of building and fitting out the warships that had been ordered. These men could only have come from the Roman naval establishment, the only warship builders in the western Mediterranean. The warships built in the short time available were galleys of the lighter or liburnian type.[11] The light Roman ships could not stand the amount of continual heavy weather of the north-west Gaulish coast as could those of the Gauls, which were superior under sail, but their one advantage lay in their superior speed and manoeuvrability in fairly calm seas, given by their greater oar-power and fine lines.

Additionally, Caesar mentions that he had ships specifically for reconnaissance in coastal waters, which he classified as *speculatoria navigia*, literally spy ships. It is not clear whether these were brought from the Mediterranean or built locally, but they were presumably smaller, lightly manned and of more shallow draft than the regular warships; they were nevertheless loaded with troops and added to the fleet strength for battle.

The first part of the ensuing campaign consisted of a series of sieges, with the Gauls fortifying themselves on headlands and promontories; the Romans laying siege and more often than not, the Gauls escaping by sea whilst the Roman ships were confined to port by heavy weather, or by simply pushing past them with superior weight and/or numbers and taking advantage of their superior knowledge of the tides, shoals and rocky inlets of the coast. The summer was marked by considerable bad weather which severely limited the use of the lighter Roman ships, designed as they were for the Mediterranean. Although it can deliver violent, short, stormy seas, the Mediterranean is very different from the long, heavy seas of the Atlantic for which the Gallic ships had been evolved.

At last however, sufficient ships had been built, equipped and manned. Ships were also brought from the Mediterranean, making the long voyage around Hispania to supplement Caesar's new, local construction.[12] The Roman fleet was ready to put to sea, under the command of Decimus Iunius Brutus, the Gauls massed their own fleet, 220 ships and in mid to late summer of 56 BC, sailed out to do battle off Quiberon Bay. The number of Roman ships is not known but it could only be those that they had been able to build between early spring and the mid to late summer of that year, together with some Gallic ships levied from the pacified and allied tribes and reinforced by the addition of the ships brought around from the Mediterranean, but which together could not have been as many as those of the Gauls.

56 BC

The Romans must have previously observed the enemy ships closely and previously tried to fight them as they had already discovered the ineffectiveness of their rams against the enemy's strong, heavy oak hulls and that the height of their decks made the use of throwing spears difficult, as was the use of normal grapnels; even the erection of towers on the larger ships did not give the Romans a sufficient height advantage over their towering adversaries. Accordingly, they had devised and equipped their own ships with a specialised weapon to deal with their enemy. 'Sharp pointed hooks, inserted into long poles', rather like the grappling hooks employed in sieges. These were used to grab and pull tight the rigging ropes of the enemy ships. The ropes were then snapped by a sudden spurt of rowing and the rig inevitably collapsed.[13] The Romans grabbed for braces (securing the ends of the yard-arm), sheets (controlling the lower corners of the sail) and even the stays (holding the mast in place).[14] As the Gallic ships relied entirely on their sails and rigging, when they lost these they were at once robbed of all power of manoeuvre. Upon disabling an enemy ship, two or three Roman ships would come alongside and the soldiers board and take it. After losing several of their ships to this tactic, the Gauls made to leave but the wind dropped and they were becalmed; one by one they were isolated and captured, only a very few managing to escape. The battle had lasted from ten in the morning to sunset and with their fleet lost, the Gauls surrendered. Caesar had meanwhile sent Crassus with his forces into Aquitania (south-west France) which was duly conquered, bringing the whole western seaboard of Gaul into Roman control.

55 BC   In 55 BC, Caesar took his army east where they bridged the Rhenus and operated to the east of the river. The river had already become the de facto boundary between ethnic Gauls and Germans and Caesar made only a punitive expedition beyond it, but no attempt at conquest. He delineated the river as the boundary of Roman Gaul.

By the late summer, Caesar turned his attention northward, to Britain, the inhabitants of which, related to the Gauls, had been supporting them and sending reinforcements against the Romans. Despite questioning traders and sailors, the Romans could get no worthwhile intelligence about the island, its size, harbours or its inhabitants, although presumably they had a copy of Pytheas' book of his travels so many years before. The Roman warships, and a number of the captured Gallic ships, had been brought around to the north coast. A warship under Gaius Volusenus was sent to reconnoitre the British coast and the army marched to the (modern) Pas de Calais. The Britons learned of Caesar's plans and sent envoys, to whom he said that he would soon visit Britain and he was assured of a friendly reception.

Volusenus returned with his report after four days. The report was of limited use, Volusenus, a cavalry officer, had cruised along the British coast making a visual note of the coastline but failing to land or reconnoitre for possible landing sites. In addition to his warships, Caesar had assembled about eighty transport ships, enough for two legions (about 10,000 men) and another eighteen ships for his cavalry.[15]

The boats of his potential enemies were long-boats of leather, stretched over a wicker-work shell, supported by wooden frames and stitched. Light and flexible, a forty foot (12m) boat could carry two tons, yet be carried by two men. They were not of course, able to oppose the big Roman ships, whose crossing was uncontested; Caesar did however note these boats and would later emulate them to provide river transports for his men. The seagoing transport ships were designated *naves onerariae* and were equivalent to contemporary merchant ships, the term also perhaps being applied to ships conscripted for use by Caesar.

The fleet sailed at midnight on 26 August and made the British coast at about nine the next morning. The cavalry transports had been delayed so the fleet waited for them, but they did not appear. The landfall had cliffs behind the beach and was not suitable for a landing, so the fleet sailed along the coast until a better landing site was found near to modern Deal and the ships were run ashore. The Britons immediately attacked the transports as they came into the beach, which because of their depth, could not be run right inshore. The water alongside them was deep, making it very difficult for the soldiers to disembark whilst fully equipped. After some hesitation by the troops, an *Aquilifer* of the Tenth Legion jumped in and waded ashore, holding the eagle aloft, which encouraged the troops to redouble their efforts and get ashore to protect him. Gradually, as more and more men got ashore and managed to form up, they prevailed in forming a beachhead.

The troops were unable to secure their landing in the face of the continuing attack and so Caesar ordered some of the lighter warships to row at full speed ashore on the flanks of the transports and use their artillery to give covering fire, driving the attackers away from the flanks of the men already ashore and allowing them to move forward.[16] This is one of the rare occasions where the use of shipboard artillery is specifically mentioned. The remaining warships lowered their ship's boats, filled with troops, to land them in support of the legionaries who were fighting their way ashore from the transports. Once enough troops had got ashore, they formed up and quickly put the Britons to flight.

The eighteen ships with the cavalry had been held back in Gaul by bad weather, but four days later managed to sail. When in sight of Casear's camp however, a storm blew up from the east and despite their efforts, the unfortunate ships were driven back to Gaul. Of Caesar's ships, the transports had been pulled off the beach or anchored offshore and the warships were beached. The same storm wrecked twelve of the transports and damaged the rest; some were driven into each other while others suffered damage to rigging and masts and lost anchors and cables; a few actually broke up. The warships had also suffered some damage from high tides. The troops had to set to and repair the damaged ships, cannibalising the wrecked ones to do so and despite beating off several attacks by the Britons, the ships were made seaworthy again. Shortly before the autumn equinox, the fleet embarked the troops, sailed and returned safely to Gaul. Caesar returned to Italy for the winter, but left orders with his commanders to repair and refit all their ships and to build new ships for his intended next campaign to Britain. He specified particularly the type of ships he wanted.

It would seem there was a standardised form of naval transport as Caesar ordered these ships to be slightly wider and slightly lower in freeboard to the normal type as used in the Mediterranean; he also required them to be suitable for oar power in addition to the normal sail power, the lower bulwarks enabling this latter.[17] The alterations were made in the light of the sea conditions encountered in the English Channel narrows and also to facilitate the loading and unloading of the ships in case of another opposed landing. The ships' equipment was ordered from Hispania and shipped to northern Gaul.

When he returned in early spring of 54 BC, Caesar found that some 600 transports of all types and sizes and another twenty-eight warships had been built and gathered. The figure is clearly an exaggeration; he only needed eighty transports the previous year to convey two legions; he now had five so presumably needed about 200 ships to carry them, plus enough for the cavalry and allowing for a greater amount of supplies than before, say 300 at most. Even allowing that the ports of Gaul had probably been scoured for anything that could make the crossing, Caesar had a considerable fleet available, which he ordered to concentrate at Gesoriacum (Boulogne). Sixty of the ships were held back by storms but by the time it was assembled the fleet was said to number about 800 vessels although it was more likely to have been half of this amount. The fleet sailed at the end of July carrying five legions and 2000 cavalry. They sailed at sunset but when the wind dropped, were carried eastward by the tide. The oars had to be used and the fleet made its intended landing place by the following midday (between modern Deal and Sandwich).[18]

The landing was unopposed and the ships drawn up on an open, soft, sandy shore; once emptied, they were pulled off shore and anchored. A force of ten cohorts and 300 cavalry were left under the command of Quintus Atrius to guard the fleet and its crews in their shore-side camp, while Caesar and the army marched inland.

That first night a great storm sprang up and many of the ships were damaged and thrown up onto the shore; the cables and anchors of others had not been able to hold and they were swept into each other. Caesar was recalled and gave orders for all the legions to detach their engineers and craftsmen to assist the sailors in repairing the ships. Some forty ships had been completely wrecked and a ship was sent back to Gaul with orders for replacement ships to be provided as quickly as possible. A further sixty ships were commandeered or built. Caesar next ordered all of the ships to be beached and enclosed within a fortified camp, which took the army ten days to complete. The same guard was again left, with the crews and craftsmen and the army marched off once more. An attack on the naval camp was beaten off by its guard.

After a successful campaign in Britain, Caesar and the army returned in late summer to the coast to find the ships repaired, but that none of the extra ships that had been ordered had arrived. To make up for the lost ships and to carry the hostages he had taken, Caesar ordered the return to Gaul be in two trips. The first contingent returned safely but when the empty ships plus

'CRUISING IN
THE MED'

In July of 51 BC, the orator and author Marcus Tullius Cicero journeyed from Athens to Ephesus to take up the post of Governor of Cilicia and was taken across the Aegean by a flotilla of warships. They sailed on 6 July and made a somewhat leisurely progress, stopping at Kea, Syros, Delos and Samos, among others, before reaching Ephesus on 22 July, after two weeks of cruising. His eventual return journey was again by warship and again took two weeks, from which one must assume that he took advantage of a regular fleet patrol 'circuit' to enjoy the voyage and a meal and night's sleep ashore each night, as a direct, non-stop voyage home on a merchantman would have taken only three or four days.[19]

the some of the new replacement ships tried to return to Britain, they were caught in the increasingly bad equinoctial weather and only a few managed to return. Nevertheless the remainder of the force managed to squeeze into the available ships and as the weather abated, returned safely to Gaul.

Upon his return, Caesar learned that his daughter, Iulia, who was married to Pompeius, had died, breaking the family bonds between them. In 53 BC one of the other triumvirs, the senior Crassus was killed in Parthia, leaving only two strongmen, Caesar and Pompeius, to vie for control of Rome and her empire.

53 BC

Affairs in Gaul occupied Caesar fully until in 50 BC, he returned to Italy. Caesar left a garrison in Gaul of initially, eight legions; four in central Gaul and the other four in the north-east, adjacent to the English Channel. Throughout all of his campaigns in Gaul, Caesar had never strayed far from a branch of the system of major rivers throughout that country and by which he was able to maintain the transport of supplies for his troops. There is no record of any further support from Britain reaching Gaul after the expedition of 54 BC and of the fleet used that year, it seems certain that some part of it at least was retained in active service to patrol the north coast. Although there was no separate naval command, as previously, a number of specialised naval personnel were retained, seconded to the commander of the legions stationed in the north, who could oversee the manning and operation of the ships used to patrol the north Gaulish coast.

CAESAR v. POMPEIUS

Political matters in Rome had deteriorated badly since the death of Crassus, a manifestation of the fact that the republican constitution itself was breaking down. By 50 BC, two factions had crystallised, the one represented by Caesar and the other by Pompeius. In December the Senate ordered both

50 BC

men to relinquish their commands but one faction of the Senate ordered Pompeius to 'defend the State' and allotted two legions to him. Caesar started to make his own dispositions and in January of 49 BC he moved with his forces into peninsular Italy and the Civil War began. After some two months of campaigning but mostly of manoeuvring the balance of forces in Italy tipped in Caesar's favour and Pompeius was forced to withdraw to Brundisium. Caesar's dash to intercept Pompeius failed and he was left to attempt to besiege and blockade him there. Strangely, neither side had naval forces available and Pompeius seized whatever merchant ships he could to use as transports.

Caesar tried to blockade the port by building moles across the narrow channel between the harbour and the sea and closing it by floating pontoons across between them, these having two-storey towers upon them, equipped with artillery. Pompeius built three-storey towers upon his largest merchant ships and also mounted artillery and every day for nine days, sallied forth to attack Caesar's forces and prevent them from sealing the harbour entrance. Finally his fleet of transports arrived from Epirus and he was able to break out and evacuate his men. Pompeius and his forces sailed for Greece, where he could expect greater support and gather all of his eastern legions and fleet.[20]

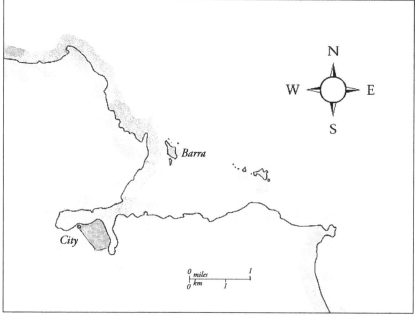

BRUNDISIUM

As Pompeius was a naval hero and the man who had really ensured the continued and permanent establishment of a sufficient navy as an essential part of the state, it is hardly surprising that most of the service joined Pompeius' cause. Of the active squadrons, those loyal to Caesar in the Channel and northern Europe were too remote to be of any help, whereas those established by Pompeius and loyal to him in the Euxine, the Aegean and the Levant were available to him. Additionally he could call upon the fleets of the allies, Egypt and Rhodes, with whom he had a good personal relationship. Caesar and his deputies who now held Italy quickly secured Sardinia and Sicily and together acquired enough of the western fleets to organise an Adriatic squadron under Dolabella, another for the western Mediterranean commanded by Decimus Brutus and a third to cover Sicily and the narrows, under Caius Curio, each of twelve ships. Several times the sources relate that generals ordered the 'building' of warships but as already discussed, these were then, as they are now, specialised, complicated and dedicated ships, totally unlike merchant ships.[21] Likewise they required shipyards experienced and familiar with the peculiarities of such ships and their design; not all shipyards could produce a warship. In Massilia, large merchantmen were converted into platforms for fighting men and artillery (but performed poorly against warships). Also, laid-up warships were refitted and put into service and these methods rather than the building of ships *ab initio*, were the sources of the ships. As for crews, there would have been in the seaports and among merchant crews, many veterans of the naval fleets who, when called to action, formed an experienced cadre of rowers, seamen and marines, well able also to train new recruits.

49 BC
APRIL

Caesar himself marched to Hispania to confront the Pompeian forces there. He was not quick enough to stop Pompeius' general, Domitius Ahenobarbus, arriving ahead of him at Massilia by sea with seven merchant ships and turning the city against him. Caesar besieged the city and blockaded it with Brutus' ships before marching on into Hispania with his remaining troops.

49 BC
MAY

The Massiliotes set about their defences and the commissioning of a fleet to break the blockade. They refitted and prepared for service such laid-up warships in the harbour that could be made sea-worthy, as many as six ships including at least two triremes, probably a quinquireme and the rest bireme liburnians. Further, they sailed out and gathered every merchant ship they could find on the nearby coast and took them back to the city. These they cannibalised and adapted to produce more fighting ships by making provision for propulsion by oars and fitting catapults and protective decking for the rowers. A further eleven fighting ships were thus produced and several smaller boats were also pressed into service. These ships were crammed with archers and fighting men and this ad hoc fleet then sailed to meet Brutus. The latter's squadron, at twelve ships, including a 'six' as flagship, was fewer in number but composed of purpose-built warships, fast and handy and the navy crews and marines aboard had been made up to strength by experienced men levied in Italy from merchant ships, stiffened by the addition of elite veteran troops from Caesar's legions.

The Massiliote ships approached in line abreast and for a while, successfully manoeuvred and shot at Brutus' ships, causing casualties with catapult shooting before closing to make attempts at shearing their oars. Gradually however they were pushed back towards the shore and became constricted in movement so Brutus' ships could grapple and board, where the superior quality of his troops soon told. The Massiliotes lost nine of their ships, three destroyed and six captured, and the survivors were driven back into their harbour; Brutus lost no ships.[22] During the campaign in Hispania, Caesar utilised the boatbuilding methods that he had observed in Britannia and had his men build similar boats which, transported by wagon, were used as assault craft on the rivers which lay across his advance.

Pompeius meanwhile, had gained the use of his own naval squadrons and sent a force of sixteen warships under Lucius Nasidius from the east, to the relief of Massilia. On his way through the Sicilian Narrows, Nasidius' fleet had entered Messana and took from there a laid-up warship, thereby increasing his strength; he next sent a light scout ship ahead to alert the Massiliotes who had managed to fit out more ships to replace those recently lost.[23] They augmented this by manning a number of open fishing boats, adding archers and catapults. This force sallied forth once more and, managing to evade Brutus, found and joined Nasidius' ships about twenty miles (35km) east of the city. Brutus' own squadron of twelve ships had been augmented by the six captured ships and despite the odds against him, he gave chase. His opponents cleared for action and formed two divisions, the Massiliotes on the right and Nasidius on the left i.e. on the seaward side.

The Massiliotes, knowing that their failure to break the blockade meant doom for their city, fought with desperation whereas Nasidius' men, far from their homes and not as zealous in pursuance of their cause, put up only a token fight before withdrawing and heading for the coast of Hispania. Brutus' men again tried to grapple and board their opponents but every time, other enemy ships and boats crowded around to pour missiles onto the attacker; in one instance, two Massiliote triremes attempted to ram Brutus' flagship from opposite sides, but he managed to extricate his ship just in time and the two ships crashed into each other instead, crippling both, which were then speedily despatched by Brutus' ships, presumably by ramming. One of the smaller Massiliote ships capsized when its deck soldiers massed on one side, trapping the rowers inside the hull. With the withdrawal of Nasidius' ships and other losses, the battle swung against the Massiliotes, who lost four ships destroyed and one capsized, four more captured and one which left with Nasidius. Brutus lost one ship, holed by several rams and swamped.[24]

Of Nasidius and his ships, nothing more is known but he presumably joined with the Pompeian forces in southern Hispania. Pompeius' commander there, Marcus Varro, ordered the 'building' (but see the previous comments as to this) or rather commissioning of several warships at Hispalis (Seville) and ten more at Gades. His fleet was concentrated at Gades but his attempted build-up of forces to oppose Caesar was foiled when they were completely outmanoeuvred by Caesar and the province and most of the troops surrendered to him. The fleet was also surrendered to Caesar, who used its ships to transport him from Hispalis back to Tarraco. Having secured Hispania in a three-month campaign, Caesar returned to Massilia which, beaten at sea and reduced by the siege, surrendered to him. With that, Caesar had secured the whole western half of the Roman domains and the western Mediterranean, which he could seek to hold with a fleet that had grown, with captured and surrendered ships, to about sixty warships.

49 BC
AUGUST

The important grain-producing province of Africa had declared for Pompeius. Curio took two of his four legions from Sicily to invade it, escorted by his squadron of twelve warships, under Marcus Rufus. In Africa meanwhile, ten old laid-up warships of which one was a trireme, had been hastily commissioned with scratch crews and put to sea. Upon sighting Rufus' ships however, their commander, (confusingly) one Lucius Caesar panicked and beached and abandoned his ship; his remaining nine ships fled southward for the safety of Hadrumentum (Sousse). The beached ship was towed off and added to Rufus' squadron. Curio landed unopposed near Clupea and marched to Scipio's old campsite, Castra Cornelia, between Carthage (now a ruin) and Utica, the provincial capital, the ships heading around the coast to meet him there.[25]

49 BC
SEPTEMBER

There were a large number of merchant ships at Utica (now blockaded) and Rufus was ordered to notify their captains to bring their ships to Curio's camp or to be sunk; with no alternative, the merchantmen obeyed with alacrity, adding their cargoes to Curio's supplies. The campaign started well but King Juba of neighbouring Numidia intervened with his army, trapped and defeated Curio; Rufus' ships withdrew with the remnants of the force and returned to Sicily. Caesar detailed Caius Antonius to march around the north of the Adriatic to deter or at least to slow any attempt by Pompeius to invade Italy by that route. Dolabella's Adriatic squadron was increased to forty ships and moved up to support Antonius. These forces advanced unopposed but incredibly, made their headquarters and camp on the island of Curicta, off the north Dalmatian coast, effectively isolating themselves if Dolabella lost command of the sea, which he soon did and as must have been anticipated given the known size of Pompeius' naval forces. Pompeius

despatched two of his four naval squadrons from the Ionian sea under
Marcus Octavius and Scribonius Libio. This fleet quickly overwhelmed
Dolabella's ships, only some of which managed to escape to Italy, leaving
Antonius cut off and besieged. Two more legions had to be sent to try to
extricate him but, with seas dominated by enemy ships, managed only to
evacuate a quarter before the rest were starved into mutiny and went over
to Pompeius' cause.

Pompeius had meanwhile organised a force of some 44,000 men and
7000 cavalry and a fleet of 300 ships, drawn from the navy and allied states

49 BC
AUTUMN

in the East.[26] These ships were organised into several squadrons; Adriatic,
under Marcus Octavius (from which Nasidius and his sixteen ships had
been detached); Achaean (the ex-Aegean flotilla) under Caius Triarius; Asian
(the ex-northern Aegean flotilla) under Decimus Laelius; Syrian under Caius
Cassius; additionally there were allied squadrons, each commanded by a
Roman officer, the Rhodian by Caius Marcellus and an Egyptian, of fifty
ships, by Pompeius' older son, Gnaeus. Overall naval command was given to
Lucius Calpurnius Bibulus, who set up his headquarters on Corcyra with a
fleet of 110 of the ships; another unit, of eighteen ships was sent by Laelius'
Asian fleet to a forward base at Oricus. These forces obviously dominated
the Adriatic and patrolled with the object of preventing any crossing by
Caesar's forces. The fleet even managed to maintain some patrols in the
'closed' winter months of 49/48 BC, considerably delaying Caesar's plans
for a confrontation. Pompeius doubtless contemplated an invasion of Italy
and Caesar had to act quickly to prevent his opponent's forces from growing
further and landing in overwhelming numbers.

Caesar managed to assemble a transport fleet and an escort squadron
of twelve warships at Brundisium and in January 48, before the end of the

48 BC
JANUARY

winter season and taking advantage of a time when the opposing fleet was
unprepared and in its harbours, managed to successfully ferry seven of his
legions (over 20,000 men) and 600 cavalry across the Adriatic.[27] With his
naval superiority, Pompeius had commandeered most of the ships in the area
and there were in fact barely enough left to carry the under-strength legions,
perhaps 100 ships or so, plus the escort. Caesar's ships had to make several
trips to get his army across. In any event, on one return trip they were
caught and attacked by the Pompeian fleet under Bibulus who managed
to capture thirty of the empty transports which he burned at sea, complete
with their unfortunate crews. Although he had landed further south than he
had wished, Caesar had done so unopposed and without loss to his army. In
risking winter crossings, Caesar's luck had held as the Bora, the winter wind
that sweeps from the north the length of the Adriatic, makes thunderstorms,
squalls and sudden gales a feature of these waters. Even in summer, vicious
squalls can appear in conditions of bright sunshine and little cloud.

Bibulus stepped up the naval patrols and extended their area, trying to cover all the possible crossing routes as well as the 94 miles (150km) from Brundisium to Dyrrhachium. Naval pressure was further increased by Octavius' Adriatic Squadron, which cruised southward along the Illyrian coast, seeking to turn the inhabitants against Caesar. They had some success until the Roman settlement at Salonae (near Spalato, Split) was reached, which remained loyal to Caesar. Octavius beached his ships and invested the town. A surprise attack by the defenders on the besiegers' camp caused many casualties and broke the siege, the survivors fleeing to their ships and sailing to join Pompeius at Dyrrhachium.

Caesar occupied Oricus then Apollonia and Pompeius moved into Dyrrhachium. In Brundisium, plans were afoot to ship reinforcements across to Caesar, who postponed the operation on receiving intelligence of enemy naval activity. One empty ship did try the passage but was intercepted and caught by Bibulus' patrols and the crew killed. Bibulus had moved the main body of his fleet to blockade Caesar at Oricus; he was however, faced by a mountainous and hostile shore. The blockading ships had to stay at sea although within the shelter of the Bay of Valona and be supplied by requisitioned merchant ships operating from Corcyra. Despite the difficulties of supply, very cramped conditions on ships not designed for crews to reside aboard and the winter weather, they managed to maintain a blockade. The privations and demands of this effort soon told however and Bibulus became ill and died. No successor was appointed as overall supreme naval commander and henceforth Pompeius' fleets operated each under their own admiral. Bibulus' deputy, Scribonius Libio, succeeded to command of the ships covering Oricus.

48 BC
FEBRUARY

Libio decided that instead of waiting for Caesar's reinforcements to attempt a crossing, he would attack their base of Brundisium. With fifty warships he crossed the Adriatic, intercepting and burning several merchantmen on the way. On arriving, he seized the small island of Barra (S. Andrea) which lies in the approach roads to the harbour; holding this meant that he could seal the harbour mouth and from it his ships started raiding the outlying garrison posts. Caesar's commander at Brundisium was Marcus Antonius, who evolved plans to reduce the enemy and break their stranglehold on the harbour; he ordered sixty ship's cutters, i.e. open rowing boats carried by ships to be used as tenders, to be concentrated and covered with fascines and mantlets, the former for camouflage, the latter for protection; troops were allotted to each and they were positioned along the shorelines leading into the harbour. Next, two newly built triremes were rowed out with much show to suggest new and inexperienced crews being trained and with few marines on deck. They rowed into the roadstead but kept clear of the island. Unable to resist the opportunity of an apparently easy kill, Libo ordered five of his quadriremes to dash out and try to capture

48 BC
MARCH

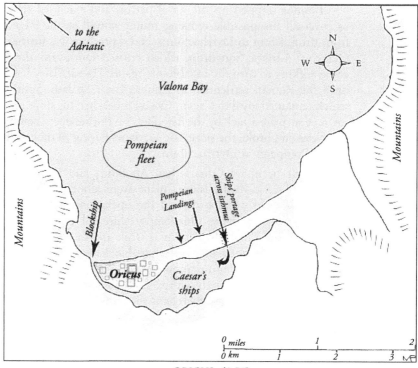

ORICUS, 48 BC

them; when they gave chase, the triremes feigned panic and ran for home, drawing the quadriremes after them, their veteran crews feeling confident of being able to catch their prey. When they drew abreast, the hidden cutters swarmed out from both shores where they had been lurking among the reeds and selecting an enemy ship, quickly overwhelmed its crew and captured it. The remainder of Libo's ships on seeing this, fearing further ambush and with little room to manoeuvre turned and fled back to Barra. To complete Libo's discomfiture, Antonius posted strong patrols along the coasts to prevent or give early warning of any landings. There is no water supply on Barra and Libo, his men prevented from being able to go to the mainland for it, was forced to evacuate and return to the Greek coast.

48 BC
April

Finally in April, Marcus Antonius managed to evade the blockade and ferry another four legions from Italy to join Caesar. The expedition very nearly ended in disaster for Antonius' fleet which was caught off the Greek coast by a southerly wind and blown northward past Dyrrhachium; there the Rhodian squadron of sixteen ships, now commanded by Caius Caponius, saw them and emerged to give chase. Antonius' ships managed to reach the harbour of Nymphaeum (Shengjin, Albania), when the wind shifted to the south-west and strengthened in a sudden squall, catching the Rhodians in the port quarter and forcing them ashore onto the rocks where the ships were lost and the survivors captured by Antonius' men. The latter had not escaped unscathed, having lost one transport and its complement of 200 new recruits, which became separated and fell into enemy hands. The transports were later sent back to Italy for more troops and the escort squadron of warships under Manius Acilius, was sent to Oricus.[28]

Both commanders now raced, Pompeius to intercept and destroy Antonius before he could join Caesar and the latter to meet up with his reinforcements. Caesar was successful and Pompeius fell back to fortify a camp in a strong position just south of Dyrrhachium. Meanwhile at Oricus, Acilius was faced with a Pompeian fleet which was, despite its losses, still greatly superior; in an attempt to defend his ships, he sent them into the lagoon at the rear of the town, using a block ship to block the narrow channel linking it with the open bay. To reinforce this, he used a merchant ship upon which his engineers erected a tower for artillery. The Egyptian Squadron, under Gnaeus Pompeius, attacked and managed to grapple and tow off the block ship and then attacked the guard-ship from the towers on their own ships. At the same time, the town walls were assaulted and the attackers seized the isthmus of the peninsula upon which the town stood. Across this, the Egyptians manhandled on rollers, four of their biremes, launching them upon the lagoon; there they immediately attacked Acilius' moored ships from the rear. By now the attackers had forced abandonment of the guard-ship opening the way for Acilius' ships to be attacked from both sides; four were towed away and the rest burnt at their moorings, while the garrison was blockaded in the town.

Pompeius had also attacked northward to Nymphaeum, where he caught and burned thirty of Antonius' transport ships which he found in the harbour there; an attack upon the town itself was repulsed. Pompeius returned to his camp and Caesar took up position between him and Dyrrhachium. The Pompeian camp was on a height on the coast, where his ships could anchor close in, and part of it was ordered to stand by the camp to cover the supply route to the east, while the rest continued to blockade Caesar and isolate him from Italy and thus any supplies and reinforcements from there. Pompeius was, as was only to be expected, making full use of his overwhelming naval superiority. Caesar had now lost his own small squadron of warships at Oricus and many of his transports. Even by denuding the west and concentrating and bringing his warships from there he would not have enough to challenge his opponent, assuming he could get dispatches to them.

Caesar resolved to isolate Pompeius from the land, which he could then forage at will. Despite having fewer men, Caesar succeeded in the face of furious opposition to complete the encirclement of Pompeius' forces. The resulting lines were some fifteen miles (24km) long. At first, Pompeius' troops enjoyed plentiful supplies, brought in by sea unopposed, whereas Caesar's men suffered privation and shortage of food, there being little around that early in the year. One advantage Caesar had was to dam the streams that ran into the enemy lines and greatly reduce their water supply. Accordingly as the siege went on into the summer, Pompeius' troops' health began to suffer and they started to desert, whereas crops inland ripened to feed Caesar's troops and ease their privations. Pompeius had to break the siege and he used his ships to assault the southern end of Caesar's line, where it ran to the sea and where the works to protect against such an attack had yet to be completed. Troops and archers were loaded aboard ship's boats and small rowed transports as the assault group; they were supported by more transports, loaded with troops as the second wave and backed by the artillery of the major warships. They attacked at dawn and got in between the lines, routing the troops there, securing the foreshore and fortifying a position themselves. Any further advance was stopped by Caesar's relieving columns and both sides then encamped in these new positions, but despite this and some further heavy fighting, the encirclement had been broken.

Finally, Caesar, unable to gain supplies from Italy because of his opponent's command of the sea and having therefore to dissipate his strength by keeping large numbers of his men occupied in the securing of supplies from inland, was forced to raise the siege and move eastward; as his troops moved along the coast, Pompeius' warships moved inshore and harried them with artillery. Pompeius followed and three weeks later in August 48 BC, the armies met at the battle of Pharsalus. Caesar won an overwhelming victory. Since abandonment of the camps, Pompeius' fleet, released from having to stand by and supply him, had again gone on the offensive. The Asian Squadron under Laelius again attacked Brundisium, seizing the island of Barra but this time arranging to have ships fitted and acting as water carriers to supply them. The defenders re-used the tactics that had been successful before, collecting and fitting out small boats and seeking to entice Laelius' ships; amazingly he fell for the same ruse and one of his quinquiremes and two smaller warships were overwhelmed and captured. The coastal patrols were reinstated but Laelius clearly intended to pursue his offensive, until news of the Battle of Pharsalus rendered it pointless and he withdrew.

At the same time, Caius Cassius with the Syrian Squadron descended in a surprise attack on Sicily. Caesar's fleet had been deployed to protect the Straits of Messana, twenty major warships and fifteen smaller under Marcus Pomponius being at Messana and the rest, under Publius Sulpicius, at Hipponium (Vibo Marina, Calabria). The force at Messana was lax, with no scout patrols or proper lookouts posted. Cassius had prepared and brought fire-ships with him, merchantmen filled with pitch, pine-resin and other inflammable materials. Having a favourable wind, he launched them against the harbour, with devastating effect, all thirty-five ships being burned to the waterline. Cassius next steered for Hipponium, where he found Sulpicius' ships moored close inshore. Another attack by forty fire-ships was made and five warships were quickly destroyed. Sulpicius' men were however more alert than those at Messana and they quickly manned their ships and counter-attacked Cassius' fleet with such ferocity that they captured the flagship, a quinquireme, Cassius only just escaping by small boat. They also captured a second quinquireme and destroyed two triremes. Cassius withdrew and once again, upon receiving confirmed news of the outcome at Pharsalus, sailed back to the east.

48 BC
AUTUMN

The Pompeian main fleet in Illyria, on hearing of the defeat at Pharsalus, tried to move its base and concentrate at Corcyra, but the men's hearts were not in it and there was great disaffection for a cause that was lost and not a little disruption as the fleet began to break up. The Egyptian, Rhodian and other allied ships went home. Cato, with the remainder, made his way south along the Greek coast, but as Caesarian forces approached, fled to join the Pompeian forces still holding Africa, losing a good many of his ships to bad weather on the way. One squadron, under Marcus Octavius and operating on the Dalmatian coast, remained in good morale and continued its resistance to the Caesarians and remained active. Pompeius himself meanwhile fled, taking ship from Greece to Asia Minor, then to Cyprus. Attempts to raise fresh forces failed and he sailed to Egypt, where he was ignobly murdered by agents of the boy-king Ptolemy XIII Euergetes.

THE ALEXANDRINE WAR

48 BC
AUTUMN

After Pharsalus, Caesar was magnanimous in his dealings with Pompeius' former supporters, including the fleet of about 200 ships of all types, which went over to him. Caesar next pursued Pompeius to Egypt, taking a force of two under-strength legions, about 3200 infantry and 800 cavalry, transported and escorted by a few Roman warships and ten Rhodian ships. Of Pompeius' former fleets (after the rest of the allies went home), it is likely that not too many of the Roman ships could be wholly relied upon in their new allegiance and certainly not those squadrons such as Laelius' and Cassius', which had been the most active against Caesar. Caesar landed at Alexandria to learn of Pompeius' ignominious end in the midst of an internecine fight for power between Ptolemy and his sister, Cleopatra VII. Egypt was nominally under Roman guardianship and Caesar felt it incumbent upon him to arbitrate and settle the matter.

Caesar set up his headquarters in the Royal Palace and billeted his men in the adjacent Bruchion district of the city and sent for Ptolemy and Cleopatra. Alexandria at that time had a population estimated at 300,000, with the native Egyptians concentrated in the west half of the city, a Jewish section in the east and the Greek population concentrated in the centre. The local populace resented the Romans' imperious attitude and encouraged by local intrigues and rabble rousing, showed rising hostility towards them; before long they were effectively isolated and shut in their area by the increasingly belligerent locals. Caesar effected and declared a resolution of the dynastic problem but in doing so, upset some of the local power factions, especially as he was forming his attachment for Cleopatra. Ptolemy's army advanced from Pelusium, at the east of the Nile Delta with 20,000 men and 2000 cavalry; they entered Alexandria and besieged Caesar's men in the Bruchion area, which they had fortified against such a possibility.[29]

Caesar's other problem was that he was also cut off by sea by the Egyptian navy, for in addition to the twenty-two ships of the resident guard squadron, the fifty Egyptian ships formerly under Pompeius' son had returned there from opposing him in the recent civil war. Caesar's own few ships were thus trapped in the small Royal Harbour by seventy-two Egyptian ships, most of them placed in the Eastern Harbour. Before they could take advantage of their position, Caesar took the initiative and a lightning attack by his troops took the Egyptian ship's crews by surprise when most of them were ashore. The troops managed to set fire to their fleet and another thirty or so ships at the harbour quays, causing enough loss and damage to break the blockade. The Romans followed this up by seizing Pharos Island thus securing the eastern harbour mouth.

Caesar was then able to send ships with requests for aid to his other commanders and before long the first reinforcements, the 37th Legion under Cnaeus Domitius Calvinus, arrived from Asia with fresh supplies. His ships were becalmed to the west of the harbour mouth and Caesar sent his remaining ships to help in towing the transports in under oar power. The Egyptian warships remaining in the Western Harbour, sallied out to intercept but were beaten off after a spirited action in which the leading Rhodian ship was set upon by four enemy ships and the rest of its countrymen immediately thereupon went to its rescue. The Egyptians lost a 'four' and many marines from two other ships but did however, manage to regain Pharos Island. The Egyptians next brought the rest of their available ships from the Nile as reinforcements and repaired and refitted as many as they could until they had a fleet of twenty-two 'fours' and five quinquiremes, as well as some smaller ships. Caesar's fleet was now composed of nine Rhodians and twenty-five Romans, of which five were quinquiremes and ten were 'fours', the remainder being triremes or smaller.

There were two ship passages through the Heptastadion, the causeway linking Pharos Island to the city and through these, the Egyptians sent fire-ships to attack Caesar's fleet in the Eastern Harbour. Avoiding this attack,

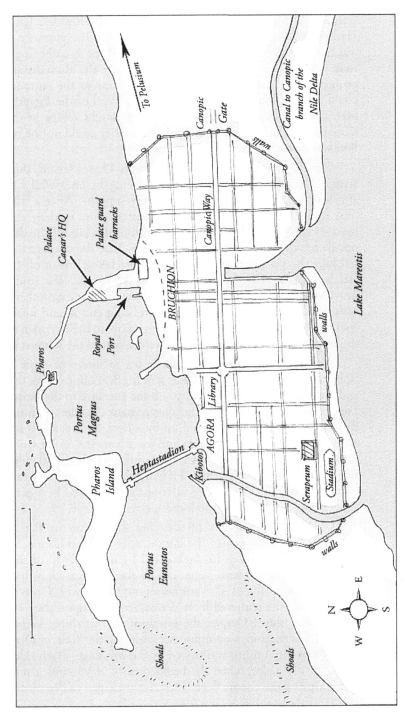

Palace
Caesar's HQ

Palace guard
barracks

Pharos

Portus
Magnus

Pharos
Island

Heptastadion

Portus
Eunostos

Shoals

Royal
Port

BRUCHION

Kibotos

AGORA

Library

Serapeum

Stadium

Canopic
Gate

Canopic Way

walls

walls

Canal to Canopic
branch of the
Nile Delta

Lake Mareotis

Shoals

To Pelusium

N
W   E
S

ALEXANDRIA, 48 BC

Caesar's thirty-four ships, under Euphranor of Rhodes, left the Eastern Harbour to mount an attack on the western. The entrance to the latter was restricted by sandbars, forcing Caesar's ships to enter singly when they were attacked by the enemy ships. Gradually the Romans and Rhodians pushed in and forced the Egyptian ships clear of the entrance until they could pull in alongside and board. After several of the Egyptian ships had been disabled or captured, the remainder sought refuge in the inner part (Kibotos) of the harbour and canal, where they could not be pursued; their fleet was nevertheless greatly weakened.

47 BC   The Romans next set out to re-capture Pharos Island, shipping troops across in small boats (Caesar himself being in one) whilst the warships attacked from seaward and gave artillery support. After a stiff fight, they took it; a subsequent attack on the Heptastadion, to deny the enemy the passages through it, failed, despite the ships driving off the defenders with missile fire to allow the troops to advance. They did manage to dump rocks to block the passageways through it before being driven off by a counter-attack, supported by boats along the western side. The Romans suffered heavy losses in being driven off the mole and had to regain their boats on its eastern side to prevent themselves from being cut off and unable to retreat back to Pharos Island. Caesar's men also set fire to the Egyptian naval arsenal, the fire unfortunately spreading to destroy part of the famous library.

The Egyptian ships again put to sea to intercept more approaching Roman reinforcements, but Caesar sent his fleet out to cover their approach and the enemy were beaten off just off the entrance to the Eastern Harbour, Euphranor being killed in the engagement. In the meantime, another Roman and allied army, backed up by a fleet, had marched from the east, captured the fortress of Pelusium and was advancing on Alexandria. Ptolemy led his army out to meet it but Caesar outflanked him and sailed to join his allies and in the ensuing battle, Ptolemy was killed and his army destroyed. Cleopatra was left as effective ruler of Egypt, backed by a garrison of four legions, and Caesar left for Judaea.[30]

Octavius' ships were still denying free access in the Adriatic and attacking Caesarian ports. The commander at Brundisium, Vatinius, had a small squadron which he augmented by using transport ships, some of which he had rigged with rams, and he also had first-class troops available to him. In the spring of 47, Vatinius set out to deal with Octavius. His ships however, became scattered by bad weather whereupon they were set upon by Octavius' ships. Despite the inferiority of his ships, Vatinius counter-attacked, his flagship, a quinquireme ramming the 'four' of Octavius, which had its ram torn off but was snared by the wreckage. Both sides' ships then joined in the melee, when the better quality of Vatinius' troops soon told and destroyed the enemy fleet. Octavius managed to flee on an escort ship, having lost a quinquireme, two triremes and eight biremes; the Adriatic was thus cleared.

Caesar returned to Rome where he had been made Dictator once more. The survivors of the Pompeian faction had been massing forces in Africa, which had remained loyal to Pompeius and also seeking to suborn the garrisons in Hispania. They included the survivors of Pompeius' fleets, with over fifty warships, which had ferried to Africa the remnants of his army and garrisons after their defeat at Pharsalus, over 40,000 men. They had managed a couple of half-hearted naval raids on Sicily and Sardinia, which achieved nothing. Caesar massed his own army at Lilybaeum in Sicily with an attendant fleet of fifty or so warships, whence, in October, it was ferried to Africa in several detachments and despite the lateness of the year, they arrived safely. The Pompeian fleet had already been laid up for the winter closed season and made no attempt at interception. Caesar systematically built up his forces, until his fleet numbered over a hundred warships, to give him overwhelming superiority at sea. Despite being confined to a small area by his enemies, while he awaited more men, Caesar's control of the seas meant that he could be supplied and maintain his position. On one

46 BC occasion, at the beginning of 46 BC, a convoy from Sicily nearing the coast mistook Caesar's blockading ships laying off Thapsus, for Pompeians and fled to seaward, taking several days to re-assemble and resume their course to join Caesar.

In the only naval action of the campaign, the Pompeian commander, Varus, sailed with fifty-five ships from Utica to Hadrumentum. Thirteen of Caesar's ships, under Aquila, were patrolling towards Hadrumentum and another twenty-seven, under Cispius, off Thapsus. Aquila's ships could not weather the point and had to seek a lee shore for the night, so Varus' ships went by undetected and fell upon and burned some transports moored at Lepcis and captured two unmanned triremes. Caesar quickly organised and led a pursuit, re-taking one of the captured ships from its prize crew. Varus managed to get to shelter beyond the point of Ruspina but Caesar could not and had to resume his pursuit the following day to Hadrumentum where Varus' ships sought refuge and refused to come out; Caesar burned some supply ships nearby and his superior fleet kept Varus bottled up in the harbour there for the duration.

The Pompeians in Africa were finally destroyed at the Battle of Thapsus in June 46 BC. Although a land battle, Caesar's fleet lay offshore in sight and ready to land marines and troops in the enemy's rear; despite the battle being won before they could do so, the presence of this force probably went a long way to breaking their enemy's morale. Pompeius' two sons and Labienus escaped to Hispania with whatever ships they could get past Caesar's blockade.[31]

Upon his return to Rome, Caesar was made Dictator for ten years and set out upon a great programme of reform and reconstruction, but he was to be murdered before most of it could be effected. For navigation, he proposed that the harbour of Ostia be greatly enlarged and that a canal be cut through the isthmus of Corinth to shorten and make safer the sea route from Italy to the east. The former had to await the reign of the Emperor Claudius in the AD 40s and the latter, until the late 19th century.

46 BC   Late in the year (46 BC), Caesar took his army back to Hispania to face the remaining Pompeians. Pompeius' elder son Gnaeus was already there with some ships, he was joined by Varus with a few more and the escapees from the African campaign. Caesar sent Caius Didius with the fleet and troops to secure the seas. Varus was driven to seek refuge in Carteia (Gibraltar) where he set up a line of archers across the harbour mouth, which surprised some of the pursuing ships and deterred the others. The Pompeians in Hispania

45 BC   were destroyed at the Battle of Munda in March 45 BC. Gnaeus Pompeius managed to get to Carteia and sailed with a fleet of thirty ships, he was caught by Didius' fleet four days later and killed in the ensuing battle. The other of Pompeius' sons, Sextus Pompeius, also managed to escape and to survive and would re-assert himself later.

Caesar returned to Rome in triumph, where he was heaped with honours and made Dictator for Life. He was already planning his next campaign, to be against Parthia and in late 45 BC, started making preparations for it. He intended to utilise a vast army and for its part, the navy had to start organising the assembly of sufficient transports and escorts to carry it, with its stores, equipment and artillery to the east and to support the effort.

44 BC   The embarkation of troops for the campaign was to start on 18 March 44 BC and arrangements were thus well advanced when the plot against Caesar culminated with his murder on the Ides (15th) of March, 44 BC. By his defeat of Pompeius and his allies, Caesar had effectively made himself the de facto ruler of a Roman world which had far outgrown its old republican system, evolved to govern a city-state but which had been overwhelmed by the rapid expansion of Rome's power and empire. The sudden removal of Caesar, in a perhaps misguided attempt to restore that already inadequate system, left a huge power vacuum at the centre, which others would be only too keen to fill.

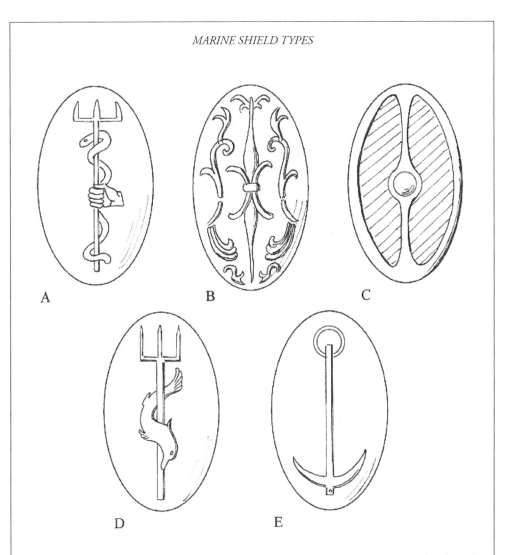

MARINE SHIELD TYPES

A B C

D E

Shield designs used by the Roman navy, and more specifically, the Roman marines serving on board naval vessels, are not well attested and source material is limited. A and B, shown above, are taken from the Praeneste Relief, C is from a sarcophagus in Naples whilst D and E are from votive altars found in the River Tyne.

Notes

1. Appian is the prime ancient source on the Mithridatic Wars.
2. Apart from Rhodes, ships were obtained from Cyprus, Pamphylia and Phoenicia and it is a moot point as to how many of them would otherwise have been classified as pirates.
3. See Fry, *Great Caesar*.
4. Fry, *Great Caesar*.
5. Appian, *The Mithridatis Wars*, but some interpretation is needed to resolve logical progression.
6. Appian and see Ormerod, *Piracy in the Ancient World*, quoting other ancient sources.
7. Ormerod, *Piracy in the Ancient World*, which includes a list of the Legates and their respective command areas.
8. James & Thorpe, *Ancient Inventions*.
9. Caesar, *The Gallic War* is obviously the source for the overall course of events in Gaul.
10. They are the only type of ship that Caesar describes in detail (*Gallic War* III.13).
11. Caesar describes them as having towers (III.14) not normally fitted on this type; however they can only have been short, more like raised platforms as they were not as high as the high poops of the Gauls' ships. To give scale, a quinquireme as has been seen, had deck ten feet (3m) above water and with a tower, at least double this height overall. It is highly unlikely that the Gauls' ships stood that high out of the water.
12. Cassius Dio says that Decimus Brutus came with 'swift ships from the Mediterranean'.
13. Caesar, *Gallic War* III.14 & 15.
14. Several translations refer to 'halliards' but as these generally run down close to the mast, to the deck, they would have needed an immensely long hook to reach them, across a deck that was higher; stays and outboard running rigging were however within reach. Of course, it may well be that the Gauls did belay their halliards to the deck edge.
15. Caesar does not say (IV.22) but presumably these ships were like those of the Veneti.
16. Presumably (IV.25) burying their rams in the beach in the process which would help to stabilise them but necessitate being towed off later.
17. Not only perhaps of transports but also of warships, *vide* the large production numbers already seen. Certainly standard transport types were used in Imperial times (see post).
18. Representing a rather slow crossing at an approximate average of three mph (5 kph) Caesar, Gallic War V.
19. For Cicero's voyage: Casson, *Travel in the Ancient World*.
20. It is Caesar's account of the Civil Wars that is followed.
21. E.g. Polybius as has already been seen.
22. Caesar's account of this battle (*Civil War* I.III.37) was presumably recorded from Brutus' report to him but also see Lucan, related in *GROW*.
23. Confirming thereby the earlier contention that warships were kept in reserve and in seagoing condition at various ports.
24. Caesar, *Civil War* II.I.6&7.
25. Once again, Caesar (II.III) is relying on the reports of his local commanders but there is no reason whatever to suppose that they are inaccurate.
26. 600 according to Appian, 100 crewed by Romans. The lesser figure is more reasonable. Caesar describes the various commands (*Civil War* III).
27. Presupposing that intelligence of this had been obtained and had been sent across the Adriatic.
28. The composition of this unit is not known, nor its previous provenance and it may have been formed from the recently 'acquired' Rhodian ships; hence the enemy's single-mindedness in seeking to destroy it.
29. Marlow, *The Golden Age of Alexandria*.
30. Apart from Caesar, The Alexandrine War is reported by other ancient writers, e.g. Plutarch (writing a century later) and Hirtius (one of Caesar's legates). Commentaries on their works are in Rodgers and *GROW*.
31. Caesar, *Civil War* III.

THE END OF THE REPUBLIC

44 BC–13 BC

With the death of Caesar, the world of Rome was once more in turmoil. Marcus Antonius, the surviving Consul, forced the conspirators to flee Rome, leaving him in control. He was backed by Marcus Aemilius Lepidus, Governor of Hispania and Gaul, who was sent to negotiate with Pompeius' surviving son, Sextus, who had already secured an army in northern Hispania. Meanwhile, Caesar's great-nephew, Gaius Octavius, learned that he had been adopted as a son by Caesar and named as his principal heir.[1]

43 BC   Antonius next went to Cisalpine Gaul (northern Italy). Octavius' faction raised support against Antonius and Octavius was sent with an army against him. Antonius was defeated and fled to Transalpine Gaul (southern France), leaving Octavius in command in Italy. The Senate declared Antonius a public enemy and appointed the plotters Brutus and Cassius to govern in the east. Caesar's former fleet commander, Dolabella, with a scratch squadron, sought to cut Cassius off from Syria, but was himself besieged in his base on the Syrian coast. A foray by his ships brought Cassius' fleet to action and after several were disabled on each side, succeeded in capturing five of Cassius' ships. In a second battle however, Dolabella's fleet was defeated and he was killed. Cassius, in command of the Eastern Fleet was next opposed by Rhodes, which refused to acknowledge his authority. Cassius could not countenance such a prominent adversary, so he attacked it. The Rhodian navy, of thirty-three ships, came out to give battle but were beaten in an action off Myndos by Cassius' larger fleet of eighty ships, including heavier ships. The Rhodians tried their favourite *diekplous* attack, but were surrounded by the Roman ships, who boarded them; they lost two ships destroyed and three more captured before breaking off and fleeing home. Cassius next massed an invasion fleet and with his eighty ships attacked the island, beating off a sally by the Rhodian fleet which cost it another two ships. Rhodes was then blockaded and preparations made for a siege, but the city was entered and fell without it.

Sextus Pompeius was given command of the navy by the Senate and appointed as the *Praefectus Classis et Orae Maritimae*. Octavius, with his army behind him, demanded and got the consulship. Lepidus in Narbonese Gaul with his army, supported Antonius. The Senate was forced to revoke the declaration against Antonius and to remove the amnesty given to the murderers of Caesar. Octavius now met Antonius and Lepidus at Bononia (Bologna) and they formed a new Triumvirate, de facto rulers of the Empire.

Octavius now sought to remove Sextus Pompeius from his command by having his appointment cancelled but the son of one of Rome's greatest admirals was not to be so lightly dismissed and retained the loyalty of his fleet of over 130 ships. With no army he could not approach Italy but he needed a secure base and with his fleet began to occupy Sicily. Octavius appointed his friend, Quintus Salvidienus Rufus, as admiral, to concentrate the remaining naval forces that were still available to him and to deal with Sextus. The two fleets met and fought an indecisive battle in the Strait of Messana, but Rufus had to withdraw to the mainland shore as it was clear that his force was insufficient to overcome Sextus' fleet.

42 BC   For 42 BC, Lepidus was made Consul and left in charge at Rome, whilst Antonius and Octavius set out to confront the armies of Brutus and Cassius in the east. These latter had built up their power base in the eastern provinces and also had a large fleet, composed of the navy's eastern squadrons and allied contingents under the command of Lucius Domitius Ahenobarbus. Brutus and Cassius learned that the still-powerful Egyptian Fleet might come to support the Triumvirs and so they sent sixty ships under Murcus to the southern Peloponnesus to forestall such a move. For her part, Cleopatra alleged plague and famine in Egypt as her reason for retaining her fleet, in reality not wishing to risk her only real weapon by becoming embroiled in their civil war. It was learned that Cleopatra's ships were at home, so Murcus' fleet proceeded to the blockade of Brundisium near to where he even managed to secure and to fortify a base on land. He was unable however, to prevent the Triumvirs from transporting their troops when the winds turned favourable especially as the transports could make way in greater numbers and in heavier weather than that in which Murcus' ships could operate. Later, Ahenobarbus arrived with fifty more ships to assist Murcus and they cut the line of supply to the Triumvirs' troops, forcing them to subsist on the scant resources of their area of operations in Greece and necessitating a short campaign on their part.

Brutus and Cassius' forces advanced westward across Greece and with their fleet blockading the Italian ports, Antonius was held at Brundisium and unable to cross to the east to join his army. At length he insisted that Octavius join him with his fleet so that their combined forces, attacking the blockade from both sides, could once the wind was favourable, break it. Together, Antonius and Octavian must have had enough ships to transport their men, but not enough to challenge Ahenobarbus' fleet of 110 ships for supremacy at sea. There is no record of any naval battle at this time and the crossing was presumably made when the enemy fleet was known to be absent elsewhere.[2] Octavius' fleet sailed to support Antonius in breaking the blockade and Sextus was therefore left in unopposed possession of Sicily and control of the western seas.

Antonius and Octavius crossed to Macedonia with twenty-eight legions and in a battle at Phillipi and another, six weeks later, defeated first Cassius, then Brutus. Some of their supporters fled to join Sextus in Sicily. On the day of the battle, a convoy with reinforcements of two legions and some cavalry, escorted by some triremes had been caught by Marcus and Ahenobarbus crossing the Adriatic when the wind failed. The escort was driven off by their attack and the transports locked themselves together to form a solid fighting platform for the troops. They were attacked with fire arrows, the first time the use of this weapon is specifically mentioned at sea in the ancient sources; many of the ships were burned and the rest surrendered, along with seventeen triremes. The republican cause was nevertheless lost and Antonius and Octavius divided the empire between them, leaving Lepidus with Africa, Antonius taking the eastern half and Octavius the west. Sextus had, meanwhile, succeeded in occupying Sicily, Sardinia and Corsica and was holding up the corn ships from Africa as well as controlling the shipments from the islands. Of the former republican fleets, a force of thirty from the Aegean and Murcus, with eighty ships, joined Sextus; the remainder, seventy ships under Ahenobarbus, continued to dominate and cause mayhem in the south Adriatic.

40 BC   In the spring of 40 BC, Antonius moved to intervene in Italy and obtained the backing of Ahenobarbus with his Adriatic fleet, as well as support from Sextus, also hoping no doubt, to gain thereby. With their joint fleets, they landed near and prepared to besiege Brundisium, when Octavius, who had superior land forces, arrived. Antonius and Octavius met and concluded a treaty between them, confirming Lepidus in Africa and their respective halves of the empire. Ahenobarbus was made proconsul of Bithynia and command of his fleet passed to Antonius. Sextus was aggrieved at being ignored by the treaty in his claims for power and continued to interfere with the corn supply to Rome, threatening the city with starvation. Under this pressure the Triumvirs met with Sextus, who arrived with a large part of his fleet at Misenum in 39 BC. It was agreed that Sextus would guarantee the corn supply and in return would be given a five-year command over Sicily and Sardinia and also Corsica and Achaea and after that, be a Consul.

THE WAR AGAINST SEXTUS

Clearly Sextus had command of the major part of the navy's western fleet and in addition had attracted to his ranks refugee republicans, escaped slaves and sundry disaffected individuals. He commanded over 200 ships. He had obtained a position of strategic dominance over Rome and the western Mediterranean and played on the obvious distrust between Octavius and Antonius. This meant that the latter, having acquired the fleet formerly commanded by Ahenobarbus, jealously kept it, rather than let Octavius use it to deal with Sextus, indicating his own preference that his only serious rival be weakened to assist Antonius' own longer-term plans. Just as clearly Octavius could not consolidate his own power in the west whilst Sextus remained in such a position, but to challenge him he would have to fight a naval war. Octavius had the navy's home bases, with their stores and those ships which had not come under Sextus' command. These would have been ships under repair or refit, those laid up and inactive, together with any new building and ships posted away from the main battle fleet, such as those in the Adriatic. Foreseeing the struggle to come, Octavius put in hand the building of new ships in yards all around Italy, with towers and heavy catapults and of all types, up to and including 'sixes'.

38 BC   War between Octavius and Sextus came before the former was ready. Antonius, perhaps once again thereby pursuing his own agenda, delayed in the handing over of Achaea to Sextus and Sextus thus resumed the blockade of Italy. Sextus' Governor of Corsica and Sardinia however offered the islands, with their garrisons and up to sixty ships, to Octavius, an offer too good to pass up, and Octavius was thus able to secure them from Sextus at no cost, the extra ships coming as a welcome reinforcement of his own fleet. For his first campaign against Sextus, Octavius planned to lead his army and his fleet under Calvisius, which with its recent additions was now of about ninety ships, south from Neapolis to Rhegium. There they would rendezvous with the Adriatic fleet under Cornificius, which was coming from Brundisium and Tarentum. The majority of Sextus' fleet were veteran and experienced crews with well worked-up ships, while those of Octavius were either recently recruited and untried, or in the case of the ships recently acquired from Sextus' former governor, probably unreliable. His only really veteran squadron was that from the Adriatic.

Octavius sailed southward with his fleet in July but after first being damaged by a storm, was met by Sextus' fleet off Cumae before he could join the ships coming from the east. Sextus had at first concentrated his own fleet of 130 ships at Messana, to block any attempt by Octavius to ferry his army across to Sicily. Doubtless learning of his enemy's preparations, leaving forty ships to guard Messana, he sallied north with the rest and caught Calvisius' smaller fleet and immediately attacked. Both fleets formed into line abreast, Calvisius resting his left flank close to the shore. From the south, Sextus' ships pushed their opponents onto the shore on the left, whereupon Calvisius moored his ships stern-on to the shore as a defence, where he could draw on support from the army. Undeterred, Sextus attacked with his left wing, massing two of his ships to one and caused a great deal of damage; Calvisius on the other wing, cut his cables and sallied forth for a counter-attack, breaking out and into the rear of Sextus' left wing, capturing the enemy's flagship and driving Sextus' fleet off. Once Sextus' fleet had returned to their bases, Calvisius gathered his surviving ships and sailed to join Octavius at Rhegium.

Octavius with his Adriatic Fleet came out to meet Calvisius and escort him in, but on seeing this movement, Sextus' fleet again put to sea to try to intercept before they could join forces. Sextus' ships began to harry the rear of Octavius' formation and so, on the mainland opposite Cape Pelorus his outnumbered ships moored stern-on to the shore, rather as Calvisius had done. Sextus' ships attacked the end ships of Octavius' line, two ships to one and started to systematically destroy them. Octavius was forced to jump overboard and get ashore when his own ship was attacked. Cornificius and the ships nearest to him cut their cables and attacked Sextus' ships and managed to seize their flagship. As Calvisius' ships could be seen approaching, Sextus broke off the action and returned to base. Many of Octavius' damaged ships, stranded on shore, were further wrecked by the worsening weather before such as could be were pulled offshore and withdrawn to safe ports. Half of the fleet had been lost and the first assault on Sextus had been a failure. Sextus proclaimed himself to be the 'Son of Neptune' and Octavius realised that he needed a bigger and better prepared fleet and a better admiral than himself.[3]

As his admiral, Octavius appointed his lifelong friend and faithful ally, Marcus Vipsanius Agrippa, who set to work energetically to revitalise and re-build the 'legitimate' navy. Extra taxes were levied to pay for construction and for the first and only time in Roman naval history, several thousand able-bodied slaves were requisitioned to be rowers, but only on the strict condition that before they went aboard the ships, they were freed in return for enlisting in the service for the duration of the campaign (manumission of a slave brought with it full Roman citizenship).[4]

Agrippa continued the building of the new ships laid down by Octavius and enhanced their protection against ramming by Sextus' smaller and handier ships by adding a belt of extra timbers around the waterline. Agrippa realised that his armoured ships sacrificed handiness for protection against Sextus' ships and that he could not expect to succeed by ramming alone, so he also had perfected and fitted a new weapon, the *harpax* or harpoon, which was a tethered grapnel attached to a shaft, seven and a half feet (2.3m) long and lined with metal strips so that it could not be chopped through. Obviously it needed a larger catapult; a two-cubit machine, a handy size well suited to shipboard use and shooting a three feet long (1m) arrow, had a stock six feet (2m) in length and it would seem therefore that the *harpax* required a somewhat larger machine to shoot it; range would also be much shorter than the conventional arrows. It was designed to ensnare an enemy ship which could then be pulled or winched in alongside so that it could be boarded.[5] Agrippa also introduced a collapsible tower to carry archers which was able to be quickly raised on going into action, but otherwise was stowed flat on deck. An improved version of the previous static towers, they were effective without adding permanent top-weight to the ships and being lighter, could probably be mounted on smaller ships. The towers were all painted in the same, distinctive colour to aid recognition between friendly ships.

With the evolution and expansion of Ostia into the major mercantile port of Rome, the navy needed a better base of its own and so Agrippa founded Portus Iulius in the lee of Cape Misenum, west of Neapolis. There he concentrated the ships and crews of the fleet. The area between Cumae and Neapolis is indented with the craters of many volcanic eruptions, some of which have filled to become lakes. Agrippa had channels dug to link Lakes Avernus and Lucrinus to each other and to the sea, with extra tunnels to permit the action of the sea to keep the basins thus formed clear and free from silting up. In the safety of these new harbours, the crews could train and work up their ships. To improve landward communication with the new base, the engineer Lucius Cocceius Auctus drove two tunnels through the Appenine spurs that reach down to the sea, one just east of Puteoli, to link with Neapolis and the other under Cumae, ten feet wide (3m) to link the route north, to Rome.[6] A subsidiary base was also established at Forum Iulii (Fréjus) in south Gaul, where the harbour facilities were improved, extended and fortified for naval use; from there the coast of Gaul and the mouth of the River Rhodanus could be controlled.

37 BC   In 37 BC, Antonius returned to Italy and the Triumvirate was renewed for a further five years. As part of an exchange of forces, Octavius was allocated part of Antonius' naval forces, namely 120 ships, commanded by Statilius Taurus, which sailed to be based at Tarentum; of these about 100 were manned and serviceable at any time. Sextus had overlooked or ignored these preparations and spent the intervening time preying on seaborne trade, virtually a pirate chieftain.

36 BC   By 36 BC, Octavius was ready to attack Sextus in Sicily, having built up an army of twenty legions and a fleet of about 150 ships of all types plus Taurus' fleet. The plan was for Taurus to attack from the east, Octavius and Agrippa from the north and the Triumvir, Lepidus from Africa. Lepidus

landed safely on Western Sicily with twelve legions and a covering fleet of seventy ships and began to overrun it from there. The other two attacks, intended to be co-ordinated with Lepidus', were driven back by severe storms, suffering some losses and over thirty ships wrecked. It was August, a month later, before the attacks could be remounted. First however, the sea passage had to be secured and Sextus well knew that if Octavius' legions could be landed in Sicily, his own land forces would be vastly outnumbered, trapped between them and Lepidus' men and in any event, no match for them and that his reign would be finished. His only hope was to win at sea and then concentrate his forces on Lepidus. His ships successfully attacked a convoy bringing reinforcements and supplies to Lepidus off Western Sicily, destroying half and scattering the rest whence they had come. Another raid by seven of his ships on the Bay of Neapolis ended when, having captured a couple of guard-ships and destroyed some merchantmen, they surrendered, presumably previously unaware of the strength of the naval establishment there and on being caught, went over to Octavius' cause. Taurus' fleet had meanwhile moved up to Calabria.[7]

Agrippa, with about 100 ships, including many quinquiremes and 'sixes', seized the Lipari Islands, north of Sicily, from which he could watch Sextus' fleet, which had been concentrated at Mylae (a re-run of the tactics of the First Punic War, by both sides). Sextus' fleet, of about 150 ships but with only one 'six', a few quinquiremes and otherwise nothing bigger than a four, commanded by Demochares, a freed slave, came out and Agrippa attacked. After the initial headlong rush at each other and much artillery shooting by the two fleets, the action settled down into a series of ship-to-ship fights. As expected, Sextus' ships relied on speed, seamanship and ramming, whereas Agrippa's main combat ships, concentrated in the centre of his line, were bigger, heavier, higher and with their added armour, virtually immune to these tactics. Use of the *harpax* and boarding gradually swung the battle in Agrippa's favour and Demochares' flagship was rammed and shattered by Agrippa's, whereupon Demochares transferred to another ship.[8] On being gradually worsted and seeing that reinforcements for Agrippa were approaching, he ordered his fleet to break off the engagement and head for Messana. Agrippa had lost five ships, but had destroyed thirty of Sextus' ships.

Covered by Agrippa's actions and joined by Taurus' ships, Octavius had also moved, landing with three legions at Tauromenium (Taormina). Unfortunately, the next day, before his transports and escort could withdraw to safety, Demochares, after his return from the battle off Mylae and having anticipated such a move by going to Messana, appeared and mounted a surprise attack, destroying or capturing about sixty of Octavius' ships.[9] Possibly the transports of Octavius' fleet were caught while landing troops and were static and not fully manned. Appian says that Octavius put to sea to meet the attack, but that in two fights lasting into the evening some of his ships were burned, wrecked or fled. Taurus' ships, even if slightly outnumbered, proved no match for those of Sextus. In any event they were badly handled and no protective screen could have been mounted. No losses are reported among Sextus' ships and Octavius immediately sent for Agrippa.

Agrippa had also landed his forces and captured Tyndaris, then advanced along the north Sicilian coast. He managed to link with Octavius' forces which had been isolated by the naval defeat off Tauromenium. While Agrippa now covered the route, Octavius was able to ship the rest of his army to Tyndaris, concentrating there instead of making another attempted landing at Tauromenium. Octavius' ships, now under Agrippa, with his own squadron and those of Taurus and Lepidus numbered altogether over 200 warships. Octavius' and Lepidus' armies were now progressively closing in on Sextus from all sides and his only option was to concentrate his fleet and gamble all in a sea battle to regain command of the seas around Sicily; if successful, the gaining of this would deny the huge amount of regular supplies needed for his enemy's large armies which, because of their size (as many as thirty-five legions), would soon suffer and deteriorate. Sextus' fleet of between 150 and 160 ships was on the east coast of the island and advanced through the Straits of Messina, commanded by Demochares and Apollophanes, to meet Agrippa. The latter's fleet had been increased to 130 ships by re-commissioning captured ships and by drafts from either or both of Taurus' and Lepidus' fleets.[10]

36 BC   In late August or early September of 36 BC, the two fleets met off Naulochus, each in line abreast with one flank near to the shore. Sextus' ships were in tighter formation than those of Agrippa, which promptly extended seaward, surrounding Sextus' offshore flank, the perfect *periplous* manoeuvre. Using the greater weight and strength of his ships, together with the *harpax*, Agrippa's ships closed on the end of Sextus' line, forcing it back and inshore and denying his ships room in which to manoeuvre. Proceeding to 'roll-up' Sextus' line, Agrippa inflicted a total defeat, sinking and burning twenty-eight ships and capturing or driving the remainder ashore. Only seventeen managed to escape, lightening ship by cutting loose and dumping their towers overboard. Agrippa lost three ships to enemy ramming. Demochares committed suicide, Apollophanes surrendered and Sextus, watching from the shore, fled to Asia with as many of his men and ships as he could. Once there, Sextus tried to find a place with Antonius, but the latter suspected him of also treating with the Parthians and thus placed him in captivity, then had him executed; the ships he took over to add to his own fleet.

Lepidus' army then joined Octavius, ending his career as a Triumvir and leaving Octavius as undisputed supreme ruler of the western half of the

Roman world. For the next couple of years, apart from a sweep to clear some piracy from the Adriatic, the navy was inactive. In his Dalmatian campaigns, Octavius had advanced down the River Savus (Sava) a navigable tributary of the Danubius (Danube) and with the help of many tradesmen and sailors from the Mediterranean fleets, had ships constructed and manned, to form a naval flotilla which was joined by allied native craft and commanded by one Menas.

This flotilla remained in service on the river at the end of the campaigns. It is most likely that Taurus and his surviving ships returned to Antonius' command in the east, any losses replaced by the salvaging of ships taken from Sextus, although in this regard the heavier 'eastern' ships were replaced by the lighter liburnian type which had formed a major part of Sextus' fleet.[11]

THE FINAL STRUGGLE, OCTAVIUS v. ANTONIUS

Antonius had campaigned extensively in the east and had formed his famous alliance with and then married Cleopatra of Egypt, an enterprise born nevertheless of mutual necessity; Cleopatra needed Antonius' troops to secure her throne and Antonius needed the riches of Egypt to support his ambitions. A contest for supremacy between Antonius and Octavius could not be far off.

33 BC   Antonius had been married to Octavius' sister Octavia but he divorced her to marry Cleopatra and hailed Caesarion, reputed to be her son by Caesar, by implication therefore denying Caesar's appointed son and adopted heir, Octavius. The latter published Antonius' will at Rome. The Triumvirate expired and Octavius duly stood down, but Antonius refused to do so. Any relationship was irreparably damaged and war followed.

32 BC   Antonius was already mustering his forces in Macedonia and he and Cleopatra then moved to Corcyra as a base for their proposed crossing to Italy. They encountered some of Octavius' scout ships watching them and as the season was late, assumed (wrongly) that Octavius had already crossed the Adriatic to Greece with his forces and so they withdrew for the winter to western Greece. Octavius' fleet had in fact, after concentrating at Brundisium, made a sweep of the Ionian Sea, seeking to confront Antonius' fleet; they failed to locate it and suffered some damage in a storm before returning to base for the winter. Antonius and Cleopatra next took up a defensive position near to Actium at the entrance to the Gulf of Ambracia. The entrance to the Gulf is only just over 400 yards (m) wide and at its narrowest, Antonius established forts on each bank from which artillery covered the entry to the anchorage within. Just outside the entrance was the small fishing harbour of Actium, where his scout ships could be based, within the cover of his nearby camp. The Gulf provided a secure and sheltered anchorage for Antonius' fleet, reinforced by the Egyptian fleet of his wife.

This northely position in Greece was to tempt Octavius to bring the
war to Antonius' 'own' territory and to avoid any problem from the reaction
in Italy if he had landed there with an Egyptian queen playing so prominent
a role. Conversely it was also an excellent jumping off point for an invasion
of Italy. The position did however, rely almost wholly on being supplied by
sea from Corinth and the Peloponnese. Their fleets were some 500 ships in
number although this total included transports. As to warships, Antonius
was well equipped, having 170 or more heavy warships including the last of
the 'super galleys', 'sevens' and 'tens'; these were most likely laid-up survivors
from the former navies of the Hellenistic states of the Levant, taken over
and re-commissioned for the occasion and probably also largely crewed
by the men of those former navies. This is the only known instance when
these large ships were part of a Roman fleet. There were also the 120 ships
returned by Agrippa.[12] This fleet was reinforced by Cleopatra's navy with
about sixty warships, which also included some of the vast ships so beloved
of the Ptolemies.

Although fighting towers (each carrying up to six archers) on the decks
of warships had been in use for many years, the relative main deck levels
of the various warships did not vary by much. Obviously a ship with three
remes was higher than a bireme and Livy refers to the four (of two remes)
being overawed by a quinqireme's higher deck (being of three remes).[13]
Mention is made of Antonius' big ships, presumably the Hellenistic multi-
remes, towering above their opponents and a couple of references are made
to 'raised decks',[14] which seem to indicate that false floors were erected over
parts of the main decks of the bigger ships to give their marines even more
of a height advantage, herein may even be the ancestor of the fore and aft
castles developed (or re-developed) from medieval times onward.

31 BC   Octavius' preparations were ready by the early spring of 31 BC. Agrippa
was once more Admiral of the Fleet, which numbered in all some 400
ships, including transports, of which some 260 were warships. The warships
comprised the fleet victorious at Naulochus (net of the ships returned to
Antonius), triremes, quadriremes, quinquiremes, the special armoured
quinquiremes and a few 'sixes' built for that campaign, totalling about 170
ships; additionally there were another 90 or so ships salvaged from Sextus'
former fleet, these being of the lighter types. Although Antonius' fleet
totalled slightly less in numbers, he had a preponderance of heavier ships,
giving his fleet greater weight.[15] Except for the ships that had served against
Sextus however, this fleet was untried in battle whereas all of Agrippa's fleet
was experienced and in a high state of readiness, their morale still flushed
with victory.

The campaign opened with Agrippa driving off Antonius' scout ships
and seizing Corcyra as a base from which to cover Octavius' armies as they

were safely transported from Brundisium and Tarentum, to land on the Greek coast, north of Actium. From there, they advanced to take up a position on high ground a little to the north of the entrance to the Gulf. Although not himself a successful admiral, Octavius, unlike Antonius, understood the value of sea power and so whilst the armies glowered at each other, he sent Agrippa, one of the best of admirals, onto the offensive.

Agrippa moved down from his base on Corcyra and with his heavy warship squadrons, under Arruntius, established a blockade of the mouth of the Gulf of Ambracia; with his fast, light squadrons, he managed to capture Methone, a regular stopping place for ships passing the south Peloponnese and from where he could intercept supply ships coming up the west coast of Greece. There was some skirmishing between units of the two fleets off the coast of Actium, in which Agrippa's ships bested those of Antonius. Next, Agrippa's fleet extended its activities into the Gulfs of Patras and Corinth, seizing those two cities in turn, to cut off Antonius' supply lines from that direction also. With a patrol line to intercept supply ships from coming up the west of the Peloponnese, Agrippa finally moved in and captured the island of Leucas, off the coast by Actium itself, closing the sea blockade as completely as was possible.

Antonius was now reliant upon such limited supplies as could be transported overland and with the increasing shortage of supplies, his position began to deteriorate, his men became restless and many began to desert to Octavius. The rest of Antonius' men became weakened and sickness began to break out in the camp. It became apparent to Antonius that he would be unable to force a decision on land. In August, one of Antonius' admirals, Gaius Sosius, attempted to break the blockade with his squadron; he was at first successful, but Agrippa soon came up with the main fleet and severely beat him, forcing a retreat and further reducing the morale of Antonius' fleet.

Antonius was in a quandary, he was in an advantageous position for his fleet to withstand an attack, but the longer that he stayed on the defensive the weaker his strength became. He had the progressively greater necessity to force action; conversely, Octavius did not oblige by taking the offensive and with secure lines of supply, he could remain on station indefinitely. Attempts at blockade-running by Antonius' ships had so far been beaten back but he now resolved to attempt a mass breakout, using the vast fleet which he still commanded. In this way, he could avoid a long overland march, which would be contested and with scant chance of foraging for enough supplies and instead, break out directly for provinces in the east, or to Egypt, where he was still secure. Without the fleet, which would have to be abandoned if he went overland, Antonius could be cut off and isolated in Greece. On the other hand, if he won at sea it would be Octavius who would be cut off and isolated in Greece and at his mercy. Some 20,000 troops and 2000 archers in addition to their regular complement of marines were embarked on the warships and any remaining ships for which there were insufficient crews, burned. The ships must have been absolutely packed with fighting men but Antonius had to utilise as many of his troops as possible for two reasons, firstly the obvious one of trying to overwhelm his enemy's marines but secondly, one of morale; if he made a break-out and got away, he would be abandoning the troops left behind and never again be trusted by the soldiers; by involving as much of the army as could be crammed aboard the ships, such a charge could not be levelled come what may.

The narrow entrance enabled the ships to form in the safety of the Gulf and to advance by divisions perhaps twenty abreast, avoiding the risk of being picked off piecemeal as they emerged. From this they could quickly deploy into their full battle formations. The fleet was arrayed in four squadrons, the right under Gellius Publicola in the north, with whom Antonius took station, the centre under Marcus Insteius and Marcus Octavius and the left, under Sosius in the south, with Cleopatra's squadron in the rear, behind Insteius. On 2 September 31 BC, the fleet, reduced to about 170 ships in total, advanced past Actium into the mouth of the Gulf and deployed into battle order of squadrons of forty or so ships each.

Waiting for them, Octavius' fleet which, without its detached light squadrons, numbered slightly more at about 200 ships was drawn up in three squadrons of about sixty-five ships each. The left wing, in the north was commanded by Agrippa himself, the centre by Lucius Arruntius and the right, in the south was under Marcus Lurius, with Octavius aboard, the whole fleet stretched out in a shallow arc about 800 yards (730m) in length. The sources quite blandly state 'that the men went aboard and formed up for battle',[16] but it is worth pausing to try to imagine, for example, Octavius' men, sailors, rowing crews, marines and extra troops attached to bolster them, perhaps as many as 60–70,000 men in all, the population of a fair-sized town, getting aboard and manning 200 ships of varying types and getting them to sea in some semblance of order. To emphasise how long it took, they started before dawn on the day of the battle, but the action did not start until noon; which in turn leads to the conclusion that Antonius' men must have started their own preparations even earlier, perhaps on the previous evening and that observation of them revealed their exact intentions soon enough to make it impossible for them to seek a surprise attack.

Antonius' fleet also formed an arc of about 500 yards (457m) in length, with both flanks secured by the shorelines and his ships close together and two or more ranks deep, preventing any attack by either of the classic manoeuvres. Both fleets faced each other about 1600 yards (1463m) apart, hoping to entice the other into an attack and thus give up their formation.

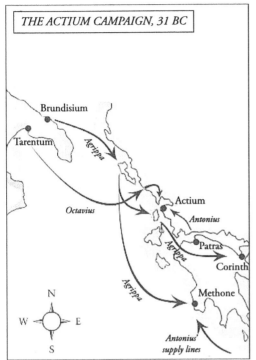

THE ACTIUM CAMPAIGN, 31 BC

Brundisium

Tarentum

Agrippa

Octavius

Actium

Antonius

Agrippa

Patras

Corinth

Agrippa

Methone

N

W   E

S

Antonius'
supply lines

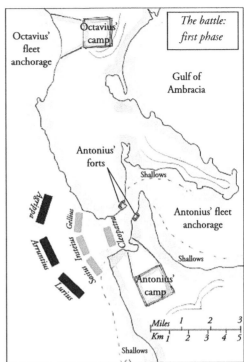

The battle:
first phase

Octavius'
fleet
anchorage

Octavius'
camp

Gulf of
Ambracia

Antonius'
forts

Shallows

Agrippa

Gellius

Antonius' fleet
anchorage

Insteius

Cleopatra

Arruntius

Sosius

Shallows

Lurius

Antonius'
camp

Miles   1   2   3

Km 1   2   3   4   5

Shallows

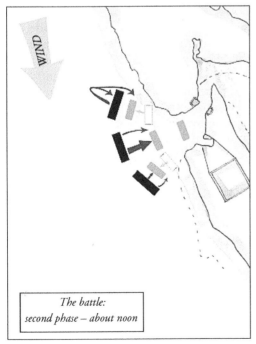

WIND

The battle:
second phase – about noon

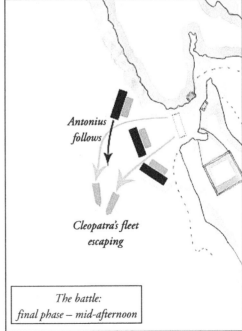

Antonius
follows

Cleopatra's fleet
escaping

The battle:
final phase – mid-afternoon

The wind started to gently blow from the north-west, down the Adriatic. After a while, having failed to entice his enemy, Antonius had to move and finally ordered his right (Gellius) to attack its opposing squadron (Agrippa) and seek to turn the flank in a *periplous* attack. Having already advanced towards Agrippa's ships which retired to draw them out and with an advance by Sosius, Antonius' squadrons were getting into more open sea and their formations becoming extended as each end tried to outflank its enemy; with Gellius' attack and that of Sosius, the integrity of their line was finally fragmented and Agrippa signalled his fleet to attack.

Once more, Agrippa had prepared for the campaign and given thought beforehand to the problem which would face his fleet; he had evolved tactics for dealing with the enemy's preponderance of larger ships. These great ships were slower in manoeuvre than the more handy, lighter ships and were also impervious to ramming attack by them. They functioned like vast slow-moving castles and woe betide any lighter ship that could be grappled and hauled in alongside, its decks swept by missiles and then swarmed over by the larger contingents of marines and soldiers of the big ship. Agrippa's ships sought to attack the oars and rudders of the big ships while avoiding their grapples. Instead of a general engagement, Agrippa's ships selected target ships and several of them, especially the lighter ones, engaged one big enemy ship. There was little sea-room for using the ram and Antonius' big ships could not attain sufficient momentum to hit Octavius' lighter ships, nor did the latter have sufficient force to inflict any but cursory damage to their large opponents, although they took every opportunity to ram, taking great care not to be trapped and caused some holing. Much use was made of fire-arrows and catapults which hurled burning pitch, despite the obvious dangers, as a way of attacking the big ships at range.[17] Traditionally, the Romans had always sought to use the advantage of their superior infantry by seeking to board an enemy but Agrippa realised that both sides had the same standard of infantry and therefore had to devise tactics for a non-boarding battle, the exact opposite of that desired by Antonius.

The battle was intense, but after an hour or more, Antonius' centre and left began to fall back. The battle was however still undecided when, for no known reason, Cleopatra formed her ships, which had not yet been engaged, into columns and emerged from the rear and fled the scene, having set sail and taken advantage of the following wind to dash through the battle-locked fleets. Antonius, on seeing this, himself abandoned the battle at its height and after managing to extricate about fifty ships, followed her. Octavius detached a squadron of liburnians in pursuit which overhauled and overcame one large enemy ship which turned to face them, its sacrifice enabling the rest to get away. The battle continued for a while but as Antonius' men learned what had happened to their leader, they quickly and not surprisingly, lost heart and the remainder of his fleet eventually surrendered or managed to

Plate I: Statue base of Valerius Valens, Praefect of the Misenum Fleet circa AD 238/240. The inscription reads 'To the great God and to make good. Valerius Valens, most perfect gentleman; Praefect of the Misenum Fleet, Erected in his lifetime, cordially fulfilled his vow'. (© Michael Pitassi)

Plate II: Warships were a frequently used motif on coins from some of the earliest of Republican issues in the 3rd century BC to at least the 'middle Empire' of the 3rd century AD. (© Michael Pitassi)

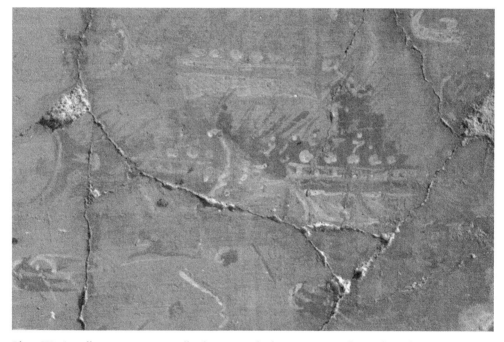

Plate III: A wall painting, now sadly deteriorated, showing a squadron of warships at sea. Each vessel's decks appear packed with troops and appear to show a single tower mounted amidships – suggesting they may well be quadriremes. The paintings probably date to the first century BC or AD. The House of the Corinthian Atrium, Herculaneum. (© Michael Pitassi)

Plate IV: A wall painting of two warships leaving harbour. Both vessels are similar in appearance and may well depict liburnians or triremes. Both ships are shown with decks packed with troops and display breaks in their forward bulwarks – most probably for use of the boarding bridge. The dotted line on the right demonstrates the 'before and after' of restoration. From the Temple of Isis, Pompeii. (© Michael Pitassi)

Plate V: Suggested reconstruction of a Corvus. Scale model, after the description by Polybius, of the device that gave the Romans their initial victories over the Carthaginians. (© Michael Pitassi)

Plate VI: A marble sculpture of a warship stem and ram at Ostia. Note that the upper piece has been moved forward from its correct position. The ram is approximately 2 feet (610mm) square across the fore end. If a full sized copy of the original then it would have only been large enough for a light type of ship. Note the horizontal and vertical vanes for cutting into an enemy hull. (© Michael Pitassi)

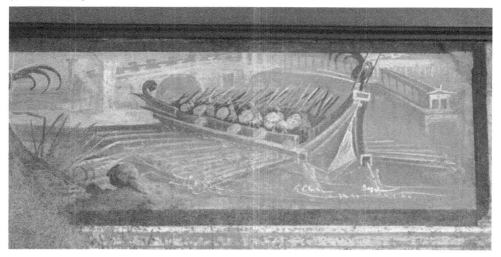

Plate VII: Detail from a wall painting from Pompeii showing a warship, its deck again apparently packed with troops, entering harbour. Seen here from the rear the twin steering oars are clearly visible. (© Michael Pitassi)

Plate VIII: Panoramic view of the harbour at Misenum taken from the lower slopes of Procida Mons. Both basins of the harbour can be clearly seen. (© Michael Pitassi)

Plate IX: A 'typical' Roman merchant ship which may well have been of the type that inspired Lucian's description of a big grain freighter. From a tomb by the Herculaneum Gate, Pompeii – and therefore dated prior to AD 79. (© Michael Pitassi)

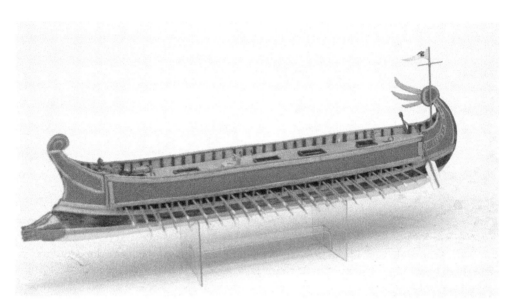

Plate X: Author's model of a trireme of the Early Empire after a relief from Pozzuoli. The ship was propelled by 122 oars (twenty-three thranite, twenty zygite and eighteen thalamite on each side) and would, in this interpretation, have had a length of 128 feet (39m) overall. Ships of this type would been a numerous and important element of the Empire's seagoing fleet. (© Michael Pitassi)

Plate XI: Petroglyph at Alta in northern Norway. It appears to represent a Mediterranean style warship complete with ram, ornate prow, steering oar and re-curved stern post. Could this be an impression of one of Agricola's long range scout ships? (© Michael Pitassi)

Plate XII: Portus Adurni (Portchester) in Hampshire. One of the chain of 'shore forts' built during the latter half of the 3rd century AD to secure the coast of Britannia. The view from the sea. Both the church and keep are Norman additions. (© Michael Pitassi)

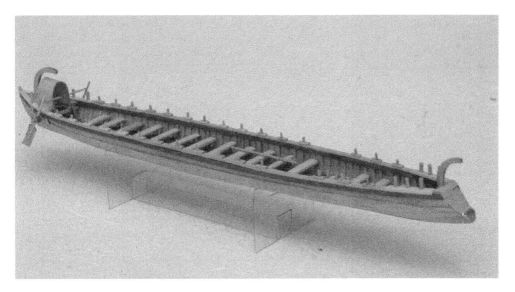

Plate XIII: Author's model of a 4th-century AD Rhine Fleet patrol vessel based upon an actual example recovered at Mainz, Germany (Moguntiacum). The ship is open and propelled by 30 oars, with one man on each oar. The original was built of oak, frame first, with iron fastenings and caulked with pitch. (© Michael Pitassi)

Plate XIV: A sixteenth-century drawing of part of the Column of Arcadius (AD 395–408) which stood in Constantinople until its destruction in 1715. This section clearly shows transport ships of a standardised type ferrying troops. (© By kind permission of the Master and Fellows of Trinity College, Cambridge)

regain their harbour, bringing to an end what would be the last great naval battle in the Mediterranean for 355 years. A week later, Antonius' abandoned army and the remnant of his fleet surrendered. Many of the ships with their dispirited crews stiffened by drafts of Octavius' men, were sent to Forum Iulii in Gaul where they were far enough away to avoid the temptation to follow Antonius and had the opportunity to join the winning side.

30 BC

After Actium, Antonius and Cleopatra fled to Egypt. Octavius and his forces moved to pursue. Early in 30 BC, he advanced into Egypt and arrived to blockade Antonius and Cleopatra in Alexandria itself. After a sortie on land, Antonius sent the ships that had come with him from Actium with Cleopatra's Egyptian ships out to face Octavius' fleet, but could only watch helplessly as they closed with Octavius' ships and raised their oars in salute to him and went over to his side. Antonius had failed and first he, then Cleopatra committed suicide. Octavius acquired Egypt and became undisputed master of the entire Roman world.

Once more it had been sea power that had been the decisive factor in the defeat of Antonius. Octavius had quickly learned that he needed sea-power to defeat Sextus and secure the west and after his initial reverses, was not too proud to relinquish command at sea to a lieutenant. His choice was fortuitous in the extremely capable Agrippa, an innovator in both weapons and tactics. After that, it was sea-power that was his chosen weapon against Antonius and Octavius would never forget the part played by 'his' navy in his climb to supreme power, and with it the establishment of the Imperial Age that now commenced.

THE PRINCIPATE

Octavius had become undisputed and sole leader of a Roman world with a total population of perhaps forty to fifty million people. It was a world which desperately needed an end to the civil wars and the internal peace and stability that he now brought to it. His changes and reforms were, although far-reaching, an evolution not a revolution and he was careful to avoid the trappings or posings of kingship, against which there remained something deep within the Roman psyche. Apart from various honours and powers that the Senate voted to him, he accepted only the honorific of 'Princeps' or 'First Citizen'.

By the end of the Civil Wars, Octavius had in total, of his own forces and those acquired from his former enemies, sixty legions with some 300,000 men and probably nearly as many again in auxiliary units; he also now had combined fleets of nearly 700 ships of all types. All of this was far more than would now be needed, or that could be sustained or afforded in peacetime. Shortly after the war, Octavian had a large monument erected on the north entrance of the gulf overlooking Actium and near to the new town that he founded there, which he named Nikopolis (Victory City) and around the base of which rams taken from captured warships were set into specially prepared mounting slots or sockets. The process was started of scrapping or burning surplus ships, while others were sent to be laid up in reserve at Forum Iulii.

To secure the Empire and his own position, Octavius needed to secure the loyalty of the military and to ensure that this was owed to him personally. He divided the responsibility for the administration of the provinces so that some were 'Senatorial;' and others 'Imperial', that is his own responsibility; he obtained effective command of the army by having most of those provinces that had garrisons as his own provinces and having the troops swear loyalty to him rather than to 'Rome'. He also gradually built up a body of professional salaried administrators and commanders throughout the empire who owed their positions and advancement to his favour.

29 BC   In 29 BC, Octavian celebrated a triple triumph at Rome and as part of the celebrations he had an artificial basin near to the Ianiculum Hill (near to the present-day St. Peter's) formed and filled with water diverted from the Tiber; in this he presented a re-enactment of the Battle of Actium with a 'sea-fight' or *naumachia* between thirty full-sized warships and many smaller craft. It was the navy's job to arrange for the 'lake' to be formed and to supply the ships, supplies and equipment required and to oversee the occasion, a task that the service would continue to perform for similar 'shows' in the future.[18] Eventually there would be two permanent *naumachia* facilities in Rome, for which Agrippa built reservoirs. Agrippa also built a naval headquarters in Rome and an arch in the Campus Martius named Portus Argonautarum, to commemorate his naval victories, with another to display a great map of the empire. Apart from his civil reforms, Octavian also set about reforming the armed services, the numbers of which he gradually reduced but whose status was enhanced to that of professional standing, volunteer forces.

28 BC   Egypt had become an imperial province with a substantial garrison. One legion and three of the cohorts were based at Alexandria together with a naval detachment, the city becoming one of the navy's permanent bases henceforth. Elsewhere in 28 BC, there had been considerable unrest in Hispania among the mountain tribes but the coasts remained secure; Carthage was restored as a colony for the settlement of discharged veterans

27 BC   and would soon again become a major seaport. In 27 BC, Octavian was renamed by the Senate with the ancient title of Augustus, by which name he was subsequently known and which became the title of every subsequent emperor.

The Arabs of the kingdom of Sabaea (Sheba) in the south-west corner of the Arabian peninsula (approximately modern Yemen) were key

INDIAN
TRADE

At about this time, one Menippus of Pergamum published an account and description of a voyage of circumnavigation of the Euxine Sea. The trade between Egypt, as the entrepot for the west, and India had grown in volume and value since the time of the early Ptolemies and had been established along routes mapped by the Greeks. The initiative for this had come from Alexander the Great when he ordered a Cretan general named Niarchos to sail back from the River Indus, to the head of the Persian Gulf. With the subsequent rise of the Parthian Empire, an alternative route avoiding their territory was to go via the Red Sea, along the South Arabian coast and across the mouth of the Persian Gulf, the smaller ships hugging the coasts and the larger ones, using the offshore, monsoon wind-assisted route. During his reign, Augustus received several embassies from India.

intermediaries in the sea trade between the Indian sub-continent and the Mediterranean world. Their degree of involvement had become a virtual monopoly and the manner of it unacceptable and so in 26 BC, Aelius Gallus, now Prefect of Egypt was sent with an expedition against them. His forces comprised 10,000 men, including contingents of 500 from King Herod of Judaea and 1000 from King Obodas of Nabatea. Despite the presence of these local allies, the expedition had not been well-enough planned and insufficient reconnaissance had been carried out. Gallus started his preparations at Cleopatris on the Egyptian shore of the Gulf of Suez. There he concentrated his own forces and had ships 'built'. There being no timber in Egypt, all materials had to be brought overland and presumably long experience of prefabrication methods were used so the ships could be assembled rather than built there; local merchant ships would have been requisitioned for transports. It is not known whether use was made of the canal between the Nile and Red Sea; it had last been cleared in 280 BC and unless maintained, was liable to silting. In view of the mass of material that was concentrated quickly, it seems likely that it remained at least partly useable and Augustus did have some restoration work to the canal carried out.[19]

26 BC

Some eighty warships and 130 transports were concentrated and with a naval complement drawn from the fleet at Alexandria, sailed and transported Gallus' army across to the eastern shore of the Red Sea, to Leuke Kome, the southernmost town of Nabatea where the allied contingents joined him. On the passage, several of the ships had been lost on the coral reefs which line the Arabian coast and the Roman sailors were also alarmed by the tides in the Red Sea. It took two weeks to ferry the army the 160 or so miles across the Red Sea and there were some outbreaks of scurvy aboard ship.

This seems a somewhat slow process to carry about 8500 men and stores, given that Caesar had needed forty ships to transport a whole legion and considering the numbers available to Gallus; the outbreak of sickness and speed of his subsequent advance indicates a slowness in command rather than capacity. Had he but known it, the Arabs had no warships to oppose him and Gallus could have saved much wasted time. As it was he abandoned his original plan to sail down the Arabian coast and attack directly but decided to advance by land, his flank covered by the navy and with supplies brought in by the ships. The Arabian Red Sea coast is hundreds of miles of waterless desert, fringed by vast coral reefs which extend far offshore and there are no good natural harbours. Great skill was required, even with the acquisition of local pilots, to bring the supply ships into shore.

It took Gallus six months to advance along the harsh Arabian coastline, but despite sickness in the ranks, the bad conditions and exhaustion, the army took towns in its path and achieved its objective; the Sabaeans were suitably overawed by the arrival of a Roman army and came to acceptable terms and were recognised with the official friendship of Rome. Gallus' army returned by a more direct route in two months and was ferried by the fleet to Myos Hormos on the Egyptian coast. The Romans did not maintain a fleet on the Red Sea; although ships were deployed there from time to time, they controlled the shores of the northern end of the sea and there was no maritime, or indeed, military challenge to them from that quarter. The best guarantee of the trade routes to India and beyond was that their successful pursuance was in the best interest and to the profit of the rulers of the peoples that bordered them.

25 BC   Ethiopian raids had started across the southern border at Elephantine (Aswan) at the First Cataract of the Nile in Egypt and in breach of a previous treaty. In 25 BC, therefore, the new Prefect, Gaius Petronius attacked and captured their capital at Nabata, placed garrisons well to the south and advanced to the Second Cataract. The expedition was well supported by ships coming up the River, which could by-pass the First Cataract and proceed upriver because of a canal first dug circa 2400 BC and which had been made deeper and wider to take ships by the Pharoah Senusret III, in 1870 BC. Petronius then instituted regular river patrols on the Nile in the section between the two Cataracts, to support and supply his southern outposts. In 22 BC the Ethiopians finally made peace and ceded the territory north of the Second Cataract to Rome and which thus became the new border of Egypt (which it remains to this day).[20]

Augustus' policy to further the security of the empire was to push its borders outwards to rest on defensible lines based on seas, deserts and major rivers. In the Euxine, Pontus and the Bosporan Kingdom of the Crimea remained as loyal friends of Rome, permitting visits by the navy to which the Euxine remained a Roman lake.

IMPERIAL FLEETS

All the while, Augustus' reforms of the army and navy had been proceeding and the future basis of the imperial forces established. Augustus never forgot that it was the navy that had given him victory over Sextus Pompeius, which secured the western base of his power and that it had gone on to give him the final victory at Actium that had made him supreme. The reforms of the navy were thorough and resulted in a service that would remain in more or less the same form for nearly three centuries, as a permanently established navy with its several separate fleets individually suited to and integrated with their local theatre of operations. Although it was one navy, the geographical separation of the fleets dictated that there could be no central command. Doubtless the 'home fleets' in Italy provided a common pool of experienced and trained officers, men and specialists in building, operating and equipping ships, to send to the other fleets; they could even furnish the basis for new fleets or formations as was to happen later when fleets were formed to control the Danubius with a cadre of personnel drawn from the Italian Fleets. To confirm this, several graves of men hailing from the Italian Fleets have been found at points all around the Mediterranean; perhaps members of the crews of visiting ships, or perhaps men from those fleets posted to other squadrons.[21]

The provincial fleets were strictly under local command. As a powerful institution of the Empire, the navy could and would on occasion involve itself in matters political. Although it remained the junior service, Augustus understood that it was essential to maintain an efficient and adequate fleet for the security of the Mediterranean, the *Mare Nostrum*, the centre of the empire. With its domination of the sea and the lack of any naval rival however, the navy's purpose would need to change to be a police force and a transport medium for armies, despatches, envoys and even on occasion, the Emperor himself and also to gather intelligence from around the seas both within and without the Empire. With no rival navies left in existence, the task of the navy was also now to ensure that naval battles would henceforth be impossible by making it just as impossible for any other navy to arise that could challenge it. As well as the policing of the seas to ensure that piracy could not recur it had to generally oversee freedom of navigation in the Mediterranean, about which the Empire and its trade revolved.

Augustus, and indeed all of the Julio-Claudian dynasty that was to follow him, were good sailors and took pleasure in the sea and boating. They had pleasure ships and yachts for their use and Augustus had a holiday villa built for himself on Capraea (Capri).

Augustus wanted the navy as a standing force to have permanent bases of its own and was determined that the neglects of the past would not be repeated. He had inherited several naval formations: firstly there was the victorious fleet recently so ably organised and commanded by Agrippa in the Civil Wars, together with the surviving ships and crews of his former opponents, all in the Mediterranean; in the north was the formation formed by Caesar to operate along the north coasts of Gaul, and those operating along the Rhenus. In the east was the fleet formed by Pompeius in the Euxine and also whatever ships had been left by Antonius in the Levant, although in both of these cases it seems that their ships had largely been removed from their stations to add to his late fleet at Actium.

The organisation of the navy was to be based on two main *Classes* (or fleets), supported by regional formations at strategic points. The position of these fleets was akin to that of the Praetorian Guard (expanded and elevated by Augustus to be the Imperial Guard) and like them, it would also intervene from time to time in politics. The fleets were to be stationed to cover each half of the Mediterranean, one westward and the other eastwards. Each fleet was a wholly self-contained entity with its own staff, responsible for its crews, ships and the provision of everything needed to operate them including weapons and shipbuilding.

Each fleet was to be commanded by a Prefect of equestrian rank, a *Praefectus Classis*, resurrecting the old term, and drawn from men who had been military officers, appointed by and taking their orders from the Emperor. There was no central navy high command at Rome or with the Emperor but a staff officer from each of the Italian fleets was attached to his staff and a senior officer for any of the other formations whose area the Emperor might visit also attended upon him. The *Quaestores Classici* seem to have survived in their posts from Republican times in charge of naval districts and for the support of visiting naval forces; where they were assigned and the precise nature of their duties are not however known. Occasionally in the future, former legionary tribunes and even imperial freedmen would achieve the rank. The former practice of consular and senatorial appointments to command fleets ceased and the senatorial class was thus prevented from attaining command of military formations with which it could threaten the Emperor.

Subordinate to the *Praefectus* was his *Sub-Praefectus* or executive officer, together with a *Cornicularius*, as next-ranking officer and a staff or *Officium* of men known by various titles. *Beneficiarii* or 'appointees', *Actuarii* or accountants and *Scribae* who were, obviously, writers made up the administrative staff and some of them were in addition rated as *sesquipliciarius* or *dupliciarius*, respectively 'one-and-one-half' and 'double' pay men, receiving those multiples of the basic pay rate. This would indicate that these staff members were ratings rather than officers and the multiple-pay men were leading ratings in the same way as they exist in today's services.[22]

Agrippa had raised and trained his civil war fleet at the northern end of the Bay of Naples and the fleet returned there to establish its permanent main western base at Misenum (Miseno) from 22 BC and become the *Classis Misinensis*. The other fleet set up its base on the Adriatic, at Ravenna, at about the same time, to become the *Classis Ravennate*. A subsidiary base was to be at Forum Iulii (Fréjus) in Gallia Narbonensis (Provence in southern France) previously used by Augustus and Agrippa in the war against Sextus and where excavations have revealed harbour walls, naval buildings and the local Prefect's house.[23] Provincial fleets were established at Alexandria in Egypt and Seleucia in Syria, each commanded by a *Praefectus Classis*, appointed by the Emperor but who was subject to the overall command of the local provincial governor. This arrangement, which obtained for all of the provincial fleets, was necessitated of course by the time that it took for communications to pass to and from Rome. Additionally there were of course the detachments already in the English Channel, the Euxine Sea and on the River Rhenus.

The *Classis Alexandrina* was not, for its part, responsible for the policing of the River Nile, which continued to be effected by the separate river police force, inherited from the Ptolemies,[24] although the Fleet could send ships and men upriver in support as and when required.[25] Its duties did include overseeing the essential grain convoys on their voyages to Italy and to police the sometimes troublesome North African coast to the west of Alexandria, later on occasion even as far as Mauretania. The *Classis Syriaca*'s two main concerns were to maintain transport and communication links between the Levant, where the Parthian threat was at its closest, and the west and secondly to ensure that there was no resumption of piracy along the once-notorious and still barely pacified Cilician coast, as well as to oversee the Aegean.

With only the addition of the fleets for the Danubius (Danube) and Britannia and some minor variations, these would remain the basic dispositions of the Roman navy until its end. Provincial naval bases were rated as '*castra*' in the same way as permanent army bases and camps. The service had already been virtually pushed out of Ostia, which was too small; the former facility at Lakes Avernus and Lucrinus was silted and interfered with civil traffic in the Bay of Naples, the harbour of Puteoli was full with merchant shipping and the base at Forum Iulii was too far away and poorly placed. The fleet needed a conveniently close but well-founded permanent home of its own.

The choice of Misenum, 125 miles (200km) from Rome, for the new base was a good one; the position is protected from the landward by the mount of Procida and hill of Bacoli and has a steep, high promontory at the point of the cape, protecting it from seaward. It has the best natural deep-water harbour on the west coast of Italy, formed from the flooding of volcanic craters. The outer crater, open to the sea, was linked to the inner by a canal, spanned by a bridge that could be moved to allow ship movements between the basins. Two tunnels were bored through hills to encourage streams of water to flow and help to scour the outer harbour and prevent silting. An aqueduct was built from the neighbouring hills to bring an adequate supply of fresh water which was stored in huge cisterns built into the hill at Bacoli.[26] The harbour at Misenum was improved by the building of protective moles for the outer harbour, equipped with pierced mooring stones set into the top, to which ships could tie up. Two moles were built parallel, projecting north-east from the headland partway across the harbour entrance; the moles were built as a succession of arches with a continuous quay along the top like a bridge; each mole had its arches offset in relation to the other, so the pillars of one coincided with the openings of the other, acting as an effective breakwater, yet allowing a flow of water to keep the harbour clear of silting; a similar, single mole was also built, projecting south-west from the opposite, Bacoli shore. Permanent barracks, storehouses, workshops and ship repair and dockyard installations were built on the flat ground between the three hills and around the craters which now formed an inner and outer harbour. Strategically, Misenum was placed to cover all of the seaports and sea routes of the Bay of Naples and the coast northward to Rome, to which it was conveniently close; it faced out to the Tyrrhenian Sea into which the power of its fleet could be easily and quickly projected to the islands and beyond, into the western Mediterranean.[27]

A naval detachment was stationed in Rome, quartered with the Praetorian Guard, for ceremonial duties and to oversee the *naumachiae*; another was still maintained at Ostia to handle visiting ships and the passage of despatches, communications, couriers and officials going to or from the provinces. A further function was to convey members of the Imperial family to and from their villas on the coasts. For really urgent despatches however, a succession of relay riders could cover the distance from Rome to Misenum in a day. This fleet also established naval stations on Sardinia, Corsica and Sicily and also at Centumcella (Civitavecchia), on the Etruscan coast, each with a resident detachment and depots to handle the ships of the fleet when they were there. Further it is logical to suppose that stores or the facility to acquire supplies for visiting ships were arranged to be available at every major port in the Empire, even though no naval personnel were permanently stationed there.[28]

The Misenum Fleet was the largest and ranked the senior and possibly had over 10,000 men with fifty or so ships. The strength and composition of the Praetorian Fleets is not known and the only real indication of this, although admittedly a poor one, is the name and type of ship shown on the gravestones of deceased personnel found at Misenum and Ravenna and a

MISENUM: 1st Century BC

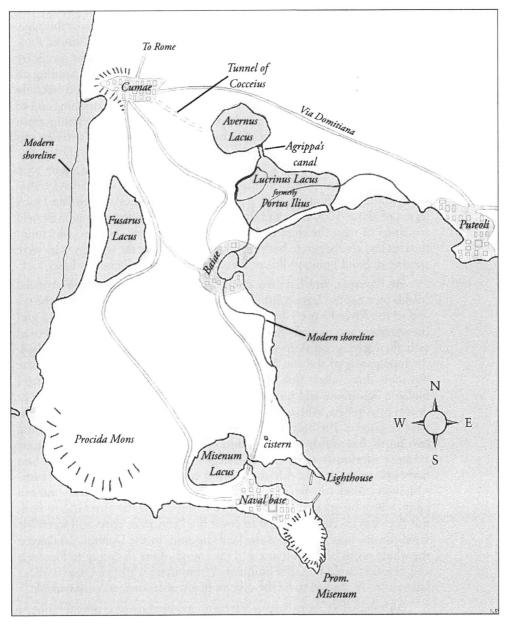

few elsewhere.[29] At Misenum, nine 'fours' and thirteen liburnians are noted
with fifty-two triremes; at Ravenna, seven 'fours' and only two liburnians,
but twenty-two triremes; on the face of it this would seem to indicate that the
trireme remained the most widely used workhorse of the fleets; conversely
it could just as well indicate some disaster involving some ships of this type,
giving a disproportionately high death toll for triremes. Several stones show
ships of the same name, either men from the same ship or from successive
ships named the same, the stones being of various dates and spanning an
unknown period. In any event, the fleet was large and powerful and certainly
set out with a 'six' as flagship (more for ceremonial use than anything and to
keep the technology of building and operating big multi-reme warships from
being forgotten), together with a few quinquiremes, 'fours' and triremes and
smaller ships. The really big multi-remes were finished and only the few
and those not of the biggest, survived in the two 'home' fleets, none were
retained elsewhere. Another indication as to the strength of the fleets is that
Nero would, in 65 AD, form a legion from the marines at each base, each
legion of about 5000 men and that even after having done so, enough men
remained to man the ships and to conduct operations. Near to Misenum,
the area had also begun to become fashionable among the wealthy, who were
starting to build holiday villas at Baiae, between Puteoli and the base.

At Ravenna, the base installations were built on stilts and artificial
islands on a natural lagoon, amid the marshes and linked by canals to the sea
and to the River Padus. Considerable excavation had to be carried out and
the waterway was named the Fossa Augusta. The site was presumably chosen
as it then gave good deep-water access, the other waterways being silted;
the topography of the area has changed radically since that time. The base
was some three miles (5km) from the town itself and equipped with quays,
moles, a lighthouse and military barracks. This fleet also set up stations or
depots at Aquileia, Ancona, Brundisium, Salonae (Split) and two more in
western Greece. The fleet could have comprised about forty ships, including
two 'fours', but mostly triremes, subject to the reservations about gravestone
evidence previously mentioned. Strategically Ravenna was one of the best
harbours on the Italian Adriatic coast, a coast with few natural harbours.
Although rather too far north to influence affairs in the Mediterranean
basin, where its operations were limited compared to the other Italian fleet,
this fleet was excellently placed to cover the Dalmatian coast and to enable
rapid connections with it and the lands beyond, to the Danubius. Likewise
the whole north of the Adriatic and the course of the Padus up to Placentia
and beyond, could be easily dominated from there whilst the base itself, as
later was to be proved to be the case on many occasions, was unassailable.[30]

Although the *Classes Praetoriae* were maintained at a level probably bigger
than strictly necessary, the support services they could offer to provincial fleets
and the fact that no incidents of piracy in the Mediterranean were reported

BUILDING
QUAYS

The Roman method of building moles, quays and other offshore works was first to drive wooden pilings into the sea bed (or riverbed for that matter) to form a fence enclosing the area to be built upon, a caisson in fact. The piles were bound and sealed and the water pumped out from within. A layer of beams was placed inside to provide a key and then a fill of limestone and rubble was poured in, mixed with pozzolana, which is a form of compressed volcanic ash, found at various places in central Italy. The Etruscan city of Orvieto is built atop a column of it and the Etruscans found that the soft pozzolana when crushed and mixed acted as a natural cement hardener, which would even set under water, literally rock-hard.[31]

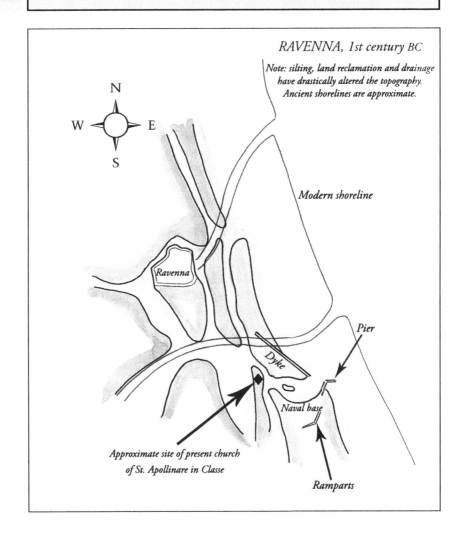

RAVENNA, 1st century BC

Note: silting, land reclamation and drainage have drastically altered the topography. Ancient shorelines are approximate.

N

W   E

S

Modern shoreline

Ravenna

Pier

Dyke

Naval base

Approximate site of present church of St. Apollinare in Classe

Ramparts

in over two hundred years justified them. Their firm financial footing made them easily affordable in the ensuing era of imperial peace and prosperity, encouraged by the absolute security of the sea-routes in turn underwritten by the navy. To fund the navy (and the army) a dedicated treasury was set up, commanded by three prefects of praetorian rank who were chosen by lot. Augustus put in 170 million sesterces and there were contributions from client kings and cities, to start the fund which was then maintained by new taxes on citizens on larger inheritances (5%) and sales (1%). Although he did not increase rates of pay, Augustus did ensure that pay and bonuses were paid promptly and reliably. As a basis for comparison, a legionary received 300 denarii per annum, less deductions for rations, clothing, boots, leather equipment, tent and arms. They would also contribute to their century's 'funeral club', a sort of savings bank that, apart from the obvious, took care of men invalided out of the service, widows and orphans. Despite this he could still save a third of his pay. Rates of pay remained unchanged in fact for about a century. Auxiliaries received a third as much but even so seem to have been reasonably well off and the rates were high enough to attract sufficient volunteers. There were four asses to a sesterce and four sesterces to a denarius.[32]

Recruitment for the navy was voluntary, open to all and appealed particularly to provincial freeborn men and also to some freedmen; Egyptians are known to have been at Misenum and Dalmatians at Ravenna and many officers were Greek. From letters home, written by Egyptian recruits at Misenum, it can be inferred that all new recruits from all over the Empire, 'joined up' locally and were then sent to the Italian bases for basic training and with it, encouragement to transfer familial and local bonds to the service, before posting to the fleets (otherwise, the said recruits would have stayed with their local, Alexandrine fleet). The official language and that used for all orders throughout the service was of course, Latin; especially necessary for example among a crew who between them might speak a dozen languages. Most non-Italians also adopted Roman or 'Latinized' names. Although lacking some of the prestige of the legions, the naval service appealed to men from the traditionally maritime peoples of the Empire.

As to the civil status of naval personnel, whereas senior officers, prefects, navarchs and probably senior trierarchs would have to be Roman citizens, the majority of seamen and rowers probably were not, although there was nothing to stop a citizen from enlisting. Slaves most assuredly were not enrolled. Marines on the other hand, at least of the Italian Fleets, must have been Roman citizens as they were rated the equivalent of legionaries in the army, and probably paid the same. Further, Nero formed two regular legions from them in AD 65; legionaries could at that time, only be recruited from among citizens and there is no report of Nero making a mass grant of citizenship to these men.

For all recruits, army and navy, the term of engagement had been twenty years but for the navy the term was increased to twenty-five years, the same as for the army's auxiliary units; even so, some men stayed on for longer. Upon discharge, non-citizens became full Roman citizens although no discharge bounty was paid; a bounty was paid on enlistment however, one of three gold aurei, equal to 75 denarii being recorded as paid in the third century. The old system whereby maritime allied and federated cities and states were required to provide drafts of men for the navy was thus superseded and abolished.

As for the army, new recruits received a medical examination and were initially posted to a naval century, which was identified by a name at a particular base, analagous to a 'stone frigate'. There they received basic training and were taught to swim, basic first aid and the use of hand weapons; from there would follow sea and perhaps more specialised training; rowers in groups to be trained to row together with a synchronised action, firstly in rowing frames set up on dry land, progressing no doubt to the base training ship. Similarly signallers would have to be trained in the use of signal flags and pennants, lamps and polished bronze mirrors, used as heliographs, as well as in the signal codes for their use. Facilities would also be provided for the training of shipwrights, boatswains, helmsmen, sailors and all of the other practices and trades needed in the working of the ships, even and by no means least, the ship's cook.

Marines were trained in the use of sword, javelin or *pilum*, together with darts and the use of the sling, in a way very similar to that of the army; in addition they seem to have carried a short boarding pike. Whether they or the sailors (or both of them) were also trained as archers and artillerymen, or only some of them, is not known, although whereas archery is specialised, all of them were probably given some basic training in the use of the catapults. There followed a posting to a century forming the crew of a ship on the establishment of the same base or to another fleet. It is not known how long a man would serve in a particular century or crew, or whether he would move to another upon promotion, be transferred to other ships, fleets or squadrons, or whether his entire century might be assigned as a whole to a different ship or posting in a subsequent sailing season.

The Roman military had always had an eye for the health of the troops and care of casualties, possibly arising from its citizen militia origins. Under the new reforms, military medical services and supplies were set up as a formal and regular part of the military establishment. Troops received first aid training and medical personnel of a physician and four orderlies per cohort (a formation of about 600 men) were added to the strength of each legion and permanent bases had military hospitals. Examples of these hospitals have been identified, complete with wards and operating theatres, at Carnuntum (near Vienna) on the Danubius and Novaesium (Neuss) on the Rhenus. It is reasonable to suppose that similar medical facilities existed at the navy's own main bases. A *Medicus* was included in the crew of a larger ship and probably an orderly in that of a small one.

With the growing preponderance of non-citizens among the rowing and seamen crews, the ships of the fleet came to resemble auxiliary units; the ship's company was still regarded as a naval century although the actual size of a crew could vary from a few dozen of all ranks on a small scout vessel, to several hundreds on a trireme or larger ship. Naval personnel were regarded as fighting men and rated as *miles* (soldier) as distinct from the *nautae* or sailors of the merchant marine. Some crewmen on their grave stelae, describe themselves as *manipularis* or member of a maniple. This was a military formation of two centuries of infantry, operating together and, by extension, by describing himself thus the crewman could be indicating that he was a member of the crew of a big ship, i.e. one with a crew number the equivalent of a maniple, rather than the 'century' of eighty or so men on a smaller one. Greek terms tended to be used for some of the ship's officers as well as Latin ones, thus Trierarch for the captain of a ship (whether or not it was a trireme). Originally of course, this rating was for the commander of a trireme but long before this it had already come to be applied to the commander of any warship, regardless of type or size and in the same way as, for example, a modern-day lieutenant, given command of a ship, is referred to and is its captain (originally an old French word and thus, ironically, derived in turn from Latin). Promotion to Trierarch was usually from the lower ranks and he could also command shore detachments. The number of officers and ratings of course varied depending upon the class of ship and therefore the size of its crew. Overall the well-established practices of the Republican navy were followed in that a crew naturally fell into three sub-divisions; the sailors (*velarii* or *nautae*); the rowers or *remiges*; finally the marines and artillerymen or *milites classiarii*.

Under the Captain, in the first category was the *Gubernator*, the sailing master, in charge of the after part of the ship and who controlled navigation, the helmsman and sailing rig; next came the *Proreta* or *Proreus*, the bow officer in charge of the fore part of the ship and the anchors, forward rig and depth-taking. The ship's other specialist ranks were also part of the 'seaman' branch of the crew and it is not clear whether they were considered as officers or, as seems more likely, as what today we would call non-commissioned officers. Thus the ship's carpenter, doctor, sail-maker, scribe or ship's clerk counted, as were senior ratings, equivalent perhaps to our modern Petty Officers; there were also *dupliciarii* on double-pay as leading ranks of all of them, perhaps Chief Petty Officers. In more detail, there was the *Secutor* or Master-at-Arms responsible for discipline, who if not an officer, would certainly rate with a modern Warrant Officer. The *Medicus* was more of a medical orderly than a physician; the ship's carpenter was a *Fabrius* or *Faber Navalis* (shipwright) and a sailor was a *Velarius*, after a *velarum* or sail. All of these ratings could also have the suffix *dupliciarius* to indicate a leading rating.

The *Remiges* or rowing crew had their own officers, the *Pausarius* or *Caleusta* commanding the rhythm of the oar-stroke, aided by a musician or time-beater, called variously a *Portisculus, Pitulus* or *Hortator*, who would beat the timing of the oar-stroke with a wooden mallet.[33] The title *Symphonianus*, an amalgam of Greek and Latin terms, is also attested and likely refers to an actual musician. Within the rowers, called a *Remex* (after *remus*, an oar), the stroke oarsmen and some of the men were styled *Dupliciarii* with double pay and were placed in charge of a section of rowers and also responsible for the relaying of orders to them. The organisation in detail of the rowing crew is not known but in the army the smallest unit was a *contubernium*, a standard army tent issued to and shared by every eight men, one of whom would be the senior, equivalent perhaps to a modern Corporal. This it is suggested could be a guide to the number of leading rates among the rowers, and for that matter also among the larger sailing crews and would fit very readily within those formations.

There were other rankings and officer's staff were variously described as *Beneficiarius* (appointee, a midshipman perhaps), *Scriba* or writer, *Librarius* or bookkeeper and an *Adiutor* or *Exceptor*, who seem to have been pursers or clerks. There are various other functions attested, such as *Nauphylax* or ship's guard and *Victimarius*, who made the sacrifice at ceremonies, but these seem more likely to have been duties carried out for the occasion by crew-members rather than actual ranks. Other were the *Urinator* or diver and *Coronarius* or someone who decorated or dressed the ship, this latter however could logically also be a signaller. In all of these cases, apart from the basic crew, the various ratings and numeries added would be according to the type of ship and its relevant crew requirement.

As to officer's pay structure, the Praefect of the Misenum Fleet, the most senior rank, was rated *trecenarius* receiving 300,000 sesterces (75,000 denarii) per annum; other Italian Fleet Praefects were rated *duocenarii* with 200,000 sesterces (50,000 denarii) per annum and Praefects and sub-Praefects of provincial fleets as *sexagenarii*, with 60,000 sesterces (15,000 denarii) per annum. A Navarch received 10,000 denarii per annum. Rates of pay for lower-ranking officers are not known.[34]

All contemporary depictions of imperial warships in the Mediterranean show armed troops on deck and one or two would appear to depict catapults mounted forward.[35] A military contingent was included in the complement of each warship, ranging from perhaps a dozen or so on a small ship, to forty or more on a quadrireme or quinquireme. These marines would be armed more or less in the same way as the auxiliary troops of the army, although the few depictions identifiable as marines indicate a more open-faced form of helmet, without crests, rather than the all-encompassing legionary types; shields are more like auxiliary types and possibly smaller to facilitate handling in the cramped confines of the ship; a shorter *hasta* or thrusting spear or pike was issued to augment the normal *pila*, sword and javelins. The heavily studded boots of the army, anathema to a ship's deck, could be supplanted by a boot with a more suitable sole, perhaps of rope; although this is pure conjecture, it seems not unreasonable. Although none are shown, archers are referred to and were an important part of the military contingent, perhaps as previously mentioned, the marines themselves or the sailors were so trained, taking up their other weapons upon closing an enemy; the same applies of course to artillery crews. Once combat was joined the sailors would, apart from protecting the helmsmen, be redundant and it could well be that they were trained to man the catapults or even to be archers, releasing the marines to fight as infantry. It is not known whether arms were also carried for rowers, probably not in the Mediterranean, where there was no opposition that the marines could not deal with; in the provincial fleets of the north and great rivers however, where landings on hostile banks were not infrequent, it is likely that weapons were shipped for every man aboard.

The marines were commanded by a Centurion, of rank according to the size of contingent. Fleet Centurions were experienced, competent men promoted from the ranks and having various grades similar to those of the army. They commanded marine units aboard ship and ashore with seniority equivalent to the size of such units. The Centurion had an *Optio* nominated ('opted') by him as his lieutenant; there was also the rank, unique to the navy, of *sub-Optio*. There was an *Armorum Custos* or armourer, responsible for maintaining weapons armour and catapults. It would seem likely that the smaller units of marines on the smaller ships, when perhaps only a dozen or so men would make up the ship's complement of marines, would have been sufficiently commanded by an *Optio* and/or a *sub-Optio*. As with the seaman branch, the marines had other rates, *Cornicen* and *Bucinator* being the same as some of the army's trumpeters, each with a differing type of instrument and few of whom are attested in naval service. There also appears a *Dolator* or 'marine with an axe', perhaps a pioneer or engineer rate. Once again, the numbers and variety of ranks making up a marine detachment would depend on and be appropriate to the size of ship to which it was posted; ashore they would have been billeted and organised as centuries in the same manner as the army. The Captain must have reigned supreme on board ship when at sea, but once engaged against an enemy at sea or ashore it seems likely that the Centurion would assume overall control.[36]

In all cases, the various functions outlined would be doubled up or reduced according to the size of a crew, one man performing two or more of such on a small ship. For the lowly rower or sailor of these fleets, the sailing season was taken up in training and cruising the sea lanes or for those ashore, in maintaining the various naval establishments; the winter season was spent in refitting their ships and gear. As in the army and despite hard discipline, with regular quarters, rations and pay, the life was not considered bad in the circumstances of the time and many sailors could afford to have and keep a slave, some had several. As previously mentioned and as in the legions, units would have their own funeral 'clubs', to ensure a proper send-off for a ship-mate and the surviving wills of some sailors show that they could amass considerable savings from their pay, for their retirement. Another rank with a Greek name, was *Navarchos*, originally 'ship master', but by about the fifth century BC, it had come to be used for the commander of a detachment or squadron of ships. In imperial service it appears to have been adopted and to have replaced the old Republican ranks of Praetor and Tribune for a commodore or squadron commander. Navarchs existed in several grades, as for the army's centurions, a senior one being rated as *Navarchus Princeps* in another mixture of Greek and Latin terms; appointment of a non-citizen to the rank generally came with a grant of citizenship and was the highest rank attainable by a non-citizen until the reign of Antoninus Pius. Navarchs were also employed as senior naval staff officers to a praefect or superior commander, even the Emperor.

Sailors have always been superstitious and wont to acquire custom, which becomes tradition. Thus, for example it was considered bad luck to sail on a Friday; ships had always been named and continued to be so; eyes or *oculi* were and are still painted on bows to guide a ship.[37] Ships had an adopted protecting deity as patron, a shrine to which was placed in the stern. On boarding, sailors would turn towards the stern and salute, offering a prayer for safe passage, a custom that survives in today's navies, of saluting the ensign at the stern upon coming aboard. A likeness of the patron was commonly placed at the bow and came to be known as a figurehead. Among sailors the Dioscuri, Castor and Pollux, were first adopted by the Greeks then by the Romans as the patrons of seamen and travellers at sea and could be glimpsed as horsemen in glittering armour when electrical storms flashed around the masts and rigging. With the acquisition of Egypt and the enlistment of Egyptian personnel, came the Goddess Isis, who appealed as a maternal figure known as 'The Star of the Sea' and popular with seamen. The spring festival to re-open the sailing season after the closed winter season was dedicated to Isis as protectress of ships, a practice continued well into Christian times and carried over into the cult of the Virgin.[38i]

EXPANSION AND NEW FLEETS

Dynastic unrest in the Bosporan Kingdom became of concern to the Romans. Situated in what is now the Crimean peninsula and parts of

Ukraine and southern Russia, it produced massive amounts of wheat, provided a stable and friendly northern shore to the Euxine, a link to and intelligence of the Scythian and Sarmatian peoples of that vast area and a buffer state to protect the north coast of Anatolia.[39] The King had been overthrown by one Scribonius who had then forcibly married his widow, Dynamis, a grand-daughter of King Mithridates VI of Pontus and using that connection, Agrippa, acting as Augustus' deputy, organised King Polemo of Pontus to depose the usurper. Agrippa gathered the 'eastern' fleet, by which is presumably meant the *Classis Syriacae* and the ships stationed in the Euxine, which he concentrated at Sinope in Pontus; there he was joined by King Herod with his fleet (this being the only mention of a Judean navy). The fleets sailed to the Bosporan capital of Panticapaeum, landed their marines and duly ejected Scribonius and installed Polemo who then married Dynamis. After a popular uprising, Polemo was killed; the Queen retained her throne and continued to be a loyal friend of Rome up to her death in AD 8. Having settled matters, the Roman fleet withdrew, content to leave the policing of the northern and eastern Euxine to the forces of the Pontic and Bosporan client states. This arrangement was not wholly satisfactory as the tribesmen of the Caucasian littoral were wont to go raiding in their native craft; there was little or no seaborne trade in the area for them to disrupt and since it was thus principally their problem, the Romans left it for their allies to deal with.

16 BC   Augustus wanted to advance the borders in Europe to more secure lines. The first part of his grand design was to advance and absorb all the territory along the entire length of the River Danubius and in 16 BC his armies occupied Noricum (roughly modern Austria). The following year Augustus' stepsons Drusus and Tiberius led their armies into the Balkans and reached the Danubius in Raetia (western Hungary) and Pannonia (Serbia). In the first stage they advanced the border from the River Savus where the existing river flotilla was once more an essential part of the advance, to the navigable River Dravus (Drava) the next northward and parallel tributary of the Danubius; the advance to and securing of the line of the Danubius itself being completed by 12 BC. The advance was then completed by incorporating all the lands up to the right bank of the Danubius, to form the new province of Moesia (Bulgaria and parts of Romania) which placed the imperial border on that bank of the river from Lake Constance to the Euxine Sea. The river was divided into upper and lower parts by the natural obstacle and gorge known as the Iron Gates (between Orsova and Turnu in Serbia, about 100 miles (160km) east of Belgrade), where the river is constricted into a torrent and is impassable to navigation.

Starting from the existing flotillas, new fleets were built up for Pannonia and the upper Danubius, known as the *Classis Pannonica* with its headquarters at Taurunum (Zamun near Belgrade) and for Moesia and the lower Danubius, the *Classis Moesica* with its headquarters at Noviodunum (Isaccea, Romania); forts on the river bank were built and equipped with quays for their ships.[40] In the latter case it seems likely that ships were brought upriver via the river mouth from the sea, as part of the invasion force and then remained to form the nucleus of the new fleet which was established concurrently with the consolidation of the new riverine frontier and province. There is significance in the siting of the *Classis Moesica's* fleet headquarters at Noviodunum, essentially at one end of its long, thin operational area. From the earliest, emphasis was given to protection of the delta and the seaborne link with the Propontis as well as the watch over the western Euxine. Upriver, legions were stationed at various points along it in whose respective operational areas, sections of the fleet were attached and with whom they sometimes shared bases. The delta, with its many courses and marshes was unsuitable for heavy infantry and at first, at least, tolerated only a low level of barbarian threat from beyond it; the defence of this area was thus almost entirely charged to the fleet.

The fleets used a riverine version of the navy's liburnian for their duties of patrolling the river frontiers, of moving men, supplies and communications between the forts and of being the essential link connecting them. As well as controlling any river traffic and preventing incursions by tribesmen from the other bank, the fleets could transport infantry or cavalry across. On a day by day basis, patrols could probably penetrate and control a belt on the other bank up to nine miles (15km), or half a day's march. In addition to the main course of the Danubius, the river system comprises numerous tributaries, large and small and navigable to a greater or lesser degree, entering the main stream from both the right or south and now Roman controlled side, where they became lines of communication and supply for the garrisons, and also on the left or barbarian side, where they gave opportunities for deep penetration or invasion by the Romans of the barbarian lands. All the while the Danubius itself was maintained as a barrier by the fleets imposing their dominance of the waterways and thus controlling all navigation and also, incidentally, overseeing the collection of customs tariffs on goods passing along and across it; for this purpose, finance officers were stationed at fleet bases.

13 BC   By 13 BC, Augustus' reforms of the military had been completed; the army was reduced to 28 legions (circa 190,000 men) plus auxilia units totalling circa 150,000. Each legion was commanded by a *Legatus*. This was to be the army's permanent establishment and was not an overlarge force considering the extent of its operational area; it allowed few reserve forces and troops had to be moved to reinforce trouble spots but in doing so, by definition, reduced cover in the area they had departed. This would provide many future problems. It should be borne in mind that the army and its engineers were normally also engaged in building roads, bridges,

fortifications, aqueducts and canals. The navy for its part had disposed of all
the older and also the large multireme ships and been reduced to a reasonable
level operating mostly triremes.[41] It still built and kept a few large ships and
had many liburnians. This latter had by now grown to become a bireme
but confusion was added by the increasing practice of referring to nearly all
warships as liburnians which thus became a generic term and increasingly
impossible to distinguish as a type. There was a further smaller type called
galea, used for reconnaissance and as a look-out. The quinquireme had
gradually been replaced by the quadrireme or 'four' and triremes.

Caesar had organised and left a fleet to operate in the English Channel
which had ensured that there had been no further problems from the
Britons, with whom trade proceeded. The client kings of the empire also
had their own fleets, probably not of any great numbers, but which played
their part; the areas controlled by them (and by their armies) being secured
for the Empire at no cost to it and relieving the Roman navy of those duties.
Polemo of Pontus, the Bosporan Kingdom and Herod of Judaea all had
fleets which had operated with the Romans. It is possible that King Juba
of Mauretania also had some ships but apart from these few, the Imperial
navy was now the only one in Europe, western Asia and North Africa. It
could always augment the ships of client states in times of crisis, or indeed,
overwhelm them should they ever indicate a possible threat, or act in a way
that the Romans might consider to be against their interests, or at any other
time, should the need arise.

Notes

1. Appian (c. AD95 to 165) and Cassius Dio (writing in the late 2nd century AD) are the main sources for this period; see Rodgers, Morrison & Coates *GROW* and Meijer. For the politics see Scullard 2.
2. Once again and despite having a land base, the blockade was largely ineffectual.
3. It might seem curious that the two fleet actions take place close together and each follows virtually the same course. Suspicions of a duplication are aroused that it was a neat device to explain how both of Octavius' fleets were beaten. The fact remains however that no attack upon Sicily took place.
4. See ante. Chapter 1, Note 28 and Suetonius, *Augustus* 16.
5. Appian, *Bello Civilis* V.118.
6. Strabo V.4.5.
7. It is noteworthy in Appian's account to see the way in which liburnians were used to maintain communication between the advancing fleets and their armies, advancing in parallel.
8. The impact was sufficient to shake men from the towers and the ship settled so quickly that some of the rowers were trapped below. Morrison & Coates *GROW* reasons that Agrippa's flagship was a quinquireme or a 'six' and Demochares' a quadrireme.
9. Demochares' ships made the long passage from Mylae despite any exhaustion from the previous day's battle, but he did have the rump of the 'old' navy and the best crews. He would also have collected any ships that had not been previously engaged.
10. It is an interesting observation that all of Sextus' admirals bear Greek names, Demochares, Apollophanes and also Menodoros and Menekrates; Octavius' admirals all had solid Roman names, Agrippa, Taurus, Cornificius and Calvisius, according to Appian.
11. Rodgers avers that Taurus returned with seventy of his ships and that Octavius paid for the sixty that were lost. Appian says (V.98–99) that he only came with 102 ships, having left the other twenty-eight at Tarentum. As war losses, it would hardly have been incumbent upon Octavius to replace lost ships with money (especially in view of their poor showing) but a division of prizes was perfectly proper.
12. But see above, they could have been anything between 70 and 130.
13. Livy XXX.25 where he says that the higher deck of a Roman quinquireme prevented Punic marines on their quadrireme 'from jumping aboard her'.
14. Cassius Dio (XL.1.2) related in *GROW*; also it seems that they may have had raised platforms on deck (Orosius in *GROW*) to increase their fighting height even more.
15. There is a reasoned calculation of the numbers in Morrison & Coates *GROW*, based on the ancient sources.
16. Orosius VI.19.
17. Plutarch (c. AD 46–120) (Anthony 66) and Cassius Dio (I.32) 'the assailants coming from many sides shot blazing missiles and with engines threw pots of flaming charcoal and pitch', quoted in Rodgers. This is the only time that such weapons are attested in a sea battle although one can presume their adoption at least from then onward.
18. A copy of a bronze tablet from late in the reign survives, listing Octavius' achievements, including details of this event.
19. Jones, *Augustus*. The full account of the expedition is by the contemporary writer Strabo.
20. Strabo gives a full account of this expedition.
21. For a listing of the inscriptions, see the Appendix and Index of Inscriptions in Starr, *The Roman Imperial Navy*.
22. See Starr (until now) the only book dedicated to the Imperial Navy and using the 'hard' evidence of inscriptions and epigraphy. Also Casson *SSAW*.
23. Bass, *A History of Seafaring*.
24. Known as the Potamophylacia, with a headquarters near the Canopic mouth of the Nile and other stations at points upriver; with its own river patrol ships and men, augmented when needed by the military, see Starr.
25. As happened in various revolts, eg. in AD 115–117.
26. The aqueduct is part of the 80-odd-mile (130km) system that started near Capua and supplied Neapolis, Baiae, Puteoli and Misenum and along another branch, Pompeii.
27. There is little to be seen today of the once-huge base. Despite the variation of the coastline caused by volcanic

movements, the suitability of the site is obvious. Ironically, the area between the two basins is now (1998) fenced off as belonging to the Italian navy.

28. Perhaps a local official was charged with this as part of their normal duties.

29. The list was compiled by Milner and is reproduced in Morrison & Coates *GROW* and also see Casson *SSAW*.

30. Nothing now remains of the base save the traces of a mole and a wall. The approximate site is now marked by the church of Saint Apollinare in Classe, the name a lone reminder.

31. Bass, *A History of Seafaring*.

32. Cowell, *Everyday Life in Ancient Rome*. There were also 25 denarii to the (gold) aureus.

33. The use of a drum is not attested, despite the movies.

34. Starr.

35. In this regard it must be borne in mind that all of the surviving wall paintings and some of the reliefs come from the Bay of Naples area and were preserved by the eruption of AD 79 and thus also represent a very limited timescale. Further, in wall paintings that were impressionistic, it was easier to paint some discs and lines to represent shields and spears and a crowded deck, than to laboriously detail each tiny figure. It is not safe to draw too many conclusions therefore.

36. There is no surviving evidence as to the chain or limits of command.

37. Names of ships are shown on sailors' tombstones and also on at least one Greek vase. *Oculi* can be seen on wall paintings, vases and statuary.

38. Venice's annual 'Wedding with the Sea' and similar rituals still occur in Italy, Greece, Spain, where icons and statuary of various saints are annually taken into or upon the sea at the opening of the sailing season.

39. For an account of the politics see Scullard 2.

40. Bounegru & Zahariade, *Les Forces Navales de Bas Danube*.

41. Although once more, this is only inferred from the grave stelae evidence and the similarity in type of most of the Bay of Naples wall paintings, they may of course not necessarily show triremes.

THE EARLY EMPIRE

12 BC–AD 70

The second part of Augustus' plan was to incorporate all of the territory between the Rhenus and the River Albis (Elbe), basically what is now western Germany and the Czech Republic into the Empire. In 12 BC the future emperor Tiberius and his brother Drusus crossed the Rhenus. In the northern sector, Drusus concentrated at Bonna the ships and boats previously used by the Romans on the river and formally consolidated them into the *Classis Germanica*, a regular fleet with its own Praefect and officers. He also reinforced the new fleet by building new ships and bringing trained crews from the Italian fleets, in preparation for the forthcoming campaigns. He had his engineers prepare a system of canals linking the Rivers Waal and Amisa (Ems) and the Rhenus via the lakes of Holland to the North Sea (or *Mare Germanica*), the Fossa Drusianae. The Zuider Zee (Ijsselmeer) had not then been formed and there existed a great lake or system of lakes (the Lacus Flevus) behind a land barrier that would later sink and be breached by the sea. The Channel fleet was brought up to augment the available forces and secure the coastline.[1]

Drusus, commanding the fleet, sailed with it down the canals and rivers to the Lower Rhenus and operated along the Dutch and German coasts and out into the North Sea. The fleet carried out exploration and reconnaissance of the area and investigated the possibility of any maritime threat to the Roman flank. One tribe only, the Bructeri, challenged the Roman ships when they sallied forth in their boats against the Roman fleet on the River Ems, but were defeated. Ships of the fleet reconnoitred the west coast of Denmark and the south of Scandinavia as well as entering into the Baltic; they reported that the native craft which they came upon were numerous, were rowed only, not sailed and were small double-enders which could be rowed in either direction but posed no threat. Drusus received the support of the tribes of north Holland, the Batavii and the Frisii, who occupied lands either side of the mouth of the Rhenus and 'around vast lagoons' on which Roman ships sailed, both of whom were Roman allies. From these advanced positions the fleet was able to reconnoitre the German coast and to explore the estuary and lower reaches of the River Visurgis (Weser) and then of the Albis itself. The *Classis Germanica* thus extended its operations along the lower Rhenus and Amisia and into the German Bight in support of the new advance. The formerly primarily river-based fleet was strengthened by the addition of seagoing ships for this extended role and to release the Channel Squadron to its former duties. Lack of experience in these new-to-them waters led to some of the ships being stranded on a falling tide on one occasion, presumably to be recovered later.

Having secured the seaward flank, the invasion of Germania could proceed; the land war could be supported by using as lines of supply the Rivers Lippe and Main, which flow into the Rhenus from the east. Naval support also enabled the legions to make simultaneous, parallel drives into enemy territory whilst retaining secure lines of supply. The border was pushed forward to the Visurgis by the following year and established on the lower Albis by 9 BC in which year Drusus died following an accident. Tiberius took overall command and continued the work of pacification and consolidation of the intended new province of Germania. By AD 4, Tiberius had the fleet operating along the Albis and north German coast. He campaigned again in AD 5 by land and sea and further exploration was undertaken by the fleet, northward up the Norwegian coast.[2]

AD 4

The next move was to be the conquest and annexation of Bohemia and with it the headwaters of the Albis. Domitius Ahenobarbus advanced northwards from Noricum, along the River Sazava (Saale) to join the upper Albis. In AD 6, when he was in the final stages of securing Bohemia, revolts broke out in Pannonia and Illyria. A hasty peace had to be made with the Marcomanni (of Bohemia) and Tiberius and his forces diverted to deal with it.

AD 6

In AD 6, after troubles there, Judea was annexed as a province; of the former navy of King Herod nothing is known, but presumably such ships and manpower as were needed by the Imperial navy to take over its duties were absorbed into that service and the rest disbanded.

Although overrun, the new province of Germania had not been consolidated and in AD 9, three legions, whilst withdrawing to winter quarters in the west, were attacked and destroyed in the Teutoburger Wald. This great disaster deeply affected Augustus and although the Rhenus frontier was quickly secured and Tiberius and his nephew, Germanicus, carried out severe reprisals and could easily have re-occupied Germania, Augustus forbade it and ordered the frontier to be fixed at the Rhenus and Germania abandoned.

AD 9

The army establishment was left at the twenty-five remaining legions and the losses were not replaced. The strength of the legions and *auxilia* totalled some 250,000 men, to cover borders now extending some 4000 miles (6400km). The navy's strength was about 15,000 in the *Classes Praetoriae* and the same number again in the various provincial fleets and squadrons, 30,000 in all or just over ten per cent. Permanent bases were set up on the Rhenus for the legions that would henceforth be stationed along it; at Vetera (Xanten), Novaesium (Neuss), Bonna (Bonn), Moguntiacum (Mainz), Argentorate (Strasbourg) and Vindonissa (Windisch in Switzerland) and quays and jetties built as riverine ports for the fleet and supply ships, known as *naves actuariae*. As on the Danubius, patrols could be transported to the east bank and the Romans did try to maintain a strip clear on that side as a 'military zone', although this seems to have been fairly lax in its enforcement and not surprisingly, was largely impracticable. The Batavii and Frisii remained friends and allies and their lands as an unofficial adjunct to the empire and the fleet could thus continue to operate and cover the southern North Sea coast but otherwise, its main focus was now to be the patrol of the Rhenus. Unlike the Albis which is wide and shallow, the Rhenus is fast and deep and formed an almost impassable barrier when patrolled as it now was. As the Roman historian Tacitus explained 'the Empire's frontiers were on the ocean or distant rivers. Armies, provinces, fleets, the whole system was interrelated.'[3]

TIBERIUS

AD 14   Tiberius was already 56 when, in AD 14 Augustus died and he became Princeps; he was the most famous general of his day and popular with the armed services. His twenty-three year tenure, although not untroubled, continued the basic stability and prosperity of his predecessor and included the unchanged continuance of the naval and military establishment already so familiar to him.

Tiberius' first test was a mutiny over conditions of service by troops in Pannonia and Germania Inferior (approximately Belgium). The Emperor's son, Drusus, was sent to deal with the former and his nephew, Germanicus, the latter. In Germania, Germanicus felt that the best course for the troops was to keep them busy and embarked upon a series of campaigns eastwards across the Rhenus. In AD 14, he advanced from Vetera along the River Lippe;

AD 15   in AD 15 he started from Moguntiacum and crossed to the River Amisia where he met with four legions which had been brought in by the fleet via the canal system and North Sea coast. This force needed some 200 ships to transport it and its supplies to the Lower Rhenus ports and many civilian ships must have been taken into service to make up sufficient capacity. With the coming of winter, the Romans withdrew and the fleet suffered losses in men and supplies on their return trip when they were caught in a severe storm off the coast.[4] In AD 16 Germanicus actually joined ships of the fleet for a North Sea cruise.

The Lower Danubius border had been a source of continual unrest from the activities of peoples, principally Dacians, living to the north. A serious irruption by them in AD 15 and the loss of a border post to the raiders led to the *Classis Moesica* transporting a large force of troops, led by Pomponius Flaccus, on punitive operations against the barbarians and after which the river remained peaceful for a long time, under the continual watch of the *Classis*.

AD 16   For AD 16, the *Classis Germanica*, with a trireme as flagship, was again augmented by impressed merchant shipping and many barges which had been built especially.[5] It again went eastward using the same routes through canals, Dutch lakes and coast, to the Amisia and thence to the River Visurgis, whence the army conducted a relentless and victorious campaign. At the close of the campaign season, most of the army returned to base overland, but part of it was embarked to return by ship from the Amisia. Despite their improved experience and all precautions, they were again beset by storms which caused serious losses to the fleet when it was caught in the open sea.[6]

For all that, Germanicus had not sought to secure territory and over-winter in the east, preferring to withdraw each year; whether the ships could have kept supplied a base at the mouth of the rivers in the face of rough winter weather is unlikely without suffering serious losses. In any event and in the absence of any consolidation of territorial gains or the discovery of any natural resource to justify it, Tiberius, already well-conditioned to Augustus' policy on borders, felt the expense of further eastward advance uneconomical and ordered Germanicus to withdraw to the Rhenus. Tiberius was content to mostly rest on the borders established by Augustus, although Cappadocia and Commagene in Anatolia were annexed. Similarly, although aware of their 'compactness', he made no attempt to increase the size of the standing AD 19   army or navy. Germanicus died suddenly in Syria in AD 19.

Also in that same year Maroboduus the King of the Marcomanni (of Bohemia), who had built up a large realm at peace with Rome, fled his collapsing kingdom, beset by envious Germanic neighbours and with Boto, a refugee Pannonian chief, sought refuge with Rome. They were settled in comfortable retirement under the aegis of the fleet at Ravenna. As part of its increasing productivity and trade, Hispania produced esparto grass used for rope-making.

AD 24   In AD 24, sailors of the *Classis Ravennate* were used in restoring order after an uprising of slaves in Brundisium. The fleet thereafter maintained a detachment there to oversee the vital sea-route across the Adriatic. Tiberius left Rome in AD 26 for the last time, retiring to Campania, then in AD 27, moved to Augustus' old holiday home on Capreae (Capri), his final home where the fleet at Misenum, just across the Bay of Naples, became his link with the outside world.

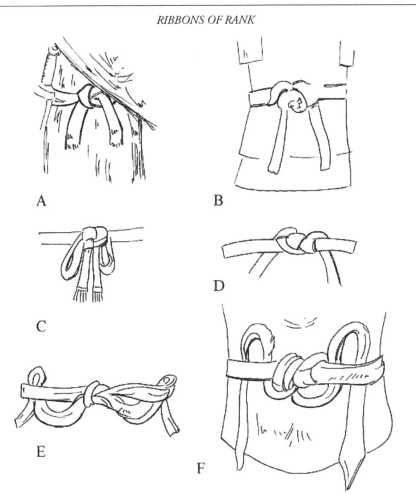

RIBBONS OF RANK

A

B

C

D

E

F

Statues of officers frequently show a ribbon tied about their armour in a number of differing styles. It is likely that many of these statues were originally painted and it could well have been that different colours, combined with different styles and methods of fastening these ribbons, distinguished individual ranks. Consuls', and later Emperors', ribbons were doubtless purple.

A. From the grave stela of a marine from Misenum. Although with an officer's ribbon this figure wears his sword on the right, indicating perhaps a non-commissioned officer.

B. Ribbon worn over a short cuirass, after a tombstone at Pompeii. The ribbon is partly obscured but a large flamboyant knot and long trailing ends are visible.

C. Marine officer on the deck of a warship. Taken from the Praeneste Relief.

D. Knot around the cuirass of an officer, thought to be a Tribune, from the Altar of Domitius Ahenobarbus in the Louvre, Paris.

E. Ornate knotted ribbon from a statue of the Emperor Nero.

F. The Emperor Vespasian, from a statue in the Temple to the Imperial cult at Misenum.

AD 28
In AD 28 the Frisii (in Holland) again revolted but this time Tiberius did not suppress them and they, being on the east side of the Rhenus, were left outside the Empire, as a buffer state between it and the German tribes. The navy now had no further reason to maintain patrols of the Visurgis or Dutch lakes to protect the Frisii and thus concentrated on the Rhenus. The Frisii did return to friendship with Rome and their waterways remained open to the navy, which, with the end of eastward expansion, had now settled into its role of the securing of the Rhenus as a permanent border. In the same way as practised by the Danubius fleets, that role was to protect the Roman or left bank by denying the river to barbarian navigation; to maintain and regulate the river as an artery of supply and communication for its garrisons and Roman trade; to control and protect traffic on the tributaries and waterways connected to the Rhenus on the Roman side, including the river mouth which was an important terminus for the sea route to northern Gaul (and later, to Britannia).

On the barbarian side or right bank, the fleet had to make reconnaissance and punitive forays to project Roman power up the tributaries joining it on that side.[7] Fleet headquarters was established at a specially built camp a short way south of what would become Colonia Agrippinensis (Cologne), with subsidiary bases downriver at Vetera and Novaesum. The main area of fleet operations seems to have been the Lower Rhenus and the fleet also built and manned several forts in the river delta, crossed as it was by many waterways and difficult to patrol on foot.[8]

On the Danubius, Tiberius settled some friendly tribes on the north bank to act as a buffer state and re-organised the provinces of Achaea, Macedonia and Moesia into one command under Caius Poppaeus Sabinus who thus became commander also of the *Classis Moesica* on the lower Danubius and the west Euxine Sea. To assist in the patrolling of the river and its traffic, Tiberius caused a road to be built along the southern or right bank, cutting through the rock faces of the Iron Gates ravine, the road linking the upper and lower parts of the river. A narrow path was cut into the rock faces lining the gorge, which could be widened with timber sections, cantilevered out from sockets in the wall to form a roadway. In AD 36, there was an outbreak of piracy on the Cilician coast and Tiberius ordered the *Classis Ravennate* to suppress it. Tiberius was with the navy at Misenum when he became ill and died there in March AD 37. He was succeeded by his great-nephew Gaius, better known to us by his nickname of Caligula. As the surviving son of Germanicus, he was popular with the armed forces but in October of AD 37,
AD 37
he suffered an illness which seriously affected his personality for the worse and he acted with increasing irrationality and tyranny.

In another famous act, Gaius set out to disprove a contention and taunt some years before by Tiberius' astrologer, Thrasyllus. The Greek had once

Gaius' spending was profligate and among his foibles was the building of two huge pleasure ships for use on Lake Nemi, in the hills south of Rome, complete with mosaic-laid decks, running water, heated baths and exotic decorations; floating palaces no less, over 230 feet long (73m).[9] He also had pleasure galleys for cruising the coast which were similarly luxuriously appointed. One item of more general usefulness found among the remains of these ships were bucket-chain bilge pumps, operated by crank-handles, whereby a chain of buckets, joined as a loop, are wound around a drum in the bilge and another on the deck, which empties the buckets into a chute and over the side (A similar installation can be seen on HMS *Victory*). This is the first reference to a proper crank handle rather than a simple windlass, i.e. which could be wound continuously and without pause to change grip;[10] its application to speed the reloading of catapults must have been obvious. He also had built a huge seagoing ship, 320 feet long by 65 feet beam (186m by 20m) for the sole purpose of bringing an obelisk from Egypt to Rome which was subsequently laid up.[11]

opined that Gaius could no more be Emperor than ride a chariot across part of the Bay of Naples from Puteoli to Baiae. The area had become a playground of the rich and famous who had built luxury villas at the resorts of Baiae and Bauli occupying the small bays between the great naval base at Misenum to the west and the busy civil port of Puteoli to the east. Having become Emperor, Gaius ordered harbour masters throughout Italy and Sicily to assemble ships of a certain size in the Bay of Naples under naval custody. When enough had been gathered (regardless of the needs of commerce) he had them moored in a double line, beam to beam with bows outward, from the docks of Puteoli to his villa at Bauli, a distance of over two miles (3km), at an average beam of say ten feet (3m), over 2000 vessels would have been needed; the sterns were sawn off level and timber laid across the ships, which was then covered with earth, to form a road some 6000 paces long. Even more ships were gathered to form 'islands', every 1000 paces along the road and on each, shops and 'villages' were erected and gardens laid complete with a drinking water system. The weather stayed mercifully calm and when all was ready, Gaius dressed in Alexander the Great's breastplate, a gold and jewel encrusted cloak, Julius Caesar's sword and the reputed axe of Romulus and shield of Aeneas; then, after making a sacrifice to Neptune, he rode his horse from Bauli across to Puteoli, followed by his cavalry guard and a mass of infantry and more cavalry, which charged into town for the last thousand paces. Gaius stayed at Puteoli until the following evening when, similarly attired, he drove a gold-plated chariot back across the 'bridge', followed by a wagon train of valuables looted from the unfortunate town, the troops and then masses of people in holiday mood. Having crossed, the Emperor was rowed in one of his pleasure barges to the centre-most 'island' where he harangued the passing throng and distributed coin. As the night wore on and the wine flowed, the revelry became more boisterous and finally, Gaius took to his naval flagship and with some other warships actually attacked one of the 'islands', just for fun, breaking the road-bridge either side of it and sinking its supporting ships by ramming; casualties are not known but must have run into hundreds.[12]

AD 39

Conspiracies started in Upper Germany by AD 39 and Gaius went there to put them down; he actually led his troops in raids across the Rhenus although more for affect than effect. After wintering in Gaul, in the spring of AD 40, Caligula massed the army on the Channel coast and put the Channel Fleet on alert for a possible expedition to Britannia. Suddenly he cancelled the enterprise and returned to Rome and the forces returned to their normal activities and stations. At this time a lighthouse was built at the harbour of Gesoriacum (Boulogne) on the north Gaulish coast, said to have originally been 200 feet (60m) high which was demolished in AD 1544. If he was serious about invading Britannia then the preparation of this harbour to service such an adventure was a desirable requisite, one that would prove its worth a very few years later. Gaius' irrationality and tyranny got worse until

AD 41

he was finally murdered in his palace in January AD 41.

The next emperor was Gaius' uncle, Claudius, who reigned for thirteen years, restoring stability and acquiring the loyalty of the forces by ensuring that they were not neglected and were paid regularly. In reforming the administration, Claudius abolished the post of *Quaestores Classici*; at Misenum and Ravenna the local Praefects of the fleet could carry out their work. Ostia was by now a wholly civilian port for which an Imperial *Procurator Portus Ostiensis* was appointed, in place of the *Quaestor Ostiensis*. The term of service for crewmen was increased from twenty to twenty-six years. Presumably as an exercise in improving the stock in coastal waters, Claudius ordered the Misene Fleet to sow oysters along the Campanian coast. These reforms were completed by AD 44. Under Claudius the whole emphasis of the administration changed from the traditional senators and equites, to a dedicated, professional bureaucracy under the Emperor himself, divided into departments, each headed by an imperial freedman. The former distinction between military and civilian staffs was ended, so that non-military men could and did become Fleet Praefects, who were also renamed as Procurators by Claudius. Accordingly the post became administrative rather than seagoing.[13]

AD 41

As a portent of things to come, in AD 41, Chauci tribesmen from the north German coast using their open boats and avoiding any Roman ships, raided along the coast of Belgica, before being caught and beaten off by local Roman forces. Claudius added five new provinces to the Empire, the two parts of Mauretania, Thrace, Lycia in Asia Minor and Britain.

BUILDING OF
PORTUS

To aid the corn supply for the capital, Claudius himself insured ships and cargoes and gave privileges to aliens who built ships. Ostia had problems with silting as well as being too small and unable to handle the volume of traffic or the largest ships that wanted to use it. Of these, it seems many preferred to use the larger harbours of southern Latium such as Antium, Formiae (Formia), Gaeta and Tarracina (Terracina) or even Puteoli and there offload onto smaller coasters for onward transport of their cargoes.[14] To overcome the problem, Claudius had built a new, large harbour, named Portus, two miles (3km) to the north of Ostia and linked by a canal to a branch of the lower Tiber. The new harbour was completely artificial and had to be totally dredged to form its basin which extended to about a third of a square mile (0.5 sq. km); it was a difficult and costly undertaking and took twelve years to build. To start forming the offshore mole and breakwaters, Caligula's huge obelisk transport was used as a blockship, filled with rocks and sunk in the desired position, after which piling was put in around it to secure it and to form the shape of the mole which was then filled. Silting remained a problem however and constant dredging was needed. It was completed with moles and breakwaters. A lighthouse was added in AD 48, four storeys high, three of which formed a square tower, surmounted by a round top storey containing the lantern and modelled on the Pharos at Alexandria. Large granaries multiplied Ostia's capacity to handle shipping for Rome although even the new sea walls did not guarantee complete protection from onshore storms.[15]

Mauretania had been in open revolt upon Claudius' accession after Gaius had its ruler murdered in Rome. In AD 41 and 42, successive campaigns brought the whole territory under Roman control and it was organised into the province of Caesariensis (the eastern part), with its capital at Caesarea, which was made a naval base with a separate naval harbour and home of a naval detachment; the western part became the province of Tingitana, with its capital at Tingis (Tangier), on the Atlantic seaboard. With most of the action taking place well inland, the navy's role was limited to the ferrying of troops and supplies, with perhaps the odd landing to turn the enemy's flank along the Atlantic seaboard.

BRITANNIA

AD 43

In AD 43 Lycia was formerly annexed and made into a province, thereby bringing the entire Anatolian coastline within the Empire. The major event of that year was however, the invasion of Britannia (the British Isles). For the previous half century or so, there had been much trade with Britannia and the other lands of the north, and Roman and Romano-Gaulish merchants had visited and even stayed there in furtherance of trade. By AD 43, therefore, the

Roman military planners would have been well apprised of the geography, harbours, estuaries and location of centres of population and familiar with the local conditions, politics, personalities and peoples of their target. Additionally, it can be assumed that they had copies of, and were familiar with, the book written by Pytheas of Massilia; an account of his travels with the astronomical and topographical observations that he recorded. The fleet organised by Caesar had patrolled the Empire's northern borders unopposed, securing that trade. Although not so far officially constituted as a *Classis*, this unit probably comprised a smallish number of ships operated by detachments of the army, possibly with a core of naval personnel. This had proved sufficient to cover the reasonably peaceful seas of northern Gaul, to ensure the prevention of piracy, to regulate navigation and doubtless to collect duties on cargoes. As to ships, those of Caesar's original fleets had, by now, long since rotted, deteriorated or otherwise been pensioned off. There is no evidence of the type of ships in use, although it is a fair assumption that in the absence of any native naval opposition requiring Mediterranean-style warships, most functions could be best carried out in suitably adapted native ships which had after all, been evolved to function in the sea conditions of that area, backed up perhaps by a few purpose built warships.

For whatever reasons, Claudius resolved to add Britannia to the Empire. For the invasion the existing rather ad hoc squadron would clearly be insufficient to attain that prerequisite for any successful invasion of the islands, as would be attested by so many failures over the coming centuries, command of the seas around them. Having established that command, it would then be necessary to establish and protect a constant procession of supply ships, reinforcements and communications between Gaul and the expeditionary forces. The expedition was to be entirely self-supporting and not at all reliant on the uncertain possibility of living even in part off the land or otherwise of acquiring supplies in Britannia. The only supply route would thus be by sea from Gaul, with the navy responsible for its maintenance and protection.

The securing of a bridgehead, which had to include a sheltered anchorage and harbour, to act as a terminal for the supply ships was therefore of prime importance. As well as the collection and building of sufficient transport ships, the naval units were now officially re-designated as the *Classis Britannica* and hugely strengthened by the drafting of officers and crews, artificers and specialists from the Italian fleets and by the building in the Mediterranean of numerous warships which were then sailed around to northern Gaul to take part in the invasion. The build-up of ships, together with the amassing of stores, materials and supplies, must in fact, have taken several years in planning and execution before the actual event, raising the question as to whether it had started under Caligula, who aborted his proposed invasion. The local merchant ships were later described by Tacitus as being 'of shallow

INCREASE
OF TRADE
UNDER
CLAUDIUS

The prolonged period of comparative peace and stability and the increased size, strength and diversity of the empire led to a vast increase in the amount of trade and goods passing in all directions. Claudius received an embassy from Ceylon, establishing friendly relations with that far-off land. The security of the seas underwritten by the navy allowed a corresponding increase in sea-borne trade; merchant ships grew to a size that would not be equalled until the 19th century AD , grain ships commonly having a capacity of 1200 tons of cargo. The merchant fleet became the biggest that the world had known and ranged from the north of Europe to India as well as operating on every major river and watercourse in the Empire. The enlarged port of Ostia must have been a hive of activity with the constant comings and goings of ships, great and small, to all parts and with every imaginable cargo. Passenger traffic was also copious with regular sailings enabling travellers to go, for example, to Gades or Rhodes in seven days, Corinth in five days, Carthage or Massilia in three days (the latter a journey of over three weeks by land), or even to Alexandria in ten days (two months by land).[16]

MERCHANT
GALLEYS

Harbours in Hispania and North Africa were enlarged and improved. Merchantmen had always shipped a few oars for manoeuvre in restricted waters, but there now evolved the merchant galley, a type that became widespread in use and whose oars, like those of the warships which inspired them, were the prime source of propulsion, with sail as an auxiliary means of power. Broader, less fast and deeper than a warship, so they could carry useful amounts of cargo, although not so much as a conventional freighter, they were reliable and twice as fast as a big sailer and specialised in the transport of higher priced goods with a short shelf-life, such as exotic animals for the arena. A further parallel with the warship was the imitation ram bow form adopted by the merchant galleys, a fashion that was carried over even into small boats. Triangular top-sails, called *supparum*, were often rigged on each side between the top of the yard and the mast, also seen on both masts of two-masted ships; the basic square sail rig remained the most common but is often shown in contemporary renditions slewed fore and aft, to take advantage of a wider variety of wind bearings.[17]

draft, pointed bow and stern and broad-beamed to withstand heavy seas';[18] barges were built with flat bottoms to ease beaching, the equivalent of landing craft; other ships had decks for the transport of animals, artillery and heavy gear, such as wagons. Sadly no indication has survived as to the sizes or capacities of the ships although the remains of a small, early 2nd century AD sailing ship found in the City of London was carvel-built over heavy frames and about fifty feet (15m) long by about twenty-two feet (7m) beam and capable of carrying nearly a hundred tons.[19]

Four legions and *auxilia* were earmarked for the task, under their commander, Aulus Plautius, who had amassed considerable experience of combined operations when working with the navy on the Danubius; from there he took with him Legio IX Hispania which was also experienced in riverine and waterborne operations. The other three legions had been stationed along the Rhenus and many of their units were ferried down that river and through the lake and waterway systems by the Rhenus fleet and its transports to the nearest convenient point for their concentration centres. The army mustered at Gesoriacum and Portus Itius (Dunkirk) where their transports had been gathered and numbered some 40,000 men, needing something over 300 ships to carry them. The invasion was to be made in three divisions, two escorted by the new *Classis Britannica* and the third by ships of the *Classis Germanica*. This last division may have mustered at the mouth of the Rhenus and, sailing on a predetermined day, taken a direct route to the prearranged landing site from there, relieving congestion on the Channel ports. Of the three divisions, the first would have been the assault troops, artillery and engineers needed to secure a beachhead and anchorage sufficient for the second wave; the latter to include cavalry to send out scouting screens and establish a piquet; finally the supporting elements, transport animals and wagons and bulk supplies to enable the army to move on. The process could have taken two or three trips to complete over the course of several days. Thereafter, ships would be deployed, partly on the cross-Channel 'supply bridge' and others from the base depots in close supply of the forces along the south and east coasts, as they advanced.[20]

The invasion plan was to land the army in the south-east 'corner' of the country (Kent) and to advance up the course of the River Tamesis, from which it could be supplied, crossing to attack the main opposition homeland in what is now Essex; here they were to be joined by the Emperor himself for the final assault and capture of the enemy capital at Camulodunum. The boundaries of the proposed new province were then to be pushed forward to a line running diagonally across Britannia, roughly from Isca Dumnoniorum (Exeter) in the south-west, to Lindum (Lincoln) in the north-east. On both flanks, seaborne support would be essential and great store was set for the use of river systems, both as supply routes and for the insertion of forces.

The Romans must have already carried out detailed reconnaissance of the whole area and its harbours and landing places, as well as the state of any local armed forces before making their final decision as to the actual landing site. For months 'innocent' trading ships and merchants must have been making careful observations and making accurate notes of the local topography. It is evident from the course taken by the invasion forces that they started out with a thorough grasp of both strategic and tactical objectives. Their use of the topography in the course of the campaign, especially in the provision of water-borne support, shows that the Romans had very good and accurate maps and charts of the country, aided and abetted by the many sympathetic and refugee Britons who had made their way to Gaul. They did not just blunder into the unknown, rather as Caesar had more or less done in Gaul. They knew the river and hill formations in their path and made use of them, time and again moving to strategic points to outmanoeuvre their opponents and to keep the opposition fragmented, while maintaining adequate and prompt supplies and reinforcements for themselves. The smoothness and efficiency with which Plautius' men effected their Channel crossing and landings is in direct contrast to the more haphazard expeditions of Caesar a century before.

After some hesitation, the fleet sailed, probably in mid-April and made an unopposed landing at Rutupiae (Richborough).[21] At that time the Isle of Thanet was separated by a wide, navigable channel (since silted and which has largely vanished) linking the estuary of the Tamesis to the English Channel and giving a sheltered passage and anchorage between the two. Rutupiae thus offered a sheltered landing site with an adjacent anchorage, which was readily defensible and within striking distance of the enemy town of Durovernum. Very early in the operation, the Romans seized and fortified Regulbium (Reculver), which controlled the northern end of the channel to the Tamesis, giving direct access to it. Control of the Tamesis was vital as it would seal the south-east corner of the country as a secure base, enable the Romans to penetrate westward deep into the country and, at the same time, enable them to support and supply operations on its north bank, for which they would thus have the initiative.

The Britons massed to oppose the invaders, but were defeated in a battle on the River Medway, after which the Romans advanced up the River Tamesis. Probably shortly after securing Durovernum, the Romans occupied the site of Dubris (Dover) and both it and Regulbium were handed over to the navy as bases. The navy, operating in the River Tamesis on the army's flank, helped with the building of a bridge across that river as well as bringing supplies forward. By operating off the coasts, menacing if not actually outflanking the enemy, the navy prevented the enemy from making any water-borne threat against the advancing Plautius. The Emperor, having sailed with his entourage and a detachment of Praetorian Guards down the Tiber, taken ship from Ostia for a stormy passage to Massilia and then by boat up the Rhodanus, joined his army and led the advance to the British capital of Camulodunum, which then became the capital of his new province. Claudius there received the submission of the Regni of Sussex and the Iceni of Norfolk, whose lands secured his flanks and then returned to Rome and triumph, awarding himself a *Corona Navalis* for crossing the Channel! Apart from securing the already part-Romanised south-east of Britannia, the Romans seem to have no clear overall plan as to the extent of their new province; unlike in Germany, where Augustus had proposed to draw his boundary between the Rhenus and Albis, no end-limit had been set and successive commanders were left to search for secure borders (as ever). They had long known, from the voyage of Pytheas for example, that Britannia was an island and that this fact would provide an ultimate limit to expansion if no interim satisfactory line could be found, unlike the limitless tracts of central Europe.

Plautius set out to expand the province, the Ninth Legion advanced north to establish a base at Lindum and the Wash; the Second, under Vespasian advanced westwards to Noviomagus (Chichester), securing the large and secure natural harbours of Chichester, Langstone and Portsmouth. From there the navy could operate, as it did, to enable him to take Vectis (the Isle of Wight). Next, Vespasian continued westward, the fleet taking advantage of the natural harbours at Christchurch and Poole (in which a navy supply base was established) and the shelter of Portland Bill to support his advance through Dorset and Devon, where a camp was set at Isca Dumnoniorum.[22] The ships of the *Classis Germanica* duly returned to their stations after the initial invasion and the *Classis Britannica* had to continue to expand to absorb its extended area of responsibility over the new and still-growing province. The maintenance of the essential link with Gaul would always remain the fleet's prime purpose and fleet headquarters was set up at Gesoriacum, although under the commander in Britannia. This was also the end of the main military highway to the Rhenus and its armies. On the British side, Rutupiae continued as a base, together with the navy's own port at Dubris (which was of increasing importance) and Regulbium, guarding the route north. The fleet's responsibility had now however changed in that it had, in effect, split into three; firstly the cross-Channel supply line; secondly the flank of the advance north-east into what is now East Anglia; thirdly the flank of the advance westward along the south coast. On both sides of the Channel and, following the advance of the provincial boundaries progressively northward up the east and west coasts of the island, the Fleet added both the North and Irish Seas to its areas of responsibility.

In the Bosporan Kingdom, dynastic upheaval had brought one Mithridates to power who almost immediately tried to turn against Rome. The Governor of Moesia therefore mounted an expedition in AD 45, loading men and supplies aboard requisitioned merchant ships, and with an escort provided by the *Classis Moesica* to counter any naval opposition (none was offered), subdued the Kingdom and placed Rome's nominee, Cotys, on the throne. At this time, in order to secure the Roman position, the Fleet founded a permanent naval base at Chersonesus (Sebastopol, Crimea) to be

AD 45

its principal base for the northern Euxine. Lying about 120 miles (200km) from the mouth of the Danubius and 100 miles (160km) from Sinope on the Pontic coast, the base was, in good weather, within a day's voyage for a warship from either point and thus readily accessible.

AD 46   In AD 46, again after local turbulence and unrest, Thrace was permanently annexed and made a province. For the purpose of the actual annexation, Claudius formed a naval formation entitled the *Classis Perinthia* to cover the operation. Whether this was composed of units drawn from the *Classis Moesica* and/or other eastern fleets is not clear and upon completion of the operation it was disbanded and its ships dispersed, presumably back to their parent fleets.[23] With the annexation of Thrace, the Empire's border was extended to include the whole Euxine coast northwards from Byzantium to the delta of the Danubius and responsibility for this coast duly fell to the *Classis Moesica*. This fleet had to adjust its focus by regarding its headquarters at Noviodunum now to be the centre of its operational area, rather then at one end of it. From the mouth of the Danubius, the fleet expanded its influence and became more involved with the active control of the western half of the Euxine, from the Propontis up to and including the Bosporan Kingdom, establishing bases and facilities at ports along the Thracian coast between the delta and Propontis. It also started to establish garrisons and facilities at the various Hellenistic settlements and cities scattered around the north-west Euxine basin, a process that would continue over the course of the next twenty years until the whole basin was under its control. The recently established base at Chersonesus was ideally placed to oversee this process and overall command of the north-west Euxine basin seems to have been vested in the military commander at Chersonesus, to whom units of the Moesican fleet were seconded. Obviously the Fleet grew with its added responsibilities and evolved different types of ship for each of its very different spheres of operation, riverine and open sea.

AD 47   By AD 47, the Roman province of Britannia had expanded to its intended border from Isca, north to the River Sabrina (Severn) and thence across to Lindum and the Wash. Although the far west of the country (now Cornwall) was yet to be occupied, to secure their gains the Bristol Channel and Sabrina estuary would have to be brought under control; ships of the navy sailed around Land's End, presumably mostly under oar westward against the prevailing winds, which could then be used to advantage for the return leg north-east to the Sabrina. Frequent stops on these dangerous coasts to allow for tides, winds and to obtain local knowledge of the coast would have been achieved with co-operation by, or intimidation of, the local peoples.

     A base was established at Glevum (Gloucester) by AD 52. Merchant ships continued to supply the troops and the navy could find no competition at sea in the north. The Roman writer Tacitus travelled with the navy on a North Sea sweep and visited Scandinavia; he described the local ships there as 'long, narrow and light, equally curved fore and aft', a general description that would not change for over a thousand years.[24] While the fleet was away in the north, a disaffected German auxiliary soldier led a fleet of boats of the Chauci to again raid Belgica in a repeat of their foray in AD 41. They attacked and burned the auxiliary fort at Valkenburg at the mouth of the Rhenus, but were then caught and destroyed by the *Classis Germanica*, which had sailed down the river.[25]

Among Claudius' civil engineering projects was the draining of Lake Fucinus (Fucino), in the Appenines east of Rome. Tunnels were dug to allow drainage and the system was completed by the late forties. To celebrate the opening, a huge *naumachia* was held on the (reduced) lake; 9000 convicts were used to man two fleets each of twelve triremes and 'fours' named respectively Rhodian and Sicilian. To encourage their efforts, troops or marines were posted on rafts. Apparently when the crews saluted the Emperor with the traditional *morituri te salutant*, he was heard to joke 'or not, as the case may be', they thereupon took this as a pardon and refused to fight. The troops threatened to massacre all of them which apparently induced a satisfactory battle.[26] Much of this tale is probably apocryphal in that, given the position and topography of the Fucine lake, the possibility of dragging triremes, let alone 'fours', to it are remote. Presumably some such celebration took place, but of more modest type and the boats used were more likely to have been the soon-to-be redundant lake craft. As always with *naumachiae*, the navy's function in arranging, organising and policing the event would have been utilised.

AD 50   Named for the Emperor's wife, Agrippina, a major veteran's colony was founded in AD 50 on the west bank of the Rhenus, Colonia Agrippinensis (Cologne). Also that year, the General Corbulo built a 23-mile (37km) long canal to link the Rivers Mosa (Meuse) and Rhenus. By AD 52 the border in Britannia was advanced on the east to the River Abus (Humber) where, to aid supply routes (which would be followed by trade), a canal was excavated to link the Wash and the River Trent.[27] In the west the Silures of South Wales continued to give trouble which was countered by naval raids along their coast and up the valleys against their villages and farms. An advance along this coast was difficult because of the successive ranges of hills that come down to the sea across a path of advance; approach from the sea by-passes such natural barriers and enabled the marines of the fleet to strike quickly and deeply into enemy territory without having to protect a line of communication and supply. The Roman ships had worked their way around the ferocious south-west coasts of Britannia using the many inlets and shelters of the Devon and Cornish coasts and had established a sea route into the estuary of the River Sabrina to their base at Glevum.

LATER TORSION-SPRING ARTILLERY

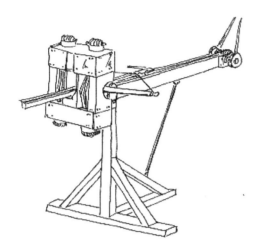

LEFT: 2nd century BC. Late Republican 'Scorpion' or small, three span, arrow-shooting catapult after an example found at Empurias in Spain. Greater use of metal parts and improved design of spring frames resulted in a more robust and reliable weapon.

RIGHT: Detail showing the armoured frontal shield for a larger type weapon. Taken from a 1st-century tomb relief. Excavated examples of the bronze face plates have depicted legionary motifs and insignia suggesting they were 'standard' issue.

LEFT: 2nd century AD. all metal framed three span catapult. An iron frame with copper alloy protective covers for the spring assemblies. Reconstructed examples have indicated that they could well have had an effective range of several hundred metres. Mass produced and widely distributed, these artillery pieces would have seen service with most military arms, including the navy.

RIGHT: A depiction of a carroballista (three span catapult) taken from Trajan's Column, Rome, that would appear to show it either being transported in, or mounted upon, a wagon drawn by mules. Such compact machines would be ideal for shipboard use.

NERO

AD 54   Claudius died in AD 54, to be succeeded by Nero, who started well, one of his first functions being to inaugurate Claudius' harbour at Portus. Nero resolved to murder his domineering mother Agrippina and in AD 59, they were at a villa at Baiae and he sent her off in a boat to convey her to her own villa across the bay. Unbeknown to her, the boat in question had been especially made or adapted to be collapsible; unbeknown to him, his mother was an excellent swimmer. The plan went awry and Agrippina swam ashore. On learning of this, Nero sent for Anicetus, his freedman who was Prefect of the Fleet at nearby Misenum and ordered him to have her killed; Anicetus got some of his sailors who, in contrast to the previous carefully contrived plans, simply battered Agrippina to death.[28]

AD 59   In Britannia, operations were mainly to quell unrest on the borders. In AD 59, Suetonius Paulinus advanced into North Wales and attacked Mona (Anglesey) to suppress the druids there. No ships were available and so to cross the Menai Strait to the island, he had flat-bottomed boats or punts made for the men and the cavalry swam across. By AD 60, the far west part of southern Britannia had been secured and added to the province.

AD 61   In AD 61, a small detachment of Praetorian Guards was sent to Egypt on an expedition up the Nile, past the Kingdom of Meroe and modern Khartoum. The reason for this is not known as these particular troops were hardly essential for an exploration or a reconnaissance or to chart the river for future navigation. Perhaps it was intended as an attempt to overawe the natives, although the local legionary garrison could do as well; perhaps the praetorians had displeased Nero and their two-year voyage was the result of his whim; perhaps to investigate rumours of riches or possible conquests to the south; or even perhaps, just for curiosity. In any event, they penetrated and mapped far up the White Nile, being eventually stopped by the impenetrable swamps and seemingly endless marshes of the Sudd region of Equatorial Africa, an achievement not to be repeated by Europeans until the explorers of the nineteenth century.[29]

AD 62   The unsatisfactorily insecure nature of the eastern Euxine was brought to prominence by a campaign against the Parthians, conducted by the general, Corbulo. At that time the road system in eastern Anatolia was undeveloped and the most direct route to the focus of operations in Armenia was by road south from Trapezus, which was thus the terminus for seaborne supplies.

AD 63   The Roman client King of Eastern Pontus, Polemo II, was 'retired' in AD 63 and his kingdom was annexed and incorporated into the province of Galatia. The Romans took over the former Royal Fleet and merged it with their own local forces, originally set up by Pompeius; the resulting squadron Nero nominated as the *Classis Pontica*, with its own praefect whose area of responsibility was the north coast of Asia Minor and the eastern half of the

CANAL
BUILDING

In AD 62, a mighty storm hit the Roman coast and the harbour of Portus, wrecking 200 ships there and also some of the Misene Fleet's ships, which were caught off Cumae. It was doubtless the constant problem of giving Rome easy access to her shipping that prompted Nero to very seriously consider, with his architects Severus and Celer, the digging of a canal to link the city with the good natural harbours around Puteoli, 160 miles (256km) away, mostly across the Pontine Marshes. Some work was actually begun and there was already an older, small canal which could be widened and incorporated for part of the route, stretching from Tarracina for nearly twenty miles (37km) parallel to the Appian Way, towards Rome.[30] The project died with the Emperor, never to be resurrected. Another investigation was made at this time, into the possibility of building another canal, this time to link the Mosella and Saune in Gaul, which would have enabled waterborne transport from the Mediterranean, via the Rhodanus, to the North Sea via the Rhenus but the project was abandoned, curiously after local opposition rather than due to any engineering difficulties, presumably from those concerned with the portage of goods between the two who would become unemployed if replaced by the canal. Also at about this time, a shipwreck disaster was recorded in the Adriatic, when a ship with no fewer than 600 passengers was lost at sea, only eighty of those aboard surviving. Presumably the ship was a passenger ferry but must have been a big ship and gives some indication of the numbers of people travelling by sea (even allowing for exaggeration). The historian Josephus quotes a similar figure for the ship on which he travelled.

Euxine. The new fleet was some forty ships in strength,[31] mostly liburnians but with a trireme and it established its principal base and headquarters at Trapezus.[32] The fleet was backed by a garrison along the coast of about 3000 troops and its new forward base enabled it to maintain a close watch on the eastern coast of the Euxine, which had otherwise been subject to piracy; control could also be extended into the Maeotis Palus (Sea of Azov), where it overlapped with the remit of the *Classis Moesica*. The *Classis Moesica* had continued to be active in the western half of the Euxine, extending Roman suzerainty to the Greek cities such as Tyras (near Akerman, Ukraine) and Olbia (Nikolayev, Ukraine) and escorting grain-carrying ships to Rome as well as the long-established shipments to Greece.

AD 64

Nero next wished to be rid of his wife, Octavia, and accused her of adultery with the same Anicetus who had been so instrumental in the disposal of his mother; she was executed and he was banished, Nero thus disposing of them both in one go. The rule degenerated, especially after the great fire in Rome and persecutions of AD 64. The rebuilding and Nero's profligacy meant increased taxes, appropriations and the debasing of the coinage and by AD 65, plots had started against him which encouraged Nero

AD 65

to become an even more ruthless tyrant. The army was starting to become disaffected and so Nero, remembering perhaps the loyal 'service' performed by the navy, took drafts from the marines of the Misenum and Ravenna Fleets to form two new legions, the Legions I and II Adiutrix respectively. These troops he kept with him at or near Rome, rather than send them back to their bases, perhaps as a counter to the unreliable attitude of the Praetorians. Presumably the fleets remained under strength for some time as later, Otho would have to augment the Misene Fleet with troops.

Years of unrest in Palestine finally broke into open revolt in AD 66 and Nero appointed Titus Flavius Vespasianus commander of the east with three legions, to deal with it. Vespasian had reduced Galilee by AD 67 and Samaria in the following year. The Romans had naval support provided most probably by the *Classis Alexandrina*, within whose remit the operational area fell. There was some naval opposition from the rebels, who equipped many ships for raiding and intercepting Roman trade, including the important grain carriers from Eqypt, along the Egyptian and Phoenician coasts. Jaffa seems to have been the centre of this activity and Vespasian sent a flying column of cavalry and troops there. On learning of the Roman approach, the rebels manned their ships and stood out to sea, only to be caught offshore by a storm and wrecked.[33]

Nero returned from Greece early in AD 68 to find great unrest. The Governor of Tarraconensis in Hispania, Servius Sulpicius Galba, declared himself *Legatus S.P.Q.R.*, or 'protector' and gained considerable support. Nero's own men started to desert him and bribed the Praetorians to support the Senate and proclaim Galba as Emperor. The Senate did this and proclaimed Nero to be a public enemy; Galba accepted and Nero committed suicide, aged 30, on 9 June AD 68, having first tried and presumably failed to persuade the navy unit at Ostia to help him to escape to Egypt. When he heard of the death, Vespasian in the east slowed his own operations right down, sensing perhaps the unrest to come.[34]

Augustus' navy base at Forum Iulii had by now become badly silted and was closed down as a permanent base and its personnel transferred to Misenum, although a small squadron remained there which declared for Vespasian in AD 69. It then ceased to be a formal naval base since, apart from serious silting, its location in a by-now pacified and secure Gallic coast away from the main foci of troubles and too far from Rome made the constant cost of trying to keep it dredged unjustifiable and unnecessary.

CIVIL WAR – CONFUSED LOYALTIES

The upheavals that shook the Roman world, following the death of Nero, in the year of the four emperors, AD 68 – 69, embroiled the Italian and Rhenus Fleets, but left the other commands virtually uninvolved. Galba and his

CORINTH
CANAL

After a brief return to Rome, Nero went to Corinth, where, in AD 67, he intended to oversee the digging of a canal across the isthmus, (which is only four miles (6.5km) wide at its narrowest and rises to 260 feet (80m) above sea level at its highest) to link the Gulf of Corinth and the Ionian Sea with the Aegean and enable shipping to avoid the long and often dangerous voyage around the Peloponnese. The only alternative was a dragway or *diolkos* whereby smaller vessels and on occasion even warships could be winched overland on rollers from one to the other. This long-established method was also some four miles in length and included lifting devices to put ships onto trolleys for the crossing; it remained in use up to about AD 900. Nero actually ceremoniously cut the first turf with a golden spade but soon tired of the project after half a mile or so had been dug; work stopped and he returned to Rome; the canal would have to wait until AD 1893 to be completed and it then followed Nero's route.[35]

TRADE IN
EXOTIC
ANIMALS

Under Claudius and Nero the trade in exotic animals for the arenas and in luxury goods and spices had multiplied and encouraged Roman seaborne trade to expand greatly; a more southerly route to India enabled ships to trade between the Red Sea and southern India and even up the east coast of India. The trading ships sailed together in fleets of up to 120 at a time and far out to sea, beyond the reach of oar-powered pirate ships. Although piracy does not seem to have been a great problem, the merchantmen carried archers and weapons. Under Nero, a polar bear appeared in the arena and in Africa, trading stations were established down the east coast from the mouth of the Red Sea to Zanzibar. During the century, shipbuilding methods started to change in that the previously closely spaced mortice and tenon joints that held the edge-to-edge butting of hull planking became more widely spaced and thus cheaper and quicker in construction. Perhaps to a degree it had been found that such close spacing with all but the very best quality of timber, could weaken it, or again that such close spacing was not so necessary to preserve strength.[36]

forces advanced on Rome in October of AD 68, to take up the reins of power and disarmed and accepted the surrender of Nero's 'naval' legions, I and II Adiutrix; in the course of so doing the latter suffered considerable casualties at the hands of Galba's men, perhaps as revenge for their loyalty to the late emperor. In any event, the ex-navy men had cause for resentment, they were however kept in quarters at Rome. Two triremes were sent from Misenum to take Galba's appointed Governor of Galatia to his posting.[37]

Galba's popularity was short-lived and by January of AD 69, the Rhenus army declared Aulus Vitellius, Governor of Germania Inferior, to be Emperor. In the unrest there, some officers were killed and the Commander of the Rhenus Fleet, Iulius Burdo was nearly a victim; he was saved by Vitellius who engineered his escape and concealment until matters had subsided and he could resume his command.

In Rome meanwhile, Marcus Salvius Otho had turned against Galba and obtained the support of the Praetorians and, not surprisingly the 'naval' legions so ill-handled by Galba. Galba was murdered on 15 January AD 69; Vitellius' forces were already moving southward and Otho had to move quickly to establish his power and to obtain forces enough to oppose him. Having the loyalty of the navy, Otho reinforced the Misenum Fleet with a contingent of Praetorians and some urban cohorts (a militia cum police force) and sent them to invade southern Gaul, which had declared for Vitellius. The 'naval' legions, he kept back as complete legionary formations to form a nucleus for his army; after concentrating his forces, Otho marched north to confront Vitellius.[38]

The Misenum Fleet, commanded by the freedman Moschus, quickly established command of the western coastal areas of the peninsula up to the border of Gaul. Discipline in the Fleet was however poor and the men unruly; they treated the coasts of Liguria and Gaul as foreign enemies, and ranged widely, raiding in search of plunder. One notable victim was the mother of the future Governor of Britannia, Iulius Agricola, who was killed when they raided the town and robbed her estate at Albintimilium (Ventimiglia).[39] In the absence of any authority, the ships' complements were using the situation as an excuse to run amok, as little attempt was made to actually invade and secure the area for Otho's cause.

The Ravenna Fleet seems to have stayed quiescent at this time. Two of its triremes escorting Galba's appointee Governor of Galatia to the east, paused on the way at the island of Kinthos (Therma) to dispose of a pretender who claimed to be Nero! Fleets in the east stayed loyal and under the orders of their local Governors.

Against the depredations of the Misenum Fleet, meanwhile, local levies had proved powerless and help was sought from Vitellius' commander in the region, Fabius Valens. A hastily assembled force under Valerius Paulinus garrisoned Forum Iulii. The fleet landed troops to the east and the Vitellians marched out to meet them. The exact location of the ensuing battle is not known, but the marines and troops from the fleet formed up on level ground between the sea and some hills. More of the men from the fleet and some local civilian sympathisers, all acting as missile troops, held the hills and the ships of the fleet came close inshore, prows on, to secure the infantry's other flank and give missile support. The Vitellians comprised part of two auxiliary

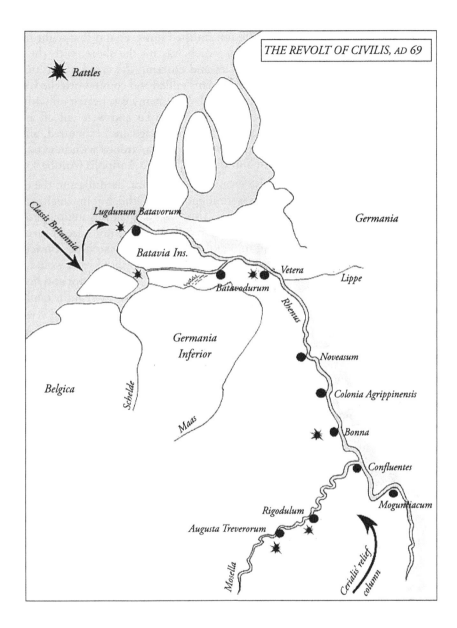

THE REVOLT OF CIVILIS, AD 69

cohorts of Tungrians (from what is now Belgium), a cohort of Ligurian levies and some Pannonian recruits and twelve squadrons of cavalry. The cavalry charged, coming under heavy missile attack and were stopped by the formed infantry and scattered; at this moment the fleet attacked with its own missiles and landed marines in their rear. The Vitellian survivors only managed to escape annihilation by the onset of dusk.

The Vitellians were not finished however and that night reinforcement attacked the fleet's camp, which was on the shore, with the ships pulled close in, killing the sentries and entering the camp. After an initial panic towards the ships, the Othonians rallied and counter-attacked, supported by a hail of missiles from their hill. The enemy was beaten off with heavy losses but a band of Othonians pursued too far and were cut off and killed. By now, neither side had a decisive advantage and, exhausted, almost by tacit agreement, disengaged. The fleet and its troops withdrew to Albigaunum (Albenga) to the east and the Vitellians to Antipolis (Antibes), to the west.

The fleet had also ensured that Corsica, Sardinia and the other western Mediterranean islands were aligned with Otho, but in Corsica, the Governor wanted to support Vitellius. There was a squadron stationed off the island, commanded by Claudius Pyrrhicus; the Governor seized him and a Roman knight who opposed him and had them both executed. Cowed at first into supporting the Governor, the people soon realised what would happen once the Fleet learned of the fate of its captain. The Governor and his accomplices were promptly seized and murdered and retribution at the hands of the fleet was avoided.[40]

Vitellius' armies continued their advance into northern Italy and between Ticinum (Pavia) and Placentia (Piacenza) they captured a unit of Otho's cavalry and rounded up about a thousand sailors, either out foraging or, not very effectively, posted to watch the River Padus crossings.

More naval personnel, under Turullius Cerialis, surrendered to Vitellius' commander Alienus Caecina as his army advanced upon Cremona. Clearly Otho had relied heavily on the use of naval personnel, quite apart from fleet operations, having marines in his bodyguard and as reconnaissance troops, to which task they were evidently unsuited. After much skirmishing the opposing armies finally clashed at the First Battle of Cremona on 14 April AD 69, at which the Legion I Adiutrix was engaged and fought well; Otho's forces were however defeated and two days later he committed suicide.

AD 69
APRIL

Vitellius, the new Emperor made a slow and riotous journey to Rome for his somewhat dissolute and brief reign. The troops were left with a lax leadership and little discipline. Many units were eventually dispersed to their original garrison areas in the provinces and along the Rhenus. Among them, the 'naval' legion, I Adiutrix was sent to Hispania, to forget its former Othonian loyalties. A cavalry officer, Sextus Lucilius Bassus, was appointed Commander of both Praetorian Fleets.

AD 69
JULY

In July, the eastern armies proclaimed their commander, Titus Flavius Vespasianus to be emperor. The *Classis Pontica* was concentrated at Byzantium to support his general Mucianus, who set off for Italy with an expeditionary force, drawn from the Syrian legions.

With the Roman world focused inward upon its internecine wars, the restless peoples beyond it's borders took the opportunity to seek plunder; there were incursions in Britannia and along the Rhenus and Danubius frontiers. An incursion of Dacians across the Danubius was beaten back by the timely arrival of Mucianus. In Pontus, following withdrawal of most of it's fleet to support Vespasian, the former commander of the old royal fleet, Anicetus (presumably another of the same name), led a rebellion, incensed the tribes to the east of the border and seized Trapezus. There the rebels concentrated all the warships they could seize and started to build more with which they intended to range at will.

Tacitus describes the boats that they built as double-ended with tumble-home above the waterline and able to add lee-boards to the bulwarks to increase freeboard and so on until totally enclosed.[41] The type was most likely developed from a local craft rather than invented *ab initio*. The 'rebels' were really just raiders and pirates and Vespasian quickly sent a force under Virdius Geminus to deal with them. This force must have been troops with ships and warships as the north Anatolian coast is backed by high mountains, isolating it from the south and making east–west advance a slow and difficult process which would have taken months; an area ideally suited to the well-practised, combined land-sea operations. Geminus' forces drove the 'rebels' to their ships, which were then pursued by his warships to the estuary of the River Chobus in Colchis (Khobi or Inguri in Georgia). At first protected by the local king, they were quickly surrendered upon his receipt of a threat of all-out war from Geminus, thus concluding this police action.

Vespasian, upon hearing of Vitellius' victory at Cremona, moved to Alexandria whence he could control the supply of Egyptian grain to Rome (perhaps a third of its requirement) and with the support of the navy's eastern squadrons, plan an invasion of Africa to gain control of another third of the grain supply.

With the Rhenus legions away supporting Vitellius, the borders were weak and defence relied solely upon auxiliary units, local levies and the fleets. A leader and commander of Batavian auxiliaries (from the west bank of the Rhenus, now in Belgium), Iulius Civilis, took the opportunity to rebel, using as his excuse ostensible support for Vespasian, but relying on his troops' resentment at perceived poor treatment from the Romans. His forces were boosted by other Batavian cohorts withdrawn from Britannia to bolster the Rhenus defences in the absence of the legions.[42]

His first act was for his troops to seize some of the *Classis Germanica's* ships and to attack and overrun by land and sea the forts of Lugdunum Batavodorum at the mouth of the Rhenus (Valkenburg and Katwijk near Leiden in Holland). The other ships of the fleet had withdrawn upriver to concentrate at a hastily improvised defensive line, which collapsed when a Tungrian cohort defected to the rebels. Some of the fleet's rowers were Batavians who disrupted its operations and later actually mutinied, murdering their helmsmen and officers who opposed them. The whole squadron of twenty-four ships deserted or were captured and with locally raised *auxilia* units defecting to Civilis. With few other troops available and indecision among their commanders, the Romans were forced to progressively withdraw upriver.

By September, the legions in the Balkans, Pannonia and Dalmatia had joined Vespasian and an advance force under Antonius Primus approached Italy. Vitellius sent Caecina and his army northward to meet it. On the way, Caecina stopped at Ravenna ostensibly to seek fleet support and to see the commander, Bassus. Whereas Caecina was lukewarm in his loyalty, if not actually trying to play a double game, the fleet, so recently a firm supporter of Otho, had no great enthusiasm for his successor. Many of the men came from Dalmatia and Pannonia, which had already declared for Vespasian, and after some political manoeuvring, the men of the *Classis Ravennate* opted also to join him, encouraged and led by Bassus. The men also decided however to prefer one of Vespasian's officers, Cornelius Fuscus, who thereupon took over command and Bassus was arrested and taken upriver to Atria (Adria) on a fast warship. Atria was then still a seaport, connected by canals to the Padus delta; it later silted and became unusable. Once there, Bassus was incarcerated by the local Flavian commander, being subsequently released by Vespasian's intervention. This defection shifted the balance decidedly in favour of Vespasian's advancing forces, who could now rely on a secure flank on the Adriatic, with concomitant secure lines of supply and domination of the Padus delta, as well as having the whole Adriatic seaboard of Italy open to them for exploitation as a military target.

The defection of the *Classis Ravennate* to Vespasian encouraged Caecina, now upriver at Hostilia (Ostiglia) to attempt to defect with his forces. His men would not tolerate this underhandedness and arrested and replaced him. They next vented their displeasure on the fleet by seizing three galleys which were on the nearby River Padus and slaughtering their crews. Following this atrocity naval personnel from Ravenna fled and, by-passing Caecina's former troops, made their way north to join Vespasian's forces there; personnel who were citizens transferred to his legions and the others joined *auxilia* units. Further recruits were brought in from Dalmatia to replace some of these crews.

FLAVIAN VICTORY – RESTORING THE RHENUS

Vespasian's forces finally brought the Vitellians to battle at the Second Battle of Cremona on 24 October AD 69; the battle was hard fought before Vespasian's men finally won. Another of Vitellius' generals, Fabius Valens, was making his way north with reinforcements. When he learned of the defeat at Cremona, his troops garrisoned Ariminium (Rimini), where they were trapped by the *Classis Ravennate*. This fleet now controlled and patrolled the Adriatic for Vespasian and enabled his forces to quickly occupy the eastern seaboard and to extend their influence into Umbria. Valens with as many of his men as possible, escaped and made his way across to Portus Pisanus (Leghorn or Livorno) on the west coast and there took ship to join Vitellius' supporters at Portus Herculis Monoeci (Monaco). Once again however, he was headed off by Vespasian's local agent, Valerius Paulinus who, with his own forces, had secured the naval base at nearby Forum Iulii and the ships and crews there. Valens sought to escape again by sea but the naval forces from Forum Iulii intercepted him and forced his ships ashore on the nearby Stoechades Isles (Iles d'Hyeres) aided by bad weather. With the capture of Vitellius' last general, the remainder of the Roman world rallied to Vespasian and in Hispania the Legio I Adiutrix, always hostile to Vitellius, led the adherence to Vespasian's cause.

On the Rhenus the Romans had been pushed back further, first to Vetera, the site of a major military hospital, then to Bonna where they suffered a defeat at the hands of the rebels. Civilis had used his ships to ferry bands of loot-seeking German tribesmen from the east bank of the river to add to his forces and to the disruption of the Roman positions and had used 'his fleet' to escort his advance up river. The remaining Romans had meanwhile concentrated at Vetera, determined to hold it and which Civilis then placed under siege.

The still-loyal remainder of the *Classis Germanica* joined a legionary force which had managed to muster at Bonna. Civilis' strength increased but his assaults on Vetera were beaten off by the stout defence. With the Flavian victories and the provincial forces swearing allegiance to Vespasian, Civilis' pretence was over. After an inconclusive battle at Bonna, the Roman forces there advanced to relieve Vetera, where they beat Civilis. The fleet could still not secure the lower Rhenus however and Civilis was able to regroup and again advance with his fleet to invest Vetera, while the Roman force had to again withdraw southward. The Romans were few in number and their morale was low, following their recent reverses, and the conflicting loyalties engendered by the power struggles were still unresolved. They eventually fell back on their main base at Augusta Treverorum (Trier) on the River Mosella, with their fleet above Confluentes (Koblenz), where the Mosella flows into the Rhenus. An attack by Civilis on Besontio was beaten off and the peoples of central Gaul hesitated to join him.

In Italy, Vitellius was not quite finished yet and sought to blockade the Apennine routes to Rome. He still had some troops and the naval Legio II Adiutrix, although how dependable this latter would be must have been open to question, as their compatriots from the *Classis Ravennate* from which it had been raised, had long supported Vespasian. The point was not to be tested as Vitellius had no sooner moved up with these troops when the *Classis Misinensis* defected to Vespasian en bloc, so he returned to Rome. The II Adiutrix were left to fend for themselves and thus went to join Vespasian's forces.

The fleet at Misenum was commanded by one Claudius Apollinaris, not a strong supporter of any faction. A centurion, Claudius Faventinus, used a forged letter which he purported to be from Vespasian promising rewards to suborn the sailors. The revolt spread up the coast to Minturnae and an attempt by pro-Vitellians to reverse the process at Capua backfired when they put their forces under Claudius Iulianus, a former naval commander from Misenum. He promptly took them over to Vespasian's cause, marching to and occupying the port of Tarracina. This ad hoc garrison of Tarracina included some gladiators and some men and ships of the fleet; there was total lack of discipline and a surprise attack by other Vitellian forces, led by the Emperor's brother, quickly overcame them. The survivors fled to the ships in the harbour in panic; six ships escaped (including Apollinaris') but the rest were captured or overloaded and swamped in the panic. Iulianus was captured, flogged and strangled.

Gradually and inevitably however, support for Vitellius fell away and his remaining forces went over to Vespasian until the latter's armies were at Rome itself. A hard core of loyal followers remained and the city was only secured after a hard fight. Vitellius himself was taken and ignominiously killed on 20 December AD 69; his brother was killed later when he surrendered Tarracina. The Senate recognised Vespasian as Emperor.

In Rome, Vespasian's younger son Domitian and his generals established his power and set out to organise an army to restore the Rhenus frontier and to deal with Civilis. Five legions were assembled and sent north; the I Adiutrix (naval) and another legion were ordered from Hispania; the *Classis Britannica* was to bring the veteran and entirely reliable XIV legion across from Britannia, the II Adiutrix being sent there to replace it. Units of the advancing army under Petilius Cerialis soon reached Moguntiacum and secured the allegiance of any wavering Gallic tribes; after sweeping aside a rebel force, they entered Augusta Treverorum. Civilis mustered his forces nearby and attacked, taking the Romans by surprise. The Romans however gradually formed up and the demoralised ex-Rhenus army troops joined in and Civilis' forces were thrown back. Meanwhile the fleet had landed units of the XIV legion, who marched inland securing the continued allegiance of more tribes. Units of the *Classis Britannica* made to raid the rebel home territory on the west bank of the mouth of the Rhenus, but were instead attacked by Civilis' fleet and lost most of their ships.

AD 69
DECEMBER

Civilis, after the defeat at Augusta Treverorum, fell back to Colonia Agrippinensis, which had already killed its rebel garrison and barred his way, then to Vetera, still holding out against him, still pursued by Cerialis whose army had grown to four legions. To strengthen his position, Civilis had the river banks breached, flooding the land in front of his positions. The Romans brought their ships down river to secure their flank, they failed however to follow up a Roman victory and Civilis was thus able to escape with his forces and to withdraw northward to his homeland (between the Maas and the Rhine). Civilis covered his retreat by cutting the mole which had been built by Drusus Germanicus (Tiberius' brother), allowing the Rhenus to flow into the Waal and cause flooding. The mole had helped to concentrate and speed the flow at the mouth of the Rhenus and to make it more easily navigable and without it, the fleet was unable to isolate Civilis from the east as the river mouth spread over its flood plain and became too shallow.

Despite a shortage of hulls for use as pontoons in bridge-building, the Romans set out to cross the Waal, II Adiutrix being detailed to build a bridge at Batavodurum (Nijmegen). Civilis mounted attacks all around but they were beaten back and the net gradually closed in on him until he had to flee across the Rhenus, near Batavodurum. The Roman fleet was still suffering low morale and the dispersal of many of its crews on military duties in the emergency and did not participate in these final actions; to be fair it seems that Cerialis moved very quickly and did not allow time for them to be reorganised and deployed.[43]

Cerialis next went to inspect the building of new forts at Colonia Agrippinensis and Bonna, then returned downstream with another naval flotilla. Fleet discipline remained poor and near to Vetera the flotilla was attacked at night by marauding Germans, coming downstream in small boats and rafts. They also attacked the crew's camp, while another party put lines on the ships, cut their cables and towed them away stern first and on up the River Lippe. Civilis now sought a naval demonstration, still having a fleet numbering some twenty-four warships, both bireme and monoreme, together with some captured merchant ships and a large number of small native craft, each carrying thirty or forty men and fitted out 'like liburnians'. They were concentrated at Helinium, a lagoon at the mouths of the Maas and Waal where he was hoping to intercept convoys bringing supplies from Gaul and Britannia.

Cerialis had not, meanwhile, been idle and had concentrated his own fleet. Although fewer in ship numbers, the Romans were better sailors than most of their opponents, with more experienced rowers and bigger ships. Cerialis had brought them up to strength and put them through some vigorous training and re-imposed strict discipline to restore their morale.

Their morale had been further boosted by their recent victories and the desire to avenge their previous reverses. The Romans moved downriver with the wind and current and the two fleet passed each other and exchanged missile fire, but could not be brought to bear for close action. Civilis retired across the Rhenus and the Romans continued to reduce his homeland. Despite the worsening weather which made the land swampy where it was not already flooded and which prevented the arrival of relief convoys, the rebels were beaten and a few days later, Civilis surrendered.

AD 70   Vespasian had remained at Alexandria but in the summer of AD 70, he sailed at last for Rome on a grain ship, the most direct and fast route back, to take up the reins of power. The military strength of the Empire now stood at thirty legions, totalling some 150,000 men and another 180,000 or so in the *auxilia* formations. The navy had regained its cohesion and settled back into its normal operational life, receiving the support of the new Emperor who, having had experience in his past campaigns of the use of seapower, appreciated the importance of its functions and was to maintain it in continued good health. He also took the view, based upon his experience, that the fleets should be commanded by 'proper' admirals and abolished Claudius' Procurators and reverted to the appointment of militarily experienced Praefects to command, effectively barring freedmen and non-military men from the posts. He also raised the status of Fleet Praefects to be in the first rank of the equestrian appointments, with commensurate salaries and second only to the Praetorian Praefect himself. The major portion of the appointment was of necessity, administrative but it also reverted to being classified as a seagoing command.

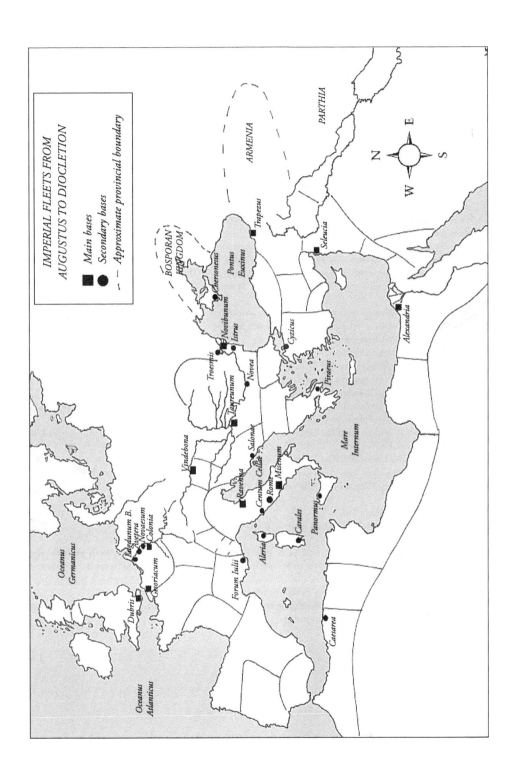

Notes

1. Scullard 2 for a precis of these campaigns; also Tacitus, *Annals*.
2. A study of maps of the area, allowing for geographical changes since, will demonstrate how the terrain and river systems dictated and were in turn used for the campaigns. Also see Starr.
3. Tacitus, *Annals* I.9.
4. Tacitus, *Annals* II.23/24.
5. Starr, quoting Tacitus, *Annals* II. It is said that ' a thousand ships' were 'built' but, as on previous occasions, exaggeration is likely given that in the previous year, 200 ships were sufficient to move four legions; in 16, eight legions were employed requiring therefore presumably no more than 400 ships, assuming them all to have been moved at once instead of in several trips.
6. It is the transports that seem to have suffered most of the losses although this does appear to be a repeat or duplication of the previous year's disaster.
7. These are applications in a riverine context of the classic naval strategies of the projection of power as expounded by Mahan; Reynolds, *Command of the Sea, The History and Strategy of Maritime Empires*. Contrast Guilmartin, *Gunpowder and Galleys* which argues against the application of Mahan doctrine to oar-powered warships at sea. Within the limited confines of the river system however, Mahan would still appear to be relevant.
8. Starr.
9. See Bass, Casson. Although destroyed in WWII there are detailed, scale models of the recovered parts of these ships in the nautical museums in Venice and La Spezia, as well as at the reconstituted museum at Nemi.
10. Sprague de Camp, *The Ancient Engineers*.
11. Pliny, quoted in Casson *SSAW*.
12. Graves, *I Claudius*; although strictly a fictional work, has a full description which conveys something of the insanity of this enterprise, while demonstrating the capabilities of the engineers and seamen.
13. Scullard 2 as to Claudius' administrative reforms.
14. Puteoli is commonly mentioned (eg. Starr, Casson *The Ancient Mariners*) and although perhaps the principal trans-shipment point, the use of the other (nearer) harbours should not be overlooked.
15. Casson, *The Ancient Mariners* (and Suetonius). Extensively investigated, most of it is now covered by Rome's Leonardo da Vinci (Fiumicino) Airport.
16. Sailing schedules, see Casson *SSAW* and *Travel in the Ancient World*.
17. Mosaics survive which show beaked, oar-powered ships which are clearly not warships, e.g. at Ostia in the Foro delle Corporazioni there are examples in the floors of shipping agents' offices.
18. Tacitus, *Annals* II.6.
19. Bass, *A History of Seafaring* ; Peddie.
20. Cottrell, *The Great Invasion* and Peddie, *Conquest, The Roman Invasion of Britain*.
21. Josephus, Jewish War II.366.
22. There has been much debate as to the precise landing site (or multiple sites); various alternatives having been suggested, but this more generally accepted site remains the only really logical choice (and see Peddie op. cit., where other sites are considered).
23. Peddie, *Conquest, The Roman Invasion of Britain*, detailing Vespasian's land campaign.
24. There is an inscription to a member of this fleet from the reign of Domitian (Starr), perhaps the grave of a veteran and not of itself evidence of its continued existence.
25. Tacitus, *Annals* and *Germania* 44.
26. Tacitus, *Annals* XI.19.
27. Sprague de Camp, *The Ancient Engineers*.
28. Selkirk, *The Piercebridge Formula*.
29. Tacitus, *Annals* XIV.4.
30. Scullard 2, referring to Pliny, *Natural History* VI.
31. Selkirk, *The Piecebridge Formula*, quoting Horace on his journey along it.
32. Starr.

33. That the Roman fleet was not offshore to intercept perhaps indicates that they were aware of the approaching storm and stayed in port. The rebels, with no alternative had to risk the storm.

34. Scullard 2. The principal ancient source for Nero remains Tacitus, *Annals*; also see Suetonius, *The Twelve Caesars*, written in the early 2nd century AD.

35. Traces of the original Roman workings are still visible at the western entrance to the canal.

36. Bass, *A History of Seafaring*; Casson *SSAW*.

37. Tacitus, *The Histories*, written only about thirty years afterwards, is the prime source for this period.

38. Tacitus, *Histories* I.87.

39. Tacitus, *Agricola* 7.

40. Tacitus, *Histories* II.14-16.

41. Tacitus, *Histories* III.47.

42. The revolt of Civilis and the campaign against him is covered in Books IV and V of Tacitus' *Histories*.

43. It is difficult to define exact movements and some locations when following the progress of this campaign, due to the drastic changes to the coastline and rivers that took place in the 3rd century AD inundations.

APOGEE AND NADIR

AD 71–AD 285

AD 71

With the establishment of Vespasian's rule, the Empire settled back into internal peace and for the navy, this meant a resumption of the various fleets' duties in their respective spheres. The new Emperor, always a firm supporter of the navy, fully appreciated the part played by its various formations in his ultimate success and in AD 71 awarded the honorific title *Praetoria* to the two Italian fleets. At the same time, many veterans retired from the service and were settled by him at Paestum in Campania for those from the *Classis Misinensis* and in Pannonia for those from the *Classis Ravennate*. He also awarded the title *Augusta* to the Alexandrine and Rhenus Fleets, which became the *Classis Augusta Alexandrina* and *Classis Augusta Germanica* respectively. He awarded the title *Flavia* to the *Classes Pannonica* and *Moesica* for supporting his cause and particularly in recognition of the very hard work that they had done to hold the line in the face of Dacian attacks when the legionary garrisons were reduced by the withdrawal of troops to fight in the Civil War. Of the 'navy' legions, I Adiutrix was confirmed as a permanent formation of the army, as was the II Adiutrix, which in recognition of its action at the Second Battle of Cremona, received the title *Pia Fidelis*.[1]

In Britannia it was realised that the border was weak and the Romans therefore sought to push it forward to a defensible line. Vespasian appointed, Petilius Cerialis, fresh from his victory over Civilis, who in the following three years extended the Roman province across the middle of England and northward, into Yorkshire.[2] The *Classis Britannica* operating in the North Sea on his right flank, conveyed troops and supplies and established a northern naval base, Petuaria, in the estuary of the River Abus (Humber, at Brough-on-Humber). In AD 71 the II Adiutrix legion was sent to Lindum to replace the IX legion which moved north with Cerialis. At this time, the *Classis Britannica* established ironworks in the forests of Kent and Essex, to produce ship's fittings and equipment for the fleet. Cerialis' successor, Iulius Frontinus, in AD 74 and 75, continued the expansionist policy and secured the remainder of South Wales; in this campaign, as with the previous one in AD 52, direct westward advance was made difficult by the succession of hills and valleys which run north and south to the sea, so early in the campaign a naval base was established at Isca (Caerleon), later to develop into a permanent legionary base. From there the fleet scouted and raided along the coast and then landed troops at various points and kept them supplied until the land advance came up with them, in the by now, traditional manner.

In Germania, the re-entrant into Roman territory formed by the westward turn of both the Rhenus and Danubius made for a very long border along the headwaters of those rivers. Moves to advance the border and to shorten it by occupying the lands in the re-entrant were started under Vespasian, his troops beginning the building of a system of interlinking forts and posts to secure the area. No record of the details of this initial advance survive, but based on the well-tried and practised methods of the Romans, the *Classis Germanica* would have detailed some of its lighter ships to scout the eastern tributaries of the Rhenus opposite and on the flanks of the advance and to transport supplies to the troops, at least until a bridge could be built to provide a permanent line of supply, which was presumably done.[3]

AD 78   The next Governor of Britannia, Cnaeus Iulius Agricola had been born at Forum Iulii, the former naval base and had already served all of his preceding military career in the province, having been a tribune under Paullinus and a legate under Cerialis. After taking over in AD 78, he attended the completion of the conquest of Wales and the founding of the legionary base at Deva (Chester) on the River Dee, with its adjacent port facilities, which would remain one of the three permanent military bases of the province until the end of the Western Empire, nearly four hundred years later.[4] In the east the *Classis Pontica* had been utilised to finally stamp out the last vestiges of piracy in the Euxine and to maintain security, retained its strength of forty ships based at Trapezus. From there it could also support the forces fronting onto Armenia, the main line of supply for which ran from the estuary of the Danubius, across the Euxine Sea to Trapezus and the protection of this important route became the responsibility of the fleet.[5]

AD 79   Vespasian died in AD 79, to be succeeded by his eldest son, Titus. Two months later, on 24 August AD 79, the famous eruption of Mount Vesuvius took place which was to bury Pompeii and Herculaneum and disrupt the surrounding area. The eruption carried to the south-east and thus away from the naval base at Misenum. The Prefect of the Fleet at that time was the author, Gaius Plinius (Pliny the Elder); staying with him at his house in Baiae was his nephew, Gaius Plinius Secundus (Pliny the Younger) who wrote a description of what he saw on those tumultuous days.[6] The disaster took about four days to unfold and on the first, the Prefect ordered the fleet to sea, having had news that the eruption had cut off the landward escape routes of many people. He was prompted by the wish to help as many as possible in what was clearly a disaster, but also by the thought that his own base area at Misenum was composed of volcanic craters and atop a still highly volatile area and the fear that the eruptions could spread; the ships should have a better chance of survival at sea. The sea was very rough as a result of the seismic disturbances and hot pumice and cinders rained down upon them, keeping the crews frantically working to prevent the ships from being set ablaze. The land along the bay had heaved and risen and the seashore had receded, leaving ships stranded and much of the port facilities dry and useless. the ships had to try and run up onto beaches in any way that they could to effect rescues. That they enjoyed some success seems probable in that Pompeii, the first big town affected had a pre-eruption population of 8–10,000 people, but it is estimated that as few as 2000 of them died in the catastrophe. Plinius himself, having been taken to Stabiae on the south side of the bay, succumbed to the fumes and died there. The fleet base remained outside of the damage and fall-out area of the eruption, damage to the ships of the Fleet was mostly superficial and none were reported as lost.

AD 80   In Rome in AD 80 the dedication took place of the newly completed Flavian amphitheatre, better known now as the Colosseum. Part of the facility was a system of awnings which could be drawn across parts of the open centre of the arena to act as sun shades for the audience and altered to match the sun's progress.[7] The navy was entrusted with rigging and operating the awnings and a naval crew was stationed in Rome for this purpose, being housed in their own nearby barracks, the *Castra Misinensis*; the Ravenna Fleet also had a detachment, housed in the *Castra Ravennensis*, situated on the west bank of the river, near to the present Vatican. Naval crews had of course previously been employed in the putting on of *naumachiae* and probably also to arrange shading at these and other venues. It must be recalled that the two Italian fleets were rated as Praetorian and in any event had each kept a small ceremonial detachment permanently in Rome as part of the guard establishment. These had previously been quartered in the *Castra Praetoria*, the guard barracks which is still today the home of the Rome garrison.

In Britannia, Agricola had continued to advance from Deva northward to consolidate north-west England and in AD 80 moved northward from the River Trent. By AD 81 he held the line between the Rivers Forth and Clyde in Caledonia (Scotland), the site of the later Antonine Wall, securing his line with a string of forts. This advance had been made with the support of the fleet on both east and west coasts. The two squadrons scouted the coasts ahead of the advance, gathering intelligence of the areas and their occupants and their strengths, seeking suitable harbours, anchorages and landing places, landing and raiding ahead of the troops to test defences or likely opposition and securing beachheads and bringing men and supplies forward to systematically envelop any suspected resistance. In addition to the scouting expeditions, the British Isles were circumnavigated by a Roman fleet for the first time. The fleet came upon and 'subjugated' the Orcades (Orkney Islands), more probably they simply landed and received the formal submission of the locals as no presence was left there and there is no mention of any return by the Romans. 'Thule' was sighted but no landing made; perhaps Pytheas had left a description which enabled this land to be identified; it could have been the Shetland Isles or even the Norwegian coast and the sea was reported as 'sluggish and heavy to the oar'.[8] There exists in fact, a petroglyph at Alta in northern Norway that could well be seen as representing a Roman warship. With confirmation of the extent of the islands, Agricola could plan his campaigns to their logical conclusion.

The II Adiutrix legion that had been formed by Nero from naval personnel fifteen years before, was still stationed in Britannia in AD 81 as Titus called upon it to provide a draft of men for his proposed German campaign for the following year; it can be distinguished from the 'regular' II legion which was named Augusta. By now however a large proportion of its original personnel must have died or retired, to be replaced by non-navy men and so it had become a 'normal' legion, any connection with its nautical origins long forgotten. Titus died suddenly in AD 81 to be in turn succeeded by his younger brother, Domitian, most of whose reign was to be dominated by campaigns firstly in Germany and then across the Danubius and in Dacia. He was popular with the forces and increased pay for the first time since Caesar, by a third; a legionary's 300 denarii per annum (paid in three instalments) being raised to 400 denarii. Other military pay rose pro rata and naval pay followed suit with varying increases according to rank.

AD 81

In AD 82 Agricola sailed around the west coast of Caledonia, north of the Clyde, securing supremacy at sea and probing the Hebridean coastal region. His ship also reconnoitred the Hibernian (Irish) coast, mapped details of the coast and harbours and questioned merchants who traded there. He followed this in AD 83 with an advance with his XX and IX legions and the II Adiutrix. The latter ironically had to make up its deficiency in numbers due to the men that it had sent to Germania, with men from the fleet. As always the advance was conducted with close co-operation from the fleet and extended to the River Tay, where the XX legion wintered in the fort which they built there; the other troops returned south for the winter, leaving the fleet to maintain communications and sea-borne supplies for this isolated forward base. For the campaign of AD 83, Agricola had once again advanced relying on the combined operations of his army and navy. As the historian Tacitus (his son-in-law, who was there) reported: 'The war was pushed forward simultaneously by land and sea and infantry, cavalry and marines often meeting in the same camp would mess and make merry together'.[9] The closeness and effectiveness of the inter-service co-operation achieved

AD 82

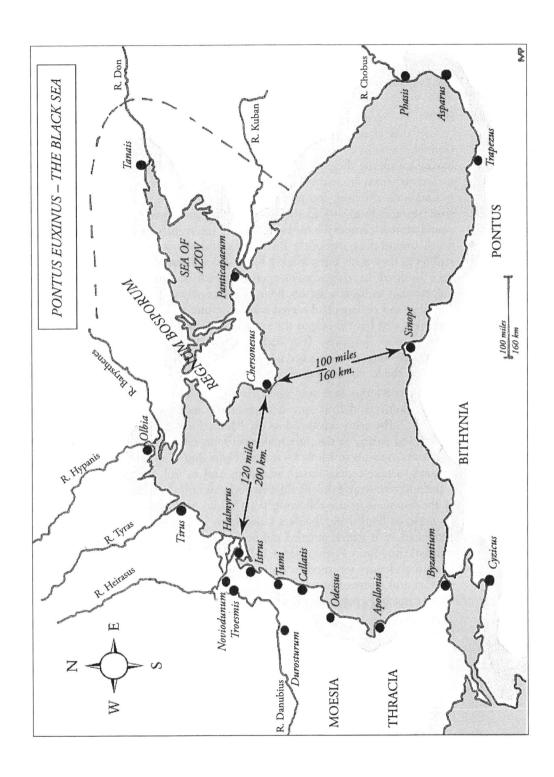

by Agricola clearly sets the standard. The natives had only small boats, no experience of ships and must have been overawed by the appearance of a great warship full of armed men and artillery, preventing them from any use of the waters of the lochs and firths, which must have gone far to demoralise them.

AD 83   In that same campaign, in the summer of AD 83, a unit of Usipii, Gemanic auxiliaries originating from the middle Rhenus, mutinied and having murdered their officers, stole three warships (Liburnicas according to Tacitus) from an anchorage on the north-west coast. They had no wish to undertake the long and potentially perilous voyage to Germania via the Irish Sea and English Channel and had they managed that journey, they would almost certainly have been quickly intercepted. Instead they sailed north around the north of the British Isles and eastward into the North Sea, raiding as they went but suffering losses to local resistance. Although it has been assumed that they were inexperienced sailors, their achievement would suggest that some at least of them had experience if not training in ship handling and perhaps had served aboard before; also as seems more logical, they may well have captured the sailors of the ships' own crews and forced them to work the ships. They had been very lucky but their luck ran out when their ships were wrecked on the coast of Holland, the survivors being 'taken by the locals' and killed or, as prisoners, sold into slavery.[10]

AD 84   In AD 84 the fleet was again sent ahead northwards 'to plunder at various points and thus spread uncertainty and terror' (in the words of Tacitus).[11] The army advanced to the Moray Firth and met and destroyed the massed enemy at the only major battle to take place in Caledonia, the unknown location of Mons Graupius. Following this victory, the fleet was ordered to take a detachment of troops and to sail around the north of Caledonia to overawe the inhabitants and scout for the intended completion of the conquest in the following year. While Agricola's men built forts as far north as Banffshire, the fleet sailed from Trucculensis Portus, the name and location of which remains unknown but is likely to have been on the south of the Moray Firth; whence they sailed and rounded Cape Wrath and beyond and then returned to their starting point. The fleet enjoyed good weather and returned in good order.[12]

At the end of the year Agricola was recalled to Rome, never to return. The conquest was never completed as in AD 85, Dacian incursions across the Danubius and serious losses on that frontier forced Domitian to order the transfer of II Adiutrix to that front to bolster the defences. Domitian was forced to choose priorities for his forces. Caledonia was a wild, poor country the conquest of which was using a tenth of the Empire's army for little or no gain. The troops were sorely needed on the Danubius, a frontier of the importance of which there could be no question.

AD 85   The Dacians from north of the Danubius mounted a major invasion in AD 85, crossing the river in force and also attacking eastward into the delta, causing serious losses to the *Classis Moesica*, the survivors of which with the remaining Roman forces had to abandon the delta area. The fleet assisted in the counter-attack, which was unsuccessful but the next year the Emperor himself led his forces to restore the position. The campaign included placing a pontoon bridge across the river and the Roman forces pursuing their enemy into his own territory. The campaigning continued into AD 87, the Romans again bridging the river and crossing to carry the war to their enemy until, finally, the Dacians were defeated and the frontier restored. Moesia was then split into two provinces, the fleet henceforth being under the overall command of the Governor of Moesia Inferior.

In Caledonia the army fell back to its main forts across the narrows between the Forth and Clyde, retaining a forward base on the Tay. For the fleet, their permanent operational area had been enormously extended to now include both western and eastern coastlines of the British Isles.

AD 89   A threatened incursion by Chatti raiders in support of a speedily put down usurpation attempt, across the frozen Rhenus in AD 89 was thwarted by the *Classis Germanica*, aided by a sudden, early thaw. In recognition of the part that it had played, a grateful Domitian granted the fleet the title '*Pia Fidelis Domitiana*'; after the Emperor's demise in AD 96, the name was reduced to '*Pia Fidelis*'.[13] Moves to advance the border between the Rhenus and Danubius and to shorten it by occupying the lands in the re-entrant, the 'Agri Decumates', had been started under Vespasian. Under Domitian, the Romans advanced deeper, absorbing more of this territory, building a new border line of forts, walls, watch-towers and palisades across country, called the *limes*. This expansion added much of the rivers Neckar and Main to the patrol and supply duties of the Rhenus Fleet. Where the river ceased to be the border, bridges were built, at Confluentes and Moguntiacum. No details survive but allowance must have been made for the continuation of river traffic, both military and civilian. The bridge at Moguntiacum was a pontoon bridge and the inclusion of a moveable centre section to allow shipping would have been simple enough. It was probably destroyed in the retreat before the invasion by Alemanni tribesmen in AD 233. Bridges were also put across the River Main but nowhere were the rivers bridged

AD 93   permanently between Roman and non-Roman territory.[14] By AD 93 the borders had been restored and peace returned but Domitian developed a fear that he was the subject of plotting against him and began a reign of terror that plagued the state until he was assassinated in AD 96.

THE ANTONINES – HIGH POINT OF EMPIRE

AD 96   After Domitian's death the reins of power passed to the ex-consul Nerva, for a brief reign from AD 96 to his sudden death in AD 98. His appointed successor was Trajan, a career soldier whose nineteen-year reign was to see internal stability allied to the external expansion of the Empire to its greatest extent.

Although progressive development and improvement to artillery pieces had improved their reliability and power, a new form of machine was perfected at about this time. The new machine had its torsion springs mounted in all-metal mountings which were covered by protective cylinders, all of which was held firm by a metal frame. The machine was more complex to manufacture, but size for size more compact and powerful as well as reliable and had an effective range of about 500 yards (457m). Made in various sizes, the smaller ones could be mounted and operated from small handcarts for use in the field, the first true field artillery. They were to be widely used in the coming Dacian Wars and were also therefore ideal for fitting to warships to replace their older-type artillery mountings, the smaller ones even being capable of deployment on ships which had been too small or light to carry the older, heavier types.[15]

AD 101

In two wars between AD 101 and 106 the Dacians were conquered and their kingdom made into the Province of Dacia, a war famously commemorated on Trajan's Column in Rome. The focus of the wars took place across that length of the Middle Danubius the responsibility of the *Classis Moesica*, which was reinforced and expanded by drafts from the other fleets, including the Praetorian Fleets and by the impress of civilian craft. Trajan's Column depicts warships of this fleet, both bireme and even a trireme in a manner stylised to emphasise the men on board, the figures of which are exaggerated in size relative to the ships which are therefore shown without covering or protective decks. Also shown several times is a form of standardised river transport which is also used as pontoons for bridging. This type continued in use for a long time, being also illustrated on the column of Marcus Aurelius, some eighty years later, in virtually the same form. Other pontoons are shown being transported on wagons, which may be the type called *ratis* or *ratiariae*, a type known for many years already and which may well have been fabricated by the army's engineers. Three pontoon bridges were built across the river for the campaigns, although no attempt was made to build permanent bridges and the pontoons were dismantled after the wars. As part of the preparations for these campaigns, in AD 100 a two and one half mile (4km) canal was constructed to the south of the Danubius on the Roman side, adjacent to the Iron Gates gorge and rapids, which were also not navigable. This canal must have had locks and forts were also built to guard them. This canal enabled the fleets in Pannonia and Moesia to link and operate together and of course for navigation to be possible over the whole length of the river.[16] The opportunity was also taken to widen the original road built under Tiberius, along the south bank of the gorge. The

Upon his return, Trajan went in for great public works, among the foremost of which was an extension to Claudius' seaport and civil harbour at Portus. The Roman harbours at Ostia and Portus were booming and more port capacity was needed. Claudius' harbour also suffered from being exposed to severe weather. Trajan, between AD101 and 106 added to it by excavating an inner, more sheltered basin with an area of one eighth of a square mile and with attendant warehouse and port facilities and a canal linking it with the River Tiber.[17] He also systematised sailing schedules. He went on to build new ports at Centumcellae (Civitavecchia) on the Etruscan coast and at Ancona on the Adriatic plus the *Naumachia Traiani* in Rome, for naval battles. A great lighthouse was built at Corunna in north-western Hispania, which although since modified, is still in use.

Classis Moesica played a major role in these campaigns, supplementing the bridges by transporting troops and supplies and penetrating as far as they could into enemy territory up the tributary rivers of the Danubius both to carry supplies as far as possible towards the foremost troops and to interdict and gather intelligence of the enemy. The fleet was also of course, almost totally responsible for keeping secure and maintaining the essential link to the sources of supply for the expeditionary forces, functions that were decisive in the success of the war.

AD 106   At the end of the campaigns, among the military decorations awarded by Trajan, were four *Corona Navalis*, to legates of consular rank who do not however, appear to have been solely fleet commanders; nevertheless the award of the old republican decoration, albeit not in its original way, surely recognised the vital role of the naval forces in the wars, despite the lack of naval opposition. After the wars and the founding of the new province, the two Danubius Fleets retained their separate identities and areas of responsibility as before and despite the canal. Operationally this made sense as, given the vast length of river to be controlled and with the pressure off the Middle Danubius as a result of the new province on the left bank, the *Classis Moesica* had in effect, to reverse its posture from one of denying that part of the river to those on that bank, to one of maintaining the links between the banks. The focus of the *Classis Moesica's* attention now therefore shifted once more, eastward to the lower Danubius, its delta and to the Euxine Sea. The south-pointing salient now formed between Dacia and the Danubius delta was fortified by a string of forts, connected by the ships of the fleet, reinforcment of the fleet headquarters at Noviodunum in the delta and the establishment of bases at Troesmis (near Galitza, Romania) and another at the Greek town of Istrus (Bobadag, Romania) on the Euxine coast.[18]

AD 106

In AD 106, the Kingdom of Nabatea was annexed to form the new province of Arabia. Although there is no evidence of corresponding naval expansion in the Gulfs of Suez and Akaba, Roman ships were known to operate in the Indian Ocean at this time and there was published an itinerary or nautical almanac, giving particulars of distances, harbours and features to be found around the coasts of the Red Sea.[19] While in Egypt, Trajan had the canal linking the River Nile to the Red Sea dredged and restored and sent a fleet through it to ravage the Arabian coast, presumably in support of his annexation of Nabatea. The canal would remain in use until the third century and the remit of the Alexandrine Fleet was extended to patrol and police it and to use it for any excursions they might make into the Red Sea; there is no indication of any permanent Roman naval presence in that sea, ships presumably being sent there from time to time only as needed. In the east, the Roman border already rested on the River Euphrates for a considerable length and after invading Armenia, which he annexed, Trajan used it as a supply artery for his march to the head of the Persian Gulf.[20]

With unrest in the Levant, Cyrene and Egypt and a revolt in Judaea to contend with, units of the *Classis Misinensis* were sent to and stationed in the east to assist in restoring order, landing marines and sailors and escorting the Emperor and generally reinforcing the local squadrons in keeping the coasts

AD 117

and sea lanes secure.[21] The Emperor died at Selinus in Cilicia in AD 117.

Trajan was succeeded by his second cousin, Hadrian, who quickly abandoned his predecessor's conquests in the east, with the exception of Arabia. Egypt had been seriously affected by the recent troubles and as part of his arrangements to secure it, naval reinforcements were sent and the *Classis Augusta Alexandrina* took over and gradually absorbed the former river police force. In about AD 131 the Governor of Cappadocia, Flavius Arrianus (Arrian) prepared an itinerary for the circumnavigation of the Euxine; he describes the sea in geographic, military, political and strategic terms and in his reports mentions a brick-built fort which had replaced an earlier one at Phasis with a garrison of 400 men with artillery on towers to protect the fleet anchorage there; there was also a five-cohort garrison at Asparis, with defences, a hospital and granaries and these were the easternmost protected harbours of the *Classis Pontica*, situated in the area of the present-day Turkish–Georgian border. The harbour at Trapezus was also improved at this time.[22]

On visiting Britannia, the Emperor decided to settle the northern border of the province upon the line of the fortified wall that still bears his name.

AD 122

In AD 122 the *Classis Germanica* ferried the Legio VI Victrix across from the Rhenus to Pons Aelius (Newcastle-upon-Tyne) to assist in the building and sailors of the fleet also probably aided the effort. As corroboration of the account of this event, two votive altars were recovered from the river at the

PTOLEMY'S
GEOGRAPHIA

In AD 127, Claudius Ptolemy published his *Geographia*, a major work that brought together much of the geographical knowledge of the second-century world into a single publication. The book contained an extensive gazetteer with notes on the latitude and longitude of the various towns and cities to be found within the Empire. Although subsequently highly influential much of Ptolemy's work was drawn from earlier works, in particular those of Marinos of Tyre. Although a work of geography it is unclear as to whether the original work published by Ptolemy actually contained any maps.

site of the Roman bridge, the actual Pons Aelius. Dedicated to Neptune and Oceanus, one has a dolphin and anchor emblem and the other an anchor, both are flanked by the letters VI, for the Sixth Legion and 'P.F.', Pia Fidelis for the Fleet, given that title by Domitian in AD 89.

At this same time, the naval base at the estuary of the Abus was rebuilt, becoming an important haven on the route between Londinium, Eboracum and the eastern end of the new wall, both as a harbour for the sea route and for the system of canals and rivers which was developed to enable water-borne trade to pass between Londinium and Eboracum without risking the open sea.[23] It was also a good operational point from which to keep an eye on the Mare Germanicum (North Sea) and its surrounding coasts. The policy was essentially defensive and apart from punitive expeditions against raiders, the border settled upon the line of the Wall, built between AD 122 and 128.

When in Egypt, Hadrian ordered a Roman naval squadron into the Red Sea on an expedition to sweep away pirates there and following which he could secure an enlargement of trade with the east. In the 130s, the Bosporan Kingdom came under considerable external pressure. Roman policy was always to support this friendly state as a useful buffer and listening-post for central Asia and so a Roman force was taken by the *Classis Moesica* and supported by the fleet, stationed at the royal Court to bolster the kingdom.[24] Roman troops were to be stationed in Crimea for over a century, supported by the fleet base at Chersonesus.

AD 132

The twenty-one year reign passed in peace and prosperity for the Empire, save for a serious Jewish revolt in AD 132, during the course of which, Hadrian transferred some Egyptian personnel from the Misene Fleet to the Legio X Fretensis to replace losses. Upon transfer to a regular legion, the men were made Roman citizens. It has been estimated that during Hadrian's reign the Roman armies totalled circa 375,000 men. For the navy an additional 50,000 to 75,000 men enabled the fleets to preserve their domination of the seas and riparian borders of the Empire.

AD 142

This stability continued into the reign of the next emperor, Antoninus Pius, who ruled a peaceful empire well for twenty-three years between AD 138 and 161. The only alteration to the Empire during his reign was under his Governor of Britannia, Lollius Urbicus who, in AD 142, advanced the border once more to the Forth–Clyde line and built the defensive wall there known as the Antonine Wall. This wall was built of turf and stone, with a ditch and palisade and forts every two miles; the fleet positioned ships to guard each end and forts were built on the south of the Firth of Forth. Ports were set up at Cramond and Troon and a garrison of 7000 *auxilia* posted to man them.[25] Although at forty miles (70km), only half the length of Hadrian's Wall, it did expose longer seaboards to be patrolled in difficult waters along the southern shores of the firths. Before the end of the reign, the border was returned to the better-built Hadrian's Wall. The lowland peoples were reasonably peaceable and formed a useful buffer between the province and the wilder tribes to the north. Without the will to conquer the whole of Caledonia, there was no point in extending further northward. The other extension of the Empire was in advancing the *limes* in Germany to the eastward by about twenty miles (30km) and establishing a new forward defensive line.

AD 152

Antoninus' reign suffered no major wars but there was trouble in Mauretania and Germania and rebellion in Egypt, Greece and Judaea as well as skirmishing against Dacians and Alans across the Danubius and Dacian borders. Vast areas of the Empire remained untroubled and navy personnel were utilised in civil engineering works in the same way as army engineers, as appears for example, from a report of AD 152 by the engineer Nonius Datus, on the building of an aqueduct at Saldae in Mauretania '... the contractor and his workmen began excavation in their presence with the help of two gangs of experienced veterans, namely a detachment of marine infantry and a detachment of alpine troops...'.[26]

Stability in government continued with the accession in AD 161 of Marcus Aurelius and his adoptive brother Lucius Verus as joint emperors. The long period of comparative peace was shattered by a Parthian offensive into Armenia and Syria. The focus of activity at sea in the east shifted from the comparative peace of the Euxine, to the threat to the Levant caused by the Parthian pressure on the Euphrates border. The *Classis Pontica* moved its main base westward to Cyzicus on the Propontis, while the *Classis Syriaca* operated between Alexandria and Seleucia, as the port for Antioch and along the Cilician coast. This fleet was also reinforced and built up to some 200 ships in strength, presumably with help from the Italian fleets. Verus went east, attended by units of the *Classis Misinensis*, which remained in that area, carrying out trooping and communications duties, until the war ended in AD 166 with the defeat of the Parthians. In AD 166, the emperors

The shipment of bulk grain from Egypt continued to be an annual event. There survives a description from the second century of one of these great ships, by the author Lucian, who saw it at Piraeus, where it had sheltered after being blown off-course by a storm: 'What a size the ship was! One hundred and eighty feet in length, the ship's carpenter told me, the beam more than a quarter of that and forty-four feet from the deck to the bottom, the deepest point in the bilge. What a mast it had, what a yard it carried, what a forestay held it up! The way the sternpost rose in a gradual curve with a gilded goose-head set on the tip of it, matched at the opposite end by the forward, more flattened rise of the prow with the figure of Isis, the goddess the ship was named after, on each side! The rest of the decoration, the paintings, the red pennant on the main yard, the anchors and capstans and winches on the foredeck, the accommodations towards the stern – it all seemed like marvels to me! The crew must have been as big as an army. They told me that she carried so much grain that it would be enough to feed every mouth in Athens for a year. It all depends for its safety on one little old man who turns those great steering oars with just a skinny tiller. They pointed him out to me; woolly-haired, half-bald fellow; Heron was, I think, his name.'[27] It was the super-tanker of its day and able to carry over 1200 tons of grain. To give some idea of the extent of the trade, it has been estimated that from the period of the early Empire, Rome imported some seventeen million bushels of grain annually, of which two million came from Sicily, five million from Egypt and ten million from Africa; a total of nearly half a million tons a year.

sent an embassy to the Emperor of China. The troops returning from the east, unfortunately brought with them the plague, which ravaged Rome in AD 167.

TROUBLED TIMES

AD 168

As if the plague were not enough, invaders struck across the Danubius in AD 168 and the Emperors marched north; the incursions were repulsed but Lucius Verus died after a stroke in early AD 169. In AD 170, barbarian raiders crossed the border of Moesia and penetrated into Greece. The *Classis Pontica* was once again moved from its base at Trapezus to Cyzicus on the Propontis to cover against any attempt by them to cross into Asia Minor. The fleet's old headquarters at Trapezus had become less important in relation to communications with Armenia, since the development and building of a more adequate road system in eastern Asia Minor and northern Syria. Conversely, an increase in military traffic across the Propontis and its strategic position at the centre of the axis of Syria and the Danubius demanded a permanent presence there and the *Classis Pontica*'s fleet headquarters would henceforth remain at Cyzicus. From there it could of course continue to patrol along the northern coast of Asia Minor and maintain detachments at all of its old bases there.[28]

AD 170

Even more trouble flared, also in AD 170, when Germanic peoples from north of the Middle Danubius invaded north-east Italy and besieged Aquileia on the northern Adriatic coast. Marcus Aurelius spent the next five years fighting to drive the invaders out and restore the border, the Danubius fleets being constantly in action, supporting and providing transport for the army along the river and its tributaries and being instrumental in helping him to pursue them into what is now the Czech Republic and across the plains of Hungary. In the winter of 170/171, the ex-Consul Marcus Valerius Maximianus was sent with detachments of men from the Italian and British Fleets to bring supplies down the Danubius for Marcus' army and was supported in this by North African cavalry scouting the banks of the river to guard against attacks on his boats. In addition to the resident fleet operations, these men had been brought from very far afield and must have commandeered virtually anything that floated, as well as building rafts and boats of their own, to haul supplies.[29] The inference is that things were reasonably quiet in Britannia at this time, whereas men could not be spared from the Rhenus frontier; the Praetorian Fleets as always, acting as a ready reserve of trained naval personnel.

The tribes south-west of Mauretania also became restive, taking to the sea and raiding the African and Hispanic coasts; in AD 170 and 171, the *Classis Misinensis* sent a major fleet force to suppress this seaborne activity, operating out onto the Atlantic seaboard and reinforcing local garrisons while the army dealt with the tribesmen on land.

Along with the general unrest among the Germanic peoples, this period saw the start of piracy and raiding by tribesmen from the north German coasts, upon the coasts of Belgica. They were driven off by local levies raised by the Governor Didius Iulianus (later to briefly be Emperor), but raiding was to continue to a greater or lesser extent from then on, ranging further to the coasts of northern Gaul and eastern Britannia. It is therefore from this period that defensive works start to be built around towns and for coastal

AD 174

forts to be constructed.[30] In the winter of AD 173/174, the *Classis Pannonica* was disabled by the freezing of the Danubius above the Iron Gates and at that time a battle actually took place on the ice to defeat raiding Iazyges tribesmen. A series of watchtowers was constructed along the Roman bank of the river, southward from Aquincum, to block obvious crossing places and to enforce the treaties which had been made with various tribes of barbarians on the other banks, which forbade them from crossing; the forts were linked and supplied by the *Classis Pannonica*.

Marcus extended the period of enlistment in the navy by two years, to twenty-eight years.[31] Although this may seem excessive, bear in mind that a man completing his twenty-two or twenty-six years of service would have found himself discharged with nothing to do, into an alien civilian world, having lived for years most probably far from his childhood home, with which he had no further connection. It may be conjecture but, many men were probably happy to go on serving past their discharge date, or if lucky, to find some shore post or job still connected with the service which had become their home, as well as that of their families, parallels to which can still be found today in 'navy' or garrison towns.

AD 180

Reverting to dynastic principles, Marcus appointed his son, Commodus to be his heir. They toured the Eastern Provinces in AD 176, but in AD 178 had once more to return to the Danubius frontier, where the Emperor died in AD 180. On his succession, Commodus precipitately made peace and ended the war in Central Europe, returning to Rome where he virtually abrogated his position as effective ruler to a number of 'favourites'. In AD 184, an uprising took place in Armorica in north-west Gaul and the *Classis Britannica* had to ferry troops across the Channel from Britannia, under Lucius Artorius Castus, to put it down. By AD 185 the Antonine Wall in Britannia had been twice breached and in that year, Ulpius Marcellus marched north on a punitive expedition, supported as always, by the fleet.

Troubles in Egypt in AD 190 caused a grain shortage at Rome and led to riots. Commodus had to assume some responsibility for government and the placing of less reliance on Egyptian grain and more from other areas. The result of this was however to demonstrate his total lack of ability and increasing signs of insanity; he even started to appear in the arena as a gladiator. It was reported that on one such occasion in the arena, the audience applauded him but he took them to be mocking and ordered the navy crews who worked the awnings to slaughter them.[32] Presumably his anger subsided as no such blood-letting took place. He was assassinated in

AD 192

AD 192.

A new emperor, Publius Helvius Pertinax, a long-serving career officer who had at one time been Praefectus commanding the *Classis Germanica* on the Rhenus, was quickly found but, just as quickly, made the fatal mistake of alienating the Praetorians, by whom he was murdered after only three months. In the ensuing power vacuum it fell to the various armies of the Empire to support three rival claimants to be emperor. Marcus Septimius Severus, Governor of Upper Pannonia and commander on the Danubius, Pescennius Niger, Governor of Syria and Decimus Clodius Albinus, Governor of Britannia. Meanwhile in Rome, the Praetorians actually held their infamous auction of the Empire, the highest bidder, one Marcus Didius Iulianus being proclaimed by them. Didius also tried to buy the

Praetorian Fleets but the Ravenna Fleet immediately went over to Severus. The Misenum Fleet was more equivocal and although Didius brought some of its men to Rome, their support of him was illusory. Upon his take-over, Severus promoted a Misenum officer to the Senate for services rendered, presumably for bringing that fleet over to his cause.[33]

Severus marched on Rome and the Senate sentenced Iulianus to death. Having secured his position at the centre and bought off Albinus with a promise of shared power, Severus took his forces eastward to deal with Niger, with the help of the Italian Fleets which ferried his men across to the Balkans. The fleets stayed with and supported Severus in his eastern campaign.[34] Niger had seized and fortified Byzantium. Severus invested the city and with the main part of his army, crossed to Asia where he defeated Niger, who was a little later killed at Issus. Byzantium, perhaps unaware of Niger's fate and unwilling to believe Severus' account of his death, still refused to surrender to him, closing its harbours with chains and mounting heavy artillery on the towers of its fortifications and harbour moles. The fleet closed in to blockade the city but in a daring attack, the defenders sent divers to cut and snare the anchor cables of some of the ships moored closest inshore; some ships were then actually pulled into the shore close enough to be attacked from the walls with rocks and baulks of timber. A sortie was also mounted by the defenders who had manned some ships in the harbour, but they were beaten back. Unable to break the blockade, the inevitable starvation set in and the City surrendered. Before leaving the east, Severus mounted a campaign into Parthia, which had given support to Niger and occupied and annexed territory to form the new province of Osrhoene, between the upper reaches of the Tigris and Euphrates.

AD 195

By AD 195 it was clear to Albinus that Severus had no intention of sharing power and so, supported by the British legions and *Classis Britannica*, he crossed to Gaul and started to consolidate and increase his power base there. Severus moved against Albinus in AD 197 and beat him after a hard-fought battle near to Lugdunum (Lyons). The troops who went with Albinus from Britannia of course reduced the garrison there and the northern border again came under pressure in AD 196; it seems likely that the garrison and its covering naval force fell back once more to Hadrian's Wall, although the navy could still dominate both east and west coasts of Caledonia at will. Severus, now undisputed ruler, was popular with the army (and presumably also with the navy which had after all, backed him), improving pay and living conditions and allowing the troops to (officially) marry and live with their families rather than only in barracks.

AD 197

The Parthians were again threatening the east and in AD 197 the Emperor once more marched to Syria. In the ensuing campaign the Romans embarked on ships and travelled down the River Euphrates, some 200 miles of whose course already formed a large part of the Roman–Parthian border.[35] At the point where the two rivers' courses are closest the Romans crossed to the River Tigris where they seized and looted Ctesiphon, the Parthian capital. Severus spent the next five years in the east, where he annexed more territory to form another new province, Mesopotamia, the last that would be added to the Empire. The standing army of the Empire now numbered thirty-three legions, plus auxiliaries and ten naval fleets. The garrison at Rome, including the Praetorians, was increased from 11,500 to 30,000 men.

AD 208   Increasing insecurity and upheaval in Caledonia, spilled over the border into the Province of Britannia and in AD 208 the Emperor with an army and his family went there, Severus intending to settle the northern border for once and for all by conquering the whole island. Leaving his younger son, Geta, in charge of the Province, the Emperor and his elder son, Bassianus, campaigned into Caledonia in AD 209 and 210, imposing terms on the tribes as his campaigns pushed northward. He made use of the *Classis Britannica* around the by now well-known northern coasts in support of his campaigns and probably re-occupied the Antonine Wall. Severus was however in failing
AD 211   health and died at Eboracum in February AD 211. Bassianus, better known to us by his nickname of Caracalla, and his brother Geta had no interest in continuing their father's campaigning only being eager to return to Rome to consolidate their power. They immediately abandoned the campaign and returned to Rome. The border was returned to rest on Hadrian's Wall, where it was to remain henceforth.

The mutually hostile brothers' rivalry and struggle to be sole emperor resulted in the murder of Geta after only ten months. Caracalla was however popular with the army, having given the troops and presumably the navy
AD 213   as well, a fifty per cent pay rise. In AD 213, Caracalla went on a tour of the Rhenus frontier and he then went eastward through Dacia, Thrace and Anatolia. While in the north Aegean in AD 214, Caracalla's galley foundered and he was rescued by an unnamed navy Prefect; in gratitude, the Emperor awarded the title *Pia Vindex* to the Praetorian Fleets.[36]

Although liked by the army, Caracalla was hated by many and plots against him finally succeeded when he was killed near to Edessa in Osrhoene
AD 217   in April AD 217 by a member of his bodyguard. Although several officers were involved in the successful assassination plot, the headquarters staff and the Commander of the Fleet were not involved.[37] The point here is that even though the Emperor was far inland, the Fleet Commander was in his entourage as part of his military staff. The commander was the senior naval officer, i.e. the Praefect of the *Classis Misinensis*, the senior fleet. The squadrons of the Praetorian Fleets which had accompanied Caracalla to the east joined with the *Classis Syriaca* and even units from the *Classis Alexandrina* in carrying troops, their equipment and supplies for the Emperor's campaign and went on to supply the men to police the coastal areas while the garrisons

were away to the east. For all his faults, Caracalla had ruled reasonably well and had maintained the military strength of the Empire and, importantly, in AD 212 had extended full Roman citizenship to all free-born and freed males in the Empire; although the cynic would say that this also had the effect of making them all liable to tax. In the military and navy this of course ended the distinction between the legions and marines, who were recruited from citizens and the *auxilia*, seamen and rowers, who were recruited from non-citizen subjects of the Empire. With his passing, there was no obvious heir and it would presage the start of nearly seventy years of turmoil and crisis for the Empire, with many short-lived emperors; a watershed that ended the continuity of the ancient world and led to the 'Late Empire', a radically different entity.

INSTABILITY AND INVASION

AD 217

The period from the assassination of Caracalla in AD 217, to the accession of Diocletian in AD 285 was one of almost constant upheaval for the Roman world, which several times came near to destroying it. There were twenty-seven recognised emperors and many usurpers and adventurers who tried for the purple with varying degrees of futility. The emperors ranged from the totally unfit, through the incompetent to stalwart and capable upholders of the Empire. The age was also dominated by unrest, indiscipline and disloyalty through much of the army, various parts of which took it upon themselves to elevate and dispose of emperors almost at a whim and certainly before any of those of real ability could achieve a position of power analogous to that of earlier emperors. The fabric of the Empire was rent from within by dissention and secession, as well as by crushing financial burdens and plague. It was only the Empire's intrinsic strength that kept it going as an institution.

As if that were not enough, the period was one of constant threat and invasion from beyond the borders. Instead of its former united front against outside enemies, the army on several occasions, dissipated its energies and strength in internecine factional fighting, providing encouragement to the ambitions of potential invaders. In the east, the ailing Parthian Empire was superseded by a new, vigorous Persian dynasty, intent on adding western provinces at Rome's expense. In Europe, the disparate tribes of Germanic peoples had started to coalesce into larger nations or confederations, better organised for what appeared to be their sole aim in life, namely assaulting the Empire. Further, the period saw the start of the phenomenon of the mass migrations of Germanic and other central, northern and eastern European peoples towards the Empire and spilling across its frontiers. The age was one of constant invasion and fighting to eject intruders and maintain the borders.

That no solution to this problem was found was due in large part to a fundamental change in the nature of the defence of the Empire. Previously the borders, particularly in Central Europe, were seen as a line to be defended and although making the line impregnable was impossible, nevertheless it was fortified and along it was stationed the entirety of the Empire's military strength. The weakness was always that to strengthen one sector meant the weakening of another from which troops had to be withdrawn. The whole strategy was to keep an enemy out, or at worst, to quickly contain and eject incursions; any fighting was to be preferably pre-emptive and on the barbarians' side of the border. In this, the strong and efficient riverine fleets were an integral, indeed essential part, making the difference between the great rivers being an actual barrier or just an obstacle. With the internal instability of the period however, more and more often troops left their stations to fight in civil unrest or to offer their strength to back a contender for the imperial title, leaving swathes of the borders unguarded and thus having to fight on the Empire's own territory to eject the intruders who had taken advantage of the invitation thus offered to them and losing the advantage of pre-emptive intelligence and action. The borders were further weakened by Emperors and pretenders preferring to have troops loyal to them actually with them wherever they were, to back them up and for their security, although this latter did not always follow. The formerly solid and strong defensive line was fragmented and the riverine fleets particularly had to limit their activities to those areas where sufficient border troops remained to support them and to secure their bases and supplies.[38]

Against this background, the navy was to suffer in different ways according to the theatre of operations, overstretched and overwhelmed on the riverine frontiers of Europe, neglected and diminished in the central fleets. It also suffered, in common with the army with which the riverine fleets were so closely linked, dissention in its ranks and lowering of morale and operational efficiency. In the Euxine and Mediterranean, neglect and a progressive weakening as the principal theatres of operations moved to the extremities of the Empire, meant that it was unable to face the first challenges to its supremacy in over two hundred years, from piracy and enemy incursions at sea. Beset by constant warring and the vast cost of and scale of simultaneous operations on several fronts to which all available manpower and financial resources had to be directed, the grand Praetorian fleets became a luxury that could no longer be afforded. The decline went further than the mere shedding of excess however and the knock-on effect upon the remaining fleets became apparent, confirming, if such were necessary, the value of the strong central establishment initiated by Augustus.

A further consideration is that none of the twenty-seven emperors were 'navy' men, unlike most of the previous incumbents who were aware of the strategic as well as the tactical and security value of a well-founded navy in maintaining the integrity of the Empire and securing its core, the sea around which it revolved. Even those among them who were soldiers had little or no appreciation of the exercise of sea-power, leading to a consequent ignoring of the needs of the navy. The beginning of the naval decline in the Mediterranean is difficult to pinpoint, but certainly the fleets were caught

AD 219

up in the general unrest among the military; on one occasion in AD 219, the *Classis Pontica* at Cyzicus sought unsuccessfully and briefly, to elevate its own commander to be emperor.[39] This was a period overall when the acceptance of central authority by the armed forces had broken down and there was a feeling that anyone could be emperor and by the troops that the making of an emperor was in their gift, which view they proceeded to prove many times. Another factor adding to the discontent in the military in general was that instability in government was coupled with serious economic inflation which in turn led to a breakdown in the adequate and regular payment of troops and naval personnel. The value of the money was unstable and so a system of payment in kind, in rations, goods and accommodation came into being. The lure of gold offered by pretenders to the purple was thus a strong one.

AD 222

The unrest, coupled with a few years of neglect and lack of firm command weakened the fleets to the extent that by AD 222, incidents of piracy were reported. It seems to have needed only a few years for the morale, *esprit de corps* and operational efficiency, as well as the numbers, of the Mediterranean fleets to have lapsed to an extent where anyone would dare to operate as a pirate. Although nowhere near as prevalent as previously, some limited piracy continued until it was once more overcome by increased naval activity in AD 235. The fleets still numbered ten commands at this time, but in what state is debateable. It was the beginning of a vicious circle, the neglect or decline of the navy encouraged incidents of piracy, which in turn unsettled maritime trade; the decline of trade lessened the amount of taxes received by the Empire and able to be spent in paying for an adequate navy and to fight increasing barbarian incursions. To meet the threats the state increased taxes anyway and at the same time had to make increased demands upon civilian shipping for troop and supply transportation, all of which of course, further depressed trade and commerce, leaving destitute seamen to turn to piracy, placing a greater burden on the navy and so on and so on. The fleets also grew smaller as part of their funding was switched to bolster the army.

AD 230

From about AD 230, the problem of raids and piracy across the southern part of the North Sea and into the Channel from the coasts of Holland, Germany and probably Denmark, to the southern and south-east coasts of Britannia and the northern coasts of Gaul by marauders became a serious problem. Their abilities in boat building and seamanship had obviously developed greatly, along with their coastal navigation and although not yet able to cross the open sea, using long, rowed boats they were increasingly making their way along the coasts and up estuaries, into the Empire. Their boats had evolved into open, double-ended, clincher-built ships, ranging from as little as twenty feet (6m) to seventy feet (22m) in length, rowed by a single reme of oars across each bulwark and resembling in appearance, the later Viking longships, with a single mast, stepped amidships upon the yard of which a square sail was rigged.[40] It would not be long before they could and would be capable of crossing the North Sea and of ranging all around the coasts of western Europe.

To counter this, the previously undefended coasts were organised into military districts and the Romans started to build a series of strong forts at various points along the British coast from the Tamesis to mid-way along the Channel and northward up the eastern side of Britannia from the Tamesis estuary to the Abus estuary, at least eleven being built between now and the end of the century. The principle was an extension of the *limes* system of the Rhenus and Danubius, into the maritime sphere, its focus being to the east and south-east, facing the threat posed by peoples in the arc of the German Bight. The sites were chosen on natural harbours, inlets or with sheltered anchorages. Coastlines adjacent to several of these bases have since changed drastically but in their time, they were all completed as bases for the support and operation of the naval squadrons stationed at each base, with their garrisons of infantry and cavalry and provided with jetties, piers, quays and slipways. The chain of forts is now referred to as the 'Saxon Shore Forts', a term unknown at the time, and the early examples resembled the earlier legionary forts, largely square in plan, with towers built into the inside faces of the curtain walls. They would soon evolve, taking greater advantage of available contours and with towers projecting beyond the curtain walls to enable enfilading cross-fire and looking more akin to the later medieval castle.[41]

The navy's personnel could be expected to have played a large part in the building of these forts and especially in the provision of harbour facilities for themselves. It is notable that this new system of fortified bases was built on virgin sites; existing ports had already of course, long been in use by the navy and had themselves gradually been fortified. With the cessation of intensive naval operations in the far north and Caledonia, the focus of the *Classis Britannica* was shifted to operations from these new bases, attempting to intercept raiders coming across the North Sea and along the northern European coast. Similarly, other forts were constructed along the north coast of Belgica and Gaul and the *Classis Germanica* was deployed in the Rhenus delta to cover that coast. Each fort had a garrison and was a depot and naval base from which patrols could be maintained and forces quickly deployed to deal with any incursion and to round up and interdict any raiders which may have evaded the patrols. This arrangement continued, was extended and remained effective until the troop withdrawals of the early fifth century left the system under-manned and unable to function properly. For this period however, these precautions seem to have sufficed as the continuing prosperity of the provinces was uninterrupted.

AD 230   In about AD 230 the process of extensive change to the North Sea coastline of what is now Holland and Belgium started with a rise in sea level and subsidence of the land which led to the sea bursting into the coastal areas, forming the Zuider Zee. The lands around the mouths of the Rhenus became untenable and economically ruined and the understandable concomitant depopulation effectively left it a waste-land, abandoned, open to barbarian incursion and almost incapable of effective defence.[42]

In AD 230 the Persians invaded and overran the province of Mesopotamia and the Emperor Severus Alexander, accompanied by the Misene Fleet, set off for the east to meet them, gathering troops from the Danubius frontier to add to his forces. The Persians were ejected after an inconclusive campaign, but the troops' morale was not high and not helped by the Emperor's attempts to reduce the military budget, attempts which doubtless included

AD 233   those most expensive of items, warships. In AD 233, German tribesmen managed to cross the Rhenus in several places; the Emperor moved to restore the situation, but by buying them off. This was too much for the army and navy on the Rhenus, who killed him.

His successor, Maximinus restored the frontier and strengthened its defences, both on the Rhenus and on the Danubius. In the latter case, the *Classis Moesica*'s responsibility was divided by the common frontier of the Province of Dacia on the north bank. On the lower reaches, below Dacia, the fleet had to cover the open frontier of Moesia, the estuary and Euxine seaboard; larger ships, wider vistas and flat, open countryside; to the west of Dacia, the fleet had only the restricted waters of the upper Danubius in which to operate, needing smaller boats. The integrity of the Danubius as a frontier had been interrupted, of little importance in the relatively quiet period just passed, but an increasing problem in the troubles now brewing. The financial burden of the large-scale, continuous military operations resulted in a heavy tax burden, which gave rise to even further civil unrest. In

AD 238   the resulting confusion, the Goths crossed the Lower Danubius in AD 238, raiding Moesia and Thrace and attacking and sacking the *Classis Moesica* base at Istrus. At the same time the Persians again invaded.

In Britannia, raiders had negotiated the North Sea and were coming down the west coast from the (Hebridean) isles off the west of Caledonia and also across the Irish Sea and attacking the western coasts of the Province, even penetrating as far as the river Sabrina in the south-west. Troops were stationed to guard and garrison strong points on the coasts of the north-west and west. Despite these threats, it seems that Britannia was not too badly affected by the raids and so, once again, the measures taken appear to have been largely effective and the defences adequately manned.[43]

For most of the rest of the century, towns, ports and even some villages across the northern provinces of the Empire would receive defensive walls and works for the first time. The system of shore forts continued to be extended, indicating a need arising due to increased frequency and proficiency of barbarian seaborne activity. However, to put this into perspective, the defensive measures and still-powerful and well-found northern fleets succeeded in keeping them at little more than irritation level. The constant land incursions were cumulatively more serious, leading to economic damage and depopulation of the worst affected areas.

The continuing turmoil in and about the Empire was bound to, and eventually did, have a deleterious effect on the northern fleets; morale and efficiency declined in men engaged in long and tedious patrols and duties, frequently in bad weather, being expected to perform even though their pay was often erratic and their loyalties were pulled different ways by competing factions. Interruptions in supplies, lack of funds for the regular replacement of worn-out ships and, as like as not, a lack of recruits, all effected a gradual reduction in the strength and effectiveness of the fleets at a time when barbarian seafaring efforts were on the increase and they were needed more and more.

At about this time there is mention of the Legio I Adiutrix, one of those originally formed by Nero from navy personnel, being based at Brigetio on the Danubius, north-west of Aquincum (Budapest).[44] It would be extremely doubtful if that unit by this time retained any connection with its origins, although it would be perfectly familiar with the riverine fleet with which it had contact.

AD 243

The Emperor Gordian III quickly dealt with the Goths and restored the frontier, then moved east by sea, concentrating large naval forces for support and defeated the Persians, driving them out by AD 243. From AD 244, units of the Praetorian Fleets were stationed at Ephesus, where they remained until AD 249. Gordian's successor, Philip, had to spend three years campaigning across the Danubius to keep potential invaders at bay and to protect Dacia. In Italy he used detachments of fleet sailors as police to combat banditry in central Italy. Following his celebration in AD 248 of the one thousandth anniversary of the founding of Rome, there was a serious uprising among the legions and fleets in Moesia and Pannonia, who sought to make their commander emperor; they quickly tired of this however and killed him instead. Their next commander was more successful, becoming

AD 249

the Emperor Decius in AD 249, who died in battle against the Goths in AD 251. Scythians, Goths and others put together a fleet in the Euxine of some 500 craft of all types and managed to get through the Propontis, into the Aegean and attacked Macedonia, Greece and Athens, Sparta and Corinth before being caught and stopped by Roman fleets.[45] Of the Roman units engaged there is no surviving information but the incursion fell within the remit of the *Classis Moesica* (the west Euxine), the *Classis Pontica* (south Euxine and Propontis) and the *Classis Syriacae* (Aegean). Whichever fleet did engage with the enemy, and it is not unreasonable to presume that all three fleets were involved to some degree, it proved to be a costly exercise for the invaders.

The fleet on the lower Danubius must have been under great pressure at this time, carrying out constant patrolling of the river and scouting of its northern banks and hinterland for signs of enemy bands, in flat, marshy and difficult terrain, with frequent fighting to hold the line. Nevertheless they could not be everywhere at once and despite all of the fleet's efforts, the Goths managed to cross and in numbers that required an army to round them up and deal with them. It was impossible for the fleet to always catch the intruders as they were crossing or preparing to do so. The Goths had by now migrated to the north of the Euxine and had sacked and burned the Bosporan city of Tanais (near to modern-day Rostov-on-Don). They were building and developing the use of boats for the sea, from those long in use by them in the years during which they had migrated from their homelands on the Baltic along the great rivers of Russia and the Ukraine. They became more adventurous with experience and undertook raiding voyages as far as the Anatolian and Balkan coasts. For its part, the Bosporan Kingdom was now dominated by the Goths and persisted in vestigial form by their grace and favour.[46]

There was still a Roman garrison and fleet presence at Chersonesus in the Crimea, but the Roman presence at other former Hellenistic settlements around the north Euxine had long since been withdrawn and effective Roman naval control of the north Euxine basin was lost. An inscription from this time records the occupation of an island in the Danubius delta by 'pirates' and from thence they could prey upon traffic in the delta; the raiders even penetrated the Propontis to make plundering raids down the Anatolian and Greek coasts. The raiders may only have had comparatively small, apparently flat-bottomed craft, but sailed together in groups, dozens strong and with hundreds of men. The Roman warships were obviously stronger and superior ship for ship but the sheer numbers and frequency of the raiding parties, as well as the area over which they could operate, made interception very difficult. The various naval squadrons that were based about the area fought the intruders in battles off Rhodes, Crete and even Cyprus. Some of the raiders at least however, must have managed to successfully return home with loot and tales to inspire others to emulate them.

AD 254   In AD 254 barbarians using Bosporan ships with captive crews, raided the northern Anatolian coast, losing heavily when they were caught ashore. The Roman writ no longer ran in the north Euxine, the Goths again raiding the south-west coasts of the sea in their small, open boats in AD 256. The Emperor Gallienus campaigned successively against invasions and across the Rhenus and Danubius frontiers for the next five years, a time of intense activity for the fleets on both rivers. The quality of the Roman forces is self-evident in that they could still beat any enemy that presented itself, the problem was that they had to fight on three of four wide fronts at the same time, against aggressive and overwhelming numbers, continuously.

AD 259   In AD 259, the Goths again attacked in force from the area north of the Euxine which they had made their own. They swept across the Lower Danubius and plundered across Moesia and Thrace, as far as the Propontis itself. They manned a fleet of 500 boats and ships of all sorts and sailed into the Propontis, sacking Cyzicus and then proceeding into the Aegean, attacking Athens and raiding as far as the southern Peloponnese and even to Epirus on the Ionian Sea; they attacked and destroyed the Temple of Diana at Ephesus, before finally withdrawing. The question is raised as to where was the *Classis Pontica*, whose base was at Cyzicus? Either it was overwhelmed and totally destroyed by the onslaught, or it was forced to retreat before them and content itself with harrying the barbarians as best it could; clearly it suffered severely.

AD 260   In AD 260, a revolt across North Africa from Mauretania, through Numidia to Africa, was dealt with and suppressed by the Misene Fleet, the only force that was available to be sent to help the small local units and obviously therefore still at this time a substantial one. In the east, the co-Emperor Valerian's forces were struck by plague and besieged at Edessa by the Persians; he attempted to negotiate with them personally but was captured, plunging the embattled Empire into a fresh crisis.

THREE EMPIRES IN ONE

Gallienus had already spent seven years trying to hold and secure the Empire and was now alone. The constant pressure and campaigning had its toll and the Emperor increasingly had to form his armies from whatever units he could draft or levy into improvised formations, turning increasingly for mobility to the widespread use of cavalry. The navy was perforce neglected and maybe even losing men to the army. For their part, the fleets of the navy, particularly in the Euxine and Mediterranean, had to be put together increasingly from whatever could be kept seaworthy and manned; the old formal fleets gave way to ad hoc squadrons operating locally. Various would-be usurpers tried their luck and were put down, but each time the Emperor's authority was challenged, valuable troops were wasted in factional fighting for and against these challenges.

Having restored the Danubius and Dacia borders yet again, he was faced with an invasion by Franks across the Rhenus, who proceeded to rampage across Gaul. Some of them got as far as Tarraco in Hispania; there, some of them seized some presumably merchant ships that were in the harbours, again presumably together with enough sailors to operate them. They sailed on to raid the North African coast; what then became of them is not recorded, but their numbers could not have been great and they were probably eventually dealt with. The Emperor, committed on the Danubius and elsewhere could do nothing to help Gaul and the Governor of Lower Germany, Postumus, had to act alone. He did destroy the raiding bands and thereupon assumed the title of Augustus and continued to secure the Rhenus

AD 261 frontier. He was recognised by AD 261 as de facto Emperor throughout Gaul and in Rhaetia, Hispania and Britannia, splitting the Empire and forming the so-called 'Gallic Empire'. He had no wider ambition and Gallienus could do little about it, although ever fearful that Postumus would be tempted to add Italy to his brief. Gallienus did station troops in northern Italy, based upon Mediolanum, to prevent such an eventuality, thereby of course, weakening the frontier defences. In Britannia, raids in the south by Saxons continued, as did raids by Scotti from Ireland, towards Hadrian's Wall and down the west coast of the Province.[47] There was success in the east however, where the Persians were beaten back by the Romans and then attacked by the Roman ally Odaenathus, ruler of Palmyra.

AD 263 The first contraction of the Empire since the abandonment of Germania in AD 9, took place in AD 263. The advanced frontier in central Germany, the *Limes*, which protected the Agri Decumates, that 'tongue' of territory formed where the Rhenus and Danubius turn south-west, was held by the forces of Postumus, but had been under constant assault for some time. In AD 263, Gallienus recovered Rhaetia from Postumus, thereby placing his loyal forces in the flank and rear of the *Limes*. Faced with this and the growing impossibility and cost of trying to maintain and garrison such an exposed frontier line, the *Limes* and Agri Decumates were duly abandoned and the frontier returned to the original Upper Rhenus–Danubius lines. To bolster the new defensive lines, Lake Constance became part of the border area for the first time and a flotilla was established to patrol it. Gallienus took an army into Gaul in AD 265 in an attempt to end the secession, which failed.

AD 266 In AD 266 and 267, Odaenathus again defeated the Persians and also a Goth incursion and restored the eastern provinces; he became effective ruler of the east but died in AD 267, to be succeeded by his Queen, Zenobia. The remaining *Classis Syriaca* withdrew from the Levantine coast to its bases in the Aegean and piracy again flared along the Cilician coast; this was put down but there continued to be the odd incident. The barbarian raids and the resumption of piracy had the timeworn familiar result of leading to a decline in merchant shipping activity, first in the Euxine, then in the Aegean. To add yet further to the problems of commerce, the Ethiopeans closed the Red Sea and the Persians closed the Persian Gulf to Roman shipping; with no naval forces in the area and no way of mounting an expedition, nothing could be done to oppose or even threaten these moves. In any event this was not as critical as it might previously have been as Roman trade with the Far East had declined steadily throughout the century until it had, by this time, all but ceased.

Gallienus' attempt to recover effective power in the east failed and he was engaged by a massive invasion by Goths and Heruli across the Lower Danubius and by sea, into Moesia and Thrace; they were met this time and defeated in the Propontis, by Roman naval forces, presumably the re-formed *Classis Pontica*. The death of their admiral, Venerianus, distracted them and the surviving Gothic boats slipped into the Aegean where they penetrated to and sacked Athens but were then stopped and again beaten at sea. Gallienus again defeated them, then returned to Italy where he was

AD 268   murdered (AD 268).

In AD 269 yet another Goth seaborne force managed to evade detection or naval challenge and slipped into the Aegean and landed to invest

AD 270   Thessalonika. The following year (AD 270), the Emperor Claudius II moved east to finish off the Goths at Thessalonika, now afflicted by plague. The remaining Gothic ships roamed the Aegean, attacking Rhodes, Crete and Cyprus with little effect before being defeated and totally destroyed in a succession of running naval battles by the *Classis Alexandrina* under Tenagino Probus, Governor of Egypt. Probus' fleet is assumed to be his province's own but could well have been reinforced by the rump of the *Classis Syriaca*. Of the *Classis Pontica* there is no mention and it or its surviving ships were presumably still in the Propontis, despite having totally failed to stop or intercept the Goths *ab initio*. By now Zenobia had assumed control of all Roman territory between central Anatolia to and including Egypt.

The Emperor Aurelian drove the by now annual and depressingly tiresome invasions back across the Danubius and Alps and ordered the building of the walls around Rome that still bear his name. Aurelian defeated

AD 272   the Goths yet again in AD 272 in Dacia, which province had by now become untenable and indefensible and he thus abandoned it, withdrawing the border to the whole length of the Danubius. He next moved east, defeating the Palmyrenes. The eastern provinces were reunited with the Empire but another Palmyrene uprising in AD 273 once more required the Emperor's attention; this time he sacked the city.

AD 274

In AD 274, Aurelian turned his attention to the rump of the 'Gallic Empire' and defeated its last Emperor, Tetricus, re-uniting the whole Empire once more, but was killed in AD 275. Aurelian's successors, Tacitus and Florianus, had to campaign in the Balkans and the next Emperor, Probus, spent his entire six-year reign opposing invaders and usurpers. Vandals and Burgundians were streaming into Gaul and it took him three years to defeat them and throw them back across the Rhenus. The depressing story continued with another irruption into Moesia.

AD 279

Probus had settled a large number of Frankish captives in Pontus, on the Euxine coast. In AD 279 this trial settlement failed when, under cover of civil unrest elsewhere, they seized a number of ships and left, raiding Greece and eastern Sicily, primarily for supplies. They were beaten off near to Carthage, but eventually made their way all the way around western Europe, to the Rhenus. If true, this is an amazing voyage by a supposedly non-seafaring people and even more amazing is that they managed it without challenge, except at Carthage, from any Roman naval force.[48] At the end of AD 280, many of the *Classis Germanica*'s ships had been laid up for winter maintenance, possibly at or near to Colonia Agrippinensis and were destroyed on the shore by a barbarian raid. By this time also, barbarian piracy around the northern coasts of the Empire had reached epidemic proportions.

AD 282

In AD 282, Carus the Paetorian Prefect was declared Emperor and Probus killed. Carus made his sons Numerian and Carinus joint rulers and, with the former, attacked Persia, where Carus died mysteriously. Numerian did not long survive and the army elected the Imperial Guard Commander, Diocletian to succeed. Carinus had successfully fought and maintained the great riverine frontiers and even campaigned in northern Britannia in AD 284. He sought to oppose Diocletian but was defeated and killed when their two forces met near Singidunum (AD 285). Diocletian was now sole Emperor and was to bring about an end to the run of successive disasters of the past seventy years, but the empire that he took over was already very different and one that his own reforms would change yet further.

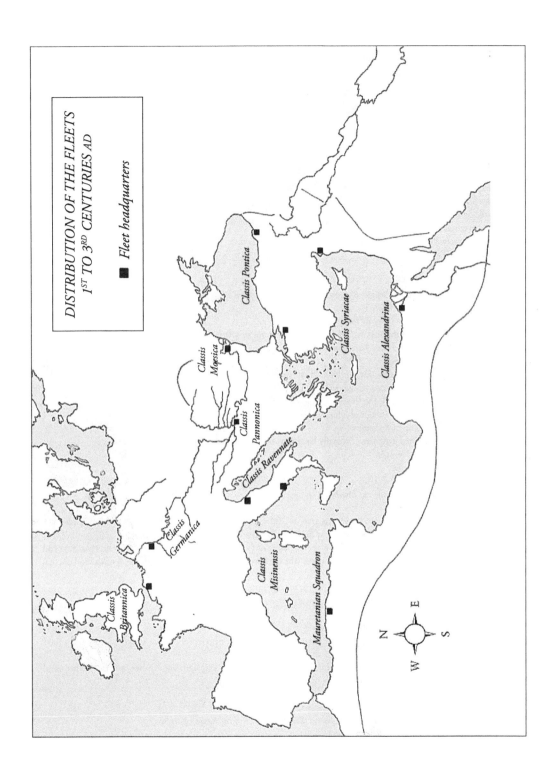

DISTRIBUTION OF THE FLEETS
1ST TO 3RD CENTURIES AD

■ Fleet headquarters

Classis Pontica

Classis Syriacae

Classis Alexandrina

Classis Moesica

Classis Pannonica

Classis Ravennate

Classis Germanica

Classis Britannica

Classis Misinensis

Mauretanian Squadron

N
E
S
W

Notes

1. Starr; Levick, *Vespasian*.
2. Cottrell, *The Great Invasion*.
3. There is of course an extensive river system to the east of the Rhenus, the Main and the Neckar being particularly useful. Austin & Rankov, *Exploratio*.
4. The historian Tacitus accompanied Agricola, his father-in-law, in Britain and wrote his biography.
5. Starr.
6. In two letters to Tacitus.
7. Called the *velarum* or sail, such an arrangement was fitted to many amphitheatres; there is a painting (now in the Naples Museum) of a riot in that of Pompeii which shows the *velarum* deployed.
8. Tacitus, *Agricola* 10.
9. Tacitus, *Agricola* 24 and 25.
10. Tacitus, *Agricola* 28.
11. Tacitus, *Agricola* 29.
12. Tacitus, *Agricola* 38.
13. Starr.
14. The earliest source for the campaigns of Domitian remains Suetonius, *The Twelve Caesars*.
15. Marsden, *Greek and Roman Artillery*.
16. See Selkirk, *The Piercebridge Formula* for a sketch of this canal.
17. Also partially now beneath the airport, although the inner basin survives.
18. Bounegru & Zahariade, *Les Forces Navales du Bas Danube*; Starr.
19. Casson, *The Ancient Mariners*.
20. There was never a naval formation for this river. Boats were used for transport downriver, especially during the various invasions mounted by the Romans. Navigation by large ships upriver however was not practicable. The river is 1700 miles (2720 km) long, of which the lower 1100 miles (1760 km) are navigable but the sometimes low water and at other times, swift current and lack of obliging winds make up-river navigation arduous.
21. Starr, referring to Eusebius and Cassius Dio.
22. Arrian wrote from personal experience, actually having cruised the sea with his squadron.
23. Selkirk, *The Piercebridge Formula*.
24. Austin & Rankov, *Exploratio*.
25. Mackie, *A History of Scotland*.
26. Starr; Sprague de Camp, *The Ancient Engineers*.
27. Lucian, *Navigium* 5.
28. Strabo (XII.8.11) says that the fleet at Cyzicus grew to 200 ship sheds with harbour facilities to match. Peddie, *The Roman War Machine*; also Starr, *The Influence of Seapower on Ancient History*.
29. One notable feature of Roman campaigning is that, unlike most of their opponents, Roman forces nearly always had plentiful supplies in the right place at the right time. The use for transport of even quite small rivers was a fundamental feature of their logistical system.
30. Pearson, *The Roman Shore Forts*.
31. Starr.
32. Birley, *Lives of the Later Caesars*.
33. Starr, *The Influence of Seapower on Ancient History*.
34. No naval opposition was encountered and one can only assume that the eastern fleets either stayed neutral and in their ports, or simply joined Severus.
35. Once more, local craft were impressed and additional craft built for the campaign, but it is not known whether naval personnel were involved on the rivers.
36. Starr.
37. Although this is disputed, Birley, *Lives of the Later Caesars*.
38. Luttwak, *The Grand Strategy of the Roman Empire*; Ferrill, *The Fall of the Roman Empire*.

39. Starr, quoting Dio, LXXIX.7.3.
40. Haywood, *Dark Age Naval Power.*
41. Pearson, *The Roman Shore Forts.*
42. Haywood, *Dark Age Naval Power;* Pearson, *The Roman Shore Forts.*
43. From this period onward, military inscriptions increasingly come from the coastal regions, particularly in the north-
     west and west, together with an increasing incidence of coin hoards, indicating a corresponding increase in raiding.
     Morris, *The Age of Arthur.*
44. Austin & Rankov, *Exploratio.*
45. Starr, *The Influence of Seapower on Ancient History.*
46. Ascherson, *Black Sea.*
47. Morris, *The Age of Arthur.*
48. Starr, quoting Zosimus, I.71.

RENEWAL AND DECLINE

AD 285–AD 476

AD 285

On becoming Emperor Diocletian realised that the imperial power structure had broken down and that, to restore the Empire to its former strength and stability, sweeping reform would be needed. To start, he brought in another military officer, Maximian to be 'Caesar' or number two and in charge of the western provinces. Diocletian was thus free to concentrate upon the affairs and borders of the eastern half of the Empire and thus founded his capital at Nicomedia (Izmit) on the Propontis. There he was equidistant between the Danubius and the Euphrates. Maximian did the same in the west, establishing his capital at Mediolanum, to place himself between the Rhenus and Upper Danubius. Rome herself thus ceased to be the effective capital and the remnants of the *Classes Praetoriae* became more remote still from the centres of power.

AD 286

Maximian was raised to the rank of Augustus or co-Emperor in AD 286. In that year he appointed a local commander, Carausius, who had been active in repelling Irish raiders from the west of Britannia, to operate against rebel bands in northern Gaul. Later, in AD 286, his command was extended to include the *Classis Britannica* at Gesoriacum in order to deal with barbarian pirates and raiders coming down the Channel and raiding the coasts of Gaul and Britannia. Carausius built up the fleet strength and efficiency, mounted patrols and attacked the raiders at sea, their light, open boats being no match for the bigger Roman warships. It was noticed eventually however, that the raiders always seemed to be caught when on their way home after a raid, never before, and the plunder recovered did not always get returned either to the victims or in default, to the Emperors; the *Classis Britannica* had in effect become pirates. The justification of course, is that the initiative always rests with the raiders, unless they are unlucky enough to run into a Roman patrol. With the Romans having little or no intelligence from the raiders' homelands as to their intentions, the raiders' existence and location could not be known until they were spotted by a lookout, or until they actually attacked. Late in AD 286, Maximian passed a death sentence on

Carausius *in absentia*, who thereupon withdrew his naval forces to British ports and declared himself Emperor in Britannia, supported by the troops there and the garrisons of Gesoriacum and Rotomagus (Rouen). Most of the fleet stayed under his command, securing his power base; some of the ships did remain loyal and made their way to loyal ports to the east and west of the disaffected area.[1]

Diocletian concentrated on building up the armies and did little for sea power, the navy in the Mediterranean having, in the instability and chaos of the previous century, become greatly run down and neglected. In AD 230 the navy had comprised ten fleets, the Italian at Misenum and Ravenna, the fleets of Alexandria, Syria and Pontica, together with the two on the Danubius, the *Moesica* and *Pannonica*, the *Classis Germanica* on the Rhenus, the *Classis Britannica* in the north and the squadron on the Mauretanian coast. The *Classes Praetoriae* were now but a shadow of their former selves and such squadrons that did manage to keep up some activity were temporary in nature, cobbled together from whatever ships and crews were available. In response to the ever-increasing barbarian activity off the north coasts of Europe and their increasing ability and expertise in seamanship, the fleet that Carausius had turned to his use had, of sheer necessity, not become so run down and was probably the best left in the Empire and continued to be so after him. The remainder of the navy was re-organised into smaller squadrons, in lieu of the great fleets of yore, each commanded by a *Praefectus* and each being based on a local centre under the overall commander of the respective districts. There were thirteen such units and they were to be the basis of naval organisation in the Mediterranean henceforth. Larger formations were to be made up from the squadrons as and when required, but it is immediately apparent that this was a devalued system compared to the previous one. With the dissipation of the ships to small, local commands, there existed no reserve or centralised force to oversee the maritime situation as a whole or any mechanism whereby fleets could be directed in concert to a particular end. Bases included a reduced Misenum, Ravenna, Arelate in Gaul, Aquileia at the northern end of the Adriatic, Alexandria, Rhodes and Byzantium on the Propontis.[2]

AD 286   Starting in 286, the long Danubius border was re-organised, the former provinces into four new areas, Moesia Prima, Moesia Secunda, Scythia and Dacia Ripensis. The riverine forces of the former *Classis Moesica* were divided into four parts, one being allotted to each new province with additional bases, half of which were also legionary bases. Presumably the responsibility for the western Euxine Basin and Thracian coast remained as before with the naval command of that part of the former fleet that controlled the delta (Scythia) as previously. With the build-up of barbarian strength to the north-west of the sea and their progressive overrunning of the former Hellenistic ports around it and consequent Roman withdrawal from the area, Roman

The period saw the introduction and use of a small, light galley with a single reme of about thirty oars, the lusoria, primarily for patrol work on the Rhenus and Danubius. This was a narrow, open boat with an unusual bow which would appear to have been formed to provide a platform to enable troops to get ashore quickly when the boat was run bow-on to a river bank. A mast-step for a light rig was included and the boats measured an average of sixty or so feet (18m) in length by ten feet (3m) beam and drew only eighteen inches (46cm). It has been estimated that they could manage seven knots cruising under oars and the crew could sling their shields along the sides for protection, the helmsman being protected by a small stern cuddy. The type seems ideally evolved to act as a raiding craft, as distinct from earlier, heavier 'pure warship' types, intended for patrol and the opposing of enemy shipping. Whereas it is of course possible that similar types existed before, nevertheless the introduction of the lusoria perhaps indicated a change in tactics to small-scale interventions on hostile river banks, whereas previously the policy had been of trying to maintain a *cordon sanitaire* on the opposite banks. These boats were built with a heavy keel, but on the 'frame first' principle, that is by first building a skeleton of frames onto which the hull-planking was fixed, carvel fashion and without mortices and tenons between the hull planks, which depended for their strength upon their fixings to the frames rather than, as previously, to each other. The changes in building methods had thus now completely, if not perhaps universally throughout the Roman world, evolved from the closely spaced mortice and tenons by which hull planks had been fastened to each other edge-to-edge, to build up a strong monocoque hull into which ribs, frames and thwarts were then fitted; to the intermediate stage of few well-spaced tenons used to locate and position, rather than to fix the hull planking and with greater reliance of the shell on the internal members for their strength; to this final, totally frame-first method.[3] The first method produced an intrinsically strong hull shell which, aided by bracing and wales was able to absorb the shock of ramming an enemy vessel, a shock that the enemy ship would find damaging and possibly fatal, a factor of almost no importance however by this time, with the demise of opposing heavy, ram-equipped warships. A further type in use at this time was possibly known as a platypegia and was especially for use in the Danubius delta, appearing also in the Nile delta. It seems to have been a punt with raised prow and poop, a stern cabin and a light sailing rig with a lateen sail.[4]

naval presence would become correspondingly reduced. The division of the *Classis Moesica* stationed in the Danubius delta had a most exposed position covering the delta with its marshes and waterways and additionally having to provide seagoing forces to patrol and protect the coasts and shipping between the delta and Propontis.

AD 288

Both emperors campaigned vigorously on the Rhenus and Danubius and, in AD 288, jointly against the Alemanni in the former Agri Decumates. They advanced from respectively the Rhenus and Danubius, in a pincer movement, although they did not attempt to permanently re-occupy the territory. An attempt in AD 288 by Maximian to end the secession of Carausius was unsuccessful, his small and inexperienced fleet being no match for the veteran *Classis Britannica*, which met and defeated it in the Channel. Carausius' superior naval forces could supply their garrisons in northern Gaul and prevent any attempt to cross to Britannia in force. In AD 290, he offered a peace treaty to the Emperors, who, being unable to oppose him and to buy more time, accepted. Carausius felt that this gave him legitimacy and for his part did in fact hold the provinces of Britannia together and stabilised their finances; he also extended the shore fort system by establishing new forts and garrisons at Rutupiae and Portus Adurni (Portchester) and maintained the fleet in good order.

AD 293

To secure the succession, in AD 293, the Emperors appointed two Caesars or 'junior emperors', Constantius and Galerius. Constantius attacked and recovered from Carausius the secessionist territory in northern Gaul. Gesoriacum was invested and a mole built across the harbour mouth, sealing the harbour and trapping several of the fleet's ships inside. Carausius was murdered and succeeded by Allectus.

AD 294

In AD 294, forts were built on the left bank of the Danubius opposite the legionary bases of Aquincum and Bononia (Vidin in Bulgaria).[5] Other fortified landing places and outposts were set up on the barbarian shore, indicating a more aggressive forward policy and one that relied entirely on the riverine fleets for its implementation; effectively a return to the old imperial policy of defending the actual borders by establishing and maintaining strong garrisons and defences at the front. These fortified landing places consisted of a gateway, built parallel to and a little way inland from the river, between two towers which were in turn linked to the river's course by flank walls of between 65 and 150 feet (20 and 45 m). They were built on the river banks opposite to Roman forts and held by a light garrison and would thus allow for the landing of troops on the river bank, within a secure perimeter. As constant contact must be maintained between the fort and its outpost, presumably at least one of the fleet's ships was permanently allocated to each such installation, others being drafted in according to the level of activity.

AD 296

In the north, Constantius had made careful preparations, enlarging his loyal part of the *Classis Britannica* by building and equipping more ships. He invaded Britannia with two forces in September of AD 296, part of his fleet under his second-in-command, Asclepiodotus, crossed the Channel under cover of fog and made a successful landing along Southampton Water. Constantius sailed from Gesoriacum with the rest of his fleet and crossed

Another innovation at this time, although it may well have been invented earlier, came into wider service use, namely a new type of artillery piece which was a torsion-spring powered catapult with a long single throwing arm, mounted vertically with one end embedded in the now horizontally mounted spring and a sling at the other, free end. The arm was wound back to the horizontal by a winch and latched, a rock or perhaps burning material was loaded into the sling; when released the arm flew up and forward against a stop, the sling releasing its missile against a target up to 500 yards (457m) distant. Not for nothing did the Romans nickname the machine an onager, after the kick of the wild ass. By its format, the onager's frame sat square on the ground and could only be trained by manhandling the whole thing; although very destructive, the machine was not capable of fine aiming and the possibility of scoring a direct hit at range from a moving deck on a moving enemy ship must have been remote. There is no record of the type being used on board ship, although for siegework or bombardment of large, static targets, it could have been useful.

Confusingly, the term 'catapults' was applied to these machines and in a reversal of nomenclature, *ballista* was applied to the former arrow-shooting pieces; the previously clear distinction in naming and differentiating the arrow-shooting from the stone-throwing artillery becomes muddled henceforth. The period also saw the introduction into infantry formations of the *manuballista*, a small, torsion spring arrow shooter and the *arcuballista*, a non-torsion, presumably composite bow-powered arrow-shooter. Whether these were simply the former *cheiroballista* re-designated and the re-introduction of an updated *gastraphetes* or belly-bow, or completely new developments is not clear; once again however, their use as infantry weapons implies lightness and handiness and thus that they were also suitable for use on board ship.[6]

to the Tamesis estuary. The rebel fleet failed to locate either of Constantius' forces and cruised off Vectis but was not engaged. Allectus' forces were defeated in battle near to Calleva Atrebatum (Silchester), following which Constantius proceeded to restore the Province.[7] He ranged widely and took steps to deal with and to strengthen the northern borders. His ships cruised as far as the Orcades which 'he made run red with the blood of the Picts' (Eumenius) in naval raids upon those islands. It is not clear but likely that he took units of the lately rebel fleet with him to exercise them and bring them back under discipline with a long and arduous cruise, the inherent dangers of which would focus their attention to their duty. This campaign produced the first recorded mention of the Caledonians by that name. Whilst in Britannia, Constantius further extended the system of shore forts from the Tamesis to the Wash. There was a considerable decline in barbarian raids and piracy in the northern seas in the next half-century or so, leading to an economic boom period in Britannia and reflecting the security afforded by the high state of efficiency and effectiveness of its protecting fleet and defensive system.

AD 297

While Maximian dealt with problems in North Africa, Galerius secured the Danubius and Constantius, after his success in Britannia, secured the Rhenus. Galerius defeated the Persians and restored Armenia, adding some extra areas to Roman territory on the Tigris. With all of the Empire's rulers for once working together, the major military crises on many fronts could be and were dealt with and the Empire was left more secure than it had been for a long time.

The administration of the Empire was totally reformed with the provinces re-grouped into twelve large dioceses, many of the old provincial borders being swept away. Each Emperor controlled about a quarter of the frontiers from his respective headquarters, keeping with him a body of cavalry and specialised units which could be deployed as required to bolster troops drawn from frontier garrisons. Dispersal of imperial power among the four rulers meant that they could each be based nearer to the scenes of action and as the political power and the centre of government followed them to their respective centres, the importance of Rome itself, as capital, continued to recede and become notional. The period also saw an increase in the strength of the army, which grew to a strength in excess of 400,000 men, assisted by a system of conscription and the re-introduction of regular pay for serving personnel to supplement, if not to entirely replace, the system of payment in kind. Additionally bonuses were paid, for example, on the Emperor's birthday. A further development which affected the frontier garrisons, including the riverine fleets, was the allocation of land to the garrison troops as virtually private property for them to grow food and produce. In return their sons were conscripted in due course and the troops' loyalty secured by their having to defend their homes and livelihoods on the frontiers. Some serving barbarians were included in the system. Although giving some economic stability, the system also rendered the units concerned immobile and although there was some exchange of units between areas, overall their loyalties became, not surprisingly, more localised and rested upon their homes and farms. This additional degree of autonomy gained by these units in being more reliant upon providing their own provisions, rather than being dependent solely upon supplies from central depots would also in time lessen the authority of the central government and serve to corrode the unity of the state.

AD 305

Both Diocletian and Maximian, uniquely, retired in AD 305, leaving Constantius and Galerius as emperors who in turn appointed Maximinus Daia and Severus as Caesars. In AD 305, Constantius campaigned against the Picts in Caledonia but then died at Eboracum in AD 306. The army

'PAINTED'
SHIPS

> A t the same time a new type of scout ship was introduced for operation ahead
> of the bigger warships and powered by twenty oars per side, rated as *scaphae*
> *exploratoriae* or scouting skiffs and nicknamed *picati* or *pictae*, meaning painted; the
> ships were painted a sea blue-green, with sails similarly coloured and the crews even
> wore uniforms in a matching camouflage colour.[8] No other details of the type survive
> to enable determination as to whether it was a completely new type, a development
> of an existing one, or simply a re-classification of a class already in service. The use
> of such total camouflage could suggest several methods of use for the ship; firstly
> on the open sea, to sit astride known routes of navigation of the barbarians, who
> presumably would shy away the moment that they saw a regular Roman warship,
> their relative speeds being too similar to permit the latter to overhaul them; the
> scaphae could sneak up close enough to foil an escape while the bigger ships came
> up. Secondly, as with the lusoriae in use on the rivers, they could have been able to
> approach enemy coasts unseen to carry out raids, there being no reason after all why
> the Romans should not have carried the fight to their enemies, as they always had
> done in the past.

there proclaimed his son, Constantine, to be Emperor in his place. Galerius
accepted him as Caesar but in Rome, Maximian's son, Maxentius, with his
father's help, staged a coup and Severus was killed. Galerius' attempt to
unseat Maxentius failed and so a conference to settle matters was held in
AD 308, resulting in a new man, Valerius Licinianus, known as Licinius,
becoming a co-emperor in the west with Constantine as his Caesar; Galerius
and Maximinus Daia continued in the east. This still left Maxentius as
de facto master of Italy and Africa. Another usurper attempted to seize
Africa, threatening Maxentius and the vital grain supply to Italy. In AD 310
Maxentius, who could command the *Classis Misenensis*, or at least the naval
forces that had succeeded it, sailed and with the fleet, suppressed the usurper
and secured the province of Africa.[9]

There was an outbreak of piracy by barbarians after AD 306, with several
wide-ranging raids by small groups of boats, one at least on Britannia and
others, ominously, out to the Atlantic coasts as far as northern Hispania.[10]

AD 310   Probably as a result of this and as a punitive response, in AD 310 Constantine
campaigned against the Franks in what is now Belgium and Holland and
re-organised the naval forces on the Rhenus.[11] Galerius died in AD 311 and
Licinius moved east in an attempt to take over there. Open war was avoided
when he agreed with Maximinus Daia that he would have the Balkans,
leaving Maximinus to hold the rest of the east. Constantine meanwhile,
resolved to deal with Maxentius and advanced into Italy with his army,

culminating in his victory on 28 October AD 312 at the Milvian Bridge on the outskirts of Rome and the death of Maxentius.

    In the east, the uneasy truce broke down when Maximinus crossed the Hellespont with an army; Licinius met and defeated him in Thrace, leaving the Empire now divided between two ambitious men, an arrangement that would not last. After a first disagreement, Constantine invaded the Balkans in AD 316, defeating Licinius' forces but then losing to him in Thrace. In the ensuing peace treaty of AD 317, Constantine nevertheless gained the Balkan provinces and from AD 321, started to build up his fleet, enlarging and deepening the harbour at Thessalonika in preparation for it. The final break came in AD 323. Constantine gathered an army and his fleet and moved east. In June of AD 323, the opposing forces met in battle at Hadrianopolis (Adrianople, Edirne) in Thrace. Licinius was defeated and retreated into Byzantium, ready to withstand a siege. The key to this position was the Propontis and Licinius' fleet, under his admiral, Abantus sought to block the narrows of the Hellespont and to prevent Constantine's fleet, under his son Crispus, from forcing the passage through to Byzantium and isolating it from its lines of supply on the Asian shore.

    There are inconsistencies in the accounts of the ensuing decisive battle of the Hellespont, which make determination of all but the outcome difficult.[12] Firstly, Constantine's fleet is said to have numbered 2000 transports (probably an exaggeration) and two hundred triaconters (to re-introduce a by-then very ancient and obsolete term) or thirty-oared galleys. Licinius' fleet was of 350 triremes from Egypt, the Levant and Anatolia; other sources claim that Constantine had only eighty of the thirty-oared warships and Licinius 200 triremes, figures which seem more reasonable, bearing in mind the reduction and subsequent neglect of Roman seapower in the Mediterranean in the previous century. Licinius' fleet was presumably a concentration by all of the eastern squadrons, but must have comprised several types, not triremes alone. Thus the first inconsistency is that even had Abantus been a raging incompetent he could not lose, a triaconter, even with its oars double-manned, standing absolutely no chance against a trireme, let alone by being heavily outnumbered. The trireme is faster, higher, just as manoeuvrable and carries several times the number of marines and archers, able to shoot down into the probably unprotected small boats, or to simply ram them. Secondly, it has been noted that Constantine had been building up his fleet in anticipation of the war for a couple of years and this fleet must in fact have been the navy's western squadrons, renovated and strengthened and with ships the equal in size and strength to their eastern rivals. The problem is of course, in the definition of the types of ship engaged; given that the two halves of the same empire were the combatants, they both had the same technology, weapons, training and tactical background. Classification of warships is far from clear, most at this time being referred to as liburnians,

AD 316

AD 323

whether they were or not within the classical meaning and similarly, the by-now unfamiliar terms triaconter and trireme could have been applied to ships vastly different from those to which the terms were originally applied centuries before. The difference noted in Constantine's ships may in fact reflect a completely new, powerful type of warship, evolved to meet and overcome what must have been known of Licinius' much greater number of triremes. This is the last occasion upon which mention is made in the ancient sources of triremes taking part in an action, thereafter they disappear as a type from the record if not in actual fact.

Abantus formed up in close formation across the narrows, while Crispus formed his ships into two looser ranks and advanced. The first of Crispus' lines broke through Abantus' formation, the second line then advancing to exploit the breaks in a classic *diekplous* attack. Abantus' ships were too closely packed to manoeuvre and, after several hours of hard fighting, he withdrew to the Asiatic coast, having lost some 130 ships. This account gives rise to the next problem, which relates directly to the tactics of the battle. The narrows are, at their tightest, almost a mile wide (5280 feet, 1.6 km). At an average beam of twenty feet (6m), with oars retracted, it would take 264 of Abantus' ships to moor in a solid wall across from shore to shore and have 86 ships in reserve (in 480 BC the Persian King Xerxes had the Hellespont bridged at its narrowest and used 674 ships of all types, tied beam to beam to form a double row). Crispus' loose formations would be repelled by the 'solid wall' of ships and his tactic would thus be to have his ships' catapults shoot incendiaries to burn his enemy out of formation. There is no account of such an occurrence and one can only assume that the two fleets met in looser formation; in which case, with oars out and at say twenty yards per ship, Abantus could have blocked the narrows with only 88 of his ships and have formed nearly four lines across. Nevertheless, the narrows were not blocked and Crispus won the ensuing melee.[13]

Abantus was not beaten (which also calls into question the figure for his losses) as he intended to resume the battle on the following day, but a storm blew up, severely damaging or destroying half of his ships and leaving him too weak to oppose Crispus. This of course, leads to the final query. If Abantus' fleet suffered so severely in the storm, as is reported, then how is it that Crispus' ships, which could not have been that far away, escaped unscathed? Whatever the facts, Abantus was unable to continue the fight, or perhaps he just left with his ships and elected to become neutral. On learning of the loss of his fleet, Licinius abandoned Byzantium, using the rest of his ships to retreat to the Asiatic shore, where the ships were subsequently abandoned. When Crispus arrived with his transports, the army was embarked and Constantine pursued Licinius to Asia and there, finally, defeated him, to become sole Emperor.

CONSTANTINE

AD 330   Constantine made many changes in the thirteen years of his sole rule, apart from the building of his new capital at Constantinople, on the site of the old Greek town of Byzantium. To feed the expanding city, grain from Egypt was diverted from about AD 330, to Constantinople. By this time the traditional source of supply into the Aegean from the Bosporan Kingdom and Euxine littoral were becoming unreliable and restricted due to increasing incursions by the Goths and other barbarian tribes who were migrating into the northern Euxine area. The population of Rome had been falling for some time, placing less demand on Egyptian grain, increased production in Africa making up any difference needed. With the ending of the city of Rome's primacy in the Empire and the final transfer of the centre of power to the new capital in the east, the centuries-old flow of vast quantities of goods to its markets via its ports of Ostia and Portus declined to a trickle and with it, the importance of those ports. Likewise, any lingering claim to seniority by the Italian squadrons and bases as institutions had finally gone to the east with the Emperor and they lost their title of *Praetoriae*, although this had probably formally disappeared contemporaneously with the disbanding of the Praetorian Guard in AD 310.

Constantine's reforming military policy was to change fundamentally the centuries-old basis of imperial defence from one of seeking to maintain and tenaciously defend the borders themselves to one of defence in depth, leaving the borders policed but comparatively lightly manned but with large forces well to the rear in 'mobile field armies' to deal with invasions.[14] This was a formalisation of the situation more or less forced on the Romans in the chaos of the third century. Whereas it enabled a strong reserve force to be available to be directed to any point at which need arose, the first, obvious drawback was that henceforth the Romans would be fighting on their own land and in reaction always to the enemy's initiative, instead of at their own initiative, fighting ahead on their enemy's lands. Wherever the battle zone, the lands upon which it was placed would be damaged and diminished and would through lack of security, become de-populated and impoverished. The next problem was that in order to form the mobile army, which acquired the status of an elite, the frontier forces were stripped of their best men; there was no glory in being stuck in a lonely and isolated frontier post when one could be comfortably billeted well to the rear in a town with all the amenities and close to the centre of power and promotion. The supreme irony is that the navy's Praetorian fleets had always been a de facto reserve for the 'border' fleets, as opposed to the army whose whole strength was previously on the borders, with little or no reserves in the rear. Now the positions were reversed, with the army building up reserves to back the border forces, but the navy losing the like capacity and capability.

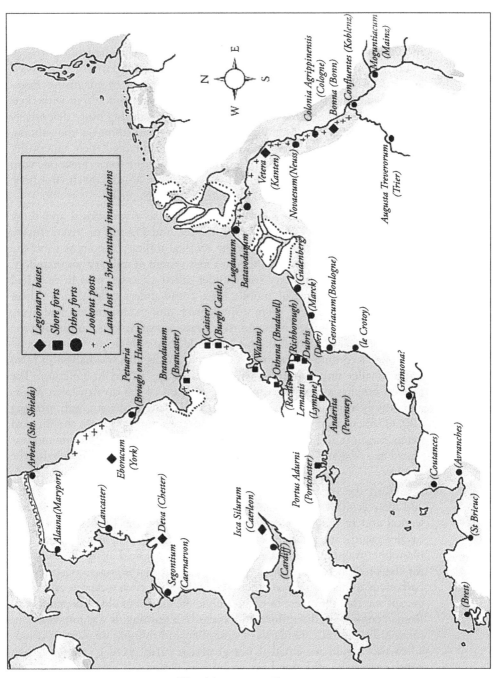

THE NORTHERN FRONTIER

The frontier troops were no longer expected to be able to stop and throw back an invader, only to hamper and hinder, but to leave them to the mobile army to catch and fight. There was no point in the frontier troops fighting all-out when they knew they were not to be supported or reinforced as previously and as the barbarians were incapable of practising siege-craft, they could shelter in their forts. Their morale sank along with their capabilities. They became a border police force, adopting more defensively sited and protected strongholds for their posts and losing in the process, that edge of discipline and training that had maintained their superiority over the barbarians for so long. The overall size of the forces grew but with falling standards, especially in the troops effectively wasted on the frontiers, the number of troops that could be rated as effective, fell.

The troops of the field army were known as *Comitatenses* and those of the frontier forces as *Limitanei* or 'border' and *Ripenses* or 'river' troops. The reforms also finally removed any residual military functions from the provincial governors, vesting them in a new system of military commanders. Each diocese had a military commander called a *Comes*, who in turn had under him several area or mobile force commanders called *Duces*. These officers were promoted from experienced unit commanders and were responsible for frontier forces and river fleets, as well as forts, combining the army and naval functions; their remit could span a single province or more than one, according to the area. The size of the legions was halved to form more, smaller units, more of which became specialised in function. The greatest emphasis was placed on the expansion of the cavalry, both scouts and heavily armoured. The field armies could have had a strength totalling 100,000 men; men who nevertheless had been removed from the forward defence against and thus deterrence of barbarian incursion. Command was vested in a *Magister Peditum* for the infantry and a *Magister Equitum* for the cavalry.

With the increasing attention and importance given to the cavalry and the recruitment of whole units of barbarians, serving under their own leaders and in their own tribal groups (including the Emperor's personal cavalry guard), the standard of infantry, even in the field army declined, in discipline, training and tactics. The morale of the field army did however, for the present, remain high. A further effect of the mass enlistment of barbarians under their own officers and with their own weapons and tribal groups was that they were in effect, unlike the *auxilia* of old, independent of Roman command, discipline and standards of training. It was impossible to impose the rigorous standards of discipline and training on Roman troops when they could see equal if not greater rewards given to the barbarian contingents who did not have to bother; without it the Roman citizen infantry lost their long-held advantage over their enemies.

The navy was also greatly affected by the changes; the Mediterranean fleets had, as has been seen, ceased to be save for a few squadrons at best of mostly smaller ships. There probably remained a reasonable force in the Euxine to cover the north Anatolian and Thracian coasts and to guard against a resumption of Gothic raids through the Propontis into the Aegean, especially with the increased importance of the area with the new capital at Constantinople. The Rhenus and Danubius fleets suffered most from the change of emphasis away from the borders and, reduced to *Ripenses* status, underwent the malaise of the other frontier forces.

The *Classis Britannica*, under a new commander, the '*Comes Maritimi Tractus*' was the least affected, as it already in effect fulfilled the functions of both the mobile army and frontier defence in one, in relation to its operational area of south-eastern Britannia and north-eastern Gaul.[15] It was thus ranked as *Comitatenses* or 'field army' and commanded by a *Comes*.

These arrangements proved helpful in enabling Constantine to campaign for power with his field army whilst leaving the borders guarded, if not entirely secure, and also at all times to keep the military power which underwrote his position close to him and avoid the rise of over-mighty generals elsewhere. All of this entailed huge military expenditure and the tax burden increased proportionately. An embassy was sent to Constantine from Ceylon at about this time, indicating that trade links with the Indian sub-continent were still in existence.

AD 332

AD 336

Threats to the Empire from outside had not entirely disappeared and perhaps realising that the defence of the Empire could not rely entirely upon reacting to its enemies initiatives, in AD 328 Constantine fought a major war against the Alemanni across the Rhenus and in AD 332 across the Danubius in the former Dacia against the Goths. He rebuilt Trajan's bridge across the Danubius and in AD 336, attacked the Sarmatians and effectively recovered much of Dacia itself for Rome, although not permanently,: it was lost after he died. Constantine built more fortified landing places on the banks opposite to Roman forts on the Rhenus and Danubius, to facilitate incursions into enemy territory; he also built permanent stone bridges at Colonia Agrippinensis and Moguntiacum over the Rhenus and at Oescus (Sistova or Svishtov, Bulgaria) over the Danubius, with protective fortifications at their ends. Both riverine fleets were bolstered by this fresh initiative on the borders and the renewal of a policy of taking the offensive to the enemy. The previous reorganisation which had taken place, with its drawbacks, remained however to continue its longer-term corrosive effects upon the fleets.

AD 337

Constantine died in AD 337, to be succeeded by his surviving sons, confusingly named Constantine II (who took Britannia, Gaul and Hispania), Constans (who took the rest of Europe and Africa) and Constantius II (who

AD 340   took the east and Egypt). In AD 340 Constantine II invaded Italy and was defeated and killed at Aquileia. The surviving brothers ruled their respective halves of the Empire for a further ten years until, in AD 350, Constans was killed and replaced by Magnentius. Constantius II moved west to defeat Magnentius in AD 351. In AD 352 he mounted a naval expedition which was sent to recapture the provinces of Africa and Hispania from forces loyal to Magnentius; of their composition nothing is known. By AD 353 Constantius II was sole ruler of the Roman world. With the Romans once more fighting each other the barbarians took their opportunity to re-commence raiding across the European frontiers, even seeking to settle on under-populated areas of the west bank of the Rhenus. The stability of the frontier was undermined and the barbarians even captured Colonia Agrippinensis. Trade on the river was effectively halted, naval patrols being difficult, indeed pointless, with both banks in barbarian hands. The Rhenus fleet had to withdraw to areas still under Roman control, such as they were, and up the tributary rivers such as the Mosella. The shipping of grain and goods from Britannia as well as the military link to the Rhenus was broken.

Barbarian seaborne raids had started once more and became progressively more frequent after about AD 350 along the coasts of Gaul and Britannia, by now on occasion in such strength that the raiders would beach their craft and penetrate inland; in the west the Irish had become restive and active and using curraghs, light but seaworthy boats made from frames covered with stretched hides and reminiscent of the coracles of the Gauls and Britons, crossed to sieze and increasingly to keep and to settle land in western Caledonia (where they were called Scottii) and also in western

AD 355   Wales.[16] In AD 355, Constantius II made his cousin Flavius Iulianus (Julian) commander of the troubled Rhenus frontier and Caesar in the west. Julian campaigned in AD 356, assisted by a simultaneous offensive northwards from the Alps by the Emperor. They drove Frankish invaders out of areas of the west bank of the middle Rhenus, around Colonia Agrippinensis and Confluentes; again in AD 357 on the upper Rhenus Julian's army inflicted a crushing defeat on the Franks near to Argentorate.[17]

AD 357   Also in AD 357, Julian learned from captured enemy scouts the location of places where the river was very low in summer and could be forded, near to Tres Tabernae (Saverne) and which the Alemanni had used; the Romans used the fords to attack the Alemanni in due turn.[18] Obviously the Rhenus fleet had not operated this far upriver. At the end of the year (AD 357) Julian blockaded a party of Franks who had secured themselves in an old Roman fort by a river. He surrounded the fort and had river patrols rowing up and down stream all night in their *lusoriae* to keep the river ice broken and to prevent any escape by that route across the otherwise frozen river. The Franks soon surrendered; that these were warships is confirmed by their being specified by the author Ammianus as 'scouting vessels'.

Julian adopted a 'forward' border policy, setting up new forts and strengthening border garrisons along the Rhenus and securing the submission of several of the tribes along its eastern banks. To protect his cross-river operations and reinforce the riverine fleet, Julian had a squadron of forty river warships built and eventually built up a fleet of 600 ships and boats of all types.[19] The fleet included many transports which he used to re-establish the link with Britannia and in convoys to bring grain from there to supply his campaigns. Julian had firmly re-established Roman control of the river and overcome all opposition on the Lower Rhenus by AD 358. In AD 360, he

AD 360

sent reinforcements to Britannia, where they drove off Pictish invaders past Hadrian's Wall and restored the northern frontier. By this time, barbarian seaborne raiding had become commonplace and the already overworked Roman defences were further stretched by the appearance of pirates and raiders emanating from Caledonia and Ireland and operating in the west. Julian was overall very successful both militarily and as an administrator and his troops declared him Augustus of the west in AD 360. In that same year, the last king of the Bosporan Kingdom died. His country having by now been absorbed by the Goths, no successor arose.

Before the looming confrontation between the two rivals came to a

AD 361

tragic conclusion, Constantius II died in November AD 361, leaving Julian as sole Emperor. He again campaigned aggressively across the Rhenus but

AD 363

was distracted by a Persian invasion of the eastern provinces. In AD 363 he moved to counter this and in turn invaded Persia, advancing to their capital at Ctesiphon. In support of this campaign, he used fifty warships and 1100 supply boats on the River Euphrates.[20] The warships one can imagine as types similar to the river patrol boats in use on the Rhenus and Danubius, with provision to rig awnings over the decks to give shelter from the summer sun. No permanent Roman fleet on the Euphrates is known despite the long border which rested upon it; probably they did have patrol boats, operated by the local military commands and not themselves amounting to enough of a permanent force to justify designation as a fleet. The fifty ships were thus those already on the river, augmented by others built there for the expedition. Julian and his forces advanced virtually unopposed down the Euphrates and utilised the major canal which ran south-west, linking it with the Tigris just north of the Persian capital. Having failed to bring the Persians to a decisive battle, Julian was in an over-extended position and he decided to withdraw northward up the Tigris in the face of increasing Persian attacks, to meet reinforcements coming down that river. First however, he ordered the burning of nearly all of the ships and boats to save having to work them upstream which would slow the army down. Conversely, the army now had to carry all of its goods and supplies, without the capacity of the river transport. In the course of the withdrawal the Emperor was wounded and died.

THE EMPIRE DIVIDED

AD 364   After the death of his short-lived successor, Jovian, the generals elected
Valentinian to be Emperor (AD 364); he appointed his brother Valens to be
co-Emperor, in charge of the east while he took over Illyria and the west,
again using Mediolanum as his capital. In AD 367, Picts, Saxons, Irish and
Franks, acting together in a pre-arranged attack, assailed Britannia from all
sides. Both of the local commanders, Fullofaudes, the *Dux Britanniorum*
and Nectarides, the *Comes Maritimae* were killed and the province was in
chaos. This is the only mention in the ancient sources of the rank of *Comes
Maritimae* and perhaps was one exclusive to the *Classis Britannica*, the only
one of the 'old' imperial formations to have remained recognisable and intact
and if anything to have continued to flourish. The fact that its commander is
ranked as *Comes* and thus senior to the *Dux Britanniorum* is also significant
in confirming that the fleet remained the prime instrument for the defence
of the province.

AD 368   Valentinian sent two expeditions to try to restore the situation, with
only limited effect. In AD 368 a new commander, Flavius Theodosius landed
with additional forces at Rutupiae. The father of the future emperor was
successful in military operations against the intruders, which included
counter-raids and interdiction by the navy against the barbarian homelands,
handing them a taste of their own medicine. Theodosius had a long chain
of signal stations erected along the coasts of Britannia, on the west stretching
from the legionary base at Deva to Hadrian's Wall and on the east, from
Hadrian's Wall southward to the mouth of the Abus, to link with the existing
system there. The stations were organised in series, each dependent on an
inland fort containing troops that could sally forth to deal with a landing
at short notice and which thus complemented those areas covered by naval
patrols. The province was restored by AD 369, but it never really recovered
from the amount of damage that had been done.[21]

Between AD 367 and 369, the Romans fought a war against Goths on
the north bank of the Lower Danubius, a period of intense activity for the
fleets of the river. The supply route for the support of the campaigns was
by sea through the Euxine, the large seagoing transports being offloaded in
the delta onto river transports for onward transmission to the garrisons and
troops along the river. The fleet also secured crossing points on the enemy
bank and oversaw the construction and protection of pontoon bridges across
AD 369   the river. Finally, upon the conclusion of peace in AD 369, the fleet secured
ships, moored mid-stream upon which the Emperor Valens met the Goth
King to sign the peace treaty.[22] The Roman base at Chersonesus in the Crimea
probably still persisted as a lone outpost in the Euxine, being reinforced
AD 372   and the fortifications enhanced as late as AD 372. Valentinian's son Gratian
succeeded his father who died on the Danubius front in AD 375. Gratian's

OXEN
POWERED
SHIPS

> An anonymous author in about AD 370, proposed a warship to be propelled by oxen, hitched to wheels at the side of a galley that would act like oars, i.e. a paddle wheel; horse-drawn ones were used in the seventeenth to nineteenth centuries AD , but in the fourth, such ingenuity found no practical application. The engineer Vitruvius also described a device to be an odometer for naval use but no indication has been found that it may have been built and used.[23]

infant half-brother, Valentinian II was then appointed his (nominal) co-emperor.

In the east, Valens had sought to increase security along the Danubius by building more forts with more garrisons and tried to hold the Lower Danubius and Balkans against the Goths. The eastern or Ostrogoths had settled around the north of the Euxine Sea. They were assailed and displaced by the onslaught of the Huns and in turn fell upon and pushed the western or Visigoths, who were settling north of the Danubius in Dacia and the Hungarian plain. These Visigoths appealed to cross into Moesia and Valens AD 376 had allowed them to seek refuge there in the summer of AD 376. Their crossing of the river was largely effected by the ships and transports of the fleet and patrols were then maintained against incursion by other barbarians, who were intercepted. The Visigoths were badly mishandled by the Roman authorities and, joined by other tribesmen, rose and attacked the Empire. Valens tried to throw them back across the river but was killed, along with the effective destruction of his mobile field army in the catastrophic battle AD 378 near Hadrianopolis in August AD 378.

Gratian, now sole Emperor, appointed Theodosius the younger as Emperor in the east in AD 379. The latter fought a four-year war against the Goths, ending with a treaty in AD 382 which allowed them to settle in Moesia along the Danubius and to live semi-autonomously. Although AD 382 they were required to supply troops, these would remain under their own leaders and organisation and thus the effect was to create an all-but independent kingdom, under its own rulers and arms, within the borders of the Empire; an entire population of non-Romans in what had become a sparsely populated area, the remaining Roman inhabitants of which were duly forced out. The effect, despite the troops which were in fact supplied in considerable numbers and who fought loyally, was to remove that territory as a province of the Empire and also therefore, to remove the Lower Danubius from Roman control and as a real border.[24] The *Classis Moesica* or what remained of it, presumably made its way either upriver to Roman territory, or towards the delta and the Thracian coast. Theodosius made an ultimately vain attempt to limit the 'settlers' by a code banning them from being trained in the building of ships, they were also if possible, to be kept from settling on coasts.

AD 383   Gratian lost military support through poor judgment and in 383, the army in Britannia declared its commander, the *Dux Britanniorum*, Magnus Clemens Maximus, to be Emperor. He then moved to Gaul, once more stripping Britannia of its best protecting troops, leaving it virtually defenceless and hastening the decline of the province. As a result, the incidence of barbarian raids all around the coasts increased. Presumably the repeated diminution of forces in Britannia also applied to naval personnel, reducing therefore the strength and effectiveness of the *Classis Britannica*, which nevertheless must also have rallied to Magnus' cause. Of the fate of the commanding *Comes*, nothing is known. Gratian was killed at Lugdunum and Magnus had effective control north of the Alps.[25]

AD 386   In AD 386 another huge number of Goths sought to migrate across the Lower Danubius which would, if permitted, have totally unbalanced the fragile peace attained with the Visigoths already there. Good intelligence enabled Theodosius to concentrate his forces against the threat of further invasion, command being vested in Petronius Probus. The Romans waited until the Goths had amassed and embarked in a vast number of boats and rafts, many of them makeshift, to make a mass crossing, probably in the area of the base at Noviodunum. At this point the Danubius fleet, reinforced with every warship that the Romans could get into the River, attacked and to quote the author Zosimus, 'when the signal was given the Romans sailed out in large ships with very strong oars and sank every boat they encountered. Because of the great weight of their armour, none of the warriors who jumped overboard were saved. The boats that escaped ran into other ships along the shore...none could penetrate this barrier of Roman ships. The slaughter was greater than in any previous naval battle and the river was choked with bodies and weapons.'[26]

AD 388   In AD 387 Magnus attempted to invade Italy, briefly occupying Rome in January of AD 388; he then marched to the northern end of the Adriatic, supported by a fleet commanded by one Andragathus, his *Magister Equitum*. The origin of this fleet is unknown, it may have been raised from the units brought from southern Gaul and Italy and with ships from Ravenna. Theodosius sent his own eastern fleet with marines to secure Sicily and to recover Italy, securing its own flank by an expeditionary force sent from Egypt to Africa. The Emperor himself took his army through Illyria to seek a confrontation with Magnus.[27] It is worthy of comment to note, even at this late stage in the Empire's fortunes, the scale of strategic planning and operations of which its military command was capable. Not content with simply gathering an army and looking for Magnus, the Emperor's campaign was planned on a continental scale, moving forces in a broad sweep across North Africa and the Mediterranean, south and west of Magnus towards Italy and Hispania while blocking him in the Balkans, forces which although unlikely to directly confront him, would progressively restrict him. They met in battle in July near Aquileia where Magnus was defeated and killed. His fleet must have escaped as it was later caught and routed off Sicily although again by whom is not clear but presumably by the fleet previously brought from the east by Theodosius, or by western squadrons that had remained loyal. Valentinian II was left as emperor in the west but in AD 392, he was murdered and succeeded by an usurper, Eugenius, who was in turn defeated by Theodosius in AD 394.

AD 392

After only a year as sole emperor, Theodosius died at Mediolanum in AD 395, dividing the Empire between his two young sons, Arcadius in the east and Honorius in the west, a division that would now be permanent and making more or less official the separation into two empires that had been made when Valentinian had split it with his brother. The armed forces of the Empire as a whole numbered about a half million men, with frontier forces and mobile armies which included a large number of specialised units. At this, the turn of the fifth century, the Empire was still largely intact both territorially and as a political entity. By now, production of military equipment and weapons had been centralised upon government arms factories, fifteen in the east and twenty in the west. In the division, Melita went to the Eastern Empire, who retained it until it was lost to the Arabs in AD 870. Effective power in the west increasingly rested with the senior army officers, by now commonly 'Romanised' barbarians whose power and influence increased in direct proportion to the weakness of the emperors. The western borders were now almost constantly overrun by raiders despite the efforts of the forces, which by now contained a large proportion of barbarian manpower, drawn from the tribes themselves or from new settlers, such as the Franks now settling in north-eastern Gaul.[28]

AD 395

The Rhenus fleet, although reduced, was still active, as was the *Classis Britannica* on the north coasts. The latter seems to have been disbanded at about this time and to have been replaced by two formations, a *Classis Sambrica* under the commander of Belgica Secunda, stationed on the Channel coast of Gaul and a *Classis Anderitianorum*, presumably based at Anderita (Pevensey), to cover the northern Channel coast; this formation is shown in the *Notitia Dignitatum* as being at Paris under the commander for Gaul but this is more likely to have been a temporary posting.[29] Overall however, the impression is gained of fleets trying to control the Channel, but losing any semblance of control over the North Sea to the barbarians and that the Romans had in fact effectively conceded the seas around Britannia, seeking only to concentrate on keeping the cross-Channel communications open. The fleets of the Mediterranean were reduced to a few squadrons, although this proved enough, in the absence of opposition, to maintain it as a Roman lake. With the destruction by the non-nautical Huns of the Goth kingdom to the north of the Euxine, pressure from that quarter lessened. The *Classis Pannonica* probably still operated but the fleet on the lower half of the Danubius had ceased to exist with the ending of unified Roman command of the river.

AD 396   Honorius' army commander, Flavius Stilicho had taken an army to Britannia in AD 396 to restore the situation there, which had once more become parlous, but had to withdraw it in AD 401 to meet a Goth threat. He did manage to strengthen the coastal defences and in the north he concluded alliances with the Votadini and Damnoni, who occupied the area north of Hadrian's Wall.[30] At this time a unit of *exploratores* is listed as serving in Britannia at Portus Adurni; this nomenclature normally refers to cavalry scouts but as these would be of little use at Portus Adurni. This unit was logically that which provided crews for the *scaphae exploratorae* stationed there.[31]

AD 397   In AD 397 the Count of Africa rebelled and Stilicho sent a force of perhaps 10,000 troops by sea to suppress him before the rebellion could affect the supply of grain to Italy. A fleet for this expedition was prepared 'in the harbours of Etruria' (according to the historian Claudian), a strange choice of description for a foray to Africa; more likely the fleet was gathered at Misenum.[32]

AD 401   In AD 401 the Visigoths under their King, Alaric, moved to invade Italy, but were repelled by an army under Stilicho outside Mediolanum. Once more troops were brought from Britannia and other areas to bolster Stilicho's forces, which went on to defeat Alaric twice more. He led a charmed life however and each time, managed to escape and re-build his forces. Together they formed a cancer roaming almost at will and forging a destructive and disruptive path through an empire which seemed to lack the will as well as the strength to eradicate them and contributing more than somewhat to its demise. He was aided in his career by the poor relationship between east and west and by increasing indiscipline in the Roman army which prevented pursuit after a battle to finish him off. Germanic people entered Italy in AD 405 and were destroyed, but in the winter of AD 406, the Rhenus froze hard near Moguntiacum, preventing the river patrols and allowing Vandals, Alans and Sueves to cross, whole tribes at a time, and they poured across Gaul in their tens of thousands. The frontier defences were greatly weakened and Gaul left virtually defenceless by the absence of the mobile army, which had been stationed in Italy to deal with the Visigoths.

            Honorius and the Court moved to Ravenna, shielded by its impenetrable marshes and guarded by its fortified naval base and what was left of the
AD 407   imperial fleet. In AD 407, the troops in Britannia tried to organise a leader and

PILGRIMAGE

By this time the practice of pilgrimage to the Holy Land from all parts of the now-Christian Empire was growing at a rapid rate, despite the early churches' condemnation of the practice, and it most probably fuelled a fair proportion of the maritime traffic of the Mediterranean. The navy could no longer guarantee total safety and freedom of the sea, as it had for so long done, and regular patrols were a thing of the past. Accordingly, pilgrims had to take their chances on seas now once more subject to some piracy, although still nowhere near to the extent of the scourge of the first century BC. The imperial navy in the east and the west strove hard to maintain control and to keep open the trade routes and ports of the basin and, of course, to deny the same to the barbarians. Overall it can be considered to have succeeded until the fall of Carthage to the Vandals.[33]

elected their Governor, Constantinus to be Constantine III and proclaimed him emperor; they next invaded Gaul restoring the Rhenus frontier once more with nearly all of the troops, unbelievably again leaving the island defenceless. Although the Rhenus frontier was restored, the barbarians who had already crossed were sealed inside the Empire; no attempt to deal with them emanated from the Emperor who seemed more concerned about the rebel Constantine, regardless of the fact that they were in truth on the same side and the barbarians were left unchallenged to roam and plunder Gaul as they fancied and proceeded to do.

AD 408

In AD 408 Alaric and his Visigoths again entered Italy and laid siege to Rome, Honorius withdrew troops from the north but failed to end the usurpation of Constantine, who remained in Britannia and Gaul. Also in AD 408, Arcadius died, to be succeeded by the infant Theodosius II as Emperor of the east, where effective power was wielded by Anthemius, the Praetorian Prefect of an east itself beset by problems and unable to lend assistance to the west. In any event, a split having been made, it perhaps already looked upon itself as a separate entity. In AD 409, taking advantage of the lack of an adequate garrison and the absence of any naval forces, the Picts and Irish again invaded north-western Britannia and western Wales.

AD 410

In late AD 409, the barbarians in Gaul had managed to evade the defences and cross the Pyrenees into Hispania. In AD 410, having first captured Ostia, gained control over the granaries and intercepted the main supply route, effectively rendering the city unable to resist, Alaric and his Visigoths sacked Rome, the first time that it had been overrun for 800 years. After this, Alaric moved through Italy intending to try and sail for Africa but such ships as he gathered were wrecked by a storm as he was preparing to cross to Sicily; he died shortly afterwards and the Visigoths made their way by land out of Italy into Gaul. The most surprising thing is that it had proved impossible for Honorius to put an army into the field to destroy Alaric, whose numbers were not great; the price perhaps of reduced recruitment of Romans and over-dependence upon barbarian levies, leading to the rapid decline of the western armies. The mobile army in Italy indeed seems to have vanished or perhaps was held close to and for the defence of Ravenna and thus easily by-passed. In any event, Honorius made ready to flee with his entourage to Constantinople and ordered his ships at the naval base of Ravenna to be prepared; just then, a force of some 4000 trained troops were ferried into Ravenna from the east to reinforce his garrison and he was persuaded to stay.

Under the pressure of these invasions, Honorius wrote, in AD 410, in response to requests for help from Britannia to say that he could do nothing and that they should look to their own defence; having suffered the successive stripping of troops from its garrison in attempts to bolster the Rhenus frontier, the province was left with little with which to defend itself. Of the northern fleets, nothing remained as an organised force and any remaining ships may have been used by local commanders on an ad hoc basis only. In AD 411 the pretender Constantine III was defeated at Arelate (Arles) in Gaul and in AD 412, Honorius was able to appoint a new *Comes Britanniorum* and to send some reinforcements.[34]

AD 412

In January of the same year, there was an edict issued in the name of the Eastern Emperor Theodosius II relating to the reinforcement of the forces deployed in the provinces of Moesia Secunda and Scythia, the former being that stretch of the Danubius opposite to what had been the province of Dacia and the latter the lowest part of the river and its delta. Both areas had been within the remit of the old *Classis Moesica* in former times. Although the fleet had been strong enough as late as AD 386 to destroy an attempted invasion by Goths across the river, it must have suffered or been neglected and had virtually ceased to exist in the depredations of the late fourth century. Now that the Visigoths had moved away to the west, the Romans could re-occupy the lands in Moesia and Thrace that Theodosius had given to them, returning their border to the line of the Danubius as previously, with the re-garrisoning of the border forts and the re-establishment of a naval presence on the river. The border needed further strengthening against future perceived threats (which would materialise in the form of the Huns) and accordingly, a new construction programme had been put in hand some time before and the ships so produced were now being allocated. A few at least of the older ships must have survived but in poor or outdated condition yet remained of sufficient value to be worth refitting for further service. The decree called for the deployment of ninety new and ten refitted ships in Moesia and 110 new and fifteen refitted ships in Scythia. The ten to be refitted for Moesia are specified as *lusoriae*, additionally for this formation, four *iudicariae* and ten *agrarienses* are required, together with another five of the former and twelve of the latter assigned to the Scythian fleet.[35]

All of these ships were built presumably to standardised designs but of the two types which are referred to as *iudicariae* and *agrarienses*, no details are known. The former may well refer to the former *codicariae* or transports or perhaps even for liaison duties and the latter for reconnaissance; it could well be that these names relate to functions rather than to specific ship-types. The fleet on the Danubius was later further strengthened following a damaging incursion by the Huns. A final observation is that there was no attempt to re-form the *Classis Moesica*, but that the two naval formations were dealt with individually and by reference to their respective provinces only.

THE FINAL ACTS

The Empire in the West was slipping away, migrations of tribes from the east beginning to settle in its territory in numbers too vast to be assimilated and changing its nature by those very numbers. The best that the 'Empire' could do was to try to retain some form of control and *Romanitas* over the increasingly disparate territories. In the east, the Huns had destroyed any last vestige of the Bosporan Kingdom and moved to the area north of the Danubius and had raided across it. By AD 418 the Visigoths had taken over Aquitania in western Gaul and established an independent kingdom there, which maintained a fleet in the Bay of Biscay, inherited from the Romans who were retained as officers to run it. Ironically, the Visigoths had to maintain it as protection against continuing piratical raids by their fellow barbarians. The Franks were doing the same in setting up a kingdom in northern Gaul, cutting off communication with Britannia and sacking the former legionary base of Augusta Treverorum in AD 419. The *Comes Britanniorum* had to withdraw with his troops to reinforce what remained of Roman Gaul.

AD 413   In AD 413 the Count of Africa, one Heraclian, sought power and rebelled; he gathered a fleet, mostly of transports (and said to have been of 3700 ships!) and sailed to take Rome. He was met and defeated in a battle on the Tiber and escaped with only one ship.[36] Nothing is known of the actual strength of his forces or of the loyal force, led by the *Magister Militum*, Constantius, which met them. It is puzzling however that Constantius could meet and deal with a rebel, but not the barbarians, also that the fleet was unable to intercept the rebels although it could well have played a part in the loss of their fleet. It is certain that Constantius did have the use of the navy and that he used it to excellent effect in retaining Roman control over the Mediterranean; he was the first and indeed the only Roman commander for a very long time to have any appreciation of the use and importance of sea power. He was further assisted by the weather when storms wrecked Goth attempts to assemble a fleet in Baetica. Large parts of Gaul and Hispania were now ruled by various barbarian tribes who acknowledged Roman suzerainty to a greater or lesser extent, but Roman control continued along the coasts of both, secured by the fleet and possession of the granary of Africa. In AD 416 this control enabled a blockade which forced the Visigoths into a treaty of alliance with Honorius, who proceeded to use them against other tribes in Hispania.

AD 416

Naval operations in the western Mediterranean became more common at this time and secured a resurgence of Roman power and influence, supported by armies which, throughout east and west, still numbered perhaps a quarter of a million men. These were however still divided with many tied down as frontier garrisons and the remainder in smallish mobile armies; above all, as has been noted, the standard of the troops was not what it had been except in cavalry. In siege warfare and the whole sphere of naval operations, the Romans still held a monopoly. Attempts continued to deny the seas to the invaders and in AD 419 an edict actually sentenced to death some Romans who had been showing the Vandals how to build ships.

AD 423

Honorius died in AD 423 but with the legitimate heir, the infant Valentinian III, absent in Constantinople, a usurper, Ioannes, siezed the initiative at Rome to become Western Emperor. Theodosius II in the east, marched against him and, supported by his fleet, took Aquileia and then in AD 425, assaulted Ravenna from the sea. In a surprise amphibious attack the usurper was killed and the new Emperor duly installed.[37] Real power was now exercised by the general Aetius, who struggled to keep the Empire together and to restore Gaul, with some success. In Britannia, Vortigern was elected leader in AD 424 and went on the offensive against the Irish settlers who were seeking to detach parts of Wales from the Empire. He dealt with them and to deter further incursions, had an adequate naval force deployed in the Irish Sea and Sabrina estuary, the last mention of an organised naval force in the province. Pleas to Aetius for reinforcements could not be met however, leading Vortigern's successor and son, Vortigern II, to the dubious solution of actually recruiting Saxons as troops, who, once in Britannia, stayed.

AD 424

The resurgence of Roman sea-power was to be shortly challenged as the Vandals, under their leader Gaiseric, had by AD 422 made their way into southern Hispania and had acquired some ships. With these they started to raid the coast of North Africa and seized the Balearic Islands. They continued their migration and despite Theodosius' law and the punishment of offenders, secured enough ships and crews to cross to North Africa from Hispania in AD 429. The ships were provided by the disaffected Roman Governor, who may of course have simply been taking any step just to keep them moving and to get them out of his area. The whole Vandal population of about 80,000 people crossed, of which some 25,000 were warriors. For

AD 429

the next ten years, they gradually made their disruptive way eastwards across North Africa.[38]

AD 432

The Roman Count of Africa, Boniface, had, at most, between 10,000 and 20,000 troops and although defeated and losing Hippo to the invaders, held Carthage. There was however, rivalry between Boniface and Aetius, which led to civil war between them. Incredibly, and despite the Vandals being in the western part of Africa, Boniface crossed to Italy with his army in AD 432 to seek power. He was met and beaten by Aetius outside Ariminium.[39] It is easy to see how this greatly helped Gaiseric by leaving Africa almost defenceless. For his part, Aetius was fully committed in Gaul where, by holding the Rhenus/Danubius line, the mass migrations from the east had been stopped. He thus had to accept the Vandals' presence and leave them to their own devices. They soon took Carthage (in AD 439) and proceeded to consolidate their occupation of the entire province by seizing the grain fleet there. From this, they proceeded to acquire and build a fleet of up to 120 warships that enabled them to dominate, and then occupy, Sardinia, Corsica and Sicily by AD 440. The Romans had lost naval supremacy in the central Mediterranean for the first time since the Punic Wars over 650 years before.

AD 440

The Eastern Emperor responded to this by immediately sending a naval expedition to oppose the Vandals. The expedition failed. At last, both Eastern and Western Emperors were united in their belief in the necessity to maintain that control of the seas which had been taken for granted for too long. However, the means of securing that control, the navy, had been reduced to such a degree that when, for the first time in four centuries, there was a naval rival in the Mediterranean, it was not only unable to prevent that rival from coming into being, its original purpose, but unable to overcome it once it had. After this hasty attempt to deal with the Vandals, the Eastern Empire was prevented from making any further attempt at dealing with them and helping the west by constant and serious attacks upon themselves throughout the AD 440s by Huns from across the Danubius.

AD 450

Theodosius II died in AD 450, to be replaced by Marcian who, although he had campaigned against the Vandals in North Africa, had no filial feeling towards the west, which had by now ceased to be an organic state anyway. Nevertheless at this time an official, the *Comes Officiarum*, who already had responsibility for the weapons factories (*fabricae*), was given the additional duty of making an annual inspection of the state of the frontiers, frontier troops and the frontier forts and guard boats and reporting their condition, at this stage a function more or less without an object. Marcian did adopt a more offensive policy towards the Hun incursions. The eastern fleets continued in existence and their eastern seas remained reasonably peaceful and secure.

The Huns, under Attila, invaded Gaul in AD 451, to be met and beaten
by Aetius at the Battle of Catalaunian Fields (Chalons). In AD 452, Attila
was back, but died the following year, his empire dying with him. Jealous
of Aetius' power, Valentinian III killed him, only to be himself killed in
turn. He was succeeded by a litany of Emperors of the West made and
unmade at the behest of Germanic warlords who effectively ruled, backed
by their largely barbarian armies; of actual 'Roman' troops little remained;
frontier troops, isolated and unpaid, had dispersed and the remnants of the
comitatenses, lacking discipline and training, were indistinguishable from the
barbarians anyway.

            In Britannia a revolt by the Anglo-Saxons led to a defeat of the Romano-
British army there and the setting up of an independent Saxon kingdom
in the south-east. This was followed by their progressive take-over of the
country; the province was lost.[40] Barbarian raiders continued to range widely
in the north, both against 'Roman' coasts and those now ruled by their own
barbarian predecessors and settlers; in AD 455 a band of Heruli some 400
strong, in seven obviously quite sizeable ships, raided as far as the north
coast of Hispania, having sailed from their homeland on the north coast of
Europe, east of the Rhenus.

            The Vandals landed at Ostia, attacked Rome and plundered it in AD
455. There were still some 'Roman' forces in the west however and the
Vandals did not have it all their own way. In AD 456 the Roman commander
Claudius Ricimer, himself a Suevian, using a Roman fleet, defeated the
Vandals in an action off Corsica. Having also stopped their advance in
Sicily, he beat them again in a naval action off Agrigentum in the same year.
Ricimer's nominee, the Emperor Majorian, repelled the Vandal fleet from
the mouth of the Tiber in AD 457. The ancient port of Ostia had continued
to decline and was by now all but abandoned. Majorian in AD 460, went on
to prepare a war fleet in Carthago Nova in Hispania, gathering some 300
ships, presumably intending a re-invasion of Africa, but before it could be
completed it was found and destroyed by the Vandal fleet.

            As to the types of these last Roman ships, the much later Eastern
Emperor Leo VI (AD 886–912) in his book *Tactica*, described three types of
ship which were called by the name of a *dromon*, a term which had come into
common use in fact by the sixth century. He defined what had obviously
become the dominant warship type as a light, swift warship powered by a
single reme, with a protective deck over the rowers; the ship had a single
mast probably with a lateen rig with a three- or four-cornered sail and with
a ram; a lateen-rigged liburnian or even a penteconter revisited. The ram had
developed into an upturned 'spur-like' form, projecting above the waterline,
designed not to puncture an enemy hull so much as to ride up and over
a bulwark, smashing it or causing the enemy to roll under it and become

swamped, an indication that the potential enemy craft tended to be smaller, open, i.e. un-decked, boats and susceptible to this kind of attack. The type was simple to build and required a modest crew and thus could be quickly deployed in numbers. These ships were circa 100 to 130 feet (30–40 m) long and up to 20 feet (6m) in beam, powered by a single reme of only fifty oars, rowed through oar ports in the sides; the type would later grow and become a bireme of greater dimensions.[41]

The south and west part of Britannia were still 'Roman' at this time although no longer under imperial control and, almost as a postscript, a contingent from there is reported to have fought for the Emperor Anthemius in Gaul. These troops were most likely ferried across the Channel by whatever ships they could commandeer and it is too much to assume that they had any but a few naval craft left to assist them from the formations that had succeeded the *Classis Britanica*.

AD 467   There was further naval activity in AD 467 when Gaiseric and his Vandal fleet raided the Peloponnese and the Empire, both east and west, decided at last to deal with the Vandal Kingdom. The Eastern Emperor, Leo prepared a huge force, scouring the eastern Mediterranean for ships to provide a fleet of, it is said, a thousand ships, most of which were transports for the army of 100,000 men, all under the command of his brother-in-law, Basiliscus. The Western Emperor, Anthemius contributed his own forces and ships, under the Count of Dalmatia, Marcellinus, who successfully cleared the Vandals from Sardinia and then joined forces with the Eastern Fleet.

The Romans landed en masse near Hermaeum but delayed instead of attacking Carthage at once. This delay gave the Vandals time to fully prepare their fleet and five days later, with the wind in their favour, they sailed to the attack. The Vandals caught the Roman fleet completely by surprise close-packed at anchor and attacked with fire-ships and rams, wiping half of it out. The rest retreated to Sicily where Marcellinus was murdered and the campaign was abandoned.[42] This is the last mention of a 'Roman' fleet in existence as distinct from the former eastern imperial squadrons, which had now become the separate Eastern Empire's own navy. That navy was, of course, the direct successor to the navy established by Augustus and would endure for centuries to come. From this point it becomes part of another story; that of the successor empire in the east, formed from what had been the eastern half of the Roman Empire. The last emperor in the west, the boy

AD 476   Romulus Augustulus, retired (or perhaps was retired) on the 4 September AD 476. Although they undoubtedly did not realise it at the time, this date signified the formal end to the Roman Empire of the West.

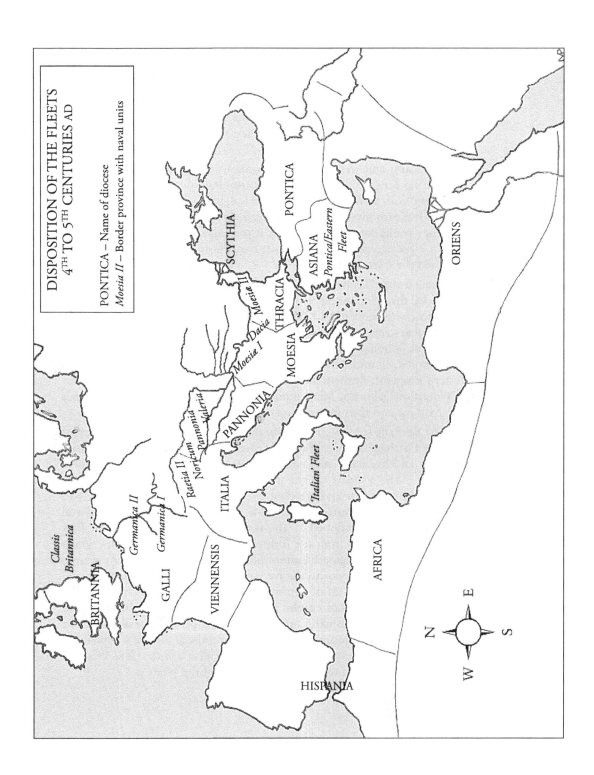

DISPOSITION OF THE FLEETS
4TH TO 5TH CENTURIES AD

PONTICA – Name of diocese
Moesia II – Border province with naval units

NOTES

1. Ashe, *Kings and Queens of Early Britain*.
2. Starr, *The Influence of Seapower on Ancient History* and *The Roman Imperial Navy*. Also Haywood, *Dark Age Naval Power*.
3. After the remains of five such vessels discovered at Mainz; similar types have been recovered from the Danube. Morrison, *The Age of the Galley*.
4. Bounegru & Zahariade, *Les Forces Navales du Bas Danube*.
5. Marsden, *Greek and Roman Artillery* and also Michael Lewis, 'Trajan's Artillery', in *Current World Archaeology* No.3. The problem is the almost total lack of any pictorial representation of artillery pieces on ships, indeed in this late period there is a dearth of pictures of ships themselves; but also see Vegetius IV.44.
6. Austin & Rankov, *Exploratio*.
7. Ashe, *Kings and Queens of Early Britain*.
8. Vegetius IV.37.
9. See Starr, an inscription of 302 by the Fleet Praefect of the *Classis Praetoria Misinensis* shows that the fleet still existed in that form at that time, but in what strength is another question.
10. Haywood, *Dark Age Naval Power*.
11. The extent and manner of this reorganisation is not known save that frontier armies and river fleets were to be commanded by a new military officer called a *Dux*.
12. Zosimus e.g.
13. The accounts also take no account of the current which runs through the narrows at a steady 2.5 knots towards the Aegean, sweeping the whole channel until it gets to Dardanos where the bend pushes it mid-stream and produces a half-knot eddy on the European side. Thus Abantus had the current with him and Crispus had to row against it.
14. Luttwak, *The Grand Strategy of the Roman Empire*.
15. Ammianus Marcellinus XXVII.8.5; in Haywood, *Dark Age Naval Power*.
16. Ashe, *Kings and Queens of Early Britain*.
17. Baverstock, *Julian the Apostate*.
18. Austin & Rankov, *Exploratio*.
19. Ammianus' figure seems excessive but could well include e.g. pontoons for bridging.
20. Peddie, *The Roman War Machine*, quoting Ammianus XXII.3.9.
21. Pearson, *The Roman Shore Forts*; Haywood, *Dark Age Naval Power*.
22. Bounegru & Zahariade, *Les Forces Navales*.
23. Jones & Thorpe, *Ancient Inventions* and see Ferrill, *The Fall of the Roman Empire* for an illustration.
24. Williams & Friell, *Theodosius, The Empire at Bay*. Ferrill, *The Fall of the Roman Empire*. It would of course become a cancer that would erode the fabric of the Empire, but did Theodosius have any option?
25. Ashe, *The Kings and Queens of Early Britain*.
26. Zosimus IV.38–39.
27. Williams & Friell, *Theodosius, The Empire at Bay*. Zosimus IV.42–47.
28. This area had been devastated by inundations and constant warfare and its population much depleted; similarly large areas of the Balkans had been de-populated by plague and it was in these vacuums that some at least of the barbarians saw their opportunity.
29. Haywood, *Dark Age Naval Power*.
30. Mackie, *A History of Scotland*.
31. Austin & Rankov, *Exploratio*.
32. There are no natural harbours in Etruria to rival Misenum, still operational at this time. No naval opposition is reported and it would be interesting, to say the least, to know how many warships/transports made up this fleet.
33. Casson, *Travel in the Ancient World*.
34. The size and effectiveness of this is highly debatable and was probably limited to manning a few forts; not enough could have been spared for re-establishment of the province which was perforce largely left to its own devices.
35. Codex Theodosianus VII.17. It also mentions fleets based at Alexandria and Crete. Constantinople was presumably the main (sea) base.

36. Orosius VII.42. Elton, *Warfare in Roman Europe*.
37. No mention is made of a Ravenna Fleet and if there still was such a formation by this time, it obviously did not support the usurper.
38. An indication of Roman weakness, if one were needed, is that such a small force, with all its accoutrements, could persist. At Cannae in 216 BC it will be recalled that the Romans fielded in one day, an army bigger than the whole Vandal nation and this was not the only occasion (and see Ferrill, *The Fall of the Roman Empire*).
39. The lack or neglect of any naval opposition is again noticeable.
40. Ashe, *Kings and Queens of Early Britain*.
41. Also Casson *SSAW*.
42. Norwich, *Byzantium, The Early Centuries*. Procopius is the ancient source.

Appendix I

The Kings and Emperors of Rome

The Kings

Traditional date for the founding of Rome	21 April 753 BC
ROMULUS	753 – 715
NUMA POMPILIUS	716 – 673
TULLUS HOSTILIUS	673 – 642
ANCUS MARCIUS	642 – 616
LUCIUS TARQUINIUS PRISCUS	616 – 579
SERVIUS TULLIUS	578 – 535
LUCIUS TARQUINIUS SUPERBUS	534 – 510

The Republic

Foundation of the Republic	510
SULLA Dictator	81 – 79
First Truimvirate;	
CAESAR, POMPEY, CRASSUS,	60 – 53
GAIUS JULIUS CAESAR	49 – 44
Second Triumvirate;	
OCTAVIAN, MARK ANTHONY,	
LEPIDUS,	43 – 36

The Emperors

AUGUSTUS	27 BC – AD 14
TIBERIUS	14 – 37
GAIUS (CALIGULA)	37 – 41
CLAUDIUS	41 – 54
NERO	54 – 68
GALBA; OTHO; VITELLIUS	68 – 69
VESPASIAN	69 – 79
TITUS	79 – 81
DOMITIAN	81 – 96
NERVA	96 – 98
TRAJAN	98 – 117

HADRIAN	117 – 138
ANTONINUS PIUS	138 – 161
AURELIUS & VERUS	161 – 169
MARCUS AURELIUS	169 – 180
COMMODUS	180 – 192
PERTINAX; DIDIUS JULIANUS;	
CLODIUS ALBINUS	192 – 193
SEPTIMIUS SEVERUS	193 – 211
BASSIANUS (CARACALLA)	
& GETA	211 – 212
CARACALLA	212 – 217
MACRINUS	217 – 218
DIADUMENIANUS	218
ELEGABALUS	218 – 222
SEVERUS ALEXANDER	222 – 235
MAXIMINUS	235 – 238
GORDIAN I; GORDIAN II	
PUPIENUS; BALBINUS	238
GORDIAN III	238 – 244
PHILIP	244 – 249
DECIUS	249 – 251
GALLUS & VOLUSIANUS	251 – 253
AEMILIAN	253
VALERIAN	253 – 260
GALLIENUS	253 – 268
CLAUDIUS II	268 – 270
QUINTILLUS	270
AURELIAN	270 – 275
TACITUS	275 – 276
FLORIANUS	276
PROBUS	276 – 282
CARUS	282 – 283
NUMERIAN & CARINUS	283 – 284
CARINUS & DIOCLETIAN	284 – 285
DIOCLETIAN	285 – 286
MAXIMIAN	286 – 305
CONSTANTIUS	305 – 306
SEVERUS II	306 – 307
MAXENTIUS	306 – 312
MAXIMIAN	307 – 308
CONSTANTINE	307 – 324
CONSTANTINE	324 – 337
CONSTANTINE II	337 – 340

The 'Gallic Empire'

POSTUMUS	259 – 268
LAELIANUS; MARIUS	269
VICTORINUS	269 – 271
TETRICUS	271 – 274

Eastern Empire

DIOCLETIAN	286 – 305
GALERIUS	305 – 311
MAXIMINUS	310 – 313
LICINIUS	308 – 324
CONSTANTIUS II	337 – 361

CONSTANS	337 – 350		
MAGNENTIUS	350 – 353		
CONSTANTIUS II	353 – 360		
CONSTANTIUS II & JULIAN	360 – 361		
JULIAN	361 – 363		
JOVIAN	363 – 364		
VALENTINIAN	364 – 367	VALENS	364 – 378
VALENTINIAN & GRATIAN	367 – 375		
GRATIAN & VALENTINIAN II	375 – 383	GRATIAN	378 – 379
VALENTINIAN II	383 – 392	THEODOSIUS	379 – 395
EUGENIUS	392 – 394		
THEODOSIUS	394 – 395		
HONORIUS	395 – 423	ARCADIUS	395 – 408
Sack of Rome	410	THEODOSIUS II	408 – 450
JOHANNES	423 – 425		
VALENTINIAN III	425 – 455	MARCIAN	450 – 457
PETRONIUS MAXIMUS	455		
AVITUS	455 – 456		
MAJORIAN	457 – 461	LEO	457 – 474
LIBIUS SEVERUS III	461 – 465		
ANTHEMIUS	467 – 472		
OLYBRIUS	472		
GLYCERIUS	472 – 474	LEO II	474
JULIUS NEPOS	474	ZENO	474 – 491
ROMULUS AUGUSTULUS	475 – 476	et seq. to	1453

Appendix II

Roman Navy Personnel

The following list and command structure is a summary, rationalised into a semblance of logical order, of the various known appointments and ranks referred to more fully in the text. The modern ranks that are mentioned are perhaps the closest approximations to many of the Roman ranks. However, it will be noted that the role of certain ancient ranks, such as *Dolator*, remain open to interpretation.

SEAGOING	ADMINISTRATION

REPUBLICAN

Consul/ProConsul *appoints*	
Military Tribune *who appoints*	
Centurion *who appoints*	(from 311 BC)
Optio	*Duoviri Navales*

(from circa 264 BC)

Praetor (for detached squadron)	*Quaestores Classici*
(under Pompeius, 67 BC)	
Legatus (11 Staff and 13 on Stations)	*Praefectus Classis et Orae Maritimae*

IMPERIAL

HIGH COMMAND

| *Praefectus Classis* (Fleet Commander) | *Quaestores Classici* |
| (both replaced under Claudius only by Procurators) | |

Navarchos Princeps (senior Admiral)
Navarchos (Admiral or Commodore)   Staff: Sub Prefect (Aide de camp)
                                                 Cornicularius (Senior Sgt)
                                                 Beneficiarius (Appointee)
                                                 Actuarius (Clerk)
                                                 Scriba (Writer)

(from 3rd Century AD)

Praepositus Reliquationis
(temporary flag rank in
absence of *Praefectus*)

(4th Century AD)
Comes Maritimae (for *Classis Britannica* only)

OTHER RANKS

Trierarchos	Ship Captain
Gubernator	Navigation and Stern Officer, First Lieutenant
Proreus/Proretus	Bow Officer, Second Lieutenant
Pausarius/Celeusta	Rowing Officer
Secutor	Master–at–arms

RATINGS

Remex	Rower	
Velarus	Sailor	
Medicus	Medical Orderly	
Fabricus	Carpenter	
Faber Navalis	Shipwright	
Coronarius	Signaller?	NB. *All rated as* miles
Urinator	Diver	*or* manipulari. *All have*
Hortator/Portisculus/Pitulus	Timebeater	*equivalent leading rates*
Symphoniacus	Musician	*named* dupliciarii.

MARINES

Centurio	
Optio	
Sub-Optio	
Armorum Custos	Armourer
Miles/Manipularis	Marine
Dolator	Pioneer/Engineer?
Cornicen/Bucinator	Trumpeters

Appendix III
Suggested Crew Levels by Ship Type

PENTECONTER – Monoreme, one man per oar

		of 20 oars	of 50 oars
Officers		2/3	4
Sailors		4	6
Marines		6	10
Rowers		20	50
	total	32	70

LIBURNIAN Bireme, one man per oar

			of 50 oars (Trajan's Col.)	of 60 oars (seagoing)
Officers			4	4
Sailors			4	6
Marines			6	10
Archers			4	6
Rowers:				
	Thranite		26	34
	Zygite		24	26
		total	68	86

LUSORIA   NB Built in various sizes and thus crew totals vary accordingly

		of 30 oars:
Officers		2
Sailors		3
Marines		8
Archers		4
Rowers/Marines		30
	total	47

TRIREME   One man per oar

	Athenian
Officers	4
Leading Ratings	6
Sailors	10
Marines	10
Archers	4
Rowers:	
Thranite	62
Zygite	54
Thalamite	54
total	204

QUADRIREME Bireme, two men per oar

	Rhodian
Officers	7
Leading Ratings	10
Sailors	10
Marines	20
Archers	6
Artillerymen	2
Rowers	
Thranite	80
Zygite	80
total	215

QUINQUIREME   Trireme, two men per oar and one per oar

Officers	8	
Leading Ratings		
Sailors	20	
Marines	40	(plus in the First Punic War, one
Rowers		century of legionaries – 80 men)
Thranite	124	
Zygite	116	
Thalamite	56	
total	364	

'SIX'   As a bireme, three men per oar

Officers			15
Sailors			30
Marines			80
Archers			30
Artillerymen			24
Rowers			
	Thranite		180
	Zygite		180
		total	539

FIFTH-CENTURY 'PRE DROMON' Monoreme, two men per oar

Officers		6
Sailors		12
Marines		30/40
Rowers		80
	total	128/138

RHINE PATROL BOAT   Monoreme, one man per oar

Officers		2
Sailors		3
Marines		12
Archers		4
Rowers		44
	total	65

Appendix IV

Glossary of Place Names

A guide to the ancient place-names used in the text with their modern equivalents.
Fl. indicates a river; Ins. an island and Prom. a promontory or cape.

Abus Fl.	Humber, England
Aegades Ins.	Egadi, Sicily
Aegusa Ins.	Favignana, Sicily
Agrigentum	Agrigento, Sicily
Albigaunum	Albenga, Italy
Albintimilium	Ventimiglia, Italy
Albis Fl.	Elbe, Germany
Amisia Fl.	Ems, Germany
Antipolis	Antibes, France
Antium	Anzio, Italy
Apollonia	near Fier, Albania
Aquincum	Budapest, Hungary
Arelate	Arles, France
Argentorate	Strasbourg, France
Ariminium	Rimini, Italy
Atria	Adria, Italy
Augusta Treverorum	Trier, Germany
Baiae	Baia, Italy
Barra Ins.	S.Andrea, Brindisi
Batavodurum	Nijmegen, Holland
Bauli	Bacoli, Italy
Besantio	Besançon, France
Bononia	Bologna, Italy
Bononia	Vidin, Bulgaria
Bonna	Bonn, Germany
Britannia	British Isles
Brundisium	Brindisi, Italy
Bruttium	Calabria, Italy
Burdigala	Bordeaux, France
Caesarea	Algiers, Algeria
Caledonia	Scotland
Calleva Atrebatum	Silchester,England
Camulodunum	Colchester, England

Capreae Ins.	Capri, Italy
Carales	Cagliari, Sardinia
Carnuntum	Near Vienna, Austria
Carteia	Gibraltar
Carthago Nova	Cartagena, Spain
Centumcellae	Civitavecchia,Italy
Cephallenia Ins.	Kefalonia, Greece
Chalcis	Khalkis, Greece
Chersonesus	Sevastopol, Crimea
Chobus Fl.	Khobi or Inguri,Georgia
Clupea	Nabeul, Tunisia
Colchis	Georgia
Colonia Agrippinensis	Cologne, Germany
Confluentes	Koblenz, Germany
Corcyra	Corfu, Greece
Cossyra Ins.	Pantellaria, Italy
Croton	Crotone, Italy
Cumae	Cuma, Italy
Danubius Fl.	Danube
Demetrias	Volos, Greece
Deva	Chester, England
Dravus Fl.	Drava, Serbia
Drepanum	Trapani,Sicily
Dubris	Dover, England
Durovernum	Canterbury, England
Dyrrachium	Durres, Albania
Eboracum	York, England
Ebusus Ins.	Ibiza, Spain
Echinus	Lamia, Greece
Ecnomus	Licata, Sicily
Elephantine	Aswan, Egypt
Empuriae	Empuries, Spain
Eryx	Erice, Sicily
Euxine	Black Sea
Formiae	Formia, Italy
Forum Iulii	Fréjus, France
Fucinus	Lake Fucino, Italy
Gadir, Gades	Cadiz, Spain
Genua	Genoa, Italy
Gesoriacum	Boulogne, France
Glevum	Gloucester, England
Hadrianopolis/Adrianople	Edirne, Turkey
Hadrumentum	Sousse, Tunisia

Hellespont	Dardanelles, Turkey
Herculaneum	Ercolano, Italy
Hermaeum Prom.	Cape Bon, Tunisia
Hibernia	Ireland
Hiera Ins.	Marettimo, Sicily
Hippo Zarhytus	Bizerta, Tunisia
Hispalis	Seville, Spain
Hispania	Spain & Portugal
Hostilia	Ostiglia, Italy
Iberus Fl.	Ebro, Spain
Isca	Caerleon, Wales
Isca Dumnoniorum	Exeter, England
Istrus	Bobadag, Romania
Kynthos Ins.	Therma, Greece
Lacinia	Capo Colonne, Italy
Lemanae	Lympne, England
Leptis Magna	Lybia
Liger Fl.	Loire, France
Lilybaeum	Marsala, Sicily
Lindum	Lincoln, England
Liparae Ins.	Eolie, Lipari, Italy
Lissus	Lezhe, Albania
Londinium	London, England
Luceria	Lucera, Italy
Lugdunum	Lyons, France
Lugdunum Batavorum	Katwijk, Holland
Luna	La Spezia, Italy
Maeotis Palus	Sea of Azov
Magnesia	Manisa, Turkey
Massilia	Marseilles, France
Mediolanum	Milan, Italy
Melita	Malta
Mercuri Prom.	Cape Bon, Tunisia
Messana	Messina, Sicily
Misenum	Miseno, Italy
Moenus Fl.	Main, Germany
Moguntiacum	Mainz, Germany
Mona Ins.	Anglesey, Wales
Mosa Fl.	Meuse, Belgium
Mosella Fl.	Moselle, Germany
Mylae	Milazzo, Sicily
Narbo	Narbonne, France
Narenta Fl.	Naretva, Croatia

Neapolis	Naples, Italy
Nicea	Nice, France
Nicomedia	Izmit, Turkey
Novae	Svishtov, Bulgaria
Novaesium	Neuss, Germany
Noviodunum	Isaccea, Romania
Noviomagus	Chichester, England
Noviomagus Batavodurum	Arentsburg, Holland
Nuceria	Nocera, Italy
Nymphaeum	Shengjin, Albania
Oblivio Fl.	Minho, Portugal
Oescus	Sistova, Bulgaria
Olbia	Nr. Nikolayev, Ukraine
Orcades Ins.	Orkneys
Oricus	Dukat, Albania
Osilipo	Lisbon, Portugal
Pachynus Prom.	Correnti, Sicily
Padus Fl.	Po, Italy
Paleopolis	Pizzofalcone, Italy
Palinurus Prom.	Palinuro, Italy
Panormus	Palermo, Sicily
Panormus	Kusadasi, Turkey
Panticapaeum	Kerch, Crimea
Petuaria	Brough on Humber, England
Phintias	Licata, Sicily
Phocaea	Foca, Turkey
Pisae	Pisa, Italy
Placentia	Piacenza, Italy
Pons Aelius	Newcastle-upon-Tyne, England
Pontiae Ins.	Ponza, Italy
Portus Adurni	Portchester, England
Portus Herculis; Monoeci	Monaco
Portus Itius	Dunkirk, France
Portus Pisanus	Livorno, Italy
Propontis	Sea of Marmara, Turkey
Puteoli	Pozzuoli, Italy
Regulbium	Reculver, England
Rhegium	Reggio Calabria, Italy
Rhenus Fl.	Rhine
Rhodanus Fl.	Rhone
Rotomagus	Rouen, France
Rutupiae	Richborough, England
Sabaea	(Sheba) Yemen

Sabrina Fl.	Severn, England
Saguntum	Sagunto, Spain
Salonae	Split, Croatia
Savus Fl.	Sava, Serbia
Scodra	Shkoder, Albania
Sinope	Sinop, Turkey
Stoechades Ins.	Iles d'Hyéres,France
Sulcis	S. Antioco, Sardinia
Surrentum	Sorrento, Italy
Tamesis Fl.	Thames, England
Tanais	Rostov on Don, Russia
Tarentum	Taranto, Italy
Tarracina	Terracina, Italy
Tarraco	Tarragona, Spain
Tauromenium	Taormina, Sicily
Taurunum	Zamun, Serbia
Thermae	Termini Imerese Sicily
Thurii	Thurio, Italy
Ticinum	Pavia, Italy
Tingis	Tangier, Morocco
Tolosa	Toulouse, France
Trapezus	Trabzon, Turkey
Tres Tabernae	Saverne, France
Troesmis	Galitza, Romania
Tyras	Nr. Akerman, Ukraine
Vectis Ins.	Isle of Wight, England
Verulamium	St. Albans, England
Vetera	Xanten, Belgium
Vindobona	Vienna, Austria
Vindonissa	Windisch, Switzerland
Visurgis Fl.	Weser, Germany
Zakynthos Ins.	Zante, Greece

Appendix V
Glossary of Nautical Terms

ABAFT – towards or relating to the stern.

AMIDSHIPS – relating to the middle portion of a ship's length.

ARTEMON – foremast and/or foresail of an ancient ship.

AWNINGS – fabric screens deployed to give shelter from sun or weather.

AUXILIARY RIG – light sailing rig used as a secondary means of propulsion.

BARGE – a broad, flat-bottomed cargo carrier of medium size.

BEAM – the width of a ship from side to side.

BIREME – a ship with two remes of oars, one above the other.

BOARDING BRIDGE – a device for bridging the space between engaged ships, to enable marines to cross.

BOOM – a spar or pole along the foot of a sail or used for holding something at length such as the foot of a sail.

BOW – the foremost part of a ship.

BRACES – ropes attached to and used to control the ends of a yard.

BRACING – extra members introduced to reinforce an existing structure.

BULWARK –the sides of an open ship above its deck.

CABLE – a heavy duty rope for mooring (q.v.).

CATCH – the point at which the oar blades enter the water at the beginning of a stroke.

CARVEL – method of hull construction where planks are fitted edge to edge.

CAULKING – the forcing of material between the planks of a hull or deck to make them watertight.

CLINCHER/ CLINKER BUILT – method of hull construction where planks are overlapped.

CORACLE – open craft with a skin of leather, stretched over a wicker or wooden frame.

CORVUS – a boarding bridge (q.v.) dropped onto an enemy deck and locked in place by a spike at the end.

CUDDY – a small deck shelter.

DECK – horizontal platform or floor in a ship.

DERRICK – a boom or pole rigged to act as a crane.

DOUBLE-ENDED – a ship whose hull tapers to a point at both bow and stern.

DRAFT – the depth of a ship in the water.

FOREFOOT – the bottom of the stempost (q.v.) where it turns into the keel.

FOREMAST – the mast nearest to the bow of a ship.

FRAMES – strengthening constructions fitted within the hull and transversely to the length.

FRAME-FIRST – construction method where a 'skeleton' is built, then covered, to form a hull.

FREEBOARD – height between the sea surface and the lowest level of a ship's side or apertures such as oarports.

GALLEY – (Latin *galea*) used as a generic term for a ship propelled by oars.

GANGWAY – plank(s) or structure used to enable access from ship to shore.

GARBOARD – the first plank of a hull, fitted either side of and immediately onto the keel.

GRAPNEL – a barbed hook attached to a line, thrown to ensnare a target.

HALLIARDS – lines between deck and masthead, used to hoist the yard or sails.

HARPAX/ HARPOON – type of grapnel (q.v.) shot from a catapult.

HATCHES – openings in a deck for access, ventilation or cargo handling.

HEADS – the ship's lavatories.

HELMSMAN – the person who steers the ship.

HULL – the 'shell' of a ship, the main body of it which floats.

INBOARD – closer to the centre-line of a ship.

JETTIED – something built out beyond the main body of a hull.

KEEL – the central spine of a hull from which the rest of the hull is built up.

KNOT – a rate of movement at sea of one nautical mile per hour.

LATEEN – corruption of 'Latin'. Type of sail and rig appearing in the late Empire.

LEEWAY – the amount by which wind and current push a ship off course.

LIGHTER – a barge (q.v.) which is not self-propelled.

MAST – pole mounted vertically for mounting yards (q.v.), sails, flags.

MAST STEP – the platform upon which the bottom of the mast rests.

MONOREME – a ship with a single reme of oars.

MORTICE AND TENON – method of joining two pieces of wood by cutting matching slots in each, bringing them together and fixing them with a piece of wood inserted in the two slots.

MOOR (to) – to fix a ship in a chosen position with ropes or anchors.

MONOCOQUE – where the strength of a structure is contained in its 'shell' or outer skin.

OAR STROKE – one complete cycle of working an oar.

OUTBOARD – from the centre-line of a ship towards the outside of the hull.

OUTRIGGER – a construction extending outboard of the hull proper to carry e.g. a thole.

PLANK-ON-FRAME – method of hull construction where a skeleton of frames is first erected and then covered by planking.

PONTOONS – floating platforms.

POOP /POOP DECK – after Latin, *puppis*; the aftermost deck of a ship.

PORT – the left-hand side of a ship when viewed from the stern.

PROW – the bow section of a ship.

PUMP, CHAIN OR BUCKET – a string of containers attached to a moving belt around a top and bottom pivot, which are filled at the bottom of their travel and empty at the top when they tilt.

PUMP, DOUBLE-ACTING – a pump which operates through a system of valves so that it works on both the up and down strokes of the operating handle.

PUNT – shallow flat-bottomed boat for use in very shallow water, propelled by a pole.

QUARTERS – the rearmost side parts of a ship.

RAM – armoured projection on the bow of a ship used to damage or puncture an enemy hull.

REME – a horizontal level of rowers.

RIG – all of the ropes, sails and tackle needed to operate a sailing ship.

RUDDER – a device for steering a ship; also steering oar.

RUDDER -BALANCED – where part of the rudder blade is in front of the shaft balancing the force of the water acting on the rear part to an extent.

RUDDERS/SIDE RUDDERS/STEERING OARS – steering devices affixed to the stern quarters (q.v.) of a ship on one or both sides.

RUNNING RIGGING – rigging which is used to operate the sails.

SEA KEEPING – the degree to which a ship can ride comfortably in a sea.

SETTLING (IN THE WATER) – process whereby a ship sinks to the level of its latent buoyancy dictated by the materials from which it is made.

SHEETS – ropes attached to and used to control the bottom corners of a sail.

SHIPPED – something which is brought onto or inboard of a ship.

SHROUDS – supporting ropes or lines secured between a mast and the sides of a ship.

SKIFF – (Latin *scapha*) light, small boat.

SQUARE RIG – where a yard and sail are rigged across the beam of a ship.

STANDING RIGGING – rigging used to support the mast(s).

STARBOARD – the right-hand side of a ship when viewed from the stern; after 'steering board', the side upon which a single side rudder was fixed.

STAYS – standing rigging (q.v.) between the top of a mast and the bow and stern.

STEM – the bow of a ship (q.v.).

STEMPOST – the foremost vertical timber of the ship, forming the point of the bow.

STEPPED (MAST) – the act of erecting a mast.

STERN – the rearmost part of a ship.

STERN QUARTERS – the rear flanks of a hull.

STERNPOST – the aftermost vertical timber of the ship.

STROKE OARSMAN – leader of a group of oarsmen who sets the pace of rowing.

SUPPARUM – triangular sails fitted above the yard and to the mast.

TENDER, SHIP'S – a small boat used for errands by its parent ship.

THALAMITE – rower of the lowest reme in a trireme arrangement.

THOLE – the pin against which an oar is pivoted and worked.

THRANITE – rower in the topmost reme of a multireme ship.

THWARTS – timbers fitted between the sides of a hull as spacers and doubling e.g. as seats.

TRIREME – a ship with three remes of oars, one above the other.

TILLER – a bar inserted into a rudder shaft used to operate it.

TOPSAIL – a sail rigged above the main or lowest sail on a mast

WALE – strengthening or protective timber fitted along a length of the outside of a hull.

WATERLINE – the level to which a hull floats in the water.

WORKING-UP – operating an untried ship and/or crew to gain experience and efficiency.

YARD – pole or spar to which a sail is attached.

ZYGITE – rower in the middle reme in a trireme arrangement.

BIBLIOGRAPHY

ABBREVIATIONS USED IN THE NOTES:
Casson *SSAW*: Casson, *Ships and Seamanship in the Ancient World*
Meijer: Meijer, *A History of Seafaring in the Classical World*
Morrison & Coates, *GROW*: Morrison and Coates, *Greek and Roman Oared Warships*
Rodgers: *Greek and Roman Naval Warfare*
Scullard: Scullard, *A History of the Roman World, 753 to 146 BC*
Scullard 2: Scullard, *From the Gracchi to Nero*
Starr: Starr, *The Roman Imperial Navy*
Tilley: Tilley, *Seafaring on the Ancient Mediterranean*

PRIMARY SOURCES:
    Lives of the Later Caesars. First part of the Augustan History. Trans: A. Birley.
    Caesar, *The Battle for Gaul*. Trans: A. & P. Wiseman.
    Caesar, The Civil War. Trans: F.P. Long.
    Livy, *The Early History of Rome*, Books I–V. Trans: A. de Selincourt.
    Livy, *The War with Hannibal*, Books XXI–XXX. Trans: A. de Selincourt.
    Polybius, *The Rise of the Roman Empire*. Trans: I. Scott-Kilvert.
    Sallust, *The Jugurthine War*. Trans: S.A. Handford.
    Tacitus, *Agricola and Germania*. Trans: H. Mattingley.
    Tacitus, *The Annals*. Trans: M. Grant.
    Tacitus, *The Histories*. Trans: K. Wellesley.
    Vegetius, *Epitome of Military Science*. Trans: N.P. Milner.

OTHER SOURCES:

Anderson R.C.	*Oared Fighting Ships*
	Argus Books 1976.
Ascherson N.	*Black Sea*
	Vintage 1996.
Ashe G.	*Kings and Queens of Early Britain*
	Methuen 1982.
Austin & Rankov	*Exploratio, Military and Political Intelligence in the Roman World*
	Routledge 1995.
Balsdon J.P.V.D.	*Life and Leisure in Ancient Rome*
	Bodley Head 1969.
Barker P.	*Alexander the Great's Campaigns*
	Patrick Stephens 1979.
Barker & Rasmussen	*The Etruscans*
	Blackwell Publishers 1998.
Bass G.F.	*A History of Seafaring Based on Underwater Archeology*
	Thames and Hudson 1972.

Bickerman E.J.	*Chronology of the Ancient World*
	Thames & Hudson 1980.
Bounegru & Zahariade	*Les Forces Navales du Bas Danube et de la Mer Noir aux Ier–VIe Siécles*
	Oxbow Books 1996.
Bowerstock G.	*Julian The Apostate*
	Duckworth 1978.
Bradford E.	*Ulysses Found*
	Hodder & Stoughton 1963.
Burn A.R.	*The Pelican History of Greece*
	Penguin Books 1966.
deCamp L.S.	*The Ancient Engineers*
	Ballantine 1974.
Casson L.	*Ships and Seafaring in Ancient Times*
	British Museum Press 1994.
" "	*Ships and Seamanship in the Ancient World*
	Princeton University Press 1986.
" "	*The Ancient Mariners*, 2nd Edition.
	Princeton University Press 1991.
" "	*Travel in the Ancient World*
	Johns Hopkins University Press 1994.
Calza & Becatti	*Ostia*, IX Edition
	Libreria dello Stato, Rome 1974.
Clayton P.A.	*Chronicle of the Pharaohs*
	Thames & Hudson 1994.
Connolly P.	*The Roman Army*
	Macdonald 1975.
" "	*The Greek Armies*
	Macdonald 1977.
" "	*Greece and Rome at War*
	Macdonald 1981.
" "	*The Roman Fort*
	Oxford University Press 1991.
Cottrell L.	*Enemy of Rome*
	Evans Bros. 1960.
" "	*The Great Invasion*
	Pan Books 1961.
Cunliffe B.	*The Extraordinary Voyage of Pytheas the Greek*
	Penguin Books 2002
Dal Maso L.	*Rome of the Caesars*
	Bonedin 1974.
David J.M.	*The Roman Conquest of Italy*
	Blackwell 1996.
Elton H.	*Warfare in Roman Europe, AD 350–425*
	Oxford University Press 1997.
Ferrill A.	*The Fall of the Roman Empire – The Military Explanation*
	Thames & Hudson 1988.
Feugere M.	*Weapons of the Romans*
	Tempus 2002.
Fry P.S.	*Great Caesar*
	Collins 1974.

Gaul S.	*Malta, Gozo and Comino*
	Cadogan Books 1993.
Gibbon E.	*The Decline and Fall of the Roman Empire*
Grandazzi A.	*The Foundation of Rome, Myth & History*
	Cornell University Press 1997.
Guerber H.A.	*The Myths of Greece and Rome*
	Harrap 1938.
Guilmartin J.F.	*Gunpowder and Galleys*
	Conway 2003.
Hague P.	*Sea Battles in Miniature*
	Patrick Stephens 1980.
Harden D.	*The Phoenicians*
	Thames & Hudson 1962.
Hawes D.	*Ships and the Sea, a Chronological Review*
	Chancellor Press 1985.
Haywood J.	*Dark Age Naval Power*
	Anglo-Saxon Books 1999.
Hourani G.F.	*Arab Seafaring*
	Princeton University Press 1995.
Humble R.	*Warfare in the Ancient World*
	Book Club Associates 1980.
James & Thorpe	*Ancient Inventions*
	Ballantine Books 1994.
Jones A.H.M.	*Augustus*
	Chatto & Windus 1970.
Kemp P.	*The History of Ships*
	Macdonald & Co. 1978.
Kepple L.	*Understanding Roman Inscriptions*
	Batsford 1971.
	Larousse Encyclopaedia of Mythology
	Paul Hamlyn 1964.
Levi P.	*Atlas of the Greek World*
	Equinox 1984.
Levick B.	*Vespasian*
	Routledge 1999.
Lissner I.	*Power and Folly, The Story of the Caesars*
	Jonathan Cape 1958.
Luttwak E.N.	*The Grand Strategy of the Roman Empire from the 1st Century* AD *to the 3rd*
	Johns Hopkins University Press 1976.
MacDowell S.	*Twilight of the Empire. The Roman Infantryman, 3rd to 6th Centuries* AD
	Osprey 1994.
Mackie J.D.	*A History of Scotland*
	Pelican Books 1976.
Mansir R.	*Ancient and Medieval Ships*
	Moonraker 1981.
Marlow J.	*The Golden Age of Alexandria*
	Victor Gollancz 1971.
Marsden E.W.	*Greek and Roman Artillery–Technical Treatises*
	Oxford University Press 1969.

" "	*Greek and Roman Artillery–Historical Development* Oxford University Press 1969.
Marsh H.	*The Caesars* David and Charles 1972.
Mason E.	*Tiberius* Panther Books 1963.
Massa A.	*The World of the Etruscans* Tudor Publishing 1973.
Matyszak P.	*Chronicle of the Roman Republic* Thames and Hudson 2003.
Meijer F.	*A History of Seafaring in the Classical World* Croom Helm 1986.
Morris J.	*The Age of Arthur; A History of the British Isles from 350 to 650* Trinity Press 1973.
Morrison J. & Others	*The Age of the Galley* Conway Maritime Press 1995.
Morrison & Coates	*Greek and Roman Oared Warships 399–30 BC* Oxbow Books 1996.
Morrison, Coates & Rankov	*The Athenian Trireme*, 2nd Edition. Cambridge University Press 2000.
Moscati S.	*The World of the Phoenicians* Sphere Books 1973.
Muir's Historical Atlas,	*Ancient and Classical.* 6th Edition George Philip and Son 1963.
Norwich J.J.	*Byzantium. The Early Centuries* Penguin 1988.
Ormerod H.A.	*Piracy in the Ancient World* Johns Hopkins University Press 1997.
Patai R.	*The Children of Noah, Jewish Seafaring in Ancient Times* Princeton University Press 1999.
Pearson A.	*The Roman Shore Forts* Tempus Publishing 2002.
Peddie J.	*The Roman War Machine* Alan Sutton Publishing 1994.
" "	*Conquest–The Roman Invasion of Britain* Sutton Publishing 1997.
Pemsel H.	*Atlas of Naval Warfare* Arms & Armour Press 1977.
Rankov & Hook	*The Praetorian Guard* Osprey 1994.
Ransford R.	*War Machines* Octopus Books 1975.
Reynolds C.G.	*Command of the Sea, The History & Strategy of Maritime Empires* Robert Hale & Co. 1976.
Rodgers W.L.	*Greek and Roman Naval Warfare* US Naval Institute 1937.
Russo F & F	*Assiedo A Pompei 89AC* Edizioni Flavius 2005
Salmon E.T.	*Samnium and the Samnites* Cambridge University Press 1967.

Scarre C.	*Chronicle of the Roman Emperors* Thames and Hudson 1995.
" "	*The Penguin Historical Atlas of Ancient Rome* Penguin 1995.
Schreiber H. & G.	*Vanished Cities* Weidenfeld and Nicholson 1958.
Scrinari V.S.M.	*Ostia, Porto* Archeological Sites and Museums 1989.
Scullard H.H.	*A History of the Roman World, 753–146 BC* 4th Edition. Routledge 1980.
Scullard H.H.	*From the Gracchi to Nero. A History of Rome, 133 BC to AD 68* 5th Edition. Routledge 1982.
Sekunda, Northwood & Hook	*Early Roman Armies* Osprey 1995.
Selkirk R.	*The Piercebridge Formula* Patrick Stephens 1983.
Simkins & Field	*Warriors of Rome* Blandford 1988
Starr C.G.	*The Influence of Seapower on Ancient History* Oxford University Press 1989.
" "	*The Roman Imperial Navy, 31 BC – AD 324* 3rd Edition. Ares Publishers 1993.
Thiel J.H.	*A History of Roman Sea-Power before the Second Punic War* North Holland Publishing 1954.
Throckmorton P.	*History from the Sea – Shipwrecks and Archeology* Mitchell Beazley 1987.
Tilley A.	*Seafaring on the Ancient Mediterranean* BAR International Series 1268, 2004.
Torr C.	*Ancient Ships* Argonaut 1964
Wallace-Hadrill J.M.	*The Barbarian West 400 to 1000* 3rd Edition. Barnes and Noble 1998.
Warner O.	*The British Navy* Thames and Hudson 1975.
Warry J.	*Warfare in the Classical World* Salamander Books 1980.
Welsh F.	*Building the Trireme* Constable 1988.
Williams & Friell	*Theodosius, The Empire at Bay* Batsford 1994.

Index

A

Abantus, Admiral 292, 293, 313
Abdera 131, 132
Abus, River 234, 253, 263, 273, 300
Abydos 121
Achaea 185, 186, 224
Acilius, Manius 173
Actium 35, 191, 193, 194, 195, 197, 198, 201, 202
Adherbal 69, 107
Adiutrix, navy legions 238, 239, 240, 242, 245–247, 253, 256, 275
Adriatic 34, 36, 44, 51, 84, 85, 86, 87, 91, 92, 93, 95, 121, 124, 130, 134, 141, 144, 158, 167, 169, 170, 171, 172, 178, 179, 182, 185, 186, 187, 191, 196, 203, 206, 222, 237, 244, 245, 286, 302
Aegades 66, 67, 70, 75, 77, 78, 79, 92, 323
Aegean 28, 86, 93, 101, 105, 106, 119, 122, 123, 124, 128, 131, 132, 147, 151, 152, 153, 154, 158, 165, 167, 170, 185, 203, 239, 294, 297, 313
Aegina 101, 105, 106, 124
Aegusa 69, 323
Aeneas, Shield of 225
Aetius, General 308, 309, 310
Aetolia 108
Aetolian League 93, 95
Aetolians 101, 104, 105, 123, 124, 126
Agamemnon 146
Agricola, Iulius 240, 251, 254, 255, 256, 258, 282
Agri Decumates 259, 278, 288
Agrigentum 54, 78, 96, 116, 310, 323
Agrippa, Marcus Vipsanius 187, 188, 189, 190, 192, 193, 194, 195, 196, 197, 198, 202, 203, 205, 214, 217
Agrippina (mother of Nero) 234, 236
Ahenobarbus, L. Domitius 167, 184, 185, 220

Alalia 4, 13, 59
Alaric, King 304, 305
Albinus, Decimus Clodius 267, 268
Albinus, Aulus Postumius 146
Albinus, Lucius Postumius 84
Albis, River 219, 220
Alemanni 259, 288, 297, 298
Alexander, King of Epirus 20
Alexander the Great 26, 31, 130, 199, 225
Alexandria 36, 85, 95, 126, 139, 149, 152, 175, 176, 178, 182, 197, 198, 199, 203, 227, 229, 243, 248, 249, 286, 313
Allectus 288, 289
Amentum (javelin sling) 19
Anatolia 27, 119, 151, 152, 155, 214, 222, 236, 292
Andragathus 302
Andriscus 136
Andros 122
Anicetus 236, 237, 243
Anicius, Praetor 132
Anthemius (Emperor) 305, 311
Antikythera computer 159
Antiochus 119, 123, 124, 125, 126, 127, 128, 130, 132
Antiochus of Syria 119
Antipolis 136, 242, 323
Antium 18, 20, 30, 92, 227, 323
Antoninus Pius (Emperor) 213, 264
Antonius, Caius 169, 170
Antonius, Marcus Snr. 35, 144, 145, 153, 155, 156
Antonius, Marcus 171, 172, 173, 183, 184, 185, 186, 188, 190, 191, 192, 193, 194, 195, 196, 197, 202, 244
Apollonia 84, 94, 116, 121, 124, 171, 323
Apollinaris, Claudius 246
Appius Claudius 52, 96
Apulia 20, 22

Apulians 32, 34
Aquileia 130, 206, 286, 298, 303, 308
Aquilifer 163
Aquincum 266, 275, 288
Aquitania 162, 307
Arcadius (Emperor) 99, 303, 305
archers 9, 12, 13, 15, 22, 31, 45, 54, 57, 97, 98,
        167, 168, 174, 180, 188, 192, 194, 209,
        212, 239, 292
Archimedes 97, 98
Arelate 286, 306
Argentorate 221, 298
Argos 123
Aricia, battle of 10
Arrianus, Flavius (Arrian) 262
Arruntius, Lucius 194
Artemon 3, 55
ARTILLERY
        Ballista 18, 289
        Catapulta 18
        Formula Artillery 37
        Gastrophetes 19, 21, 289
        Onager 287
        Torsion Artillery 23, 235
Asclepiodotus 288
Asia Minor 26, 93, 121, 122, 123, 124, 126, 128,
        130, 132, 144, 175, 226, 236
Asparis 262
Athenian 13, 15, 17, 40, 56, 80, 92, 121, 321
Athens 80, 101, 116, 121, 122, 134, 151, 152,
        157, 165, 265, 276, 277, 279
Atlantic Ocean 43, 107, 134
Atrius, Quintus 164
Attacking tactics (Naval) 14, 127, 128, 183, 190,
        196, 293
Attalus, King of Pergamum 93, 105, 106, 119,
        120, 124
Attila 310
Atilius, Praetor 124
Auctus, L. Cocceius 188
Augusta Treverorum 241, 245, 246, 247, 295, 307
Augustus (Emperor) 198, 199, 200, 201, 202,
        203, 208, 214, 215, 217, 219, 220, 221,
        222, 232, 238, 271, 278, 285, 299, 311
Aurelian (Emperor) 279, 280
Aurelius, Marcus (Emperor) 260, 264, 266
auxilia 39, 215, 220, 230, 244, 248, 296

B

Babylon 3
Baiae 205, 206, 217, 225, 236, 254
Balearic Isles 43, 108, 144
ballista 18, 289
Basiliscus 311
Bassus, Sextus Lucilius 242
Batavii 220
Batavodurum 241, 247, 295
Belgica 226, 234, 241, 266, 273, 303
Bibulus, L. Calpurnius 170, 171
bireme 13, 17, 22, 24, 29, 87, 94, 106, 135, 155,
        167, 173, 179, 192, 216, 247, 311, 322
        evolution of 13
Biscay, Bay of 159, 160, 307
Bithynia 139, 151, 185
Blaesus, Cnaius Sempronius 66
Boarding bridges 109
Boeotia 124
Boeotian 124, 131
Bomilcar 93, 100
Bomilco 96
Boniface 309
Bonna 219, 221, 241, 245, 247, 295
Boodes 56
Bosphoran Kingdom 158, 200, 213, 216, 232,
        233, 257, 276, 277, 294, 299, 307
Bosporus 154
Britannia (Britain) 12, 25, 149, 160, 162–165,
        168, 203, 224, 226–228, 230, 232–234,
        236, 240, 241, 243, 246, 247, 250,
        253–256, 262, 264, 266–269, 272–275,
        278, 280, 285, 286, 288–291, 297–300,
        302–308, 310, 311, 313, 314
Brittany 159, 160
Brundisium 56, 84, 93, 94, 96, 116, 124, 152,
        157, 166, 170, 171, 174, 178, 184, 185,
        186, 191, 193, 195, 206, 222, 323
Bruttians 34, 36
Bruttium 104, 105, 108, 323
Brutus, Decimus Iunius 161, 167
Burdigala 159, 323
Burdo, Julius 240
Bythinia 153, 154
Byzantium 233, 242, 257, 268, 286, 292, 293,
        294, 314

C

Carcina, Alenus 242, 244
Caesar, Gaius Julius (Emperor) 153, 158, 159,
    160, 161, 162, 163, 164, 165, 166,
    167–180, 182, 183, 184, 191, 200, 202,
    216, 225, 228, 231, 285, 291, 298
Ceasar, Lucius 169
Caesarea 227, 249
Caligula (Emperor) 224, 226, 227, 228
Caligula's ships 225
Calleva Atrebatum 289
Calvinus, Cn., Domitius 176
Calvisius 186, 187
Camarina 72
Camouflage (on ships) 171, 291
Campania 1, 2, 26, 28, 34, 44, 66, 92, 146, 222
Camulodunum 230, 231
Cannae 91, 92, 114, 314
capitacensi 22, 24, 88, 142
Caponius, Caius 172
Cappadocia 151, 222
Capraea (Capri) 201
Caracalla (Emperor) 269, 270
Carausius 285, 286, 288
Caria 119
Carinus (Emperor) 280
Carthage (Punica) 1–2, 4, 8, 10, 12, 17, 19–20,
    26–27, 31–32, 36–40, 43, 46, 50–54, 56,
    59–61, 63–67, 69–78, 80, 83, 86–90,
    92–96, 98, 100–102, 105–108, 110–114,
    116–117, 124–125, 136–138, 140, 143,
    147, 149, 159, 169, 198, 229, 280, 305,
    309, 311
Carthago Nova 90, 102, 107, 310, 324
Carthalo 69, 71, 72, 74
Carus (Emperor) 280
Cassius, Caius 170, 174, 175, 183, 184, 185
Castra Cornelia 110, 169
Castra Misinensis 255
Castra Praetoria 255
Castra Ravennensis 255
Catalaunian Fields, Battle of the 310
Catulus, Caius Lutatius 76
catapulta *see* Artillery
Cato, Marcus Portius 110, 159, 175
Censorinus, Lucius Marcus 136
Centumcella 204

Centumulus, Cnaius Fulvius 84
Cephallenia 130, 324
Cerialis, Petilius 241, 242, 246, 247, 253, 254
Cerialis, Turullius 242
Chaeronea 151
Chalcedon 154
Chalcis 106, 116, 122, 124, 324
Chalkidiki 106, 122
Chalkis 131
Charybdis, whirlpool of 51
Chersonesus 232, 233, 249, 257, 263, 276, 300
Chios 35, 40, 56, 80, 119, 132
Cicero, M. Tullius 165
Cilicia 144, 153, 154, 157, 158, 159, 165
Cincius 104
Cinna 146, 151
Civilis, Iulius 217, 243, 244, 245, 246, 247, 248,
    251, 253
CLASSIS
    Classis Praetoriae 206, 221, 285, 286
    Classis Alexandrina 203, 238, 269, 279,
    281
    Classis Anderitianorum 303
    Classis Augusta Alexandrina 253, 262
    Classis Augusta Germanica 253
    Classis Britannica 228, 230, 232, 246,
    253, 267, 268, 269, 273, 285, 286, 288,
    297, 300, 302, 303, 311
    Classis Germanica 219, 220, 222, 230,
    232, 234, 243, 245, 254, 259, 262, 267,
    273, 280, 286
    Classis Misinensis 203, 246, 253, 262,
    264, 266, 269, 291
    Classis Moesica 215, 222, 224, 232, 233,
    237, 259, 260, 261, 263, 274, 276, 286,
    287, 301, 306, 307
    Classis Pannonica 214, 253, 266, 304
    Classis Perinthia 233
    Classis Pontica 236, 242, 254, 262, 264,
    265, 266, 272, 276, 277, 279, 281
    Classis Ravennate 203, 222, 224, 244,
    245, 246, 253, 281
    Classis Sambrica 303
    Classis Syriaca 203, 264, 269, 278, 279
    Classis Syriacae 214, 276, 281
Claudius (Emperor) 52, 68, 92, 94, 96, 113, 124,
    180, 226–229, 231–234, 236, 239, 242,
    246, 248, 250, 261, 263, 279, 310

Claudius, Caius 52
Cleopatra, Queen of Egypt 175, 176, 184, 191,
    192, 194, 194, 197
Clupea 63, 64, 78, 113, 169, 324
Colchis 243
Colonia Agrippinensis 224, 234, 241, 247, 280,
    295, 297, 298
Comes Maritimae 300
Commodus (Emperor) 267
Conditions (on ships) 55, 56
Confluentes 241, 245, 259, 295, 298
Constans (Emperor) 297, 298
Constantine (Emperor) 99, 291, 292, 293, 294,
    297, 298, 305, 306
Constantinus (Constantine III) 305, 306
Constantius (Emperor) 288, 289, 290, 297, 298,
    299, 307
Coracaesium 157
Corbulo, General 234, 236
Corcyra 56, 80, 84, 92, 101, 122, 124, 170, 171,
    175, 191, 192, 193, 324
Corycus, Cape 125
Corinth 37, 101, 103, 105, 106, 116, 122, 130,
    137, 180, 192, 193, 195, 229, 239
Corinth, Gulf of 101, 103, 105, 106, 130, 239
Cornelius, Publius 32, 102
Cornificius 187
Corona Muralis 102
Corona Navalis 59, 232, 261
Corsica 4, 10, 32, 43, 51, 59, 60, 83, 91, 93, 114,
    131, 185, 186, 204, 242, 309, 310
Corvus, the 57, 58, 59, 63, 64, 66, 70, 75, 109
Corycus 125, 128
Cossyra 64, 78, 324
Cotta, Caius Aurelius 66, 154
Crassus, Publius Licinius 155, 159, 160, 162, 165
Crassus, T. Otacilius 100
Cremona 91, 242, 243, 244, 245
Crete 130, 134, 139, 144, 147, 154, 155, 156,
    159, 313
Crispus 292, 293, 313
Ctesiphon 269, 299
Cumae 2, 8, 10, 22, 186, 188, 205, 237, 324
Curio, Caius 167, 169
Cyllene 105
Cynoscephalae, Battle of 122
Cyprus 139, 159, 175, 182
Cyrene 146, 152, 154, 156

Cyzicus 249, 257, 264, 265, 266, 272, 277, 282

D

Dacia 256, 260, 261, 269, 274, 275, 278, 279,
    286, 297, 301, 306, 312
Dalmatia 85, 244, 311
Dalmatian 84, 144, 155, 169, 175, 191, 206
Danubius, River 154, 191, 201, 203, 206, 210,
    214, 215, 221, 222, 224, 230, 233, 243,
    254, 256, 258, 259, 260, 261, 264, 265,
    266, 267, 273, 274, 275, 276, 277, 278,
    279, 285, 286, 287, 288, 290, 297, 299,
    300, 301, 302, 304, 306, 307, 309, 324
Darius I, king of Persia 5, 10
Decius (Emperor) 275
Delos 134, 151, 156, 165
Delphi 18
Demetrias 26, 31, 106, 124, 324
Demetrias, of Macedon 31
Demetrius, of Pharos 86
Demochares, Admiral 189, 190
Democrates 101, 120
Deva 254, 255, 295, 300
Didius, Caius 180
Didius Iulianus 266, 267
Diekplous attack 14, 127, 128, 183, 293
Dimale 86
Diocletian (Emperor) 270, 280, 285, 286, 290
Dolabella, G. Cornelius 167, 169, 183
Domitian (Emperor) 246, 250, 256, 258, 259,
    263, 282
Douro, River 140
Drepanum 66, 67, 68, 69, 70, 71, 73, 74, 75, 76,
    77, 78, 324
Drusus 214, 219, 220, 221, 247
Dubris 231, 232, 249, 295
Duilius, Caius 56, 59
Duoviri 30, 32, 38, 44, 156, 318
Duoviri Navales 30, 44, 318
Durovernum 231
Dux Britanniorum 300, 302
Dyrrachium 108, 116, 324

E

Eboracum 263, 269, 290, 295
Ebusus 90, 324
Echinus 101, 324

Ecnomus 61, 62, 63, 64, 78, 135, 324

Ecnomus, Cape 61

Edessa 269, 277

Egypt 5, 9, 10, 26, 36, 37, 38, 46, 119, 130, 134, 140, 146, 154, 159, 167, 175, 178, 184, 191, 193, 197, 198, 199, 200, 203, 213, 225, 236, 238, 292, 294, 298, 302, 324

English Channel, battle in 288

Ephesus 123, 125, 126, 127, 128, 158, 165

Epidamnus 84

Epipolae Plateau 98

Epirus 20, 36, 84, 93, 132, 136, 151, 166

equites 88, 226

Eraclea 61, 71, 72, 78

Eretria 122

Eryx 67, 73, 75, 78, 324

Etruria 53, 121, 157, 304, 313

Etruscans 1, 2, 3, 4, 8, 10, 13, 18, 22, 26, 27, 32, 38, 40, 43, 44, 204, 207

Euboea 101, 106, 122, 124, 131, 132, 151

Eudamus 127, 128

Eugenius 303

Eumenes (of Pergamum) 124, 125, 127

Euphranor (of Rhodes) 178

Euphrates, River 262, 264, 268, 285, 299

Euripus 106

Euxine Sea 139, 151, 154, 155, 156, 157, 158, 167, 199, 200, 202, 203, 214, 215, 224, 233, 236, 237, 254, 261, 262, 264, 271, 274, 275, 276, 277, 279, 280, 286, 294, 297, 300, 301, 304

F

Fabius, Marcus 114

Falto, Praetor Quintus Valerius 76

Faventinus, Claudius 246

Figulus, Gaius Marcus 131

Fimbria 151, 152

Fire weapons 126, 174, 175, 196, 311

Fiume 134

Flaccus 151, 152, 222

Flaminius, Titus Quinctius 122

Florianus (Emperor) 280

Forum Iulii 188, 197, 198, 203, 238, 240, 245, 249, 254

Fossa Augusta 206

Frisii 219, 221, 224

Fullofaudes 300

Fuscus, Cornelius 244

fustibulus 21

G

Gabinius, Aulus 156

Gades 106, 107, 116, 134, 147, 169, 229, 324

Gadir 3, 324

Gaeta, Gulf of 28

Gaiseric 308, 309, 311

Gaius (Emperor) 102, 131, 142, 153, 154, 162, 183, 193, 200, 224, 225, 226, 227, 254

Galatia 236, 239, 240

Galba, Publius Sulpicius 101, 103, 105, 121, 122

Galba (Emperor) 238, 239, 240

Galerius (Emperor) 288, 290, 291

Gallia Narbonensis 141, 203

Gallienus (Emperor) 277, 278, 279

Gallus, Aelius 199, 200

Gastraphetes see artillery

gastraphetes 21, 289

Gaul 25, 32, 84, 89, 91, 108, 112, 117, 130, 141–143, 145, 157, 158–165, 182–184, 188, 197, 202, 224, 226, 228, 231, 232, 237, 240, 245, 247, 266–268, 272, 273, 278, 280, 285, 286, 288, 297, 298, 302–311

Gauls 32, 84, 86, 91, 108, 112, 141, 160, 161, 162, 182, 298

Gela, Battle of 72

Geminus, Gnaeus Servilius 91

Geminus, Virdius 243

Genthius, King 132

Genua 117, 121, 134, 147, 324

Germania 220, 221, 240, 241, 250, 254, 256, 258, 264, 278

Germanicus 220, 221, 222, 224, 247, 249

Gesoriacum 164, 226, 230, 232, 249, 285, 286, 288, 295, 324

Gibraltar, Straits, battle of 107

Gordian (Emperor) 275

Gratian (Emperor) 300, 301, 302

Greece 10, 26, 41, 88, 95, 105, 106, 108, 121, 122, 123, 124, 130, 131, 132, 134, 136, 137, 149, 151, 152, 166, 175, 184, 191, 192, 193, 194, 206, 218, 237, 238, 324, 325, 327

Gythion 123

H

Hadrian (Emperor) 262, 263, 264, 268, 269, 278,
    299, 300, 304
Hadrianopolis 292, 301
Hamilcar Barca 60, 61, 74, 75, 76, 77, 86, 87
Hannibal 56, 69, 86, 87, 89, 90, 91, 92, 93, 94,
    95, 96, 98, 100, 101, 104, 105, 106, 107,
    108, 112, 113, 114, 117, 123, 126, 127,
    143
Hanno, of Carthage 12, 61, 76, 77
Harbour works
    Ostia 141, 207
    Portus 227, 259
Harpax 187, 189, 190
Hasdrubal 66, 105, 108
Helinium 247
Hellespont 56, 80, 119, 121, 123, 125, 126, 127,
    128, 149, 152, 292, 293, 325
Hellespont, Battle of the 292, 293
Helvetii 159
Hemiolia 27, 29, 87, 155
Heracleum 131, 132
Heraclian 307
Herculaneum 254
Hermaeum 8, 20, 63, 64, 78, 311, 325
Herod, King of Judea 199, 214, 216, 220
Herodotus 5, 40
Hexeres 23, 29
    evolution of 23, 135
Hiera 76, 325
Hierkte, Mount 74, 75, 78
Hieron, Tyrant of Syracuse 10, 93, 94
Himilco 12, 89, 90
Hipparchus of Bithynia 139
Hippo Zarhytus 74, 78, 110, 325
Hispania 20, 51, 86, 87, 88, 89, 90, 91, 92, 93,
    94, 101, 102, 103, 105, 106, 107, 108,
    114, 123, 134, 140, 141, 143, 153, 155,
    158, 160, 161, 164, 167, 168, 169, 179,
    180, 183, 198, 222, 229, 230, 238, 242,
    245, 246, 261, 278, 291, 297, 298, 303,
    305, 307, 308, 310, 325
Honorius (Emperor) 303, 304, 305, 306, 308
Hostilia 244
Huns 301, 304, 306, 307, 309, 310

I

Iberus, River 86, 87, 90, 101, 143, 325
Iceni 231
Ilipa, Battle of 106
Illyria 87, 92, 93, 94, 101, 103, 106, 132, 160,
    175, 220, 300, 302
Illyrian 51, 84, 85, 86, 87, 88, 94, 132, 134, 155,
    171
Illyricum 136
India 9, 141, 199, 200, 229, 239
Insteius, Marcus 194
Instruments 27
Ionian Sea 92, 104, 122, 191, 239
Iron Gates Gorge 214, 224, 260, 266
Isauria 153
Isca 233, 254, 295
Isca Dumnoniorum 230, 232
Istria 130, 131
Istrian peninsula 130
Istrus 249, 257, 261, 274
Italiote Greeks 1, 22, 26, 28, 38, 44
Iulianus, Claudius 246
Iulianus, M. Didius 266
Iunius 68, 69, 71, 72, 73, 140, 161

J

Jovian (Emperor) 300
Juba, King of Numidia 169
Juba, King of Mauretania 216
Judaea 158, 178, 199, 216, 262, 264
Jugurtha, King 142
Julian (Emperor) 298, 299, 313

L

Labienus, Quintus 179
Laelius, Decimus 170, 174, 175
Laelius, Gaius 102, 103, 107, 108, 110, 111, 113,
    170, 174, 175
Laevinus 93, 94, 101, 104, 105, 113, 121, 122
Lampsacus 123
La Spezia 34, 84, 250, 325
Latium 2, 26, 28, 227
Lemboi 84, 85, 86, 87, 94, 132, 155
Lemnos 105, 106, 154
Lepidus, Aemilus 153, 183, 184, 185, 188, 189,
    190
Leptis Minor 112

Printed and bound by CPI Group (UK) Ltd, Croydon, CR0 4YY
13/04/2025
14656527-0001

Lesbos, Isle of 125, 153
Leucas 122, 193
Lex Gabinia 156
Lex Rhodia 10
Libio, Scribonius 170, 171, 172
liburna 87
liburnae 88, 110
liburnian 155, 160, 191, 215, 310
Licata 61, 63, 72, 324, 326
Licinius (Valerius Licinianus) 151, 155, 159, 291, 292, 293
Liger, River 160
Liguria 108, 240
Ligurians 83, 86, 108, 112, 136, 141
Lilybaeum 43, 44, 66, 67, 68, 69, 71, 72, 74, 75, 76, 78, 89, 91, 94, 100, 179, 325
Lindum 230, 232, 233, 253
Lipara 56, 58, 60
Liparae Islands 18, 66, 78, 89, 189, 325
Lissus 85, 132, 325
Livius 86, 124, 125, 127
Livy 40, 41, 53, 80, 95, 117, 149, 192, 217
Locris 106
Londinium 263
Longutica 90
Lucanians 36
Luceria 32, 325
Lucretius, Gaius 131
Lucullus, Lucius Licinius 151, 152, 153, 154, 155, 156
Lugdunum 241, 243, 249, 268, 295, 302
Luna 84, 121, 147, 325
Lurius, Marcus 194
Lusitanian War 134, 140
Lusoriae 291, 285, 298, 306
Lycia 153, 226, 227

M

Macedonia 26, 85, 86, 95, 119, 122, 123, 132, 136, 137, 140, 151, 152, 185, 191, 224
Madeira 43
Maenius, Caius (Consul) 20
Magnentius (Emperor) 298
Magnesia, Battle of 130
Magnus 158, 177, 302, 303
Mago, Admiral 36, 46, 106, 107, 108, 111, 112, 117
Majorian (Emperor) 310

Mancinus, Lucius Hostilius 137
Marcellinus 311, 313
Marcellus, Caius 170
Marcellus, Marcus Claudius 92, 94, 96, 98, 117
Marcian (Emperor) 309
Marcius, Ancus (King) 1
Marcius, Marcus 111
Mare Germanicum 263
Marinos of Tyre 263
Marius, Gaius 142–146
Maroboduus, King of Marcomanni 222
Massilia 4, 25, 40, 83, 86, 89, 90, 116, 134, 136, 141, 147, 167, 168, 169, 228, 229, 231, 325
Massinissa 108, 136
Mauretania 203, 216, 226, 227, 264, 266, 277
Maxentius (Emperor) 291, 292
Maximian (Emperor) 285, 288, 290, 291
Maximianus, Marcus Valerius 266
Maximinus (Emperor) 274, 290, 291, 292
Medicine, shipboard 147, 209
Mediolanum 278, 285, 300, 303, 304
Megara 136, 137
Melita 60, 64, 77, 78, 88, 116, 303, 325
Merchant ships 3, 35, 229, 265
Mesopotamia 3
Messalla, Valerius 101
Messana 89, 168, 174, 175, 184, 186, 189, 325
Messina 51, 52, 53, 56, 61, 78, 190, 325
Metapontum 100
Metaurus, Battle of 105
Metellus, Quintus 141, 156
Miletus 119, 153
Minturnae 246
Misenum 185, 188, 203, 204, 205, 206, 208, 211, 217, 222, 223, 224, 225, 226, 236, 238, 239, 240, 246, 249, 254, 255, 268, 286, 304, 313
Mithridates 151, 152, 153, 154, 155, 156, 158, 214, 232
Moesia 214, 224, 232, 259, 260, 265, 274, 275, 277, 279, 280, 286, 301, 306, 312
Moguntiacum 221, 241, 246, 259, 295, 297, 304
monoreme 13, 29, 247
Moschus 240
Motya, Siege of 23
Mucianus, General 242, 243
Munda, Battle of 180

Murcus 184
Mylae 52, 53, 58, 60, 80, 189, 217, 325
Myndos, Battle of 183
Myonnesus 128, 129
Mytilene 153

N

Nabis, Tyrant of Sparta 123
Narbo 147, 159, 325
Narenta, River 134
Nasidius, Lucius 168, 169, 170
Nassus 101
Naulochus, Battle of 190
naumachiae 204, 234, 255
navarchs 24, 208
naves onerariae 162
Navigation 3, 85, 139, 141, 159, 263
Navpactos 105
Neapolis 2, 24, 28, 32, 39, 78, 113, 186, 188,
     189, 217, 326
Necho II, of Egypt 3
Nectarides 300
Nero (Emperor) 206, 208, 223, 236, 237, 238,
     239, 240, 251, 256, 275
Nerva (Emperor) 259
Nicea 136, 326
Nicomedes, King 153
Nicomedia 285
Niger, Pescennius 267, 268
Nile, River 3, 10, 38, 176, 177, 199, 200, 203,
     217, 236, 287
Nile Delta 3, 10, 176, 177
Nile-Red Sea canal 3, 199, 262
Nonius Datus 264
Normandy 159, 160
North Africa 138, 154, 157, 216, 229, 290, 303,
     308, 309
Notitia Dignitatum 303
Novaesum 224, 249, 295
Noviodunum 215, 233, 257, 261, 302
Noviomagus 232
Nuceria 32, 326
Numantia 140
Numerian 280
Numidia 108, 136, 169

O

Oblivio, River 140
Obodas, King of Nabatea 199
Octavia 191, 237
Octavius, Gnaeus 111, 112
Octavius, Marcus 170, 171, 175, 178, 194
Octavius/Octavian, Gaius 183–194, 196–198
Odaenathus 278
Oeniadae 101
Olbia 59, 60, 78, 237, 326
Onusa 90
Orcades (Orkney islands) 25, 256, 289, 326
Oreus 106, 122
Oricus 94, 116, 170, 171, 172, 173, 326
Ortygia 98, 117
Osilipo 134, 140, 147, 326
Ostia 1, 18, 28, 36, 40, 44, 90, 91, 92, 93, 102,
     105, 113, 141, 156, 180, 188, 203, 204,
     226, 227, 229, 231, 238, 250, 294, 305,
     310
Otacilius 93, 100
Otho, Marcus Salvius (Emperor) 238, 240, 242,
     244

P

Pachynus, Cape 72, 78, 94
Padus, River 84, 91, 112, 121, 130, 143, 206,
     242, 244, 326
Paestum 39, 78, 101
Paleopolis 28, 326
Palinuros, Cape 66
Pamphylia 144, 153, 182
Panaetius 137
Pannonia 134, 214, 220, 221, 244, 253, 260, 267,
     275, 312
Panormus 60, 65, 66, 71, 74, 75, 78, 81, 126,
     249, 326
Paterculus, Caius Sulpicius 60
Patras, Gulf of 122, 131
Paulinus, Suetonius 236
Paulinus, Valerius 240
Paullus, Marcus Aemilius 64, 132
Paulus, Lucius Aemilius 86
Pelorum, Cape 52
penteconter 1, 11, 13, 15, 22, 24, 47, 310
Pergamum 93, 105, 108, 119, 121, 124, 127, 141,
     147, 199

Periplous attack 14, 190, 196

Perseus (King of Macedon) 131, 132, 136

Personnel, recruitment etc. 22, 24, 30, 143, 208, 267, 270, 290, 296

Pertinax, Publius Helvius (Emperor) 267

Petronius 64, 80, 200, 302

Petuaria 253, 295

Pharos of Alexandria 36

Pharsalus, Battle of 174

Philip of Macedon 23, 87, 92, 93, 94, 95, 96, 101, 104, 105, 106, 119, 120, 121, 122, 123, 124, 126, 131, 149, 275

Phillippi, Battle of 185

Philus, Publius Furius 92

Phintias 62, 72, 326

Phocaea 128, 326

Phoenician 1, 3–5, 12, 13, 40, 60, 80, 126, 133, 149, 159, 238

Pillars of Hercules 3, 107, 157

pilum 209

piracy 3, 4, 10, 34, 38, 83, 84, 86, 127, 134, 137, 141, 144, 147, 152, 156, 157, 191, 201, 203, 206, 224, 228, 237, 239, 289, 291, 305

Piraeus 40, 122, 249

Pisae 89, 91, 134, 326

Placentia 91, 206, 242, 326

Plautius, Aulus 230, 231, 232

Plinius, Gaius 254, 255

Polemo 214, 216, 236

Polybius 40, 41, 46, 48, 49, 58, 77, 80, 81, 112, 117, 119, 137, 149, 182

Polyremes 27, 35

Polyxenidas 125, 126, 127, 128

Pompeii 2, 32, 35, 41, 99, 109, 146, 217, 223, 254, 255, 282

Pompeius, Cnaeus 152, 153, 155, 156, 157, 158, 159, 165, 166–171, 173, 174, 175, 176, 179, 180, 183, 184, 201, 202, 236, 318

Pompeius, Cnaeus Jnr. 170, 173, 179, 180

Pompeius, Sextus 179, 180, 183, 184, 186–190, 197

Pomponius 111, 174, 222

Pons Aelius 262, 263

Pontia 28

Pontus 151, 154, 155, 158, 200, 214, 216, 236, 243, 249

Portus Adurni 288, 295, 304

Portus Itius 230

Postumus 278

Praefecti 44, 48, 156

Praefectus Classis 156, 184, 202, 203

Praefectus Classis et Orae Maritimae 156, 184

Praetorian Guard 202, 204, 294

Primus, Antonius 244

Probus (Emperor) 279, 280, 302

Procurator Portus Ostiensis 226

Propontis 119, 151, 152, 215, 233, 264, 265, 276, 277, 279, 285–287, 292, 297, 326

Proretus 46, 319

Ptolemy 5, 26, 27, 37, 38, 95, 119, 146, 152, 159,

Ptolemy II Philadelphus 5, 38

Ptolemy IV 95, 119

Ptolemy V 119

Ptolemy IX 152

Ptolemy XIII 175, 176, 178

Publicola, Gellius 194, 196

Pulcher, Publius Claudius 68, 69, 70, 71, 73, 96, 97

Pullus, Lucius Iunius 68

Pumps and dry docks 137

Puteoli 101, 188, 203, 205, 206, 217, 225, 227, 237, 250, 326

Pydna, Battle of 132

Pylos 86

Pyrgi 4, 40

Pyrrhic War 36

Pyrrhicus, Claudius 242

Pyrrhus, King of Epirus 36, 59

Pyrrhus of Epirus 36

Pytheas, voyage of 25, 41, 162, 228, 232, 256

Q

Quadrireme 38, 41, 79, 80, 88, 106, 117, 119, 122, 171, 172, 192, 211, 216, 217
evolution of, 17

Quaestores Classici 44, 202, 226, 318

Quaestor Ostiensis 44, 226

Quiberon Bay, Battle of 161

Quinctus, Decimus 101, 102, 104, 117

Quinquireme 23, 29, 31, 35, 41, 43, 45–47, 52–54, 56–58, 61, 68, 69, 75, 79, 89, 91, 95–97, 100–104, 106–108, 112, 113, 117, 119, 121–125, 127, 136, 167, 174–179, 182, 192, 211,
evolution of, 45

R

Ravenna 203, 204, 206, 207, 208, 222, 226, 238,
    240, 244, 249, 255, 268, 286, 302, 304,
    306, 308, 314
Ram
    evolution of, 133
    use of, 8, 12
RANKS
    26, 30, 44, 46, 88, 202, 210–212, 296
    Auletes (musicians) 15, 45
    Centurion 24, 102, 246
    Dupliciarii (leading hands) 15, 210, 319
    Gubernator (lieutenant) 26, 44, 45, 210,
    319
    Keleusta (rowing officer) 15
    Magister Navis (ship master/captain) 26,
    44, 45
    Optio (junior centurian) 24, 46, 212, 318,
    319
    Pausarius (rowing officer) 26, 45, 46, 211,
    319
    Pentecontarchos (1st officer) 15
    Prorates (bow officer) 15
    Secutor (master-at-arms) 26, 210, 319
    Thalamite (bottom-most rowers) 15, 29
    Thranite (top-most rowers) 15, 29, 120
    Trierarch (captain) 15, 24, 44, 208, 210
    Zygite (middle level rowers 15, 29
    ribbons of 223
Red Sea 3, 5, 10, 38, 141, 199, 200, 239, 262,
    263, 279
Regillus, Lucius Aemilius 125, 127, 128
Regni 231
Regulbium 231, 232
Regulus, Caius Atilius 60, 61, 63, 64, 65
Rhaetia 278
Rhegium 36, 51, 52, 78, 101, 186, 187, 326
Rhenus, River 159, 162, 202, 203, 210, 219–222,
    224, 226, 230, 232, 234, 237, 238, 240,
    241–243, 245–248, 253, 254, 258, 259,
    262, 266, 267, 269, 273, 274, 277, 278,
    280, 282, 285–288, 290, 291, 297, 298,
    299, 303, 304, 305, 306, 309, 310, 326
Rhodanus, River 89, 143, 188, 231, 237, 326
Rhodes 10, 38, 93, 119, 121, 124, 126, 127, 128,
    134, 139, 145, 151, 152, 153, 157, 167,
    178, 182, 183, 229, 286

Rhodian 13, 16, 17, 29, 38, 46, 69, 75, 119, 121,
    122, 123, 125, 126, 127, 128, 129, 134,
    152, 155, 170, 172, 173, 175, 176, 178,
    182, 183, 234, 321
Ricimer, Claudius 310
Rimini 34, 245, 323
Rome 1–4, 8, 10, 12, 18, 20, 22, 24, 26, 28, 32,
    34, 36, 38–41, 43, 44, 46, 51, 54, 56,
    59, 60, 73, 74, 83, 84, 86–88, 90–96,
    100, 101, 103, 105, 108, 111, 112, 114,
    116, 119, 121–124, 128, 130–132, 134,
    136, 137, 140–143, 145–147, 149, 151,
    152, 153, 154, 156–159, 165, 179, 180,
    183–186, 188, 191, 198, 200, 202–205,
    214, 218, 222, 224–227, 232, 234, 235,
    237–240, 242, 243, 245, 246, 248–250,
    285, 290, 291, 292, 294, 297, 302, 305,
    307, 308, 310, 315, 317
Romulus (King) 225, 311
Romulus Augustulus (Emperor) 311
Rotomagus 286
Rowing systems 33
Rufus, Q. Salvidienus 169, 184
Rutupiae 231, 232, 288, 300

S

Sabellian 10, 34
Sabellians 34
Sabinus, Caius Poppaeus 224
Sabrina, River 233, 234, 274, 308
Saguntum 86, 87, 101, 116, 327
Sails
    flax 9
    hemp 9
Salamis, Battle of 15, 18, 54
Salinator, Claudius Livius 124
Salinator, Marcus Livius 86
sambucae 97
Samnites 10, 20, 24, 26, 28, 32–36, 41, 80, 146
    Samnite War, First 20
    Samnite War, Second 20, 26
    Samnite War, Third 32
Samos 119, 165
Samothrace 152
Sardinia 1, 4, 10, 18, 20, 43, 51, 56, 59, 60, 83,
    91, 93, 100, 105, 108, 112, 114, 117, 131,
    141, 157, 167, 179, 185, 186, 204, 242,
    309, 311, 324, 327

Sarpedonium, Cape 130
Scipio 27, 56, 59, 89, 90, 92, 93, 102, 103, 105, 106, 107, 108, 110, 111, 113, 114, 125, 137, 138, 139, 169
Scodra 132, 327
Scribonius 170, 171, 214
Seleucia/Seleucid Empire 26, 119, 123, 132, 134, 144 203, 249
Selinus 262
Sempronius, Publius 108
Sempronius, Tiberius 88
Senusret III, Pharaoh 200
Sertorius, Quintus 153
Servius Fulvius Nobilior 64
Severus, Marcus Septimius (Emperor) 237, 267, 268, 269, 282, 290, 291
Severus Alexander (Emperor) 274
Shipbuilding 5, 53, 285
        times/rates 48–50, 95
Sicilian 50, 51, 56, 60, 61, 69, 71, 76, 80, 105, 131, 156, 157, 168, 190, 234
Sicily 1, 4, 10, 18, 23, 32, 36, 43, 44, 51, 52, 53, 54, 56, 60, 61, 63, 64, 65, 66, 67, 68, 71, 72, 73, 74, 75, 76, 77, 80, 87, 89, 91, 92, 93, 94, 95, 96, 100, 101, 104, 105, 108, 110, 111, 113, 114, 121, 124, 141, 157, 158, 167, 169, 174, 179, 184, 185, 186, 188, 189, 190, 204, 217, 225, 302, 303, 305, 309, 310, 311, 323, 324, 325, 326, 327
Side, Battle of 127
Signals, shipboard 27
Singidunum 280
Sinking, Ships of 4
Sinope 158, 214, 233, 327
Sirte, Gulf of 66
Skiathos 132
slingers 9, 12, 22, 31, 97
Smyrna 123, 128
Social War, The 146, 149
socii navales 34
Sosius, Gaius 193, 194, 196
Sparta 116, 123
Spartacus 155
speculatoria navigia 160
Steering oar 9, 330
Stilicho, Flavius 304
Suetonius Paulinus 236

Suez, Gulf of 3, 5, 199
Sulci 60, 78
Sulla (Dictator) 35, 146, 151, 152
Sulpicius, Publius 174, 175
Sumerians 25
Sundials 143
Surrentum 2, 327
Syphax 108
Syracusans 10, 19, 21, 23, 27, 31, 34, 36, 37, 53, 54, 57, 92, 94, 96, 97, 100, 117
Syracuse 10, 12, 17, 23, 36, 51, 52, 53, 61, 72, 74, 78, 80, 93, 94, 96, 98, 100, 116
Syria 119, 158, 183, 203, 222, 286

T

Tacitus 221, 228, 234, 243, 250, 251, 256, 258, 280, 282
Tagus, River 134
Tamesis, River 230, 231, 273, 289
Tanais 257, 276
Taranto, Gulf of 22, 34, 36, 54, 92, 104
Tarentines 34, 100, 101, 102
Tarentum 20, 34, 36, 38, 39, 43, 44, 78, 96, 98, 101, 104, 105, 116, 117, 186, 188, 193, 195, 217, 327
Tarquinia 3, 4
Tarquin the Proud, King (Etruscan) 8
Tarraco 89, 90, 101, 116, 169, 278, 327
Tartessos 3
Tauromenium 189
Taurus, Statilius 189, 190, 191
Temple of Apollo (Delphi) 18, 97
Teredo beetle (shipworm) 5, 9
Tetricus 280
Teuta, Queen 84, 85
Thapsus 96
Thapsus, Battle of 179
Theodosius, Flavius (Emperor) 300, 301, 302, 303, 305, 306, 308, 309, 313
Thermae 66, 78, 327
Thermopylae 124
Thermus, Marcus Minucius 153
Thessalonica 131
Thessalonika 279, 292
Thessaly 124, 151
Thrace 128, 131, 151, 226, 233, 269, 274, 277, 279, 292, 306
Thurii 34, 39, 327

Tiber, River 1, 2, 4, 10, 18, 198, 227, 231, 307, 310

Tiberius (Emperor) 88, 214, 219, 220, 221, 222, 224, 247, 260

Tiberius Sempronius 88

Ticinum 242

Tigris, River 268, 269, 290, 299

Timsah, Lake 3

Titus (Emperor) 100, 122, 238, 242, 254, 256

Towers, on ships 157, 188, 192

Trade

        development 131

        exotic animals 239

        growth under Claudius 227

        with India 143, 199

        Pilgrimage 305

Trajan (Emperor) 235, 260, 261, 262, 297, 313

Trapezus 236, 237, 243, 249, 254, 257, 262, 265

Trasimenus, Lake 91, 92

Trebbia, Battle of 91

Triarius, Caius 170

trihemiolia 29

triremes 12, 13, 15–19, 21, 24, 26, 27, 29, 31, 34, 40, 41, 43, 45–48, 52–56, 58, 61, 79, 87–89, 101, 102, 107, 108, 112, 114, 117, 120, 122, 124, 126, 127, 136, 149, 155, 167–169, 171, 172, 175, 176, 179, 185, 192, 206, 210, 216, 218, 222, 234, 237, 239, 240, 292, 293, 330

Troesmis 249, 257, 261

Tunisia 8, 43, 114, 324, 325

Tyndaris 60, 78, 81, 190

Tyre 31, 80

Tyrrhenian 10, 24, 83, 94, 121, 140, 144, 158, 204

Tyrrhenian Sea 10, 24, 83, 94, 140, 204

Tyrrhenian seas 121

U

Ulpius, Marcellus 267

Urbicus, Lollius 264

Utica 100, 110, 111, 112, 113, 114, 136, 169, 179

V

Valens, Fabius (Emperor) 240, 244, 245, 300, 301

Valentia 140, 147

Valentinian (Emperor) 300, 301, 303, 308, 310

Valerian (Emperor) 277

Valerius Licinianus (Emperor) *see* Licinius

Valerius, Marcus 53, 93

Valerius Messalla 101

Vandals 280, 304, 305, 308, 309, 310, 311, 314

Varro, Marcus Terentius 154, 169

Varus, Publius 179, 180

Vatia, Publius Servilius 153, 154

Vatinius, Publius 178

Veii 18

Velia 66, 78, 101

velites 47

Venerianus, Admiral 279

Veneti 130, 182

Verus, Lucius (Emperor) 264, 265

Vespasian, Titus Flavius (Emperor) 223, 232, 238, 242, 243, 244, 245, 246, 248, 250, 253, 254, 259, 282

Vetera 221, 224, 241, 245, 247, 295

Visigoths 301, 302, 304, 305, 306, 307, 308

Vitellius, Aulus 240, 242, 243, 244, 245, 246

Volscians 20

Volusenus, Gaius 162

Vortigern 308

Vulso, Lucius Manlius 61, 63, 130

W

Warship evolution 9

X

Xenophanes 92

Z

Zama, Battle of 113, 114

Zakynthos 5, 101, 327

Zenobia, Queen 278, 279